T

Church of Christ

An Apologetic and Dogmatic Treatise

by

E. SYLVESTER BERRY, S.T.D.

Professor of Apologetics

Wipf and Stock Publishers
EUGENE, OREGON

NIHIL OBSTAT:
> EDWARD A. CERNY, S.S., S.T.D.
>> *Censor Librorum*

IMPRIMATUR:
> FRANCIS P. KEOUGH, D.D.
>> *Archbishop of Baltimore*

May 6, 1955.

Wipf and Stock Publishers
199 W 8th Ave, Suite 3
Eugene, OR 97401

The Church of Christ
An Apologetic and Dogmatic Treatise
By Berry, E. Sylvester
ISBN 13: 978-1-60608-802-9
Publication date 5/5/2009
Previously published by Mount Saint Mary's Seminary, 1955

FOREWORD

The present volume, being the outgrowth of lectures delivered in the classroom, was originally written in Latin with the intention of supplying a textbook suited to the needs of those beginning the study of theology in our seminaries. But upon the advice of friends—professors of theology as well as priests engaged in parochial duties,—the matter has been completely recast into English. It is believed that in this form the work will be of wider utility than in Latin. It is hoped that the detailed explanations and the simplicity of language will render the work intelligible and useful to a large portion of the laity.

With the exception of the Sacraments, there is, perhaps, no subject of more practical interest to clergy and laity alike than that of the Church, yet there are few works in English treating the subject in full. The author trusts that he has made some contribution in this matter by giving a connected and rather detailed account of the origin, constitution and powers of the Church from the dogmatic as well as from the apologetic point of view.

Many questions not found in ordinary Latin treatises on the Church have been introduced, not only because of the interest that attaches to these questions themselves, but also because they help to make the true nature of the Church better understood.

There is no claim to originality, except, perhaps, in the order and method of treatment. Much time and labor have been expended to put the subject into logical order and to state clearly and distinctly the precise doctrine to be proved in every instance. Proofs are useless unless there is some definite clear-cut proposition to be proved. To prove, for instance, that the Church is holy, without knowing exactly what is meant by holiness, and in what manner the Church is said to be holy, is simply to confuse the issue. For this reason much space is given to explanations; every question is resolved into its component parts and each proved separately from reason, Scripture, and Tradition. Moreover, a doctrine can scarcely be accepted as definitely established unless the arguments brought against it can be satisfactorily answered. On this account considerable attention has been given to objections, many of which have been taken directly from non-Catholic authors.

The scholastic method has been employed to a certain extent by setting forth the doctrine in the form of theses, followed by explanations, proofs, corollaries, and objections. This may seem a little formal

to those not accustomed to it, but there is no method better adapted
to beget order, clearness, and precision. It will also make the work
more convenient for the use of theological students trained to the
scholastic method. Practically all quotations have been taken directly
from the authors quoted, and a special effort has been made to preserve
the sense as well as the words of the original. The quotations from the
Fathers of the Church and from other ecclesiastical writers are from
Migne's Latin and Greek Patrologies, designated P.L. and P.G. respectively in the references, where the first number indicates the volume, the others the columns in which the words quoted may be found.
All passages marked by an asterisk in the footnotes are quoted according to the English translations of the Fathers prepared by non-Catholic
scholars and published by Scribner.[1] Decrees and acts of councils are
quoted from Denzinger-Bannwart's *Enchiridion Symbolorum et De-
finitionum*[2]—a work easily accessible to all students. Decrees not found
there are taken directly from the collections of councils by Mansi or
Labbe-Cossart.

The humble efforts of the author will be amply rewarded if they
but serve to arouse greater appreciation and deeper love for the Church,
to whose infallible authority he unreservedly submits every statement
of doctrine contained in the following pages.

The Author.

Mt. St. Mary's Seminary
   Emmitsburg, Md.

---

[1] Roberts-Donaldson, "Ante-Nicene Fathers"; Schaff-Wace; "Nicene and Post-
Nicene Fathers"; Schaff, "Nicene and Post-Nicene Fathers."
[2] From the edition prepared by Fr. Umberg, S.J., Herder, 1922.

PREFACE

Divine Revelation was given to the world by Jesus Christ the Son of God made man for all men of all time. The sublime teaching spoken by the Savior by lake shore and on mountain side was meant to be a guide for all mankind. It was to be known and accepted by all men. It was stamped with the hall mark of eternal truth. It was true twenty centuries ago; it is true today. He who gave it to the world was none other than the God of Truth.

In order that divine Truth might be brought home to all men Jesus Christ established a Church, a teaching organization, to speak to the world in His name and with His own authority. To that Church He gave a very clear and unequivocal mission. It was to teach men whatsoever He had taught—nothing more, nothing less. On all men Christ placed the obligation of hearing His Church as they would hear Himself. He promised to remain with His teaching Church. He sent down the Holy Ghost on its first teachers selected by Himself in order that they and their successors might be illumined and assisted in the work of continuing the teaching and sanctifying mission of God's own Divine Son.

The Church established by Jesus Christ is the Church known to the world as the Catholic Church. Its center of authority to the world is designated by the word Roman, but that word in no way changes the connotation of the "Ecclesia Catholica." The Church founded by the God of all must necessarily be Catholic or Universal in time, place and doctrine. The Catholic Church is the true Church. No other Church received its mission from Christ. No other Church is Catholic. No other Church can trace its authority to Him who said, "Going therefore teach all nations." Every other so-called Church must, and in fact does, trace its origin to some mere man or woman. All of the protesting bodies are in rebellion against Christ's authority as exercised by the Church He Himself founded. Daily they are becoming more and more confused, a babel of contradictory voices, unable to agree on any point of faith, unable to lead men to Christ by any sure path. Thinking men outside the Catholic Church are growing tired of the hydra-headed Protestantism all around them.

Protestantism after its four centuries of revolt is absolutely bankrupt as a moral force. In America, as everywhere else, it is distinctly Erastian. It flies to the State for protection. It seeks strength in the

v

secular arm to enforce morality. It depends on man-made laws to keep the people's feet on the pathway of virtue.

Jesus Christ was not a God of confusion. He did not breathe hot and cold in the same breath. The sixteenth century revolt was begotten in blasphemy. It accused the Church of Christ of error, of teaching what was false and immoral, of having been conquered by the "gates of hell." The fomentors of revolt might very properly have accused individuals in God's Church of wrong-doing. That would be quite different from giving the lie to the God of truth. Today we see the harvest of the sixteenth century sowing,—growing infidelity, indifferentism, religious chaos, consequent moral decadence, blind leaders united in only one thing,—opposition to the Church of Jesus Christ. They rejoice in its sufferings in Mexico or Russia. They approve any programme against it regardless of the character of those responsible for such a plan.

The Catholic Church is the most interesting and the most remarkable fact in the world. Kingdoms and empires have grown in their greatness, have sickened and died. The man-made churches of today shall be no more in comparatively few years. The names may be in use but they shall be only names. Twenty centuries have seen a great many changes, a great many ups and downs. But twenty centuries have seen no change in the Catholic Church,—no change in teaching, no change in principles, no change in her attitude towards sin, no change in her mission to teach Christ crucified and His doctrines to all mankind, no change in her consciousness of her own authority and right to speak to the world. Twenty centuries have seen her grow and expand despite all the forces of earth and hell arrayed against her. In a world of doubt and religious confusion the Catholic Church stands "like Teneriffe above the restless ocean's foam." Men may hate her as men hated and still hate Christ; one thing men cannot do,—they cannot neglect her. They must be either with her or against her. She arrests the attention of men more every day.

It is about the Catholic Church founded by Jesus Christ that Dr. Berry speaks. It is her claims he states and for them he gives proof. It is her position in the world as a divinely authorized teacher he emphasizes. Succinctly yet clearly he marshals his arguments to bring conviction to the mind of the reader that the Catholic Church is what she has ever claimed to be,—the Bride of Christ, the mouthpiece of Christ.

He has done his work well. He places all of us under an obligation to him for his lucid explanation of the Church's position and teaching. Let us have an end of indefinite, vague terminology. Let us speak out the truth plainly without apologies, without fear. The world is looking for it. We repeat that the Catholic Church and she alone is the true Church of Christ. The teachings of Jesus Christ are found in their fullness and completeness in the Catholic Church alone. The Catholic Church is the Christian Church. Christianity is Catholicism. There is no Catholicism where there is no recognition of the Vicar of Christ. "Where Peter is, there is the Church."

✠Michael J. Curley,
Archbishop of Baltimore.

CONTENTS

Page

Preface v

Introduction xv

Works Consulted xvii

PART I. APOLOGETIC

Chapter I. ORIGIN OF THE CHURCH

Art. I. Origin and Meaning of the Name Church 3

Art. II. Christ Founded a Church Under the Form of a Society 6
    1. Nature of a Society 6
    2. Errors Regarding the Origin and Nature of the Church 7
    3. Christ Personally Founded His Church as a Society 9
    4. The Church Distinct From the Synagogue 12
    5. Objections Considered 14

Art. III. Christ Founded But One Church 18

Art. IV. Purpose and Nature of the Church 21
    1. Purpose of the Church 21
    2. General Nature of the Church 22
    3. The Church and the Kingdom 25

Chapter II. ATTRIBUTES OF THE CHURCH

Art. I. Perpetual Indefectibility of the Church 29
    1. The Nature of Indefectibility 29
    2. Erroneous Doctrines 30
    3. The Church of Christ Perpetually Indefectible 31
    4. Objections Answered 34

Art. II. Visibility of the Church 36
    1. The Nature of Visibility 36
    2. Errors Concerning the Visibility of the Church 37
    3. The Church of Christ formally Visible 39
    4. Objections Answered 41

Chapter III. PROPERTIES OF THE CHURCH

Art. I. Unity of the Church 45
    1. The Nature of Unity 45
    2. Unity of Government 47

   Page

        3. Unity of Faith 50
           a) Unity of Doctrine 52
           b) Unity of Profession 53
        4. Unity of Worship 54

Art. II. Holiness of the Church 56
        1. Nature of Holiness 56
        2. Physical Holiness of the Church 57
           a) Passive Holiness 57
           b) Active Holiness 58
        3. Moral Holiness of the Church 59
        4. Manifestative Sanctity of the Church 61
        5. Objections Answered 64

Art. III. Catholicity of the Church 67
        1. Use and Meaning of the Term 67
        2. The Church Catholic by Actual Diffusion 70
        3. Catholicity of Church Further Defined 72
        4. Perfect Catholicity To Be Attained 74

Art. IV. Apostolicity of the Church 77
        1. The Nature of Apostolicity 77
        2. The Church of Christ Apostolic 79

               Chapter IV. MARKS OF THE CHURCH

Art. I. Requisites for a Mark of the Church 82
        1. The Nature of a Mark 82
        2. Marks Claimed by Non-Catholics 83

Art. II. The Four Marks of the Church 85
        1. Unity as a Mark of the Church 85
        2. Sanctity as a Mark of the Church 85
        3. Catholicity as a Mark of the Church 86
        4. Apostolicity as a Mark of the Church 88
        5. Persecution as a Mark of the Church 88
           Conclusion 89

Art. III. Marks of the Church Applied 89
        1. The Catholic Church Possesses
           a) Unity of Faith, Worship, and Government 89
           b) Manifestative and Causative Sanctity 90
           c) Universality of Diffusion 93
           d) Apostolicity of Succession 94
           e) Objections Answered 94
        2. Protestant Churches 97
        3. The Anglican Church 99
        4. Schismatic Churches of the East 103

Page

PART II. DOGMATIC

ORGANIZATION AND POWERS OF CHURCH
Chapter V. THE MYSTICAL BODY OF CHRIST

Art.　I. The Church as the Body of Christ 109

Art.　II. The Soul of the Church 115

Chapter VI. MEMBERS OF THE CHURCH

Art.　I. False Conditions of Membership 121
　　1. Predestination as a Condition 121
　　2. The State of Grace as a Condition 122
　　3. Objections Considered 123

Art.　II. True Conditions of Membership 125

Art. III. Persons Excluded From Membership 127
　　1. Manifest Heretics and Schismatics 128
　　2. Excommunicates 130

Art. IV. Persons of Doubtful Membership 132
　　1. Persons Invalidly Baptized 132
　　2. Occult Heretics and Schismatics 133

Art.　V. Necessity of Membership 134
　　1. Twofold Necessity of Membership 134
　　2. Membership a Relative Necessity 136

Chapter VII. AUTHORITY OF THE CHURCH

Art.　I. Authority to Govern 140
　　1. Threefold Power of Government 141
　　2. Right of Temporal Punishment 143
　　3. Right to Inflict Corporal Punishment 144
　　4. Persons Subject to Punitive Powers 145

Art.　II. Nature of Church Powers 146

Chapter VIII. RULERS OF THE CHURCH

Art.　I. Erroneous Doctrines 151

Art.　II. A Ruling Body of Divine Institution 152
　　1. Apostles Alone Receive All Authority 153
　　2. Apostolic Power Descends by Succession 155

Art. III. The Successors of the Apostles 157
　　1. True Successors of the Apostles 157
　　2. Other Ministers of the Church 159

Page

Art. IV. Apostolic Prerogatives 163
      1. The Apostolic Office 163
      2. Special Prerogatives 165

Chapter IX. THE PRIMACY PROMISED

Art.   I. The Preeminence of Peter 169

Art. II. Peter the Rock Foundation 173
      1. St. Peter the Rock 173
      3. Primacy of Jurisdiction Symbolized 175
      3. Objections Answered 177

Art. III. Peter the Key-Bearer 179

Art. IV. Peter the Law-Giver 182

Art. V. Peter Confirmer of the Brethren 185

Chapter X. THE PRIMACY CONFERRED

Art.   I. Institution of the Primacy 188
      1. Peter Constituted Chief Pastor 188
      2. Objections Considered 189

Art. II. The Testimony of Tradition 191

Art. III. St. Peter and the Other Apostles 193

Art. IV. The Primacy a Permanent Institution 195

Chapter XI. SUCCESSORS TO ST. PETER (The Roman Pontiff)

Art.   I. The Doctrine and Its Proofs 198

Art. II. The Testimony of History 200
      1. Witnesses From the Fifth Century 200
      2. Witnesses From the Fourth Century 204
      3. Witnesses From the Third Century 207
      4. Witnesses From the Second Century 209
      5. Witnesses From the First Century 212

Art. III. Objections Considered 215

Chapter XII. PRIMACY AND EPISCOPATE

Art.   I. Nature of Powers and Tenure of Office 225
      1. Nature of the Powers Exercised by the Roman Pontiff 225
      2. Tenure of the Supreme Pastoral Office 227

Art. II. The Pope and the Bishops Severally 231

Page

Art. III. The Pope and the Bishops in Council 235
    1. Nature and Various Kinds of Councils 235
    2. Rights of the Roman Pontiff in Regard to Ecumenical
       Councils 237
    3. Objections Considered 241

Chapter XIII. THE INFALLIBLE TEACHING AUTHORITY

Art. I. The Teaching Authority of the Church 243

Art. II. Infallibility of the Church 247
    1. Nature of Infallibility 247
    2. Active Infallibility of the Church 248
    3. Passive Infallibility of the Church 254
    4. Objection Answered 256

Chapter XIV. INFALLIBILITY OF THE BISHOPS

Art. I. Infallibility of Ecumenical Councils 260

Art. II. Infallibility of the Bishops in Their Ordinary Teaching
    Capacity 266

Chapter XV. THE INFALLIBILITY OF THE ROMAN PONTIFF

Art. I. The Doctrine of Papal Infallibility 270

Art. II. Objections Against Papal Infallibility 283

Chapter XVI. THE EXTENT OF INFALLIBILITY

Art. I. Primary Extent of Infallibility 288

Art. II. Secondary Extent of Infallibility 289

Chapter XVII. CHURCH AND STATE

Art. I. Various Theories Advanced on Church and State 293

Art. II. Catholic Doctrine on Church and State 296
    1. Church and State Distinct and Perfect Societies 297
    2. State Indirectly Subordinate to the Church 298
    3. State and Church in Mutual Support 301

Art. III. Mutual Rights and Duties 303

Art. IV. Practical Application of Principles 307

Art. V. The Roman Pontiff and Secular Rulers 309
    1. Secular Rulers Indirectly Subject to Roman Pontiff 309
    2. Roman Pontiff Exempt From Civil Authority 311
    3. Temporal Power Necessary 312

Index 314

INTRODUCTION

Purpose of This Work

Since Christianity embodies the final revelation of God to man,[1] there must be some means instituted by God to preserve it from age to age and propagate it among men. The various societies known as Christian Churches claim to be that means. Hence the first purpose of this work is to inquire whether Christ really established a Church, and if so whether he established one or many.

If Christ established but one Church, it becomes necessary to discover which of the many now existing is, in very truth, the Church of Christ. This can be done by comparing the various Christian churches of today with the Church of Christ as set forth in the Gospels, where its nature and characteristics are portrayed in unmistakable terms. The Church that possesses these characteristics in their fullness today must necessarily be the *one true Church of Christ*.

Having discovered the true Church of Christ, the work of the *apologist* is finished and it becomes the duty of the *dogmatic theologian* to investigate its inner nature. Hence the present work is divided into two parts,—*Apologetic* and *Dogmatic*. The one points out the true Church of Christ; the other investigates its organization and powers.

---

[1] Proof of this may be found in treatises on Revealed Religion.

WORKS CONSULTED

The following are a few of the more important works consulted in connection with the various questions,—apologetic, dogmatic, and historical,—concerning the Church. Other works occasionally referred to are quoted in the references.

*Androutsos, Chrestos
"Dogmatike tes Orthodoxou Anatolikes Ekklesias," Athens, 1907.
Ballerini, Peter
"De Vi ac Ratione Primatus Romanorum Pontificum," Rome, 1849.
Batiffol, Pierre
"Primitive Catholicism" (Tr. by Brianceau), London, 1911.
Bellarmine, Robert, S.J.
"Disputationes De Controversiis Fidei," Naples, 1856.
Benni, Cyril Behnan
"Tradition of the Syriac Church of Antioch," London, 1871.
Billot, Ludovicus, S.J.
"Tractatus de Ecclesia Christi," Rome, 1921.
"De Habitudine Ecclesiae ad Civilem Societatem," Rome, 1922.
*Bright, William
"Canons of the First Four General Councils," Oxford, 1892.
Cercia, Raphael, S.J.
"De Ecclesia Vera et de Romano Pontifice," 2 vols., Naples, 1858.
Chapman, John, O.S.B.
"Bishop Gore and Catholic Claims," London, 1905.
D'Ales, A.
"Dictionnaire Apologetique de la Foi Catholique," Paris, 1911-.
D'Herbigny, Michael, S.J.
"Theologiaca de Ecclesia," 2 vols., Paris, 1921.
Dieckmann, Herman, S.J.
"De Ecclesia Tractatus Historico-Dogmaticus," 2 vols., Freiburg, 1925.
Dorsch, Aemil
"De Ecclesia Christi," Innsbruck, 1914.
Duchesne, Louis
"The Churches Separated from Rome" (Tr. by Mathew), New York, 1907.
Finlay, Peter, S.J.
"The Church of Christ," London, 1916.

---

*Indicates non-Catholic author.

Fortescue, Andrian
"The Orthodox Eastern Church," London, 1907.
Franzelin, John Baptist
"De Ecclesia Christi," Rome, 1887.
Funk, Francis X.
"Patres Apostolici," 2 vols., Tubingen, 1901 (latest edition by Bihl-
meyer).
Hefele-Leclercq
"Histoire des Conciles," Paris, 1904-1923.
Hurter, H., S.J.
"Theologiae Dogmaticae Compendium," Innsbruck, 1900.
Jungmann, Bernard
"Dissertationes Selectae in Hist. Eccles.," 7 vols., 1881.
Lightfoot, John
"Horae Hebraicae," Canterbury, 1658.
Macguinness, John, C.M.
"Commentarii Theologici," Paris, 1911.
Mazzella, Camillus, S.J.
"De Religione et Ecclesia," Rome, 1880.
*Middleton, Edmund S.
"Unity and Rome," London and New York, 1922.
Murray, Patrick
"Tractatus de Ecclesia Christi," 6 vols., Dublin, 1860.
Nilles, Nicolaus, S.J.
"Kalendarium Manuale," 2 vols., Innsbruck, 1896.
*Palmer, William
"Treatise on the Church," 2 vols., London, 1838.
Palmieri, Dominic, S.J.
"Tractatus de Romano Pontifice," Prato, 1891.
*Puller, F. W.
"The Primitive Saints and the See of Rome," London, 1900.
Rivington, Luke
"The Primitive Church and the See of Peter," London, 1894.
Ryan-Millar
"The State and the Church," New York, 1924.
Salembier, L.
"The Great Schism of the West" (Tr. from French), London, 1907.
*Salmon, George
"Infallibility of the Church," London, 1890.

*Indicates non-Catholic author.

*Schaff, Philip
"The Creeds of Christendom," 3 vols., New York, 1877.

*Schaff-Herzog
"Encyclopedia of Religious Knowledge," 12 vols., New York, 1908.

Segna, Francis
"De Ecclesia Christi," Rome, 1900.

Straub, Anton, S.J.
"De Ecclesia Christi," 2 vols., Innsbruck, 1912.

Suarez, Francis, S.J.
"De Fide," Paris, 1878.

Tanquerey, Adam, S.S.
"Synopsis Theologiae Dogmaticae," Paris, 1923.

Vacandard, E.
"Etudes de Critique et d'Histoire Religieuse," 3 vols., Paris, 1909-1911.

Van Noort, G.
"Tractatus de Ecclesia Christi," Amsterdam, 1909.

*Wilberforce, R. I.[1]
"Principles of Church Authority," Baltimore, 1855.

Wilmers, William, S.J.
"De Ecclesia Christi," Ratisbon, 1897.

---

*Indicates non-Catholic author.
[1] Wilberforce became a Catholic shortly after writing the work mentioned.

PART I

Apologetic

THE TRUE CHURCH OF CHRIST

"You shall know the Truth and the Truth shall make you free."
—St. John VIII, 32.

CHAPTER I

Origin of the Church

Synopsis.—1. Origin and Meaning of the Name.—2. Christ Founded a Church Under the Form of a Society.—3. Christ Founded But One Church.—4. Purpose and Nature of the Church.

ART. I. ORIGIN AND MEANING OF THE NAME CHURCH

Ecclesia, the Greek and Latin word for *Church*, is derived from *ekkalein*, which means *to call together; to summon. Ekklesis* is the act of calling together, *ekklesia* is the result of that act,—the assembly of persons called together. Hence *ecclesia* originally signified an assembly for any purpose whatsoever. It was used in this sense by all ancient writers both sacred and profane; e.g., "All the tribes of Israel met together in the assembly (*ecclesia*) of the people of God."[1] "I have hated the assembly (*ecclesia*) of the malignant; and with the wicked I will not sit."[2] "Now some cried one thing, some another; for the assembly (*ecclesia*) was confused."[3] "The Athenians coming together (*poiesantes ekklesian*) signified their intentions by ballot."[4]

In the course of time the word *ecclesia* was restricted to a religious assembly and then to a religious society, particularly to a Christian society. Even in this sense the word is variously used:

1. *Ecclesia* designates all rational creatures subject to Christ as their head. In this sense the *Church* consists of three parts,—the *militant* Church, composed of all the faithful on earth; the *suffering* Church, which consists of the souls detained in Purgatory; the *triumphant* Church, including both the saints and angels in Heaven. "It is manifest," says St. Thomas, "that both men and angels are ordained for the same end; viz., the glory of the Beatific Vision. Hence angels as well as men belong to the mystic body of the Church."[5]

2. In a somewhat more restricted sense *ecclesia* refers to all those who have been faithful to God in every age, from the beginning of mankind. Thus St. Gregory the Great says: "The holy ones who have lived before the law (of Moses), those who lived under the Law, and

---

[1] Judges xx, 2.
[2] Ps. xxv, 5.
[3] Acts xix, 32.
[4] Thucydides, "Historia," i, 139.
[5] "Summa Theologica," 3a qu. 8, and 4.

3

those living under the dispensation of grace,—all these being members of the Church, constitute the body of the Lord."[6] In like manner St. Augustine says: "Christ is our head and we the body. What say I? we alone and not those also who were before us? Assuredly all the just from the beginning of the world have Christ for their head. They indeed believed in Him to come, whom we believe to have come."[7]

3. Kahal, the Hebrew equivalent of *ecclesia,* is frequently used to designate the people of Israel,—the Church of the Old Law. This is especially true of those passages in which the people of Israel are set forth as a type or figure of Christ's Church in the New Law; e.g., "I will declare thy name to my brethren; in the midst of the church will I praise thee."[8] "I will give thanks to thee in a great church; I will praise thee in a strong people."[9] "This was he that was in the Church (*ecclesia*) in the wilderness with the angel who spoke to him on mount Sina."[10]

4. In the *language* of the Fathers *ecclesia* usually means the society of all the faithful who adhere to Christ Incarnate as their Head and thus constitute the Church of the New Law. In the writings of the Apostles the faithful are the *"called"* of Jesus Christ; *called* according to His purpose; *called* to be saints."[11] Taken collectively, they constitute a community,—the community of the *called,* i.e., the *Ecclesia* or Church of Christ, who used the word in this sense when He said, "Upon this rock I will build my Church (*ecclesiam*)."[12]

5. The word *church* (*ecclesia*) is also frequently used to designate the faithful of a particular district or country. Thus we speak of the French Church, the Roman Church, the American Church, etc. This use of the word is common with St. Paul in his salutations; e.g., "Paul, called to be an apostle . . . to the Church of God that is at Corinth."[13] In like manner St. John speaks of the seven churches of Asia.[14] Even the faithful who worship together in the same place were called a *church.* St. Paul says: "Aquila and Priscilla and the church which is in their house, salute you."[15] In like manner parishes and dioceses are today often called churches.

6. By an easy transition the word *ecclesia* was applied to the edifice

<hr>

[6] "Letter to John the Bishop"; P.L., 77, 740.
[7] "Expositio in Psalm," xxxvi; P.L., 36, 385.
[8] Ps. xxi, 23.
[9] Ps. xxxiv, 18; cf. Num. xix, 29; xx, 4; Deut. xxiii, 3.
[10] Acts vii, 38.
[11] Rom. i, 6; 1 Cor. i, 2.
[12] Matt. xvi, 18.
[13] 1 Cor. i, 1; vii, 17; Rom. xxi, 4.
[14] Apoc. i, 4; ii, 1; iii, 11.
[15] 1 Cor. xvi, 19 Rom. xvi, 5.

in which the faithful met for divine worship. Hence we have the Spanish *iglesia,* the French *eglise,* and the Italian *chiesa,* to designate both the society and the edifice. In the early ages of the Church the edifice for worship was appropriately called the house of the Lord,— *domus dominica,* or simply *dominicum.* The Greek equivalent, *oikia kyriake,* was similarly contracted into *kyriakon.*[16] This shortened form was corrupted into *kyreiko* by the Goths and then passed into German as *kirche,* into English as *church.* In the Slavonic languages it became *cirkev* or *cerkov.*

It is interesting to note that in the Romance languages the word for *church* properly refers to the society. It is only by metonymy that it can be applied to the edifice. In the Germanic languages we find the very opposite. Slovak seems to be unique in having distinct terms for these two ideas; *cirkev* is the society, *kostol* the building. The latter is equivalent to our word *castle,* both being derived from the Latin *castellum*—a fortified place.

Synagogue

Under the Law of Moses the Chosen People were sometimes called a *church* (*kahal*) but more often the *synagogue* (*edah*) of Israel.[17] This is especially true after the time of Christ, when the Church was often contrasted with the Synagogue. The word is derived from the Greek *synagein—to drive together.* Hence it signifies an assembly of persons brought together by physical or moral force. Commenting on the difference between *ecclesia* and *synagoga,* St. Augustine says: "By the *synagogue* we understand the people of Israel, because *synagogue* is the word properly used of them, although they were also called the Church. Our congregation, on the contrary, the Apostles never called *synagogue,* but always *ecclesia;* whether for the sake of distinction, or because there is some difference between a congregation whence the Synagogue has its name, and a convocation whence the Church is called *ecclesia:* for the word congregation (or flocking together) is used of cattle, . . . whereas convocation (or calling together) is more of reasonable creatures such as men are. . . . Hence the worthier name is ours on account of our being *called.*"[18]

The name *synagogue* was also used to designate the Jewish faithful who frequented the same house of prayer; hence we read of the "synagogue of the Libertines, and of the Cyrenians, and of the Alexandrians, and of them that were of Cilicia and Asia."[19] At first the

---

[16] St. Cyril of Jerusalem, Catecheses xviii, 26. P.G., 33, 1943.
[17] Cf. Ex. xii, 3, 6, 47; xvi, 1, 2, 9; Num. xxvii, 17; xxxi, 16; Levit. iv, 13, 45.
[18] "Expositio in Psalm," lxxxi; P.L., 37, 1047.
[19] Acts vi, 9.

edifice in which a particular congregation of Jews met for prayer and instruction was called *house of the synagogue,* but in the course of time it came to be known simply as *the synagogue.*

ART. II. CHRIST FOUNDED A CHURCH UNDER THE FORM OF A SOCIETY

Synopsis.—1. Nature of a Society.—2. Errors Regarding the Nature and Origin of the Church.—3. Christ Personally Founded a Church as a Society.—4. The Church a Society Distinct from the Synagogue. —5. Objections answered.

1. Nature of a Society

A society may be defined as a union of intelligent beings, entered into for the purpose of attaining a common good by united efforts. A number of individuals is the *material element* necessary for the formation of a society, but they do not form a society unless banded together for the attainment of a common end by united efforts. Hence the union of wills toward a common end is the *formal* element of every society. The specific nature of a society may be literary, political, or religious, according to the end to be attained, and the organization of the society will vary accordingly. Hence the end to be attained may be called the *external formal element.*

The end to be attained by a society must be more or less permanent. A number of men uniting their efforts to extinguish a fire in a neighbor's house would not constitute a society. The fact that the purpose of a society is to be attained by the united efforts of all its members, does not mean that each and every member must contribute the same kind of effort or perform the same duties. In this respect a society resembles a physical body in which there are many members, each with its own peculiar function, yet all contribute to the well-being of the whole body, which in turn redounds to the good of each member.

Finally, no purpose can be accomplished unless suitable means are used and properly directed. To this end authority is necessary to co-ordinate and direct the members in the use of these means. Without authority there can be nothing but confusion and discord, and the society itself would soon perish. Those who exercise authority in a society are its *superior* or *officials;* those subject to this directing or ruling authority are *inferiors* or *subjects.*

Practically speaking, authority is the formal element of every society since it is authority that preserves and strengthens all the bonds by which the members are held together.

From the above considerations we deduce the following conditions necessary for a society:

a) a number of individuals;
b) a moral union, i.e., a union of wills;
c) a common end to be attained;
d) suitable means to attain that end; and
e) adequate authority.

These five conditions are essential and sufficient to constitute a society. If they are found realized in the Church founded by our Lord, then that Church is a true society.

2. Errors Regarding the Origin and Nature of the Church

The various errors concerning the origin and nature of the Church may be classed as Protestant, Rationalist, and Modernist.

1. PROTESTANTS for the most part believe that all Christian churches owe their existence in some way to Christ; but few would admit that Christ personally founded any particular society that can claim to be His Church, to the exclusion of all others. In a general way they seem to hold that Christ proclaimed a doctrine, or rather an ideal of life, which He wishes all His followers to realize. For this purpose they are free to form societies or churches in which to practice the Christian religion as they see fit. "Those believers who dwell together in one place become a church by their recognition of each other and their mutual agreement to observe Christ's ordinances in one society. Thus the visible church is one of the forms through which the kingdom of God is manifested among men."[20] Those who are not satisfied with one church may betake themselves to another or establish a new one to their own liking.[20a]

Protestants were forced to adopt this loose conception of the Church in order to justify the introduction of new churches by the so-called Reformers in the sixteenth and following centuries. If Christ personally founded one definitely organized society to continue as His Church through the ages, then all others must be counterfeits.

II. RATIONALISTS also deny that Christ founded a Church. According to David Friedrich Strauss, Christ was merely the founder of a new school of philosophy. Only in the second century did His dis-

---

[20] Clarence A. Beckwith, "Outline of Christian Theology," p. 208.

[20a] In citing Protestant theories on this and other questions, we can give only the opinions of individual Protestant writers. Their churches as such cannot be said to teach anything. Many of them have official creeds, but no two members of any church hold the same views even on matters contained in the creed.

ciples conceive and carry out the idea of forming societies similar to
the Jewish synagogues.[21] Adolph Harnack and Weizsäcker maintain
that Christ taught no particular doctrine, but simply strove by word
and example to win all to the practice of a spiritual life. The *Kingdom*
which Christ proclaimed, they contend, is within the soul,—it is purely
spiritual. "It is in the nature of a spiritual force, a power which sinks
into a man within and can be understood only from within. . . . It is
not here or there, it is within you."[22]

This interior communion with God is proclaimed as the essence of
Christianity; its collective and social character is only a secondary feature. It was owing entirely to external circumstances that the disciples
of Christ finally separated from the Synagogue and formed local societies, which gradually coalesced into one larger society, known as the
Church. The doctrines of the Church were elaborated with the assistance of Greek philosophy, and its organization was borrowed from
Rome.[23]

III. THE MODERNISTS agree with the rationalists in denying that
Christ intended to establish a Church. According to their teaching, religion consists entirely in certain experiences arising from the action
of God upon a religious sentiment, which they call the *need for the Divine*. In the first century the faithful began to form local societies to
further their common interests. In course of time (in the second or
third century according to Sabatier) these local societies began to unite,
and the Church in the Catholic sense of that term sprang into being.
Therefore the origin and present state of the Church are due to evolutionary forces. The *Kingdom of God* announced by Christ is essentially
collective and social, i.e., it is a real society, but purely eschatological;
it is the kingdom of justice to be inaugurated at the end of the world,
which Christ believed near at hand.[24]

A detailed criticism of these theories is unnecessary; they are sufficiently refuted by proving that Christ actually did establish a Church
under the form of an external and visible society. It may be noted,
however, that Harnack and Loisy are right in making spiritual regeneration an essential element of the *Kingdom of God,* but they are wrong
in making it the only one. Our Lord often contrasted the spiritual
character of His kingdom with the external formalism of the Old Law;
in the new kingdom God is worshipped in *spirit and in truth*.[25] At the

---

[21] Strauss, "Das Leben Jesu."
[22] A. Harnack, "Das Wesen des Christentums," p. 39.
[23] A. Harnack, "Lehrbuch der Dogmengeschichte," I, 140 sqq.; Weizsäcker, "Das Apostolische Zeitalter"; cf. D'Ales, "Dictionnaire Apologetique," art. "Eglise."
[24] Cf. A. Loisy, "L'Evangile et l'eglise"; G. Tyrrell, "Scylla and Charybdis"; A. Sabatier, "De l'Essence du Christianisme."
[25] Cf. Matthew v, 1 sqq.; John iv, 24.

same time the social element is no less essential; the kingdom of God on earth is to be a real kingdom,—a real society, in which interior perfection is demanded.

3. Christ Personally Founded His Church as a Society

It is an article of faith that Christ personally established a church under the form of a true society visibly existing among men. This was decreed by the Vatican Council in the following words: "In order to perpetuate the saving work of Redemption, the eternal Pastor and Bishop of souls decreed to establish a holy Church, in which all the faithful might be gathered together by the unity of faith and love as in the house of God."[26] The same doctrine is also taught by the condemnation of the following proposition of Modernism: "It was not the intention of Christ to establish a Church as a society destined to continue upon earth through a number of centuries; in fact, according to the teachings of Christ, the Kingdom of Heaven was to come only with the end of the world."[26a]

DEMONSTRATION. The fact that Christ personally instituted a Church is proved: from His own promise to do so; from the institution of the Apostolic ministry; from prescription. The social nature of the Church is also proved from the same sources and clearly indicated by the various figures or symbols under which the Church is depicted in the Gospels and in the writings of the Apostles.

1. THE PROMISE. "Thou art Peter and upon this rock I will build my Church."[26b] In these words our Lord promises to establish a Church, and the promise is absolute; its fulfillment is subject to no condition whatsoever. The very name *church* (*ecclesia*) indicates a society.[27] Moreover, Christ uses the word *build,* thus comparing His Church to an edifice in which parts are joined to parts and so ordered that a completed structure rises from the foundations. Thus also shall it be with the Church: the faithful as living stones shall be built up into a spiritual house.[28] In a word, the Church which Christ promises to establish, shall be a true society of men amongst men.

2. THE APOSTOLIC MINISTRY. The founder of a society need only formulate the necessary plans and authorize suitable persons to put them into execution. Christ did this in regard to the Church, when

---

[26] Denzinger, n. 1821.
[26a] Decree "Lamentabili," 3, July, 1907; Denzinger N. 2052.—Note—In this part of our work, definitions of councils and decrees of popes are not cited as proof of a thesis, but simply to prove what is the defined doctrine of the Church.
[26b] Matt. xvi, 18.
[27] See above, p. 3.
[28] 1 Peter ii, 5.

he instituted the Apostolic ministry, sending forth the Apostles with authority to teach, govern, and sanctify, and obliged all men to submit to their threefold authority. A few texts will be sufficient to show this triple power granted to the Apostles:

a) Authority to Teach. "Go therefore and make disciples of all nations . . . teaching them to observe all that I have commanded you."[29] And again He said to them "Go into the whole world and preach the gospel to every creature."[30]

b) Authority to Govern. "Whatsoever you bind upon earth shall be bound also in heaven; and whatsover you loose upon earth shall be loosed also in heaven."[31] Again: "All power is given to me in heaven and on earth . . . as the Father hath sent me I also send you."[32] With these words our Lord conferred upon His Apostles the same power and authority that He himself had received as divine legate from His Heavenly Father.

c) Power to Sanctify. "Go, therefore and make disciples of all nations, baptizing them in the name of the Father and of the Son and of the Holy Spirit."[33] Again: "Whose sins you shall forgive, they are forgiven them, and whose sins you shall retain they are retained."[34] "This is my body which is being given for you; do this in remembrance of me."[35]

The authority to teach, govern, and sanctify, undeniably conferred upon the Apostles, implies the corresponding duty to accept their teaching, to observe their precepts, and to receive at their hands the means of sanctification. The duties are also clearly enunciated by our Lord:

a) The Duty of Accepting the teachings of the Apostles is proclaimed in these words: "Go into the whole world and preach the gospel to every creature. He who believes and is baptized shall be saved, but he who does not believe shall be condemned."[36]

b) The Duty of Obedience is no less stringent: "He who hears you, hears me; and he who rejects you rejects me. And he who reject me, rejects Him who sent me."[37] Speaking of the man in need of correction Christ said: "Appeal to the Church, but if he refuse to hear even the Church, let him be to the as the heathen and the publican."[38]

---

[29] Matt. xxviii, 19.
[30] Mark xvi, 15.
[31] Matt. xviii, 18.
[32] Matt. xxviii, 18; John xx, 22.
[33] Matt. xxviii, 19-20.
[34] John xx, 22, 23.
[35] Luke xxii, 19.
[36] Mark xvi, 16.
[37] Luke x, 16.
[38] Matt. xviii, 17.

c) The Duty of Receiving the Means of Sanctification is also inculcated: "Amen, amen I say to thee, unless a man be born again of water and the Spirit he cannot enter into the kingdom of God."[39] Elsewhere we read: "Unless you eat the flesh of the Son of man and drink his blood, you shall not have life in you."[40]

Christ having conferred upon His Apostles authority to teach, govern and sanctify, sent them forth into the world to make disciples: "Go, therefore, and make disciples of all nations." A rite of initiation was also prescribed: "Baptizing them in the name of the Father and of the Son and of the Holy Spirit." All the requisites for a true society were fully realized,—superiors endowed with adequate authority, subjects constituted by a special rite of initiation and brought together in a unity of government, faith, and worship. Hence, Christ personally founded His Church under the form of a true society by the very act of instituting the apostolic ministry.

3. PRESCRIPTION. Down through the centuries from the days of the Apostles there has existed a true and visible society claiming Christ as its author,—a claim that was recognized as just by all antiquity. St. Cyprian may be quoted in this connection: "Our Lord first gave this power to Peter, upon whom he built His Church, and from whom He ordained that unity should have its origin."[41] Likewise the Apostles, who certainly must have known the mind of their Divine Master, always looked upon themselves and their associates as the rulers of a society founded by Christ from whom they derived all authority. Thus, for instance, St. Paul writes: "God indeed hath set some in the Church; first apostles, secondly, prophets, thirdly, teachers . . . for the work of the ministry, for building up the body of Christ."[42]

4. SYMBOLS OF THE CHURCH. The social nature of the Church is also clearly indicated by the many symbols or figures under which it is depicted in Holy Scripture. It is often called a *flock,* a *sheepfold,* a *house,* or a *body.* Christ says: "Other sheep I have which are not of this fold; them also I must bring, and they shall hear my voice, and there shall be one fold and one shepherd."[43] St. Paul thus addresses the clergy of Ephesus: "Take heed to yourselves and to the whole flock, in which the Holy Spirit hath placed you bishops, to rule

---

[39] John iii, 5.
[40] John vi, 54.
[41] "Epistola ad Jubaianum"; P.L. 3, 1114. Further testimony will be found in the article on the apostolicity of the Church; *infra.*
[42] 1 Cor. xii, 28; Ephes. iv, 11. Other texts will be found in the following section on the Church and the Synagogue.
[43] John x, 14-16.

the Church of God."[44] Writing to Timothy he says: "That thou mayest
know how thou oughtest to behave thyself in the house of God which is
the Church of the living God."[45] To the Ephesians he writes: "And all
things he (God) made subject under his (Christ's) feet and he gave him
as head over all the Church which indeed is his body, the completion of
him who fills all with all."[46]

No symbol could be found more suggestive of a society than that of
a fold or flock, in which the sheep are united under the care of a shepherd, whose voice they hear and obey. In fact, so appropriate is the
comparison that the rulers of the Church in all ages have been known
as *pastores,*—the Latin word for *shepherds.* Scarcely less significant is
the comparison with a house or a body, for in both there is union and
order of parts to constitute a complete whole. When men are thus united
they form a *society.*

4. The Church Distinct From the Synagogue

Many rationalists deny that Christ had any intention of founding a
society distinct from the Synagogue.[47] They maintain that the influence
of St. Paul finally led the disciples to withdraw from the Synagogue and
form separate societies, which gradually coalesced into the one society
known as the Church of Christ. This theory is sufficiently refuted by
establishing the following thesis concerning the origin of the Church:

Thesis.—The Church Was Established by Christ as a Society Distinct
From the Synagogue

PROOFS. I. *From Reason.* Societies having different authors, different members, different superiors, and striving by different means to
attain separate ends, must be recognized as entirely distinct societies. But
this is precisely the case with the Church and the Synagogue. Moses was
the immediate author of the Synagogue, whereas Christ was the immediate and personal author of the Church. For this reason St. Paul contrasts Moses with Our Lord: "Moses indeed was faithful in all his house
(the Synagogue) as a servant . . . but Christ is faithful as the Son over
his own house (the Church)."[48]

The Synagogue was limited in its membership to one nation; the

---

[44] Acts xx, 28.
[45] 1 Tim. iii, 15.
[46] Ephes. i, 22, 23.
[47] *Synagogue* is here used to designate the Mosaic religion,—the Church of the
Old Law.
[48] Heb. iii, 5, 6.

Church was established for all men: "Going therefore, teach all nations." The Synagogue was intended primarily as a preparation for the coming of Christ; it was "our tutor unto Christ, that we might be justified by faith."[49] The Synagogue wrought sanctification for one people only, and that a mere legal sanctity, produced by sacrifices and sacraments that were but types and figures,—"weak and beggarly elements."[50] The Church, on the other hand, works a real supernatural sanctification for all men by means of a sacrifice and sacraments efficacious in themselves. Finally, the rulers of the Synagogue belonged to the priesthood of Aaron, with which the ministers of the Church,—the Apostles and their successors,—have no connection.

II. *From Scripture.* The Acts of the Apostles always portrays the Church as a society having a separate and independent existence. On Pentecost the disciples already constituted a society, to which a large number was added by the rite of Baptism: "Now they who received his (Peter's) word were baptized and there were added that day about three thousand souls, and they continued steadfastly in the teaching of the apostles, and in the communion of the breaking of bread and in prayers."[51] Again we read: "Now in those days as the number of the disciples was increasing, there arose a murmuring among the Hellenists against the Hebrews that their widows were being neglected in the daily ministrations. So the Twelve called together the multitude of the disciples and said. 'It is not desirable that we should forsake the word of God and serve at tables. Therefore, brethren select from among you seven men of good reputation, full of the Spirit and of wisdom that we may put them in charge of this work. But we will devote ourselves to prayer and to the ministry of the word' . . . These they set before the apostles, and after they had prayed they laid their hands upon them. And the word of the Lord continued to spread, and the number of disciples increased rapidly in Jerusalem; a large number also of the priests accepted the faith."[52] These passages obviously refer to a society distinct from the Synagogue,—a society having its own officials, its own peculiar doctrines, and a distinctive worship.

After the martyrdom of St. Stephen "there broke out on that day a great persecution against the Church in Jerusalem, and all except the apostles were scattered abroad throughout the land of Judea and Samaria."[53] These words depict the Church as a society subject to persecution at the hands of the Jews which could not be the case were the

---

[49] Gal. iii, 24.
[50] Gal. iv, 9.
[51] Acts ii, 41, 42.
[52] Acts vi, 1 sqq.
[53] Acts viii, 1 sqq.

Church not recognized as something different from the Synagogue and opposed to it. St. Paul leaves no room for doubt in the matter: in his Epistle to the Hebrews he makes a lengthy comparison between the Synagogue and the Church, thereby proving that they were absolutely different institutions.[54] When writing to the Corinthians, he also distinguishes between the Church and the Synagogue: "Do not be a stumbling-block to Jews and Greeks and to the Church of God."[55]

III. *From Roman Law.* The laws of Rome allowed the Jews freedom of religious worship and conferred upon them many privileges, yet the Church was cruelly persecuted from its very beginning. Scarcely thirty-five years after our Lord's death, Nero decreed that it was not lawful to be a Christian,—"*Christianos esse non licet.*"[56] Hence the Roman government must have looked upon the Church as a society entirely distinct from the Synagogue.

5. Objections Considered

OBJECTION I.—Christ expected to return soon after His death to judge the world. This is evident from His words to the Jews: "Amen I say to you, there are some of those standing here who will not taste death, till they have seen the Son of Man coming in his kingdom."[57] On another occasion He described the signs preceding the second coming, and then added: "Amen I say to you that this generation shall not pass till all these things be done."[58] His words to the Apostles convey the same meaning: "Amen I say to you, you will not have gone through the towns of Israel before the Son of Man comes."[59] It is evident, then, that Christ had no intention of founding a Church, or kingdom on earth. The kingdom announced by Him was purely eschatological,—a kingdom to be inaugurated at His second coming.

ANSWER.—Taken by themselves, the passages quoted might suggest that the end of the world and the second coming of Christ were near at hand, but other and clearer texts leave no doubt that our Lord neither expected nor proclaimed His second coming as an event of the near future. He said to the Apostles: "Behold I am with you all days even to the consummation of the world."[60] The tenor of these words implies at least several centuries intervening before the end of the world. At an-

[54] Heb. iii, 1 sq.
[55] 1 Cor. x, 32.
[56] Tertullian, "Apology," iv; P.L., 1, 285.
[57] Matt. xvi, 28.
[58] Matt. xxiv, 34.
[59] Matt. x, 23.
[60] Matt. xxviii, 20.

other time He said: "This Gospel of the kingdom shall be preached in the whole world for a witness to all nations, and then shall the end come."[61] This presupposes a considerable lapse of time; the preaching of the Gospel to the whole world and to all nations was not a work to be accomplished in a few months or years. Again, in foretelling the destruction of Jerusalem, Christ said: "They will fall by the edge of the sword, and will be led away captive into all nations; and Jerusalem will be trodden down by the gentiles till the times of the nations be fulfilled."[62] This indicates a considerable period of time between the destruction of Jerusalem and the end of the world.

It is a recognized principle of interpretation that the obscure passages of a work must be explained in the light of clearer texts bearing upon the same subject. Hence the rather obscure texts quoted in the objection must be interpreted according to other passages whose meaning is clear. To consider each one in particular: (a) "Some that stand here shall not taste death till they see the Son of man coming in His kingdom," i.e., according to some interpreters, until they see the Son of man reigning in His kingdom, the Church which was spread far and wide even during the lifetime of some who heard these words of our Lord. Other scholars take the words "coming in His kingdom" as a reference to our Lord's coming in judgment at the destruction of Jerusalem. Still others take them as a reference to the Transfiguration, which occurred six days later.[63] On this occasion our Lord was speaking not to the people, but to His Apostles, three of whom were privileged to see Him in that fleeting moment of glory on the mount. (b) "This generation shall not pass till all these things be done," i.e., the Jewish people shall not perish from the earth until the things foretold shall come to pass. If this be the correct interpretation, the prophecy is wonderfully fulfilled. No other people known to history ever preserved its identity during long centuries of exile like the Jews. (c) "You shall not have gone through the towns of Israel till the Son of Man come," i.e., before you have preached the Gospel in all the cities of Israel, I shall come in judgment against the city of Jerusalem for its sins of infidelity. In the Old Testament God is often said to come in judgment when there is question of some special manifestation of His justice against iniquity.[64]

Whatever be the interpretation of the texts just considered, it has been proved beyond doubt that Christ not only planned a Church, but

---

[61] Matt. xxiv, 14.
[62] Luke xxi, 24.
[63] Matt. xvii, 1.
[64] Cf. Is. iii, 14; xxx, 27.

actually established it. This fact cannot be overcome by objections taken from one or another text of uncertain meaning.

OBJECTION II.—Christ frequented the Temple and the synagogues, and observed the rites of the Mosaic Law; in fact, he openly declared that He had come, not to destroy, but to fulfill the Law.[65] The disciples also frequented the Temple as we read in the Acts: "And continuing daily with one accord in the temple."[66] These facts prove that neither Christ nor His disciples had any idea of a society distinct from the Synagogue.

ANSWER.—The conclusion does not follow from the facts adduced. It is possible for a person to belong to two or more societies at the same time, if those societies are not opposed to one another. The Acts of the Apostles relates that the disciples attended the Temple daily, but it also states that they "continued steadfastly in the teaching of the apostles and in the communion of the breaking of the bread and in the prayers."[67] They formed a society under the leadership of the Apostles with their own doctrines and their own distinct worship. They went to the Temple to pray, as they were accustomed to do, but they afterward met in their own homes to celebrate the Eucharist,—"breaking bread in their houses."[68]

Up to the time of Christ's passion and death the Mosaic Law was in full force; the disciples and Apostles were strictly bound by its precepts and ceremonies, and although Our Lord was not bound by the Law, He observed its ordinances, that He might show Himself an example to those who were. Therefore it was necessary for the disciples of Christ to attend the services of the Temple before His death. After that they would only gradually give up practices to which they had been accustomed all their lives.

It is also true that Christ came to fulfill the Law: He came to fulfill the prophecies contained therein, and to establish the Church long prefigured by the institutions of the Law. He came to establish the kingdom promised to the seed of David.

OBJECTION III.—The ceremonies of the Old Law were a profession of faith in a Messias to come. The disciples of Christ believed Him to be the Messias already come, hence their observance of the Law was a virtual denial of this new faith, for as St. Paul observes: "If you be circumcised, Christ will be of no advantage to you . . . you

---

[65] Matt. v, 18.
[66] Acts ii, 46.
[67] Acts ii, 42.
[68] Acts ii, 46.

are estranged from Christ; you have fallen away from grace."[69] It is evident, therefore, that those first disciples did not consider themselves as forming a society distinct from the Synagogue until they had come under the influence of St. Paul, the author of the separatist movement.

ANSWER.—The objection has no bearing on the question at issue. The disciples believed Our Lord to be the long expected Messias, whether He established a Church independent of the Synagogue or not. Their observance of the Mosaic Law would be no greater denial of faith in one case than in the other. It has been proved that Christ did establish a Church as a society distinct from the Synagogue. It is also certain that the first disciples continued to frequent the Temple and observed the Mosaic Law to some extent. Whether they were right in so doing is another question. On this matter Tanquerey says: "The Synagogue was a figure of the Church and a preparation for it; hence the change from one to the other was not a change from a false to a true religion, but from one form of true religion to another. For this reason the change was made gradually in order to win the Jews more securely to the new faith. . . . The Apostles themselves observed certain ceremonies of the Law lest they give offense to their brethren, but when converts from among the Pharisees wished to impose the Mosaic Law upon gentile converts, St. Peter openly declared that it was no longer obligatory.[70] But since both Jew and Christian worshipped the same God and observed the same moral code, and since the new religion, preached first to the Jews, differed but little in doctrine from the old, we should not be surprised to find that at first the separation of the Church from the Synagogue was not complete."[71]

St. Augustine clearly explains the relation of the Synagogue to the Church by distinguishing three stages in the history of the Mosaic Law. These stages he designates as the *living,* the *dead,* and the *deadly.* Before the passion and death of Our Lord the Mosaic Law was obligatory (*living*) upon every member of the Jewish nation. After the death of Christ the Law ceased to bind; it was *dead,* yet the Jews were free to observe it until the Gospel of the New Law was duly promulgated. After due promulgation of the Gospel the Old Law was both dead and *death-dealing;* those who still observed its ceremonial precepts thereby denied that the Law of Christ is sufficient for salva-

---

[69] Gal. v, 2 sq.
[70] Acts xv, 10, 11.
[71] Tanquerey, "Synopsis Theol. Dogm.," Vol. I, p. 317 (6th ed.).

tion. For this reason St. Paul says: "You are estranged from Christ, you who are justified in the law; you are fallen from grace."[72]

On the same subject Father Semeria says: "Christianity was a new fruit coming to maturity on an old vine: it was a new life developing from one that had passed maturity and was now growing decrepit. A number of causes, both human and divine, bound this new life to the Jewish religion. According to a happy expression of the Fathers, 'the Synagogue was being buried with honors.' God did not wish a sudden and violent transition, but the infant Church contained within itself an element which soon developed and brought about a complete separation. It was a case of historical biology."[73]

ART. III. CHRIST FOUNDED BUT ONE CHURCH

Protestants in general believe that one Christian church is as good as another, since all owe their existence equally to Christ; but they deny that He established any one to the exclusion of all others. Protestant theologians of the sixteenth century introduced the doctrine of a twofold Church,—the one visible, the other invisible. They were forced to this doctrine when asked to explain where the Church of Christ existed before the Reformation, since they taught that the Catholic Church had long since fallen into error and corruption and had ceased to be the Church of Christ. They solved the difficulty by claiming that the true Church of Christ is invisible and comprises all the just, or all those predestined to eternal life. The visible Church is composed of the various religious organizations, or churches, which are but so many external manifestations of the Church invisible. The just and the just alone belong to the invisible Church, regardless of what visible church organization they may belong to. In fact, they may belong to the invisible Church even though they have no connection with any organized church society.

There are some who maintain that Our Lord simply proclaimed the ideal of a Church and left it to His followers to organize actual churches, which realize more or less perfectly the ideal proposed by Him. This doctrine likewise leaves a multitude of churches, in all of which salvation may be obtained with equal security. Hence the belief that one church is as good as another.

These theories are refuted in part by the fact already proved, that Christ actually instituted a real Church under the form of a visible

---

[72] St. Augustine, "Letter to St. Jerome," P.L., 33, 156.
[73] Semeria, "Venticinque Anni di Storia," p. 92.

society.[74] The question now arises whether Christ established one Church or several. The answer to this question is of supreme importance. If there is but one true Church of Christ, all others must be false claimants, with no right to existence. If there is but one true Church, our eternal salvation depends upon finding and embracing it, and the doctrine that one church is as good as another must be rejected.

Thesis.—Christ Founded But One Church

The doctrine stated in the above thesis is not only historically certain, but also a defined dogma of the Church, as is evident from the

PROOFS. I. *From Reason.* Had Our Lord established two or more churches, all would have to teach the same, or different doctrines; employ the same, or different means of salvation. If they taught the same doctrines and employed the same means of salvation, it would be difficult to assign a sufficient reason for their separate existence. If they taught different doctrines or used different means of salvation, one only would be teaching *all* the doctrines of Christ or using *all* the means established by Him for salvation; yet the Church of Christ must "observe all things whatsoever I have commanded you."[75] Again, if several churches teach opposing doctrines, all save one must necessarily teach falsehood, whereas the Church of Christ must ever be "the pillar and mainstay of truth."[76]

Nicene Creed: "believe in ONE holy, catholic and apostolic Church."

II. *From Scripture.* Sacred Scripture always speaks of the Church as one,—the one kingdom of God on earth; the single mustard seed that grows into a tree filling the whole earth; the one net cast into the sea; the one field in which the wheat and cockle grow together until the harvest.[77] Again, the Church is the *spouse* of Christ, and the union between Christ and His Church is held up as the model for the union between husband and wife,[78]—a union between one man and one woman; not a polygamous union with several wives. The Church is also the *body* of Christ,[79] but Christ is no monster having several bodies.

Our Lord Himself explicitly states that His Church shall be one: "Upon this rock I will build my Church."[80] He does not say *churches*.

---

[74] The visible nature of the Church will be discussed more at length in the following chapter.
[75] Matt. xxviii, 19.
[76] 1 Tim. iii, 15.
[77] Ephes. v, 25.
[78] Matt. xiii, 24 sq.
[79] Ephes. i, 22, 23.
[80] Matt. xvi, 18.

He also says: "There shall be one fold and one shepherd."[81] St. Paul gives the reason why the Church should be one: "One body and one Spirit; as you are called in one hope of your calling. One Lord, one faith, one baptism, one God and Father of all."[82] The Church, which is the body of Christ, should be one, since there is but one God and Father of all, one faith, one baptism, one and the same eternal life to be attained.

III. *From Tradition.* To quote the words of early writers on this question seems a needless task. Neither the Fathers of the Church nor the early heretics ever dreamed of denying that the Church of Christ must be one and only one. A few examples from the early Fathers will suffice for a doctrine so clearly and forcibly stated in Holy Scripture.

a) *The Didache.* "Remember thy Church, O Lord! Deliver it from all evil and establish it in thy love. Gather it from the four winds into thy kingdom which thou hast prepared for it."[83] The author of this ancient work evidently recognized but one Church of Christ,—the Church spread over the four quarters of the earth, whence it shall be gathered into the heavenly kingdom of the Church triumphant.

b) *St. Cyprian:* "There is one God, and Christ is one, and there is one Church and one chair founded upon the rock by the word of the Lord. Another altar cannot be constituted nor a new priesthood be made except the one altar and the one priesthood. Whosoever gathereth elsewhere, scattereth."[84]

c) *Clement of Alexandria:* "From the very reason that God is one and the Lord one, that which is in the highest degree honorable is lauded in consequence of its singleness. In the nature of the One, then, is associated in a joint heritage the one Church which they (heretics) strive to cut asunder. . . . Therefore in substance and idea, in origin, in preeminence, we say that the ancient and Catholic Church is alone . . . passing all things else and having nothing like or equal to itself."[85]

d) *St. Ambrose.* "Let us follow this one congregation of the Lord; let us recognize the one Church. . . . From every valley a catholic people is brought together; there are no longer many congregations but one, there is only one Church."[86]

---

[81] John x, 16.
[82] Ephes. iv, 3-6.
[83] *Didache Apostolorum,* x, 5; cf. Funk, "Patres Apostolici," I, 25.—This work known as "Teaching of the Apostles," was written in the first century, probably between A. D. 80 and 90.
[84] "Epistola ad Plebem"; P.L., 40, 336.*
[85] "Stromata," vii, 17; P.G., 9, 551.*
[86] "Hexaemeron"; P.L., 14, 146.

ART. IV. PURPOSE AND NATURE OF THE CHURCH

Synopsis.—1. Purpose of the Church.—2. General Nature of the Church.—3. The Church and the Kingdom of God.

1. Purpose of the Church

FINAL PURPOSE. The Church, in common with all the works of God, must have for its final purpose the manifestation of God's glory. For this reason St. Paul says: "In whom (Christ) we also have been called by a special choice, having been predestined . . . to contribute to the praise of his glory. . . . He is the pledge of our inheritance for a redemption of possession, for the praise of his glory."[87] Elsewhere he says: "Christ loved the Church and delivered himself up for her . . . that he might present her to himself in all her glory."[88]

The Church is eminently fitted to give glory to God by its wonderful manifestation of His power, wisdom, and goodness in providing such efficacious means of salvation for all men at all times, whatever be their condition or state in life.

IMMEDIATE PURPOSE. The immediate end of the Church is twofold,—one to be attained by the Church herself acting as a society; the other, by individuals acting in subjection to her authority. To point out the end to be attained by the Church herself is simply to state what position she holds in the economy of Redemption; to determine the end to be attained by the individual in the Church is to say why Christ commands all men to enter her fold.

a) *The Church.* Christ's greatest work was accomplished when He offered Himself on the Cross for our redemption and thereby merited for us every grace. This work, known to theologians as Redemption *in actu primo,* was personally wrought by Our Lord for all time, "for by one oblation He hath perfected for ever them that are sanctified. . . . He was offered once to exhaust the sins of many."[89] But the price of our redemption being offered, there was still a further work to perform; the merits of Christ's suffering and death must be applied to individual souls through all the centuries. This is known as Redemption *in actu secundo.* Since Our Lord was not to remain upon earth in His bodily presence, there was need of some agency to carry on this work; therefore, in the words of the Vatican Council, "the eternal Pastor and

---

[87] Ephes. i, 11-14.
[88] Ephes. v, 25-27.
[89] Heb. x, 14; iv, 28.

Bishop of souls decreed to establish a holy Church in order to perpetuate the saving work of Redemption."[90]

Christ proclaimed His doctrines, gave His precepts, and instituted
the Sacraments to enable all men to participate in the fruits of the
Redemption. He then instituted the Apostolic ministry to perpetuate
this work in the world. He sent forth the Apostles with authority to
teach and govern all men and to administer to them the means of salvation. But as already shown, Christ instituted His Church by instituting the Apostolic ministry. It follows, then, that the Church was
established to perpetuate the work of the Redemption by applying it
to the souls of men. In a word, the Church was instituted to save all
men, or, as St. Paul expresses it: "In order to perfect the saints for a
work of the ministry, for building up the body of Christ, until we all
attain to the unity of the faith and of deep knowledge of the Son of
God, to perfect manhood, to the mature measure of the fullness of
Christ."[91]

b) *The Individual.* Since the Church was instituted to save mankind
by bringing souls to eternal life, the ultimate end to be sought by the
individual in and through the Church can be no other than eternal
salvation, as Christ Himself admonishes: "Seek ye first the kingdom
of God and his justice."[92] The immediate end to be attained must be
that which Christ enjoined upon all men and which the Apostles demanded of those who entered the Church, i.e., to submit to the authority of the Church, to be instructed by her in all revealed truths, to
receive the Sacraments, and to offer true worship to God,—in a word
to practice the Christian religion and thus prepare for eternal life.

2. General Nature of the Church

THE CHURCH A RELIGIOUS SOCIETY. The end for which a
society exists determines to a great extent the nature of that society. The
Church, therefore, is a religious society, as all admit, and since it owes its
existence to Christ, is known as a Christian society. In fact it is the only
means established by Christ to teach His doctrines, to inculcate His moral
precepts, to administer the Sacraments, and to regulate and direct divine
worship. No one can practice the Christian religion otherwise than as
Christ Himself has ordained; whoever would be His disciple and embrace

---

[90] Denzinger, n. 1821.
[91] Ephes. iv, 13.—The Church is directly concerned only with man's spiritual welfare, but since the temporal reacts upon the spiritual, she must also give some attention to his temporal well-being. The Church greatly promotes temporal happiness
by her care for spiritual things.
[92] Matt. vi, 33.

His religion must submit to the authority of His Church, be taught and ruled by it, and receive through it all the means of salvation. This is evident from the commission which Christ gave to His Apostles when He sent them forth to teach all nations. The Church, then, is not an institution of Christianity; it *is* Christianity existing in the concrete.

THE CHURCH A SUPERNATURAL SOCIETY. The end to be attained by the Church, and most of the means to that end, are purely spiritual and supernatural. The Church has Christ for its author and exercises a supernatural power conferred by Him. Her members are raised to a supernatural state and consecrated in a special manner to God by the grace and spiritual character of Baptism. Therefore, the Church is a supernatural society in its origin and purpose, in its authority and means of sanctification, and likewise in its members. For this reason Christ could say: "My kingdom is not of this world."[93]

THE CHURCH A DIVINE-HUMAN SOCIETY. The Church, being the work of Christ and holding authority from Him, must be divine in its origin, in its constitution, and in its authority. On the other hand, it is a society of men and for men, and therefore human. In the words of Leo XIII, "the Church is a society divine in its origin, supernatural in its end and means, yet because it consists of human members, it is a human society."[94] This twofold element in the Church explains the seemingly contradictory characteristics ascribed to it by our Lord Himself. It is a kingdom not of this world, perpetual, ever opposed yet never overcome, ever displaying the vigor of youth, because, unlike other societies, it is not subject to the law of decay; it is a divine institution. On the other hand, Christ clearly foretells evils in His Church: it is the field in which cockle grows with the wheat; it is the net taking fish both good and bad. It is necessary that scandals come because the Church is a human society subject to human evils.

THE CHURCH A PERFECT SOCIETY. A perfect society, in this connection, is not one free from defects and imperfections, but one having everything necessary to make it a *complete* society. In this sense a sovereign state is a perfect society, although there may be many and serious imperfections in its government. Certain conditions are necessary to constitute a perfect, or complete society:

(1) It must be independent of all other societies, both in its existence and in its actions. A corporation is not a perfect society, since it depends upon the State for its existence and is regulated by the State in its actions.

---

[93] John xviii, 36.
[94] Leo XIII, "Satis cognitum," July 29, 1896. Denzinger, n. 1959.

(2) It must not be part of another society, for a part is necessarily incomplete.

(3) Its end must not be subordinate to that of any other society in the same order, otherwise it will also be subordinate to that other society, and therefore not independent in its actions.

(4) It must have at its command the means necessary for its own conservation and for the attainment of its own proper end, otherwise it will be dependent upon some other society for these means and therefore not perfect in itself. A society may possess necessary means either *in re* or *in virtute,* i.e., it may have them in actual possession or it may have the right to demand them of some other society, which is bound to supply them.

These four conditions being fully certified in the Church, constitute it a perfect society. It does not depend upon any other society for its existence; its end is supreme in its own order and cannot be subordinated to any higher order since it seeks man's highest good,—his eternal salvation. The Church is also independent in all its actions, as the works of Christ clearly prove: "Whatever you bind upon earth shall be bound also in heaven; and whatever you loose upon earth shall be loosed also in heaven."[95] Since the actions of the Church are ratified in Heaven, no power on earth can modify or nullify them. Christ has also promised that His Church shall endure until the end of time despite the opposition of worldly powers: "Behold I am with you all days even to the consummation of the world."[96] David's prophecy concerning Christ is equally true of His Church: "The kings of the earth stood up, and the princes met together against the Lord and against his Christ. . . . He that dwelleth in heaven shall laugh at them, and the Lord shall deride them."[97] Hated, opposed, and persecuted, the Church shall remain victorious to the end, because she has within herself all means necessary to attain the purpose of her existence.

Objections Considered

OBJECTION I.—The Church cannot be a perfect and independent society, as it has no dominion, no territory of its own, in which to exercise authority.

ANSWER.—It is not necessary that a society have a dominion, or territory, by right of ownership; a territory in which to exercise authority is dominion sufficient for any society, and this the Church has.

---

[95] Matt. xviii, 18.
[96] Matt. xxviii, 20.
[97] Ps. ii, 2-4.

Her Dominion is the world: "Go ye therefore into the whole world and preach the Gospel to every creature."[98] The Church has received her dominion from Him to whom belongs "the earth and the fullness thereof; the world and all they that dwell therein."[99] One and the same territory belongs to the Church and to the civil powers,—to the Church for the exercise of spiritual jurisdiction; to the civil powers for the exercise of temporal jurisdiction.

OBJECTION II.—In this case two independent societies would be exercising supreme jurisdiction in one and the same territory, which is contrary to the axiom that *a State within a State is a contradiction.* Hence the Church cannot be a perfect society.

ANSWER.—Two societies exercising supreme authority in the same territory is a contradiction if both are concerned about the same things; if they have different ends in view, there is no contradiction, unless those ends are incompatible. The ends sought by the Church and the State are different, but not incompatible; in fact they are mutually helpful.

OBJECTION III.—Without religion there can be neither peace nor happiness in the State. Therefore, religion, or at least religious worship, must be subject to State regulation.

ANSWER.—It is a truth too often neglected today, that there can be no peace or happiness without religion; but it does not follow that religion must therefore be subject to the State. Many things are needed by an individual for his peace and happiness, but he is not thereby justified in becoming a highwayman to obtain them; he must have recourse to the lawful methods of barter. In like manner, if the Church has in her possession anything deemed needful or necessary for the public good of the State, let those in authority seek it from the Church, as they would from a neighboring State, i.e., by mutual agreement.[100]

3. The Church and the Kingdom

Throughout the writings of the New Testament we find frequent mention of the *Kingdom of God,* or, as St. Matthew usually terms it, the *Kingdom of Heaven.* These terms are evidently synonymous, for, as Lightfoot has pointed out, the Jews frequently put *Heaven* for *God,* just as we do today in such phrases as "Heaven forbid," "heaven be pleased," etc.[101] St. Matthew, writing for Jewish Christians of Palestine,

---

[98] Mark xvi, 15.
[99] Ps. xxiii, 1.
[100] See *infra,* p. 293 sq.
[101] J. Lightfoot, "Horae Hebraicae"; on St. Matthew, iii, 2.

used expressions to which they were accustomed. For this reason he has "Kingdom of Heaven." The other Apostles and Evangelists wrote principally for Christians of gentile origin and consequently gave the Greek equivalent for the Aramaic expression found in St. Matthew and most likely used by Our Lord Himself.

The *Kingdom* so often referred to by Our Lord and His Apostles is evidently the Messianic kingdom, foretold by the prophets, prefigured by the people of Israel, and promised to David and his seed forever. "In the days of those kingdoms, the God of heaven will set up a kingdom that shall never be destroyed, and his kingdom shall not be delivered up to another people and it shall break in pieces and shall consume all these kingdoms and itself shall stand for ever."[102] This kingdom is the stone cut from the mountain without hands which in turn became a mountain filling the whole earth.[103] It is the eternal kingdom promised to the house of David: "Thy house shall be faithful, and thy kingdom for ever before my face, and thy throne shall be firm for ever."[104] "Once have I sworn by my holiness: I will not lie unto David: his seed shall endure for ever. And his throne as the sun before me; and as the moon perfect for ever."[105]

At the time of Our Lord's public ministry the Jews were still looking forward with confidence to the establishment of this Kingdom under the leadership of the Messias, but their conception of the Messias and His Kingdom had sadly degenerated since the days of the prophets. They now looked upon the Messias as a great national leader to restore the kingdom of Israel and to make of it a world power to dominate the gentile nations. For this reason Herod was greatly disturbed when the Magi inquired, "saying, Where is he that is born king of the Jews?"[106] The disciples were imbued with this idea when they "disputed among themselves which of them should be the greatest,"[107] and again when the mother of James and John asked Our Lord that "these my two sons may sit, the one on thy right hand and the other on thy left in thy kingdom,"[108] she was seeking high official positions for her sons in the worldly kingdom which they believed Our Lord would soon establish. Even after the Resurrection of Our Lord, the Apostles could not entirely rid themselves of this belief. When Christ was telling

---

[102] Dan. ii, 44.
[103] Dan. ii, 34, 35.
[104] 2 Kings vii, 16.
[105] Ps. lxxxviii, 36-38.
[106] Matt. ii, 2.
[107] Mark ix, 33.
[108] Matt. xx, 20, 21.

them to wait in Jerusalem for the coming of the Holy Ghost, they asked Him: "Lord, wilt thou at this time restore again the kingdom of Israel?"[109]

During His public life, Our Lord strove to correct this false conception of His kingdom. He clearly and emphatically proclaimed that it was not to be an earthly one, such as they expected. When the Pharisees asked Him, "when is the kingdom of God coming? He answered and said to them 'The kingdom of God comes unawares,' "[110] i.e.. it shall not be inaugurated by the marching of armies, the shouts of victory, or the trappings of royalty. "My kingdom is not of the world."[111]

What then, is the real character of this Kingdom? Harnack says that it signifies a purely spiritual and interior reign of God in the soul: "The kingdom of God comes by coming to the individual; by entering into his soul and laying hold of it."[112] Protestants in general hold a similar view; some, however, seem to identify the *Kingdom* with the invisible Church which they postulate: "The kingdom of God includes all those who yield themselves in glad obedience to the will of God."[113] In either sense, it excludes any external or visible society, such as the Church in the Catholic sense. Modernists admit that the *Kingdom* is a real external society, but belongs to the future: "according to the teachings of Christ, the kingdom of heaven was to come only with the end of the world."[114] In opposition to these views we sometimes find Catholic interpreters and theologians identifying the *Kingdom* with the Church. A study of the parables in which Our Lord explains the nature of His Kingdom will show how far the above views may be accepted, and to what extent they fall short of the truth. It is evident that the words are not always taken in the same sense; at least three distinct, though related, meanings are attached to it.

a) The Kingdom is the mustard seed that becomes a tree and fills the whole world; it is the field with wheat and cockle growing together until the harvest; it is the net cast into the sea which takes fish both good and bad.[115] There can be no doubt that these parables depict the Kingdom as an external society existing on earth,—a society composed of members both good and bad. In this sense the *Kingdom* is identical with the Church, in which St. Peter exercises the power of the keys:

[109] Acts i, 6.
[110] Luke xvii, 20.
[111] John xviii, 33-37.
[112] A. Harnack, "Das Wesen des Christentums," p. 36.
[113] Clarence A. Beckwith, "Outline of Christian Theology," p. 208.
[114] Denzinger, n. 2052.
[115] Matt. xiii, 24 sq.

"Upon this rock I will build my Church . . . and I will give to thee
the keys of the kingdom of heaven."[116]

b) The Kingdom of Heaven is also a hidden treasure, a pearl of
great price, a leaven permeating and transforming the meal.[117] In these
and similar passages we see the *Kingdom* in its interior and spiritual
aspect: it is the power of grace transforming and elevating the soul,—
the reign of God in the heart. In this sense the Kingdom is something
different from the Church, considered as an external society.

c) Finally, the Kingdom is the eternal banquet of heavenly bliss,[118]
the place for the just from the foundation of the world,[119] the land
that belongs to the poor in spirit,[120] and which the rich man shall hardly
enter.[121] These passages present the *Kingdom* in its eschatological aspect, as the glorious reign of Christ with His saints, which shall be
inaugurated at His Second Coming. In this sense the *Kingdom* is
identical with the triumphant Church.

When Christ said to Nicodemus: "Unless a man be born again, he
cannot enter into the kingdom of heaven,"[122] He was probably using
the term in its threefold sense. Baptism is the door by which we enter
the Church on earth; it is the beginning of God's reign in the heart by
regeneration, without which eternal happiness is impossible.

The above considerations bring out clearly the relations between the
Church and the Kingdom of Heaven. The Church, as an external society carrying on the ministry of Christ, *constitutes* the Kingdom in
its exterior social aspect. In the work of sanctifying souls the Church
produces the Kingdom in its interior and spiritual aspect. By accomplishing the work of salvation on earth the Church *prepares* for the
kingdom in its eschatological aspect; it is preparing to become the
Church triumphant in heaven.[123]

---

[116] Matt. xvi, 18, 19.
[117] Matt. xiii, 24 sq.
[118] Luke xxii, 29, 30.
[119] Matt. xxv, 34.
[120] Matt. v, 3.
[121] Luke xviii, 24.
[122] John iii, 5.
[123] Cf. D'Ales, "Dictionnaire de Apologetique," art. Eglise; Hastings, "Dictionary
of the Bible," art. Kingdom of God; B. Bartmann, "Das Himmelreich und sein
Konig," Paderborn, 1904.

CHAPTER II

Attributes of the Church

The Church as a society instituted to perpetuate the mission of Christ on earth, must be endowed with certain qualities necessary for the proper performance of that work. Necessary qualities are those so essentially bound up with the Church that the loss of any one of them would make the Church other than that established by Christ and render it incapable of accomplishing the purpose of its existence. From the teachings of Christ and His Apostles, and from a study of the Church as set forth in the prophecies of old and in the writings of the Fathers, it will be seen that the principal qualities or characteristics essentially necessary to the Church are *unity, sanctity, catholicity, apostolicity, perpetuity, indefectibility, visibility,* and *infallibility.* The first four of these, known to theologians as *properties,* manifest themselves externally and thus serve as a means to identify the true Church of Christ. The others, not externally evident, are called *attributes,*—in Latin, *dotes.*

As a matter of convenience the *attributes* of the Church are treated separately in the present chapter; *perpetuity* and *indefectibility,* being intimately related, are considered together in the first article. *Visibility* is treated separately in the second article. *Infallibility* will be treated at length in another part of the work.

ART. I. PERPETUAL INDEFECTIBILITY OF THE CHURCH

Synopsis.—1. Nature of Indefectibility.—2. Erroneous Doctrines.—3. The Church Perpetually Indefectible.—4. Objections Answered.

1. The Nature of Indefectibility

The general notion of indefectibility is indicated by the word itself, which is derived from the Latin *in* (*not*) and *deficere* (*to fail*). Hence *indefectibility* is inability to fail, to fall short, to perish. Applied to the Church, it means that she cannot be deprived of any essential power or quality so long as she continues to exist. *Perpetuity* is indefectibility of existence. Strictly speaking, *indefectibility* pertains to the essential qualities of the Church, *perpetuity,* to her existence. These two attributes, though really distinct, are so closely related that it is difficult to treat them separately. If the Church is indefectible in her essential qualities and perpetual in her existence, she must be perpetually indefectible in all essential qualities. Therefore, the two attributes may be combined as *perpetual indefectibility.*

It should be noted that *indefectibility* does not exclude such accidental changes as are incidental to growth and development, nor those necessary to adapt the Church to her surroundings. As the Church increases in numbers and extent, new agencies are needed to cope with her increased activities. For this purpose archdioceses and patriarchates were introduced, religious orders established, schools and other institutions founded. Rites and ceremonies, the celebration of feasts, the laws of fasting and abstinence, and other disciplinary regulations may be changed to suit the needs of time and place. These are all accidental changes which prove that the Church is a living organism that "can keep its identity without losing its life, and keep its life without losing its identity; that can enlarge its teachings without changing them; that can always be the same, and yet always developing."[1]

Indefectibility has been promised to the Church as a whole, not to its various parts. The Church as it exists in particular places may fail; even the Church of a whole nation may fall away as history abundantly proves. The Apostolic See of Rome is the only particular Church to which the promise of perpetual indefectibility has been made.

2. Erroneous Doctrines

PROTESTANTS. The defectibility of the Church is one doctrine upon which all Protestants agree. They hold that the Church not only can fail, but that she did fail sometime before the pseudo-Reformation of the sixteenth century. They were driven to this in self-defense, for if the Church as founded by Christ did not and could not fail, there was neither reason nor excuse for the institution of other churches. Those who maintain the existence of a visible and an invisible Church make the one defectible, the other, indefectible.

MODERNISTS. Modernism holds that the Church cannot be indefectible, since it is the result of evolution and therefore continually subject to evolutionary processes that affect its very constitution. "The organic constitution of the Church is not immutable; the Christian society, as well as human society, is subject to perpetual evolution."[2]

RATIONALISTS. Critics of the rationalistic school practically hold

---

[1] W. H. Mallock, "Is Life Worth Living?" p. 13.
[2] Denzinger, n. 2053.

that the Church failed in the days of the Apostles. They deny, of course, that Christ founded a Church, since that was the work of the disciples themselves after Our Lord had left them. But these critics maintain that the disciples almost immediately separated into two antagonistic schools under the leadership of St. Peter and St. Paul, respectively. Towards the end of the second century, some one in Asia Minor or Alexandria wrote the Fourth Gospel in an effort to reconcile and reunite the Judaising party of St. Peter with the universalist followers to St. Paul.[3] Schelling, Fichte and others proclaimed a threefold Church which they called *Petrine* (Catholic), the *Pauline* (Protestant) and the *Johannine* (Church of the future).

FUNDAMENTALISTS. A considerable number of Protestants in the various denominations today are known as *Fundamentalists,* because they defend what they term fundamental doctrines against the attacks of the growing modernistic element in their respective churches. Many of these Fundamentalists look forward to a more perfect kingdom to be established on earth in the near future and ruled by Christ in person. Their distinctive doctrine is, "I believe in the literal, personal, bodily, visible, imminent return of the Lord to this earth as king."[4] This is similar to the doctrine known in the early ages of the Church as *Chiliasm,* from the Greek word for *thousand.* The early Chiliasts taught that Christ would return to reign on earth with His saints for a thousand years after the last judgment. Their error was due to a false interpretation of a passage in the Apocalypse.[5] The Fundamentalists, however, seem to place this personal reign of Christ before the last judgment and thereby make it supersede the Church as it now exists.

3. The Church of Christ Perpetually Indefectible

Thesis.—The Church of Christ Is Perpetually Indefectible in All Its Attributes and Properties

The proposed thesis does not determine the attributes and properties of the Church; it simply states that, whatever they may be, the Church can never lose a single one of them, nor fail in her existence. In other words, it means that the Church founded by Christ must exist until the end of time without any essential change. In this general sense the thesis is *proxima fidei,* i.e., all but an article of faith, being clearly implied in the words of the Vatican Council: "The eternal Pastor and Bishop of

---

[3] Cf. F. Christian Baur in "Theol. Jahrbucher," 1844.
[4] Rollin Lynde Hart in *The World's Work,* Sept., 1923, p. 469 sq.
[5] Apoc. xx, 1-6.

souls decreed to establish a holy Church to *perpetuate* (*perenne reddere*)
the saving work of salvation."⁶ The doctrine is also implied in the condemnation of the following proposition of Modernism: "The organic
constitution of the Church is not immutable."⁷ Leo XIII wrote to the
same effect when he said: "The Church must carry far and wide to all
men *and for all time* the salvation wrought by Jesus Christ and the
blessings flowing therefrom. . . . Hence the Church *must be one and
perpetual*."⁸

PROOF. I. *From Reason.* Christ instituted the Church for the salvation of all men, and endowed it with certain powers and characteristics
necessary for this work. If the Church should lose any one of these
necessary qualifications, it would not be capable of doing what Christ
intended it to do; in fact, it would cease to be the Church instituted by
Him. Moreover, if the Church could fail in any of its essentials, even
for a time, it would lose all authority to teach and to govern, because
the faithful could never be certain at any time that it had not failed,—
that it had not ceased to be the Church of Christ, thereby losing all
authority. But an authority that may be justly doubted at all times is
no authority; it commands neither obedience nor respect as is evident
in churches that reject the claim to indefectibility.

II. *From Scripture.* a) *Prophecies.* Daniel represents the Church of
Christ as a kingdom standing forever unconquered and unconquerable.
"But in the days of those kingdoms, the God of heaven will set up a
kingdom that shall never be destroyed, and his kingdom shall not be
delivered up to another people, . . . and itself shall stand for ever."⁹
Isaias says: "A child is born to us and a son is given to us and the
government is upon his shoulders. . . . He shall sit upon the throne of
David, and upon his kingdom; to establish it and strengthen it . . . from
henceforth and for ever."¹⁰ According to these prophecies it was announced: "The Lord God will give him (Christ) the throne of David his
father . . . and of his kingdom there shall be no end."¹¹ In these passages
the Kingdom can be no other than the Church to be established by
our Lord.

b) *Testimony of Christ.* Our Lord himself distinctly proclaimed the
perpetual indefectibility of His Church: "Upon this rock I will build

⁶ Denzinger, n. 1821.
⁷ Decree "Lamentabili," July 3, 1907; Denzinger, n. 2053.
⁸ Leo XIII, "Satis cognitum," June 29, 1896; Denzinger, n. 1955.
⁹ Dan. ii, 44.
¹⁰ Is. ix, 6, 7.
¹¹ Luke i, 32.

my Church, and the gates of hell shall not prevail against it."[12] The Church is an impregnable fortress against which the powers of darkness shall ever beat in vain. There is no force, either internal or external, that can cause it to crumble or fall. Christ is the wise man of the parable who built his house upon the rock, "and the rain fell, and the floods came, and the winds blew and they beat upon that house and it fell not for it was founded upon a rock."[13]

When Our Lord instituted the Church by sending forth the Apostles with authority to teach, govern, and sanctify men, He said: "Behold, I am with you all days even to the consummation of the world."[14] In these words Christ promised to be with His Church, protecting it at all times, even to the end of the world. But if Christ is *for* the Church, who can prevail *against* it? Our Lord also compares His Church to a field in which the wheat and cockle grow together until the harvest, which, He tells us, is the end of the world. Therefore, the Church must continue unchanged until the end, for, although it contains much cockle, it ever remains a wheat-field.[15]

c) *Testimony of St. Paul.* In his Epistle to the Hebrews St. Paul makes a lengthy comparison between the Church and the Synagogue. He represents the one as permanent, the other as transitory. He quotes the words of the prophet Aggeus: "Yet once more, and I will move not only earth, but heaven also,"[16] and applies them to the Old Law saying: "Now by this expression *yet once more,* he announces the removal of things which can be shaken—created things—in order that the things which cannot be shaken may remain. Therefore, since we receive a kingdom that cannot be shaken, we have grace, through which we may offer service pleasing to God with fear and reverence."[17] In this passage St. Paul distinctly says that the temporary institutions of the Old Law have been succeeded by the *immovable Kingdom* of the New. Therefore the Church, the immovable Kingdom of the New Law, must be perpetual and indefectible.

---

[12] Matt. xvi, 18.—Ancient cities were surrounded by high walls to protect them against their enemies. Entrance to the city was by way of gates in its walls. Before the invention of battering-rams the strength of a city lay in the strength of its gates. For this reason *gates* soon came to mean strength or power. Hence *gates of hell* refer to the forces of evil, which Christ well knew would be loosed against His Church. Many non-Catholic scholars take *gates of hell* as equivalent to sheol, i.e., the place of the dead, and then death itself. Taken in this sense, the words of Christ are even more striking, for if death can never prevail against the Church, neither can it perish or fail. Death to a society can be only its destruction by dissolution or essential change.

[13] Matt. vii, 24, 25.

[14] Matt. xxviii, 20.

[15] Matt. xiii, 24 sq.

[16] Aggeus ii, 7.

[17] Heb. xii, 26-28.

III. *From Tradition.* a) *Pseudo-Ambrose,* the author of an ancient work formerly attributed to St. Ambrose, refers expressly to the indefectibility of the Church: "We behold in the Church a ship sailing the seas of this world . . . though tossed by the storms and buffeted by the waves, it can never suffer shipwreck because Christ hangs upon its mast which is the cross, the Father sits enthroned upon its stern, and the Holy Spirit the Paraclete, as helmsman guides the prow. Through the straits of the world twelve oarsmen (the Apostles) guide it safely into port . . . it can never crash upon the rocks nor founder in the deep."[18]

b) *St. Chrysostom* is not less positive in his statements: "Do not hold aloof from the Church, for there is nothing stronger than the Church. The Church is your hope; the Church is your salvation; the Church is your refuge. It is higher than heaven and broader than earth. It never grows old, but ever keeps the vigor of youth. Wherefore Scripture, wishing to show forth its firmness and stability, calls it a mountain."[19]

c) *St. Augustine* says: "The Church cannot be overcome nor rooted up; it cannot yield to any trials whatsoever until the end of this world come."[20]

d) *St. Jerome* expresses a similar faith: "We know that the Church will be harassed by persecution until the end of the world, but it cannot be destroyed; it shall be tried, but not overcome for such is the promise of an omnipotent God whose word is as a law of nature."[21]

4. Objections Answered

OBJECTION I.—The Synagogue, the Church of the Old Law, failed at different times in its history, e.g., when the people forsook their God to worship the golden calf erected by Aaron. Again, during the time of the Judges and still later, under the Kings, the people often fell into idolatry by worshipping the gods of surrounding nations. Now, if the Church of the Old Law could fail, then also the Church of the New.

ANSWER.—There is no parity in this matter between the Church and the Synagogue, for it was never said of the Synagogue that "the gates of hell shall not prevail against it." Neither was it said to the priests of old: "Behold I am with you all days even to the consummation of the world." Moreover, it may well be denied that the Synagogue ever really failed even for a day. It is true that many forsook the ways

---

[18] Pseudo-Ambrose, "Sermo de Salomone"; P.L., 17, 697.
[19] St. John Chrysostom, "Quod Christus sit Deus"; P.G., 52, 402.
[20] St. Augustine, "enarratio in Psalm," lxii; P.L., 36, 726.
[21] St. Jerome, "In Isaiam," iv, 6; P.L., 24, 74.

of the Lord and worshipped strange gods; but even in the worst days of Israel, there was a goodly number of faithful souls to perpetuate the church of their fathers. Even when Aaron set up the golden calf at Sinai, twenty-two thousand sons of Levi remained faithful under their divinely appointed leaders.[22]

OBJECTION II.—It must be admitted by all that the Synagogue with all its observances came to an end at the death of Our Lord, despite many prophecies regarding its perpetual existence.[23] Therefore, there is no reason why the Church may not fail in like manner, despite the promises of Christ.

ANSWER.—The Synagogue was succeeded by the Church of Christ because the Mosaic Law was only a preparation for the more perfect Law of Christ; it was a mere *paidagogos,* leading man to His Divine Teacher.[24] This preparatory character of the Law and its future abrogation was clearly foretold by the prophets. Thus, e.g., Daniel prophesied the destruction of Jerusalem and the worship of the Old Law: "And in the half of the week the victim and the sacrifice shall fail; and there shall be in the temple the abomination of desolation, and the desolation shall continue even to the consummation and to the end."[25] And Jeremias foretold the establishment of a new covenant to succeed the Law of Moses: "Behold the days shall come, saith the Lord, and I will make a new covenant with the house of Israel and with the house of Juda. Not according to the covenant which I made with their fathers."[26]

Regarding the promises of perpetuity seemingly made to the Synagogue of old, St. Augustine says: "The priesthood of Aaron was but a shadow of the eternal priesthood to come; when promises of perpetuity were made, they were not made to the shadow and figure itself, but to that which was foreshadowed and prefigured. And lest the shadow itself should be thought permanent, its abrogation was foretold."[27]

St. Paul also brings out in bold relief the temporary character of the Synagogue in opposition to the perpetuity of the Church by comparing the one to Agar, the repudiated wife of Abraham, the other to Sarah, who was never put away.[28]

OBJECTION III.—Christ Himself foretold the abrogation of His Church and the institution of a Church of the Holy Spirit: "And I will

---

[22] Cf. Ex. xxxii, 26 Num. iii, 39.
[23] Cf. the promises made to David that his kingdom and his throne should stand firm forever: 2 Kings vii, 16; Ps. lxxxviii, 36-38; Is. lx, 1 sq.
[24] Gal. iii, 24.
[25] Dan. ix, 27.
[26] Jer. xxxi, 31.
[27] St. Augustine, "De Civitate Dei," vii, 6; P.L., 41, 536.
[28] Gal. iv, 22 sq.

ask the Father, and he shall give you another Advocate to dwell with you forever."[29]

ANSWER.—These words of Christ refer to the internal mission of the Holy Spirit in the souls of men, and especially to His continual presence in the Church to preserve it from all error. This is explained by Christ Himself in the same passage. "He (the Advocate) will teach you all things, and bring to your mind whatever I have said to you."[30] Christ promised the Holy Spirit as an Advocate, i.e., a Helper or Protector for the Church already established, not as the Author of a Church to be established in the future.

ART. II. VISIBILITY OF THE CHURCH

Synopsis.—1. Nature of Visibility.—2. Errors Concerning the Visibility of the Church.—3. The Church Formally Visible.—4. Objections Considered.

1. The Nature of Visibility

Visibility primarily signifies the capability of being perceived by the sense of sight; then, by extension, it refers to the capability of being perceived by any of the five senses. Finally, it means the capability of an object being perceived or known by the intellect because of the sensible qualities adhering in that object. Hence the division into *material* and *formal* visibility. A thing is *materially visible* in its external, sensible qualities; it is *formally visible* when it can be recognized by these qualities as having a certain nature. For example, a man, considered according to the external qualities of his body, is materially visible,—he can be perceived by the senses; when the soul manifests itself by speech or other external sign, he becomes formally visible,—he is known to be a rational being, called man.

A society is materially visible because its members, its rites and ceremonies, and its places of meeting can be seen or perceived by the senses; when, through these external signs, it may be known that certain individuals are thus banded together, the society is formally *visible as a society*. If there are no external signs by which it can be known that these individuals are banded together, the society is *invisible* as a society, although the members are perfectly visible as individuals. Furthermore, a society may, and usually does, have certain external characteristics by which it may be recognized as a particular kind of society, e.g., a religious society. In that case it is *formally visible as a religious society*. If there

---

[29] John xiv, 16.
[30] John xiv, 26.

are certain marks to distinguish it as a Christian religious society, it is formally visible as a Christian church, which may be further distinguished from other Christian churches. It then becomes formally visible as a Catholic, Protestant, or Greek Church, as the case may be. Again, if there be marks to identify it as the Church actually founded by Christ, it is formally visible as the one true Church of Christ.

When we say that the Church of Christ is visible, we mean primarily, that it is a society of men with external rites and ceremonies and all the external machinery of government by which it can easily be recognized as a true society. But we further maintain that the Church of Christ also has certain marks by which it may be recognized as the one true Church founded by Christ when He commissioned the Apostles to convert all nations. In other words, we maintain that the Church of Christ is formally visible, not only as a society known as a Christian Church, but also as the one true Church of Christ. Furthermore, we maintain that the Church of Christ is so clearly visible that it may easily be recognized by all as the true Church. It has marks so evident that all who see it may say with certainty: "This is the true Church of Christ." This, of course, does not mean that all will actually recognize it as such; those blinded by passion and prejudice can no more recognize the true Church than the Pharisees of old could recognize its Divine Founder. The man who closes his eyes cannot even see the sun in its noonday splendor.

2. Errors Concerning the Visibility of the Church

Non-Catholic teaching on the visibility of the Church seems hopelessly involved. Scarcely any two Protestant theologians hold the same views, and even one and the same author frequently expresses contradictory views on the matter. Luther, for example, says that "the Church is hidden in the spirit and known only by faith."[31] "But you may say, if the Church be entirely in the spirit and of a nature thoroughly spiritual, how can we discern where on earth any part of it may be? The necessary mark whereby we recognize it, and which we possess, is Baptism and the Lord's Supper, and above all the Gospel."[32] Here, then, we have a Church wholly invisible that may be recognized by visible marks! In another work Luther teaches that there is both a visible and an invisible Church: "Because communion with the visible Church constitutes no communion in the invisible, and because many non Christians are found in the visible Church, so no visible Church

---

[31] "De Abrogatione Missae," p. 1.
[32] "Resp. ad Lib. Ambros. Cathar.," tom. ii, 376, 377.

is at all necessary."[33] Melanchthon in his later writings emphasizes the conception of the Church as a visible organization in which the pure Word of God is taught.[34] Buddeus, a later Protestant theologian, says: "When there is question of the congregation of true believers who constitute the Church properly so-called, it is evident that it is invisible."[35]

According to Luther, the just alone constitute the Church of Christ; Calvin taught that it embraces only the predestined. But as the just and the predestined are known to God alone, so in this hypothesis the Church must remain ever invisible to all save God alone. Hence Calvin said: "It is necessary to believe that the Church, invisible to us, is known to God alone."[36] Yet both Luther and Calvin defined the Church as the congregation in which the pure word of God is preached and the sacraments rightly administered.[37] The Augsburg Confession contains the same contradictory teachings: "The Church is the congregation of *saints* in which the Gospel is rightly taught and the sacraments rightly administered."[38]

These various teachings seem to have settled down to a general belief that there is both a visible and an invisible Church. This was the doctrine of Zwingli: "We believe that the Church is both visible and invisible. In the invisible Church are found all those throughout the world who believe. It is called invisible, not because those who believe are invisible, but because it is not patent to human eyes who the believers are. The visible Church is composed of all those throughout the world who have given their name to Christ."[39] In like manner Reinhard wrote: "The visible or external Church is the universal society of those who profess the Christian religion publicly; the invisible Church is the society of those who, through the doctrine of Christ are truly regenerated. The visible Church is broken up into many societies, to any one of which a man may join himself, as he sees fit."[40]

The Westminster Confession proclaims the same doctrine: "The Catholic or universal church, which is invisible, consists of the whole number of the elect that have been, are, or shall be gathered into one under Christ the head thereof. . . . The visible church, which is also catholic or universal under the Gospel, consists of all those throughout the world that profess the true religion, and of their children; and

[33] "On the Papacy."
[34] Cf. Schaff-Herzog, "Encycl. of Relig. Knowledge," art. "Church."
[35] Johan F. Buddeus, "Institutiones," V, III, sec. xiv.
[36] "Institutiones," IV, 1, n. 7.
[37] *Ibid.,* IV, 1.
[38] Augsburg Confession, Art. IV.
[39] Zwingli, "Expositio Fidei."
[40] Franz V. Reinhard, "Vorlesungen uber Dogmatik," 169 sq.

is the kingdom of the Lord Jesus Christ . . . out of which there is no ordinary possibility of salvation."[41]

The advocates of the *Branch Theory* in the Anglican Church[42] maintain that the Church of Christ is essentially visible, but consists of three parts or branches,—the Roman, the Greek, and the English. This is simply the ordinary Protestant doctrine limited in its application; instead of all Christian churches, it includes only three in the visible Church of Christ. In either case the visibility of the Church is destroyed, since the various Christian churches are not united into any external visible society that can be called *a* church in any true sense of the word. There can be no living branches unless they be united in a living trunk but in the *Branch Theory* there is no living trunk visible. If there be one, it must be invisible.

The various Protestant doctrines just reviewed, all agree in denying that there is any one visible society which can claim to be the Church of Christ to the exclusion of all others. The reason for this was candidly stated by a writer in the *British and Foreign Evangelical Review* some years ago: "Everything depends upon the answer to the question, 'What is the Church?' If it be an external society of professors of the true religion, then it is visible as an earthly kingdom; if that society is destroyed, the Church is destroyed, and everything that is true of the Church is true of that society. Then, in short, Romanism must be admitted as a logical consequence."[43] As a matter of fact the pseudo-Reformers of the sixteenth century at first held the Church to be visible, but were soon forced to change their doctrine, as Palmer explains in his work on the Church: "The Reformed seem generally to have taught the doctrine of the visibility of the Church, until some of them deemed it necessary, in consequence of their controversy with the Romanists who asked them where their church existed before Luther, to maintain that the church might *sometimes* be invisible."[44]

3. The Church of Christ Formally Visible

Thesis.—The Church of Christ Is Formally Visible Not Only as a Church, but Also as the True Church of Christ

This is an article of faith, having been defined by the Vatican Council in the following words: "God established a Church through His

---

[41] Westminster Confession, XXV, 1, 2; cf. Schaff, "Creeds of Christendom," Vol. III, p. 657.

[42] Under the name Anglican Church we include the Established Church of England and the Protestant Episcopal Church of America.

[43] British and Foreign Evangelical Review. June 1855, p. 295.

[44] William Palmer, "Treatise on the Church," Vol. I, p. 35.

only begotten Son, and endowed it with manifest marks of its institution, that it might be known by all as the guardian and teacher of the revealed word."[45] This is a clear and comprehensive definition of formal visibility. The Church has certain evident marks by which it can be recognized as the true Church of Christ, the guardian and teacher of the revealed word.

The thesis contains two propositions: (a) The Church is an external society that can be recognized as such by all,—it is formally visible as a religious society or Church; (b) This society has certain marks by which it may be distinguished from all other churches and recognized as the true Church,—it is formally visible as the true Church. It will be sufficient to prove the second proposition, since no society can be recognized as the *true* Church unless it is first recognized as *a* church. Moreover, it has been amply proved that Christ established His Church under the form of an external visible society.[46]

PROOFS. I. *From Reason.* When Christ instituted the Church, He demanded submission to its authority under pain of eternal damnation: "Go, therefore, and make disciples of all nations, baptizing them in the name of the Father and of the Son and of the Holy Spirit. . . . He that believeth and is baptized shall be saved; but he that believeth not shall be condemned."[47] Again Christ says: "If he refuse to hear even the Church, let him be to thee as the heathen and publican."[48] How could any one be obliged, under pain of eternal damnation, to hearken to the teachings of the Church and obey her precepts unless there be some means of recognizing it as the true Church endowed with authority to teach and govern? Assuredly, Our Lord in His divine wisdom has not obliged all men to do something impossible.

II. *From Scripture.* a) The prophet Isaias represents the Church as a house built upon the topmost peak of the highest mountain, where it may be seen by all nations far and near: "And in the last days the mountain of the house of the Lord shall be prepared on the top of mountains, and it shall be exalted above all hills and all nations shall flow unto it." It shall be recognized as the house of the Lord, for the people will say: "Come and let us go up to the mountain of the Lord, and to the house of the God of Jacob."[49]

b) When praying for His Apostles, Our Lord said: "And not for them only do I pray, but for them also who through their word shall

---

[45] Denzinger, n. 1793.
[46] Cf. above, pp. 6 sq.
[47] Matt. xxviii, 19; Mark xvi, 16.
[48] Matt. xviii, 17.
[49] Is. ii, 3.

believe in me; that all may be one, as thou Father in me and I in thee; that they also may be one in us that the world may believe that thou hast sent me."[50] Christ prays that His disciples be so closely united to one another that this very union will be a proof of His divine mission. In a word, He prays that His Church, the society of His disciples in all ages, shall be recognized because of its perfect unity.

c) In Holy Scripture, the Church is always represented as an external society that may be known by all; it is a *kingdom*, a *city*, a *house*, a *sheep-fold*, a *field*. It is also a *mustard seed* that grows into a tree filling the whole earth, and is easily recognized as such, for all the birds of heaven (i.e., all nations) fill its branches and feed upon it. In fact almost every page of the New Testament and the prophecies of the Old depict the Church as an external society so eminently visible that even "fools shall not err therein."[51]

III. *From Tradition.* The Fathers were wont to compare the Church to the sun and the moon, because, like them she sheds her light upon the whole world and is known to all peoples. ST. ATHANASIUS, e.g., says: "The Church of Christ in her splendor illuminates the world and remains forever as the sun and moon."[52] ST. JOHN CHRYSOSTOM says: "Neither is the sun so resplendent nor the moon so bright as those things which pertain to the Church, for the house of God is upon the pinnacle of the mountains."[53] Even more striking are the words of ST. AUGUSTINE: "When anyone would see the moon, people say to him: Behold the moon; there it is! And if there are any who do not know where to look, it is pointed out with the finger. Now, my brethren, do we thus point out the Church? Is it not plain? Is it not evident? Do not all peoples know it?"[54]

4. Objections Answered

OBJECTION I.—Our Lord Himself indicates the invisible character of His Church when He compares it to a hidden treasure: "The Kingdom of heaven is like a treasure hidden in a field."[55] What is hidden is undoubtedly invisible.

ANSWER.—It has been noted already[56] that in this and similar passages the *kingdom* is presented in its inner spiritual aspect, and

---

[50] John xvii, 19 sq.
[51] Is. xxxv, 8.
[52] "In Psalm," lxviii, 38; P.G., 27, 391.
[53] "In Isaiam," ii. 2; P.G., 56, 29.
[54] "In Epist. Ioannis ad Parthos," P.L., 35, 1988.
[55] Matt. xiii, 44.
[56] Cf. above, p. 27.

therefore is not to be identified with the Church, which is the *kingdom* in its external or social aspect. The parable teaches us the inestimable value of the blessings to be obtained in and through the Church; they are such that every other good must be accounted as nothing in comparison. Even if the parable be referred directly to the Church, it proves nothing against its visibility; the treasure was not invisible, since it was found and recognized as a veritable treasure, for which the finder sacrificed all his possessions. If the parable be applied to the Church, it clearly teaches that the man who has found the true Church of Christ must be ready to sacrifice everything to embrace it.

OBJECTION II.—On another occasion Our Lord distinctly announced that His kingdom would be purely spiritual,—a kingdom in the hearts of His faithful: "The kingdom of God cometh unawares. . . . For lo, the kingdom of God is within you."[57]

ANSWER.—The words quoted in the objection were spoken by Our Lord in answer to a question put by the Pharisees, who had long expected the Messias to come as an earthly king with all the trappings of royalty. They expected Him to restore the lost glory of Israel and subjugate the surrounding gentile nations. They now ask when these things shall come to pass: "Being asked by the Pharisees when the kingdom of God is coming? He answered and said to them: The kingdom of God comes unawares . . . for behold the kingdom of God is within you." The question asked by the Pharisees was probably intended as an insinuation that Christ was not the Messias, since He did not come as they had expected. Whatever the purpose of the question, it implied a twofold error: (1) that the Messianic kingdom had not yet begun, and (2) that it would be a great earthly power to rule the world. Our Lord corrected the latter mistake by telling them that the *kingdom of God cometh not with observation*, i.e., it will not be clothed with the outward signs of earthly power and glory. He also corrected the first error by announcing that the kingdom of God was already in their midst, since He, its founder, had already begun His mission on earth: "The kingdom of God is within you."

The best Scripture scholars, both Catholic and non-Catholic,[58] agree that the Greek phrase should be rendered *among you*, instead of *within you*, as the Latin and English texts have it. Hence the whole objection rests upon a faulty translation that makes Our Lord's words ridiculous. He was speaking to the Pharisees, who rejected Him and sought in every way to turn the people against Him. Then if the *kingdom of God* is the

---

[57] Luke xvii, 20.
[58] Among others we may mention Rosenmiller and Moffat.

reign of Christ in the soul, we hear Him telling these Pharisees that they already possess this kingdom in their hearts: "The kingdom of God is within you."

OBJECTION III.—The Church must be invisible since the worship due to God is purely internal and invisible; a worship in spirit only, for Christ has said: "God is spirit, and they who worship him must worship in spirit and in truth."[59] Where then is the need of an external visible society of worshippers?

ANSWER.—The objection illustrates the old saying that "who proves too much, proves nothing." If the worship of God is purely internal and spiritual, as the objection asserts, why should any Christians have churches, ministers, sermons or public worship?

Scripture scholars do not agree in their interpretation of the words "in spirit and truth." The circumstances under which they were spoken will give some insight into their meaning. They were addressed to the Samaritan woman, who had asked Our Lord about the legality of sacrifice offered on Mount Garizim. He tells her that the worship of the Old Law, both in Jerusalem and on Mount Garizim, must soon give way to a worship *in spirit and truth.* Worship *in spirit* is probably a sincere worship, welling up from the heart, as opposed to any mere formal worship. A similar contrast is found in Isaias, where God complains of His people because "with their lips they glorify me, but their heart is far from me."[60] In like manner, worship *in truth* is opposed either to the worship of false gods, or to the ceremonies of the Old Law, which were but types and figures of the realities of the New. There is not a word in the whole passage that can be construed into an argument against the visibility of the Church.

OBJECTION IV.—St. Paul teaches the invisibility of the Church by contrasting it with the Synagogue, the visible Church of the Old Law. He says that, in coming to the Church, the Hebrews have not "come to a mountain that may be touched, and to a burning fire, a whirlwind and darkness . . . but you have come to mount Sion and to the city of the living God, the heavenly Jerusalem."[61]

ANSWER.—In this passage St. Paul shows the superiority of the Church over the Synagogue by contrasting the circumstances under which the two laws were promulgated: one, being a law of fear, was promulgated on Mount Sinai amid lightnings, whirlwinds, and darkness; the other being a law of love, was promulgated on Mount Sion,

---

[59] John iv, 24.
[60] Is. xxix, 13.
[61] Heb. xii, 18 sq.

the symbol of heavenly peace and joy. "The latter dispensation is not, as was the Mosaic, severe, onerous, and minatory; but promises salvation, and instills joy, peace, patience and confidence."[62] There is no contrast between a *visible* Synagogue and an *invisible* Church; both are symbolized by a mountain and therefore equally visible.

OBJECTION V.—St. Peter admonishes the faithful to be "as living stones built up, a spiritual house."[63] Therefore he conceives the Church to be an invisible spiritual society.

ANSWER.—A society spiritual in every respect would necessarily be invisible but the Church is not such a society. It is spiritual because it is striving for a spiritual good and the means to that end are in large measure spiritual. It is also a visible society composed of men,—*living stones,*—externally organized and using visible signs and ceremonies in its worship.

OBJECTION VI.—In the Apostles' Creed we say: "I believe in the holy Catholic Church." Therefore the Church is an object of faith and must be invisible, for otherwise it would be an object of knowledge. What we see and know cannot be an object of faith.

ANSWER.—It is by no means certain that an object of knowledge cannot also be an object of faith; but even granting that it cannot be, it does not follow that the Church must be invisible. The Church has a human element that is visible and capable of being known. It also has a divine element which is invisible and therefore capable of being an object of faith. This fact may be illustrated by the example of St. Thomas the Apostle, who saw and knew Our Lord's human nature and believed in His divinity.

OBJECTION VII.—A body must participate in the nature of its head, but Christ, the Head of the Church, is invisible. Therefore, the Church, which is His mystical body, must also be invisible.

ANSWER.—Christ in His human nature is visible; therefore, the Church, His mystical body, must also be visible in its human element. Christ is said to be invisible because He is no longer on earth by bodily presence, but that does not change the nature of His body.

---

[62] Bloomfield, "Greek Testament with Notes," Vol. II, p. 472.
[63] 1 Peter ii, 5.

CHAPTER III

PROPERTIES OF THE CHURCH

Since the Church is a society that may be recognized by all, it must have certain visible characteristics, so distinctive that they cannot be found together in any other society. In the present chapter we shall consider the nature of these characteristics, or *properties*, and prove that the Church of Christ possesses them. In the following chapter we shall determine in how far they serve as *marks* to identify the true Church.

Cardinal Bellarmine enumerates fifteen characteristics of the Church that may be used as distinguishing *marks;* Bozius, an Oratorian, mentions ninety-nine, but all of these, as well as those mentioned by Cardinal Bellarmine, are simply different aspects of the four properties set forth in the Nicene Creed; *viz., Unity, Sanctity, Catholicity* and *Apostolicity,* —"I believe in one, holy, Catholic and Apostolic Church."[1]

ART. I. UNITY OF THE CHURCH

Synopsis.—1. Name of Unity.—2. Unity of Government.—3. Unity of Faith.—4. Unity of Worship.

1. The Nature of Unity

Unity may be taken in opposition to *plurality* or to *division.* When applied to the Church in the former sense, it means that there is but *one* true Church of Christ. This is often called *unicity,* to distinguish it from *unity* in the second sense, which means that the one true Church is not subject to division of any kind in regard to things essential. The *unicity* of the Church was established by proving that Christ founded but one society, which He called *His Church.*[2] We shall now consider the *unity* of the Church, by which its members throughout the world are so bound together as to form a society that is justly said to be *one.*

BONDS OF UNITY. No material bonds,—no fetters of steel,—can bind men together in a society. This must be accomplished by moral bonds that unite the souls of men through the faculties of intellect and will. Intellects are united by the acceptance of a common doctrine; wills

---

[1] Denzinger, n. 86.
[2] Cf. above, p. 18 sq.

45

are joined by submission to a common authority. Therefore the very existence of a society depends upon this twofold unity,—a unity of government to which all members must submit, and a unity of doctrines proposed to and accepted by all. From these two bonds of unity a third necessarily follows. The internal acts of man naturally tend to manifest themselves externally; his internal acts as the member of a society,— his submission to authority and his acceptance of the doctrine proposed, —will be expressed by external acts, for the most part symbolic. These *symbolic actions* constitute the ritual or ceremonial of the society, which must be essentially the same for all members, since it expresses acceptance of one and the same doctrine and submission to one and the same authority. Moreover, every member must strive in some measure to attain the end for which the society exists, for he who rejects the purpose of a society, thereby rejects the society itself and ceases to be a member. But to attain an end, certain means must be employed which are adapted to that end and, therefore, essentially the same for all members.

Applying these principles to the Church, we readily see that it must have (a) unity of government or social unity; (b) unity of doctrine taught and accepted or unity of faith, and (c) unity of external acts symbolizing its doctrines and government, and also unity in the use of means necessary to attain the end for which it exists. As the Church is a religious society, all these external acts pertain to the worship of God and their unity constitutes a unity of worship.

ERRORS. No one denies that the Church of Christ must possess unity of some sort. The Scriptures proclaim this fact so clearly and persistently that not even the pseudo-Reformers of the sixteenth century or their followers have ever dared to question it; but opinions differ widely when it comes to defining the nature of this unity. Protestants, for the most part, maintain that this necessary unity consists in the union of all Christians with Christ by faith, hope, and charity, in obedience to Christ as the one supreme Pastor, and in the worship of the one true God. This, they say, constitutes the unity of *doctrine, organization* and *worship*.

The Orthodox Churches of the East teach that sufficient unity is had when Christians are united by faith and by the law of God in the use of the same Sacraments under the authority of the hierarchy. But they maintain that this unity is not broken by the division of the Church into a number of totally independent national churches. "The separateness of their visible organization does not hinder them from being all spiritual great members of the one body of the Universal Church, from having one Head, Christ, and one spirit of faith and grace."[3] Practically the same doctrine is maintained by advocates of the *Branch Theory* in the Anglican Communion. According to them the universal Church is composed of the Greek, the Roman and the Anglican Communions, entirely independent, yet forming one society. These various errors are sufficiently refuted by proving that the Church of Christ must ever be essentially one (a) in government, (b) in faith, and (c) in worship.

2. Unity of Government

PRELIMINARY REMARKS. Unity of government, known also as social unity, requires that the members of the Church and all its parts be so united under one supreme authority as to form but one single society. This excludes any division by which parts of the Church would have their own independent government; it also excludes any mere federation of independent churches. Unity of government is by far the most important of the unities, because without it no other form of real unity could be maintained for any length of time.

Protestants in general seem to hold that some form of unity is necessary for the Church of Christ, but the unending multiplicity of sects forces them to adopt the theory of Jurieu, who taught that "the universal church consists of *all* societies agreeing in fundamental doctrines, even though mutually excommunicated and anathematized; that the only true unity of communion consists in spiritual union with Christ, and therefore, that the formation of new sects is in no degree blamable."[4]

Many Anglicans of the High Church party follow the lead of Palmer and Pusey in admitting that unity of government in the Catholic sense is at least desirable, and perhaps even a matter of divine ordination; but they deny that it is so essentially necessary that it may not be dispensed with for grave reasons.[5] Such reasons, of course, were found at the time of the Greek schism and again at the time of the so-called Reformation in England; but efforts should be made to restore the lost unity. These High Churchmen look upon the Anglican Church as "Providentially called to be the healer of the breach for a divided Christianity."[6] Many societies have been formed within their ranks for the laudable purpose of bringing about such a "healing of the breach."

---

[3] Philaret's Longer Catechism of the Eastern Church, n. 261; cf. Schaff, "Creeds of Christendom," Vol. II, p. 485.
[4] P. Jurieu, "Vrai Systeme de l'Eglise."
[5] Cf. William Palmer, "Treatise on the Church," Vol. I, p. 71 sq.
[6] Cf. "The World's Parliament of Religious," Vol. II, p. 1387.

Thesis.—The Church of Christ Is Necessarily One by
Unity of Government

The doctrine set forth in the above thesis is a dogma of the Church
defined by the Vatican Council: "In order to preserve the multitude of
the faithful in the unity of faith and communion, Christ placed the
blessed Peter at the head of the other Apostles, thus making him a
perpetual source and visible foundation of this twofold unity."[7] Pius IX
gave expression to the same doctrine in these words: "There is no other
Catholic Church save that built upon the one Peter and *united into one
compact body* by the unity of faith and charity."[8]

PROOFS. I. *From Reason.* Unity of government means simply that
the Church must have one supreme authority, to which all its members
and its every part are subject. This is really a self-evident truth that
needs no demonstration, because the very moment the Church becomes
divided between two or more supreme authorities, it ceases to be one
society; there is no longer one, but several churches, contrary to the
truth already established that the Church of Christ is and must ever
remain one.

II. *From Scripture.* Sacred Scripture constantly represents the Church
as a *Kingdom,* a *city,* a *house.* Therefore, it was instituted, and must
continue to exist, after the fashion of a kingdom, a city, or a house;
but Christ Himself has said: "Every kingdom divided against itself is
brought to desolation, and house upon house will fall."[9] And again:
"Every city or house divided against itself will not stand."[10] Therefore,
if the Church is to continue until the end of time, as Christ has promised,
it must ever remain a *united* kingdom.

Our Lord also beautifully illustrated the unity of His Church when
He compared it to a sheep-fold by saying: "Other sheep I have that
are not of this fold; them also I must bring and they shall hear my
voice, and there shall be ONE FOLD and ONE SHEPHERD."[11]
What more impressive comparison could have been addressed to a
pastoral people? "All the sheep of a flock cling together. If they are
momentarily separated, they are impatient till reunited. They follow in
the same path. They feed on the same pasture. They obey the voice of
the same shepherd, and fly from the voice of strangers."[12]

Our Lord not only foretold that His Church should be one; He also

---

[7] Denzinger, n. 1821.
[8] Denzinger, n. 1686.
[9] Luke xi, 17.
[10] St. Matt. xii, 25.
[11] John x, 16.
[12] Cardinal Gibbons, "Faith of Our Fathers," p. 7.

prayed that it might possess the most perfect unity. He prayed that it be one even as He and the Father are one: "Yet not for those (the Apostles) only do I pray, but for those also who through their word are to believe in me; that all may be one even as thou, Father, in me and I in thee; that they also may be one in us, that the world may believe that thou hast sent me. . . . I in them and thou in me; that they may be perfected in unity."[13] Does a chimerical Church composed of innumerable warring sects fulfill this prayer of Christ for perfect unity?

St. Paul always presents the Church as the mystical body of Christ, and liken it to the natural body in man: "As the body is one and has many members, and all the members of the body, many as they are, form one body, so also is it with Christ. For in one Spirit we were all baptized into one body."[14] Therefore, according to St. Paul the unity of the Church must be similar to that of a human body wherein all the members are so united that if one be separated it loses the life of the body, and if the body itself be divided it perishes. So likewise the Church, if it be divided, must perish, and any one separated from the body of the Church ceases to be a member.

III. *From Tradition.* The Fathers always insisted upon the unity of the Church in the strongest terms, and stoutly defended it against the authors of schism, whom they accounted the most wicked of men because they sought to rend the seamless garment of Christ. In this they followed the example of St. Paul, who classes schism along with adultery, murder, and idolatry: "The works of the flesh are manifest, which are immorally . . . idolatry . . . parties (Schisms) . . . envies, murders."[15] A few quotations from the early Fathers will suffice:

a) *St. Ignatius Martyr:* "Be not deceived; if anyone follow the author of a schism, he shall not possess the inheritance of the heavenly kingdom."[16]

b) *St. Irenaeus:* "Those who cause schism . . . rend and divide the great and glorious body of Christ, and so far as they can, destroy it. . . . No reparation they can make will ever equal the evil of their schism."[17]

c) *St. Cyprian:* "God is one, and Christ is one, and His Church is one; the faith is one and the people is one, joined into a substantial unity of body by the cement of concord. Unity cannot be severed; nor can the one body be separated by division, nor torn asunder."[18] "This

---

[13] John xvii, 20 sq.
[14] 1 Cor. xii, 12 sq.
[15] Gal. v, 19-20.
[16] "Epist. ad Philatel.," III; Funk, I, 267.
[17] "Adversus Haereses," IV, 33; P.G., 7, 1076
[18] "De Unitate Ecclesiae," 23; P.L., 5, 517.

sacrament of unity, this bond of concord inseparably cohering, is set forth where in the Gospel the coat of the Lord Jesus Christ is not at all divided nor cut, but is received as an entire garment. . . . Who then is so wicked and so faithless; who is so insane with the madness of discord, that he should believe the unity of God can be divided, or should dare to rend the garment of the Lord,—the Church of Christ?"[19]

d) *St. Gregory Nazianzen:* "We are all one body in Christ, each one a member of Christ, and all members one of another. Some being placed in command, govern, others obey and are governed. All do not have the same duty, for to rule and to be ruled are not the same, yet all are conjoined and built up by the same Spirit into one body in the one Christ."[20]

3. Unity of Faith

PRELIMINARY REMARKS. Faith necessarily implies a doctrine taught (*objective faith*), its acceptance by those to whom it is taught (*subjective or internal faith*), and an outward manifestation, or profession of that internal faith. Accordingly, unity of faith will be threefold, —unity of doctrines proposed, unity in their acceptance on the part of the faithful, and unity in their outward profession. Unity of doctrine and unity in the profession of faith are essential to the unity of the Church, but it is a disputed question whether unity of internal faith is also necessary. It must be well understood that there is no question about the necessity of internal faith for salvation. Christ plainly stated: "He that believeth not shall be condemned."[21] The question here raised concerns the necessity of internal faith for the unity of the Church, and as the same question arises under a slightly different form in connection with membership in the Church, it will there find sufficient consideration.[22]

Protestants, following their fundamental principle of private interpretation, deny that unity of faith in the Catholic sense is necessary in the Church. At first they taught that unity of faith is had by the acceptance of all doctrines contained in Holy Scripture; but private interpretation of the Scriptures led to such confusion of opposing and contradictory doctrines that some other theory had to be invented. This was found in the distinction between *fundamental* and *non-fundamental* doctrines. According to this theory, *fundamental* doctrines are those

---

[19] "De Unitate Ecclesiae," 7, 8; P.L., 4, 504, 506.
[20] "Orationes," 32; P.G., 36, 186.
[21] Mark xvi, 16.
[22] Cf. below, p. 133.

which must be accepted by all who would retain the name of Christian; *non-fundamental* doctrines are such as need not be accepted even though clearly revealed in Holy Scripture. It is evident that such a distinction cannot be maintained. Christ sent forth His Apostles with the command to teach "all things whatsoever I have commanded," and all men were obliged to accept this teaching in its entirety without distinction of fundamental and non-fundamental: "He that believeth not shall be condemned." Moreover, the very essence of faith is the acceptance of truth on the authority of God; therefore every doctrine must be accepted in its entirety, once it is known to be the revealed word of God. He who rejects a single truth known to be revealed by God is guilty of blasphemy because such rejection is a denial of God's veracity.

Even in practice the theory of fundamental doctrines failed to produce that unity for which it was invoked; there could be no agreement in deciding what are fundamental and what are non-fundamental doctrines. Waterland, a Protestant theologian, says: "There are almost as many *rules* for determining fundamentals as there are different sects or parties."[23] As a consequence, Protestants for the most part now maintain that it matters little what one believes, provided he lead a good moral life. Hence, a dogmatic religion, i.e., a religion that requires belief in certain, definite doctrines, is considered a relic of unenlightened ages.

Catholic theologians also distinguish between fundamental and non-fundamental doctrines, but with them fundamental doctrines are either those from which other truths may be deduced by reason, or which must be known and believed explicitly by all. Non-fundamental doctrines are those which need not be known by all; it is sufficient if they be implicitly believed in the general will to believe all that God has revealed. But once known to be revealed truths, they must be accepted without hesitation or doubt. Such a distinction is immediately seen to be reasonable and necessary, because many persons have neither the opportunity nor the ability to know all revealed truths.

Thesis.—The Church of Christ Is Necessarily One by Unity of
Doctrine and by Unity in the Profession of That Doctrine

The proposed thesis is a doctrine defined by the Vatican Council: "The eternal Pastor and Bishop of souls decreed to establish a holy Church, in which all the faithful should be held together by the bonds of ONE FAITH and a common charity . . . and preserved in the UNITY OF

---

[23] Daniel Waterland, "Works," Vol. VIII, p. 90 (old ed.). Cf. Murray, "De Ecclesia," Disp. VI, n. 401 sq.

FAITH and communion by THE MINISTRY OF A UNITED
PRIESTHOOD."[24]

A. Unity of Doctrine

PROOFS. I. *From Scripture.* Christ commissioned His Apostles to
"make disciples of all nations . . . teaching them to observe all that I
have commanded you."[25] He also promised to be with them "all days
even to the consummation of the world,"[26] and to send upon them the
Spirit of Truth to abide with them forever, and to bring to their mind
all things whatsoever He had taught them.[27] Consequently the Church
must teach them to all nations and at all times, even to the consummation of the world,—a mission made possible by the abiding presence of
the Holy Spirit, the Spirit of Truth. But in thus proclaiming *all* the
doctrines of Christ, to *all* people, at *all* times, the Church enjoys the
most perfect unity; her doctrines are the same at all times and in all
places. She cannot teach contradictory doctrines in different places or
at different times; she cannot even teach a part of her doctrines in one
place or in one age, and another part in another place or another age.
She must teach *all* truths at *all* times and in *all* places.

St. Paul admonishes the Galatians in most emphatic terms that there
is but one doctrine to be received by all: "But even if we or an angel
from heaven should preach a gospel to you other than that which we
have preached to you, let him be anathema. As we have said before, so
now I say again: If anyone preach a gospel to you other than that which
you have received, let him be anathema."[28] These words of St. Paul
prove that the doctrines of the Church can suffer no change because they
are not from man but "by the revelation of Jesus Christ." St. Jude likewise admonishes the faithful "to contend earnestly for the faith once
delivered to the saints."[29] It is a faith delivered once for all, incapable
of improvement, addition or change of any sort; it is the faith in which,
as St. Paul says, they must "stand fast and hold the traditions which
you have learned whether by word or by our epistle. . . . One Lord,
one faith and one Baptism."[30]

II. *From Tradition.* a) *St. Irenaeus* treats at length on the unity of
faith in the Church; after mentioning the doctrines handed down from

[24] Denzinger, n. 1821.
[25] Matt. xxviii, 19-20.
[26] Matt. xxviii, 20.
[27] John xiv, 16 sq.
[28] Gal. i, 8-12.
[29] Jude i, 3.
[30] 2 Thess. ii, 14; Ephes. iv, 5.

the Apostles, he says that the Church "proclaims them, and teaches them, and hands them down with perfect harmony as though she possessed but one mouth. For although the languages of the world differ, yet the import of the tradition is one and the same. For the churches which have been established in Germany do not believe or hand down anything different, nor do those in Spain, nor those in Gaul, nor those in the East, nor those in Egypt, nor those in Libya, nor those which have been established in the central regions of the world. But as the sun is one and the same throughout the whole world, so also the preaching of the truth shineth everywhere and enlightens all men that are willing to come to the knowledge of truth. . . . The Catholic Church possesses one and the same faith throughout the whole world."[31]

b) *St. Cyprian* says: "God is one, Christ is one; His Church is one and the faith is one." In the same work he also says: "The Church flooded with the light of the Lord, sheds forth her rays over the whole world, yet it is one light that is everywhere diffused, nor is the unity of the body separated."[32]

c) *Tertullian:* "The Apostles proclaimed the same doctrine of the same faith to the nations. Then they in like manner founded churches in every city, from which all other churches, one after another, derived their traditions of the faith and the seeds of doctrine, and are every day deriving them that they may become churches. Indeed it is only on this account that they will be able to deem themselves Apostolic."[33]

B. Unity of Profession

Unity in the profession of faith is a natural consequence of the unity of doctrine; a mere corollary to be explained rather than proved. Members of a society must accept its principles, or teachings, at least in word and action, for he who rejects the very principles of a society by word or act, thereby rejects the society itself and ceases to be a member. Therefore, every member of the Church must accept its teachings, i.e., he must make at least an outward profession of faith, "for with the heart we believe unto justice; but with the mouth, profession of faith is made unto salvation."[34] Since this outward profession concerns the one faith taught by the Church, it will be essentially the same for all its members; in other words, there will be unity in the outward profession of faith.

Unity in the profession of faith also follows from the fact that every

[31] "Adversus Haereses," I, 10; P.G., 7, 550.
[32] "De Unitate Ecclesiae," XXXIII, v; P.L., 4, 517, 502.
[33] "De Praescriptionibus," XX; P.L., 2, 32.
[34] Rom. x, 10.

member of a society must cooperate to some extent in attaining the end
which it seeks to realize; therefore, he must use, according to his position in the society, the means necessary to attain that end. But in the
Church the very use of those means,—the Sacraments, sacrifice, prayer,
and other acts of worship,—not only demand, but in fact are, outward
professions of faith, and that the one faith taught throughout the world.

It were useless to quote individual Fathers on this question for it is
a well-known fact that the Church has always demanded the strictest
unity in the profession of faith; those who refused to profess even a
single doctrine, were condemned as heretics who had already ceased
to be members, because, as St. Paul says, they are "self-condemned."[35]
For this reason Tertullian said: "Those who are heretics cannot be
Christians."[36]

4. Unity of Worship

PRELIMINARY REMARKS. Unity of worship, known also as
liturgical unity, refers especially to acts of public worship, in which the
faithful participate in their capacity as members of a society, the Church.
It applies only to those things that are of divine institution, which may
be summed up in the Sacrifice of the Mass and the Sacraments. Unity is
not necessary in those things which Christ left to the discretion of the
Church, to be changed according to the needs of time and place. The
various rites used in the Church in the celebration of the Holy Eucharist,
or in the administration of the Sacraments, do not affect the unity of
worship provided the essential nature of the Sacrifice and the Sacraments, as instituted by Christ, be left intact. Neither is unity of worship
disturbed by the use or the neglect of devotions which are not essential,
such as the invocation of saints, prayers for the dead, pilgrimages, and
the like. Denial of their efficacy or lawfulness would constitute heresy,
which is opposed to the unity of faith, but lack of uniformity in their
use does not break the unity of worship. Practically, then, unity of worship means that all members of the Church be initiated by the same
sacramental rite of Baptism, participate in the fruits of the same sacraments, and worship God by the same Eucharistic sacrifice.

According to the Protestant teaching, all men are free to worship God
according to the dictates of their own conscience. This doctrine is widely
proclaimed today as "freedom of conscience" or "freedom of worship."
It simply means that every man is free, not only to believe according to

---

[35] Tit. iii, 10, 11.
[36] "De Praescriptionibus," XXXVII; P.L., 2, 51.

his own interpretation of the Scriptures, but also to worship God in his own way. This either denies that Our Lord established any definite form of worship in the New Law, or maintains that we cannot know with certainty what it is, for surely no Christian could believe that he is free to worship as he pleases, if he admits that Christ has established a definite form of worship to be used by His followers.

Thesis.—The Church of Christ Is Necessarily One by Unity of Worship

PROOFS. I. *From Reason.* Unity in the outward profession of faith and in the use of the means necessary to attain the purposes for which the Church was instituted, constitutes unity of worship, because in the Church, which is a religious society, all these things pertain to worship. Furthermore, no one can deny that God has the right to demand one and the same form of worship from all His faithful children in the New Law as He did in the Old. The fact that unity of worship was demanded in the Old Law makes it very probable that a like unity is demanded in the more perfect Law of Christ, which was prefigured by the rites and institutions of the Old Law.

II. *From Scripture.* A comparison of the Church with the Synagogue makes it very *probable* that one form of worship is demanded of all the faithful in the New Law; the words of Christ made it *certain.* All men must be initiated into the Church by one and the same sacramental rite: "Make disciples of all nations, baptizing them in the name of the Father and of the Son and of the Holy Spirit."[37] For this reason St. Paul says: "In one Spirit were we all baptized into one body."[38] All must likewise partake of the same Eucharistic Bread: "Amen I say unto you; unless you eat the flesh of the Son of man, and drink his blood, you shall not have life in you."[39] St. Paul also teaches that the reception of the one Eucharistic Bread is not only a sign, but also a wonderful source of that unity whereby the faithful are united with one another and with Christ their Head: "And the bread that we break, is it not the partaking of the body of the Lord? Because the bread is one, we though many, are one body, all of us who partake of the one bread."[40]

At the institution of the Holy Eucharist, Christ said to the Apostles: "Do this in remembrance of me."[41] And again: "As often as you shall

---

[37] Matt. xxviii, 19.
[38] 1 Cor. xii, 13.
[39] John vi, 54.
[40] 1 Cor. x, 16 sq.
[41] Luke xxii, 19.

eat this bread and drink the cup, you proclaim the death of the Lord until he come."[42] This is the institution of that clean oblation which shall be offered in every place from the rising of the sun even to the going down,[43]—one and the same sacrificial worship to be offered at all time and in all places, *until He come.*

Unity of worship in the Sacrifice of the Mass and in the Sacraments of Baptism and the Eucharist are expressly demanded by Christ Himself; the necessity for unity in the use of the other Sacraments is equally evident from the very nature of a Sacrament. Christ alone has authority to say how grace shall be given; He alone can institute Sacraments to confer it, and no one can change them, abolish them, or add to their number. They must remain the same for all men at all time. But since the Sacrifice of the Mass and the use of the same Sacraments constitute the essential elements of worship, that worship must be the same for the whole Church, i.e., there must be essential unity of worship.

ART. II. HOLINESS OF THE CHURCH

Synopsis.—1. Nature of Holiness.—2. Physical Holiness of the Church.—3. Moral Holiness of the Church.—4. Manifestative Holiness. —5. Objections Answered.

1. Nature of Holiness

The English word *holiness* originally meant *wholeness, soundness,* or *health.* It is now used almost exclusively as an equivalent of the Latin *sanctitas,* from the verb *sancire, to set apart, to dedicate.* Therefore a thing is *holy* (*sanctum*) when set apart or devoted in some manner to God, and *holiness* or *sanctity* is the state or condition of the thing thus set apart and devoted to God. *Holiness* also includes the idea of being pleasing to God because of some union or conformity with Him. Finally, that which serves to manifest holiness is also said to be holy. Hence we have a threefold holiness,—*physical, moral,* and *manifestative.*

a) *Physical Holiness* consists in the consecration or dedication of a thing in some manner to the honor and glory of God. It is also called *real* because it is often connected with inanimate things (*res* in Latin). In this sense a church, an altar, or a chalice is said to be holy. Persons are also holy in this sense if consecrated to God in some special manner as, for example, by Holy Orders or religious vows.

[42] 1 Cor. xi, 26.
[43] Mal. i, 11.

If the person or thing consecrated to God is instrumental in producing moral holiness in others, it is said to possess *active* or *causative* holiness; otherwise it has mere *passive* or *ontological*[44] holiness. The Sacraments, the laws of God, the precepts of the Church and the hierarchy, all possess *active* holiness because they are instruments for producing holiness in the souls of men. A chalice, on the other hand, possesses mere passive or ontological holiness.

b) *Moral Holiness* consists in the consecration of the will to God by conforming it to His will. Moralists usually define it as that moral uprightness by which a person is made like to God and united with Him through charity. It is also called *personal* holiness, since it belongs to persons only. In the present order of things, all personal sanctity involves divine grace and is, therefore, supernatural.

c) *Manifestative Holiness*, as the name indicates, is any external evidence that a person or thing is holy and pleasing in the sight of God. As applied to the Church, it signifies rather the abiding power to produce such evidence when needed, and since miracles are practically the only proofs of sanctity, it may be defined as the permanent power of the Church to perform miracles when needed to manifest her physical or personal holiness.

In the Apostles' Creed we profess our faith in "the HOLY Catholic Church." The Vatican Council has also declared that the "eternal Pastor . . . decreed to establish a HOLY Church."[45] It is therefore an article of faith that the Church of Christ is holy, but in what particular sense is not defined. Theologically, it is certain that the Church must be holy in every respect. Physical sanctity, both passive and active, is an essential property; personal and manifestative sanctity also belong to the Church, if not as essential elements, then certainly as qualities contributing to her perfection according to the will of Christ.

2. Physical Holiness of the Church

Thesis.—The Church of Christ Possesses Physical Holiness, Both Passive and Active

I. PASSIVE HOLINESS. The Church of Christ must be eminently holy, since her Divine Founder is infinite Holiness itself, and because the very purpose of her existence is eminently holy. She possesses passive or ontological holiness by virtue of her intimate union with Christ. The Church is the mystical body of Christ; therefore, the union

---

[44] From the Greek, *things*.
[45] Denzinger, n. 1821.

58 The Church of Christ

between Christ and the Church must be as intimate as that between head and members in a physical body. Again, Christ is the *spouse* of His Church and His union with it is proclaimed the exemplar for that union which should exist between husband and wife, who are "two in one flesh."[46] The only union between God and a creature more intimate than that between Christ and His Church, is the union of the Word with human nature in the person of Jesus Christ. Hence the Church possesses ontological holiness to a degree surpassed only by the human nature of our divine Lord. Well, then, does St. Paul say: "Christ loved the Church and delivered himself up for it that he might SANCTIFY IT, CLEANSING IT . . . that he might present it to himself a glorious Church not having spot or wrinkle or any such thing, but that it should be HOLY AND WITHOUT BLEMISH."[47] Clement of Alexandria, writing of the Church, says: "Shall we not with propriety call the Church holy, made for the honor of God, sacred to God, of great value, and not constructed by mechanical art, but by the will of God fashioned into a temple?"[48]

The ontological holiness of the Church consists principally in the union of its members with Christ through Baptism and the Holy Eucharist. By Baptism the members of the Church are engrafted, as it were, into the body of Christ,—coincorporated with Christ, as St. Paul says,[49] and as Christ Himself indicates when He says: "I am the vine, you are the branches."[50] This union is strengthened and preserved by the Holy Eucharist so that the members of the Church ever remain "members of this body, made from his flesh and from his bones."[51] They become "a chosen generation . . . a holy nation, a purchased people,"[52] On this account St. Paul addresses all the faithful as "saints, i.e., holy ones,"[53] because all members of the Church retain in some degree this ontological holiness of union with Christ, so long as they remain within the bosom of the Church.

II. ACTIVE HOLINESS. There can be no question in regard to the active holiness of the Church, because its sole reason for existence is to produce sanctity in her members and thus lead them to eternal life. Among the many means at her command to produce sanctity are the Sacraments, the Holy Sacrifice of the Mass, the sacramentals, the

[46] Ephes. v, 23.
[47] Ephes. v, 25-27.
[48] "Stromata," VII, 5; P.G., 9, 438.*
[49] Rom. vi, 5 (Greek text).
[50] John xv, 5.
[51] Ephes. v, 30.
[52] 1 Peter ii, 9.
[53] Philip. i, 1; 2 Cor. i, 1.

preaching of the Gospel, the authority to teach and govern, and even the hierarchy, as representatives of Christ and bearers of His Person, have a wonderful power for the sanctification of men. This sanctifying power of the Church is symbolized by the "leaven which a woman took and hid in three measures of meal till the whole was leavened."[54]

3. Moral Holiness of the Church

PRELIMINARY REMARKS. *Moral* or *personal* sanctity may be either *perfect* or *imperfect,* and both admit of varying degrees. Perfect sanctity is the effect of sanctifying grace and the infused virtues of faith, hope, and charity; imperfect sanctity requires the infused virtues of faith and hope, and the exercise of, at least, some acts made supernatural by the aid of actual grace.

Moral sanctity, being a quality of the soul, can be predicated in the strict sense of persons only; the Church is said to possess it only in so far as her members are personally holy. Consequently the moral sanctity of the Church may vary from time to time, according to the number of holy persons within her fold, and also according to the degree of their sanctity. But this moral sanctity of the Church can never be entirely lost; there must ever be found a goodly number of holy persons in the Church,—persons who are holy because of her sanctifying powers. Moreover, the Church will always be noted for persons of eminent sanctity.

Many early heretics, especially the Novatians, Donatists, and Pelagians, exaggerated the moral sanctity of the Church by teaching sinners cannot belong to the Church. "The Wicliffites taught that the Church includes only the predestined. The Anabaptists and the English dissenters asserted that it consists only of those who are visibly holy in their lives . . . therefore they departed (from the Anglican communion) to form a pure society of saints in which no sinner was to find place."[55] Many of the early Reformers held a similar doctrine; others went to the opposite extreme by teaching that the Church of Christ may become so corrupt as to lose all personal sanctity. All Protestants today seem to agree in taking little or no account of extraordinary or eminent sanctity. It could not be otherwise, since they reject the most fruitful means of sanctity,—the Sacraments, the practice of the Evangelical Counsels and works of supererogation. The Articles of the Anglican Church say: "Voluntary works, besides, over and above God's commandments, cannot be taught without arrogancy and

---

[54] Luke xiii, 21; Matt. xiii, 33.
[55] William Palmer, "Treatise on the Church," Vol. I, p. 134.

impiety."[56] It is true that Baptism and the Lord's Supper (the Eucharist) have been retained as Sacraments by most Protestant sects, but they have been completely devitalized by teaching that the Eucharist is a mere memorial service, and Baptism a rite of initiation similar to that used by any ordinary society.

Thesis.—The Church of Christ Possesses Moral Sanctity, i.e., She Must Always Number Among Her Children Many Persons of Sanctity, Even of Eminent Sanctity

PROOFS. I. *From Reason.* Christ instituted the Church to sanctify and save all men; "for this is the will of God, your sanctification."[57] Is it possible that this purpose of Christ can be frustrated, even for a single day? Is it possible that at any time all the means of holiness especially instituted by Christ for the sanctification of souls, shall utterly fail in their efficacy? To assert such a possibility, would be to accuse Christ of failure.

II. *From Scripture.* Our Lord proclaimed the moral sanctity of His Church by comparing it to a field of wheat oversown with cockle; it contains much cockle, but still remains a *wheat-field* until the harvest.[58] The good shall never entirely fail in the Church; in fact, the parable leads to the inference that the good shall always predominate. The same idea is suggested by the parable of the wedding-feast, in which Christ compares the Church to a banquet, at which one alone was found unworthy.[59] The Church is also a net cast into the sea of this world; it takes both good and bad fish, and they shall be separated only on the shores of eternity. This indicates that there shall always be good and holy persons in the Church.

St. Peter calls the faithful "a chosen race, a royal priesthood, a holy nation, a purchased people; . . . who in times past were not a people, but are now the people of God; who had not obtained mercy, but now have obtained mercy."[60] These words presuppose a considerable number of holy persons in the Church at all times to make it *a chosen generation, a holy nation.* The Prophets of old speak in similar terms. Ezechiel, for example, speaking in the name of God concerning a new covenant to be established, says: "And I will put my spirit in the midst of you and I will cause you to walk in my com-

---

[56] The Thirty-Nine Articles, Art. xiv.
[57] 1 Thess. iv, 3.
[58] Matt. xiii, 24 sq.
[59] Matt. xxii, 11 sq.
[60] 1 Peter ii, 9-10; Osee ii, 24.

mandments and to keep my judgments and do them . . . and you shall be my people and I will be your God."[61] These words intimate that in the new covenant,—the Church of Christ,—there will ever be faithful souls to walk in His precepts and keep His judgments.

EMINENT HOLINESS.—The dignity and holiness ascribed to the Church in Holy Scripture cannot be justified by anything short of extraordinary sanctity in many of her children. She is represented as the *body* of Christ and, therefore, intimately united with Him, who is the fountain of all holiness. She is also endowed with the most wonderful means of sanctification in the Sacraments, especially in the Holy Eucharist. Such union with Christ and such means of grace cannot fail to produce corresponding effects in some souls at least; neither would the Church be a body suited to her divine Head were she not resplendent with sanctity in some of her members.

The Church is also represented as the *bride* of Christ, and should, therefore, be adorned with sanctity befitting her Divine Spouse, according to the words of the royal Psalmist: "The queen stood on thy right hand in gilded clothing, surrounded with variety."[62] She should also bring forth children worthy of such a union;—children eminent for sanctity and the practice of those counsels so often commended by Christ in the Gospels.

4. Manifestative Sanctity of the Church

PRELIMINARY REMARKS. Sanctity itself is something internal and invisible, but it may be manifested by external signs. This outward manifestation is called *manifestative sanctity*. There are various means of judging with more or less probability that a particular person or thing is pleasing and acceptable to God; but there is only one means of certain knowledge,—the testimony of God Himself, given through *miracles*, wrought under circumstances that leave no doubt that the person or institution through which they are performed, is pleasing to Almighty God. Miracles, therefore, constitute manifestative sanctity, but as miracles are facts, they cannot be a property or quality of the Church. Hence, manifestative sanctity, as a property of the Church, is rather *the permanent power of the Church to perform miracles*, or at least *a permanent right to have them performed, when necessary to prove her sanctity and her divine mission.* "The Church is said to be

---

[61] Ez. xi, 19; xxxvi, 26 sq.

[62] Ps. xliv, 10. This text is more appropriately rendered thus: "The queen stands at thy right hand, adorned with gold and embroidery." (Cf. Berry, "Commentary on the Psalms," pp. 332-334.)

holy on account of her miraculous powers, because such powers prove
that she is pleasing to God who dwells within her and continues to
operate through her; they prove her divine mission in the most convincing manner. For this reason the power of miracles will be most
prominent when evidence for the truth and sanctity of the Church is
most needed."[63]

Protestants, with few exceptions, deny the power of miracles in the
Church today, although many admit the occurrence of miracles in the
first ages. Middleton, a non-Catholic, says: "The most prevailing opinion is that they subsisted through the three first centuries, and then
ceased in the beginning of the fourth." But he himself rejects this opinion, because, "by granting but a single age of miracles after the times
of the Apostles, we shall be entangled in a series of difficulties whence
we can never fairly extricate ourselves till we allow the same powers
to the present age."[64] Although universally condemned by Protestants
of his day, the opinion of Middleton is quite logical. If miracles ever
existed in the Church, there is no reason why they should cease at the
end of the third century rather than in the tenth, or the nineteenth,
or any succeeding century. The circumstances that made them necessary or useful in the second or third century, may be present in any
other century, until the end of time. Hence, we must either sweep aside
the testimony of all antiquity and deny the existence of miracles in
every age, or admit that the Church is endowed with miraculous powers
for all time, unless it can be proved that Christ has ordained otherwise.

Thesis.—The Church of Christ Possesses Manifestative Sanctity, i.e.,
She Has a Permanent Power of Performing Miracles When
Circumstances Make Them Necessary or Useful

PROOFS. I. *From Reason.* The Church as viceregent of Jesus
Christ, carries forward His mission on earth. Therefore, she should
have the same means for proving her mission and establishing her
authority that Christ Himself used to establish His own. For this purpose Christ performed miracles; therefore, the Church also should
have power to perform miracles when circumstances demand the exercise of such power.

II. *From Scripture.* St. Paul represents the Church as the body of
Christ animated by the Holy Spirit, who manifests His indwelling
presence through the working of miracles: "To one through the Spirit
is given the utterance of wisdom . . . to another the gift of healing in

[63] Dorsch, "De Ecclesia Christi," p. 500.
[64] C. Middleton, "Introductory Discourse," pp. 46, 96.

the one Spirit; to another the working of miracles; to another prophecy; to another the distinguishing of spirits; to another various kinds of tongues; to another interpretation of tongues. But all these things are work of one and the same Spirit who allots to every one according as he wills. . . . For in one Spirit we were all baptized into one body."[65] Therefore, so long as the Holy Spirit dwells within the Church to animate it and guide it, we shall expect these external manifestations of His presence and power by the working of miracles.

When Christ sent forth His Apostles to preach the Gospel and organize His Kingdom, He said to them: "And these signs shall attend those who believe: in my name they shall cast out devils; they shall speak in new tongues . . . they shall lay hands upon the sick and they shall get well."[66] In these words Christ promised the power of miracles to His disciples,—a power connected with the profession of the true faith, and unlimited as to time and place. This promise, as we know, is not fulfilled in Our Lord's disciples as individuals, for no one will maintain that all members of Christ's Church have the power of working miracles. Therefore, the promise must be fulfilled in the disciples taken collectively as a society, which is the Church, and Holy Scripture testifies that such was the case in the days of the Apostles. They wrought miracles to prove their mission and confirm their teachings; in this manner many were brought to the knowledge of truth and won for Christ. St. Peter healed the lame man at the gate of the Temple, and "many of them who heard the word believed, and the number of the men was made five thousand."[67] At Lydda, he also healed Eneas of the palsy and "all that dwelt at Lydda and Saron saw him, who were converted to the Lord."[68] In Joppe, he raised Tabitha to life and "it was made known throughout all Joppe; and many believed in the Lord."[69] At Paphos, St. Paul wrought a miracle upon Elymas the magician and "the proconsul, when he had seen what was done, believed, admiring at the doctrine of the Lord."[70] When writing to the Galatians, the same Apostle appeals to the miracles wrought in their midst as a confirmation of his teaching: "He therefore who gives to you the Spirit, and works miracles among you; does he do it by the works of the Law or by the message of the faith?"[71]

---

[65] 1 Cor. xii, 8 sq.; 27 sq.
[66] Mark xvi, 17
[67] Acts iv, 4.
[68] Acts ix, 38 sq.
[69] Acts ix, 33-35.
[70] Acts xiii, 8 sq.
[71] Gal. iii, 5.

If miracles were necessary, or at least useful, for the Apostles when carrying the Gospel to those who had never heard of it, or who denied the Apostolic mission to preach a new faith, are they not likewise necessary under similar conditions in every age? Christ did not promise to be with His Church for a few years, or a few centuries only, but for all time, "even to the consummation of the world."[72]

III. *From Tradition.* Practically all the early Fathers appeal to the miracles wrought in the Church as proof of her divine mission. Middleton, a non-Catholic scholar, candidly admits this: "It must be confessed, in the first place, that this claim of a miraculous power, which is now peculiar to the Church of Rome, was universally asserted and believed in all Christian countries and in all ages of the Church till the time of the Reformation."[73] In view of this fact, it will suffice to quote but one early Father on the matter. In his work against heresies, St. Irenaeus says: "Those who are in truth His disciples, receiving grace from Him, do in His name perform miracles, so as to promote the welfare of other men according to the gift which each one has received from Him. For some do certainly and truly drive out devils, so that those who have been thus cleansed from evil spirits, frequently both believe and join themselves to the Church. . . . Others heal the sick by laying their hands upon them, and they are made whole. Yea, moreover, as I have said, the dead even have been raised up and remained amongst us for many years. And what shall I say more? It is not possible to name the number of gifts which the Church scattered throughout the whole world has received from God in the name of Jesus Christ . . . and which she exerts day by day for the benefit of the gentiles."[74]

5. Objections Answered

OBJECTION I.—All members of Christ's Church are free moral agents, capable of falling from grace at any time. Therefore, all may fall at the same time, leaving the Church deprived of moral sanctity.

ANSWER.—Sanctity in the individual depends upon his own free-will at all times; sanctity in the whole body of the faithful depends upon the will of Christ and the providence of God. By the distribution of efficacious graces God can provide unfailing sanctity for His Church without destroying man's free-will. In the Old Law God's purposes in regard to the Chosen People were not, and could not be

---

[72] Matt. xxviii, 20.
[73] "Introductory Discourse," p. 44.
[74] "Adversus Haereses," II, 32, 4; P.G., 7, 829.

defeated, yet each and every member of the Hebrew nation was left to the full exercise of his free-will. In like manner God will carry out His purposes in the New Law by preserving personal sanctity in His Church and free-will in the individual.

OBJECTION II.—The Church, as the mystical body of Christ, must follow the analogy of a physical body, which is said to be sick, or unsound, when any single member is diseased. Hence the Church loses her moral sanctity by the presence of a single sinner within her fold.

ANSWER.—A natural body is not rendered unsound throughout by the unsound condition of one or more members, unless they be vital members. In the Church the vital members are Christ and the Holy Spirit, who are sanctity itself. A body with an unsound member is not *perfectly* sound; it is diseased, because the unsound member reacts upon the whole body thereby causing pain, discomfort or *dis-ease*. In like manner the presence of sinners in the Church deprives her of *perfect* moral holiness, because, as stated above, the Church has moral holiness in so far only as her members are personally holy. The presence of sinners causes her pain and sorrow (*dis-ease*); she sorrows over sinners as she rejoices over the good: "If one member suffer anything, all the members suffer with it; or if one member glory, all the members rejoice with it."[75] The infection of one member cannot spread to the whole body of the Church, as often happens in a physical body; her powers of resistance are always sufficient to prevent such general infection.

OBJECTION III.—Our Lord did not intend His Church to have the power of miracles; in fact, He warns against the workers "of great signs and wonders," who will act as agents of Satan to deceive the faithful: "False Christs and false prophets will arise, and will show great signs and wonders, so as to lead astray, if possible, even the elect."[76]

ANSWER.—Christ is here warning the faithful against the prodigies that the agents of Satan will produce in the days of Antichrist, to deceive them if possible. Such prodigies are not miracles, but as St. Paul says, "signs and lying wonders." This very warning on the part of Our Lord presupposes the power of miracles in the Church, for otherwise there would be no reason for Satan to attempt such counterfeits. There can be no counterfeit coins where there are no genuine coins to counterfeit. The prophecies of the Apocalypse show that Satan

---

[75] 1 Cor. xii, 26.
[76] Matt. xxiv, 24.

will imitate the Church of Christ to deceive mankind; he will set up a church of Satan in opposition to the Church of Christ. Antichrist will assume the role of Messias; his prophet will act the part of Pope, and there will be imitations of the Sacraments of the Church. There will also be *lying wonders* in imitation of the miracles wrought in the Church.[77]

OBJECTION IV.—Miracles are no proof of sanctity, for Christ has said that on the day of judgment many will say to Him: "Lord, Lord, have not we prophesied in thy name, and cast out devils in thy name, and done many miracles in thy name? And then I will declare to them, 'I never knew you. Depart from me, you workers of iniquity.' "[78]

ANSWER.—Not every miracle is a proof of sanctity in the person through whom it is wrought, nor in the society in which it is wrought. The circumstances and purposes of miracles must be taken into account. For example, the prophecy of Balaam was no proof of sanctity on his part, but the circumstances and purpose of the prophecy gave undeniable proof that the people of Israel were under the special protection of God. In like manner, a miracle wrought through the use of relics, or the intercession of a saint, shows beyond doubt that the veneration of relics and the intercession of saints are practices pleasing to God, since He has scanctioned them by direct intervention of His own power to perform a miracle. When God wrought miracles through the Apostles and thereby brought many souls into the Church, did He not thereby show that the Church is holy and pleasing to Him? What was true in the days of the Apostles, is true at all times in the Church.

OBJECTION V.—"The performance of miracles is *not essential* to real sanctity. It will surely not be pretended, even by Romanists, that all those who are honored by the Church as saints must have wrought miracles."[79]

ANSWER.—There is no claim that the power to perform miracles constitutes sanctity or is in any way necessary for its existence. Miracles are simply the means, and the only certain means, to make known the presence of sanctity in a person or an institution. But as there is no necessity for sanctity to be made known in all cases, so neither was there any necessity for all the saints to perform miracles.

OBJECTION VI.—If miracles were a property of the Church, they would have to be wrought continuously, because a property, being

---

[77] Cf. Berry, "The Apocalypse of St. John," pp. 138 sq.
[78] Matt. vii, 22; cf. Palmer, "Treatise on the Church," Vol. I, pp. 142 sq.
[79] Palmer, "Treatise on the Church," Vol. I, p. 143.

essential, can never be lacking. But miracles rarely occur in the Church today.

ANSWER.—Miracles themselves are not a property of the Church: the power to perform miracles when necessary constitutes the property which is ever present in the Church. It is not necessary that this power be constantly exercised. Christ did not perform miracles at all times, yet He possessed the power at all times. Miracles are performed in the Church only when necessary according to circumstances of time and place; consequently they will be more frequent in one age than in another. In the first ages they were more necessary than at present, for, as St. Gregory the Great says, "Miracles were necessary in the beginning of the Church that the faith might grow by their nourishment. In the same way we water newly planted trees until we see they have taken root in the soil; then we cease to water them any longer."[80] In like manner Lacordaire: "When Jesus laid the foundations of His Church, it was needful for Him to obtain faith in a work then beginning; now it is formed, although not yet completed. You behold it, you touch it, you compare it, you measure it, you judge whether it is a human work. Why should God be prodigal of miracles to those who do not see *the* miracle?"[81]

As the Church becomes better established and more widely known, the need for miracles decreases, and they become less frequent, but they have never entirely ceased.[82] Changed circumstances of future years may make them as necessary as they were in the first ages of the Church.

ART. III. CATHOLICITY OF THE CHURCH

Synopsis.—1. Use and Meaning of the Term.—2. The Church Catholic by Diffusion.—3. Catholicity of Church Further Defined.—4. Perfect Catholicity To Be Attained.

1. Use and Meaning of the Term

A DISTINCTIVE TITLE. The Church has been called *Catholic* from the earliest years of her existence. St. Ignatius Martyr, in his letter to the Christians of Smyrna, written about the year 107, says: "Wherever Christ is, there is the *Catholic* Church."[83] A few years later (A. D. 140) an account of the sufferings and death of St. Polycarp

---

[80] "Homily in Evang.," 29; P.L., 76, 1213.
[81] Lacordaire, "Jesus Christ," Confer. ii, p. 39 (English tr.).
[82] Cf. below, p. 90.
[83] "Epist. ad Smyrnaeos," VIII; Funk, Vol. I, p. 283.

was addressed "to all the parishes of the holy *Catholic* Church throughout the world."[84] The same title is applied to the Church in an ancient document known as the *Fragment of Muratori*, which was written about A. D. 200. All Christians still profess their faith in the *holy Catholic Church* as often as they recite the Apostles' Creed, which dates back to the days of the Apostles, or at least to the years immediately following.

From the earliest times the word *Catholic* has been used as a proper name to distinguish the true Church from heretical sects. St. Cyril of Jerusalem thus addressed his catechumens in the year 348: "If ever thou art sojourning in cities, inquire not simply where the Lord's House is, for sects of the profane also attempt to call their dens *houses* of the Lord. Neither do you ask merely where the Church is, but where is the *Catholic Church,* for such is the peculiar name of this holy Church, the mother of us all, which is the spouse of our Lord Jesus Christ."[85] In like manner St. Augustine says: "The Church is called *Catholic* by all her enemies as well as by her own children. Whether they wish it or not, heretics and schismatics, when speaking with those outside their own sects, can call the Church by no other name than *Catholic,* for they would not be understood unless they used the name by which the Church is known to the whole world."[86]

MEANING OF THE WORD CATHOLIC. The word *Catholic* is derived from the Greek kath' holon, which means *concerning all, embracing all.* Hence *Catholicity* implies universality of some sort. When applied to the Church, it may mean (a) that the Church is to endure for all time; (b) that she teaches all the doctrines of Christ and uses all the means instituted by Him for salvation; (c) that she is destined for all men; or (d) that she is spread throughout the whole world, kath' holen ten gen. St. Cyril of Jerusalem briefly explains the Catholicity of the Church in these various senses: "It is called Catholic, then, because it extends over all the world from one end of the earth to the other; and because it teaches universally and completely one and all the doctrines which ought to come to man's knowledge concerning things both visible and invisible, heavenly and earthly; and because it brings into subjection to godliness the whole race of mankind, governors and governed, learned and unlearned; and because it universally treats and heals the whole class of sins which are committed by soul and body, and possesses in itself every form of virtue which

[84] Martyrdom of Polycarp, Funk, Vol. I, p. 315.
[85] "Catecheses," XVIII, 26; P.G., 33, 1043.*
[86] "De Vera Religione," 7; P.P., 34, 128.

is named, both in deeds and in words, and in every kind of spiritual gifts."[87]

CATHOLICITY OF DIFFUSION. The idea of diffusion, or extension, throughout the world has so predominated in the notion of universality that the term *Catholic* is now used almost exclusively in that sense. The other forms of universality are easily identified with other properties or attributes of the Church. The universality of time is simply the perpetuity of the Church; universality in doctrine and means of salvation pertain to the perpetual unity of faith and worship.

Catholicity of diffusion may be either *de jure* or *de facto*. The Church is catholic or universal *de jure* (*by right*) because it is destined for the salvation of all men, and therefore endowed with the ability to spread to all parts of the world to fulfill that mission; it is catholic *de facto* (*in fact*) when actually diffused or spread throughout the world. All who admit that Christ founded any church at all, must admit that it is Catholic *de jure*,—that it was commissioned by Christ to carry salvation to all nations, and that it was consequently endowed with the ability to spread throughout the world for this purpose. Hence *de jure* Catholicity is an essential property possessed by the Church of Christ from the first moment of her existence. It is immediately evident that *de facto* Catholicity could come only with the lapse of time, and gradually increase with the passing centuries, until the Church becomes completely *Catholic*, embracing all nations, tribes and tongues. Therefore *de facto* Catholicity is not an essential property of the Church in the sense that it must have been present at all times from the very beginning; it is an essential property in the sense that it necessarily flows from the very nature of the Church as a society destined to carry the Gospel to all nations. Starting at Jerusalem, the Church was to spread to all parts of the known world and to extend its limits as new countries were discovered; when once spread over the world it was never to be reduced again to the narrow limits of a nation, or other relatively small portions of the world. This is clearly indicated by the parable of the mustard seed, "which is indeed the smallest of all seeds," yet it gradually grew into a tree greater than all herbs, "so that the birds of the air come and dwell in its branches."[88] The same idea is expressed by Daniel when he compares the Messianic Kingdom to a small stone that "became a great mountain and filled the whole earth."[89] Christ Himself plainly indicated the progressive expansion of His

---

[87] "Catecheses," XVIII, 23; P.G., 33.
[88] Matt. xiii, 31, 32.
[89] Dan. ii, 35.

Church when He said to the Apostles: "You shall be witnesses for
me in Jerusalem, and in all Judea, and Samaria, and even to the very
ends of the earth."[90] Many other texts of Scripture could be quoted in
this matter, but these few are sufficient.

All Christians admit that the Church of Christ must be *de facto*
universal in some sense, but Protestants maintain that the Church
Catholic is an intangible something of which all Christian churches
are but so many parts. It has been proved already that the Church of
Christ is a visible society that enjoys complete unity in government,
faith, and worship. Therefore, if the Church is to be Catholic in fact,
its members and all its parts throughout the world must be so united
as to form but one society,—a visible society with unity of government,
faith, and worship. Hence the words of St. Augustine to the Donatists
of Africa: "Dissension and division make you heretics; peace and
unity make Catholics."[91] It is not sufficient for actual Catholicity that a
Church have members scattered far and wide throughout the world;
the Church itself, as a society, must exist in the various parts of the
world to exercise its authority and carry on the mission of Christ. In
other words, the Church of Christ must be *formally* universal. Neither
will mere numbers constitute universality; a large number of members
confined to a relatively small portion of the world does not constitute
universality.

2. The Church Catholic by Actual Diffusion

Thesis.—The Church of Christ Possesses de Jure Catholicity of
Diffusion as an Essential Attribute, From Which de Facto and
Progressive Catholicity Necessarily Follows, Thus Con-
stituting a Property of the Church

The doctrine, as stated, seems so self-evident that proofs are really
unnecessary. Any one who admits that Christ instituted a Church to
save all men, must admit that He intended it to become actually universal and to remain so for all time. To ascribe any other intention to
Christ would be to accuse Him of folly.

PROOFS. I. *From Scripture.* The Church of Christ must be as depicted in Holy Scripture, but, as St. Augustine says, "almost every
page of Scripture proclaims Christ and the Church spread throughout
the whole world."[91a] In fact, the Prophets single out universality as the
chief mark of the Messianic Kingdom. Thus they oppose it to the

---

[90] Acts i, 8.
[91] "Contra Litteras Petil." 11, 95; P.L., 43, 333.
[91a] "Sermon," 46; P.L., 38, 289.

Mosaic dispensation, which was limited to the one nation of the Chosen People. Isaias says: "And in the last days the mountain of the house of the Lord shall be prepared . . . and all nations shall flow unto it."[92] Zacharias: "He shall speak peace to the gentiles, and His power shall be from sea to sea, and from the rivers even to the ends of the earth."[93] Daniel compares the Church to a mountain that fills the whole earth; he represents Christ as a king whom "all peoples, tribes, and tongues shall serve."[94] Malachias foretold the offering of a new sacrifice in all places and among all peoples from the rising of the sun to the going down.[95] The Church in which this sacrifice is offered must therefore be universal.

Christ distinctly proclaimed the universality of His Church when He said to the Apostles: "Go ye into the whole world and preach the Gospel to every creature."[96] On another occasion: "This Gospel of the kingdom shall be preached in the whole world, for a witness to all nations."[97] Again: "You shall be witnesses for me in Jerusalem, and in all Judea, and in Samaria, and even to the very ends of the earth."[98]

Many other texts could easily be quoted to the same effect, but these are amply sufficient.

II. *From Tradition.* "The primitive Church always understood the prophecies relating to the universality of Christianity (the Church) as descriptive of its permanent condition; for we find the Fathers not merely asserting the fact that the Church of Christ was really diffused throughout the whole world, but arguing that the Church of which they were members must be the true Church, because it was so diffused, and that the societies of heretics which claimed to be the only true Church could not be so from their deficiency in this essential characteristic."[99] A few quotations from the Fathers will prove the justice of this statement of a non-Catholic author.

ST. CYRIL OF JERUSALEM: "The Church is called Catholic because it is spread all over the world from one end of the earth to the other."[100] ST. AUGUSTINE: "The Church is given the Greek name *Catholic,* because it is spread over the whole world."[101] ST. OPTATUS

---

[92] Is. ii, 2.
[93] Zach. ix, 10.
[94] Dan. ii, 35 sq.; vii, 14.
[95] Mal. i, 11.
[96] Mark xvi, 15.
[97] Matt. xxiv, 14.
[98] Acts i, 8.
[99] W. Palmer, "Treatise on the Church," Vol. I, p. 150.
[100] "Catecheses," XVIII, 23; P.G., 33, 1043.
[101] "Epist, ad Severianum," P.L., 33, 194.

OF MILEVE argues thus with Parmenian, the Donatist: "Thou has said, brother Parmenian, that the Church is only amongst you . . . therefore that it may exist with you in a part of Africa,—a corner of a small region. It must not be amongst us in the other part of Africa, nor in Spain, Italy, Gaul, where you are not. . . . Where then is the propriety of the name *Catholic,* since the Church is called *Catholic* because it is diffused everywhere,"[102] ST. ATHANASIUS and the bishops of the Alexandrian patriarchate use the same argument in their letter to the Emperor Jovian. They tell him that the Catholic faith must be the true one because it is the faith held universally throughout the world, whereas the Arian doctrines are professed by a few only.[103]

3. Catholicity of Church Further Defined

The Church of Christ must be universal, or Catholic, by diffusion throughout the world, but this diffusion may be either *physical* or *moral, simultaneous* or *successive, absolute* or *relative.* Therefore, it may be asked, what is the precise nature of the universality necessary for the Church, and also whether this universality must be perpetual.

MORALLY CATHOLIC. Physical universality would be realized if the Church were so completely spread over the earth that she actually exercised her authority over every portion of the inhabited world. It is evident that the Church has never been so diffused, and therefore such universality cannot be necessary. The early Fathers evidently held this view; even in the third and fourth centuries they proclaimed the Church already universal because of her diffusion, yet as St. Augustine said: "It still had much room to increase before the prophecy concerning Christ, prefigured by Solomon, would be fulfilled: 'He shall rule from sea to sea, and from river unto the ends of the earth.' "[104]

It is sufficient, then, that the Church be *morally* universal, i.e., that she be so wide-spread throughout the world that she may easily be known even in those regions in which she does not actually exist; or, as Suarez puts it: "If she has such universal renown that she may be known and distinguished from all heretical sects."[105]

SIMULTANEOUSLY CATHOLIC. The Church might have a successive existence in various parts of the world, dying out in one place as it springs up in another, until finally the Gospel would have been announced in all parts of the world. This would constitute *successive* catholicity, but it is evident that such universality is not sufficient, be-

[102] "De Schismate Donatistarum," II, 1; P.L., 11, 942.
[103] Theodoret, "Church History," IV, 3; P.G., 82-1126, 1127.
[104] "Epist, ad Hesych.," P.L., 33, 922; cf. Ps. lxxi, 8.
[105] "Defensio Fidei," I, xvi, 10.

cause at no time would the Church be really Catholic in any true sense of the word. Therefore, the Church must be *simultaneously* Catholic, i.e., it must be present throughout the whole world at one and the same time. It is true, of course, that the Church may cease to exist in this or that part of the world, but it must ever remain at least morally universal, as explained above.

ABSOLUTELY CATHOLIC. *Absolute* Catholicity is the universality of the Church, considered in itself, regardless of any other religious society. *Relative* catholicity refers to the universality of the Church as compared with that of some other society. In this latter sense, the Church will be Catholic if it is more widespread than any other single church. As already noted, mere numbers do not constitute universality; one church is not more Catholic, or universal, than another because of the mere fact that it numbers more adherents.

Absolute Catholicity is necessary in the true Church as shown above, but relative Catholicity does not seem necessary; at least, its necessity can be proved neither from Scripture nor tradition, and there seems to be no reason why a false sect might not become universally distributed over the world, unless perhaps God in His providence prevents it, of which we have no assurance.

PERPETUALLY CATHOLIC. The reason for the Church's universality demands that it be also perpetual; in so far as the Church might fail in her universality at any time, in just that far must she also fail in her mission of carrying the Gospel to all nations. Moreover, all the prophecies of old and all the promises of Christ concerning the universality of the Church were made without restrictions or limitations as to time. They never contemplate any failure; they never so much as intimate that the Church will ever be reduced to narrow or insignificant limits. Cardinal Bellarmine held that the Church might be so reduced in extent as to be confined *for a time* to one single country or province, provided it were still recognized as the Church that had been universally spread over the world.[106] This opinion has been rejected by theologians in general, yet it seems quite evident from the Apocalypse of St. John that just such a situation will be realized in the days of Antichrist. In chapter xii the Church is symbolized by a woman who is pursued and persecuted by a dragon (Satan). "And the woman fled into the wilderness where she has a place prepared by God, that they may nourish her a thousand two hundred and sixty days."[107] And again, "there was given to the woman the two wings of

---

[106] "De Ecclesia," iv, 7.
[107] "Apocalypse," xii, 6.

the great eagle, that she might fly into the wilderness unto her place, where she is nourished for a time and times and half a time, away from the serpent."[108] These words clearly indicate that the Church will be forced to seek retreat in some friendly nation or province where she can be protected from destruction for the three and one half years of Satan's reign. During this time of retreat the Church will be greatly limited in her diffusion, but she will still be *morally* universal,—she will still be known throughout the world; her very persecution will make her known far and wide through the nations of the world. Today we see the forebodings, if not the actual beginnings, of the situation just described.[109]

4. Perfect Catholicity To Be Attained

Thesis.—The Church of Christ Shall at Length Attain Perfect Catholicity, i.e., It Shall Finally Embrace All Nations and All Peoples Without Exception

Although *moral* universality is sufficient to make the Church truly Catholic, the prophecies of old certainly demand something more for their adequate fulfillment; one and all announce a kingdom that shall be universal to the last degree. A few examples will make this clear: (a) "He shall rule from sea to sea, and from the river unto the ends of the earth . . . and all kings of earth shall adore him; all nations shall serve him. . . . And in him shall all tribes of the earth be blessed; all nations shall magnify him."[110] (b) "And all the nations thou hast made shall come and adore before thee, O Lord; and they shall glorify thy name."[111] (c) "His empire shall be multiplied and there shall be no end of peace."[112] (d) "And judgment shall sit . . . that the kingdom, and power, and the greatness of the kingdom under the whole heaven may be given to the saints of the most High; whose kingdom is an everlasting kingdom, and all kings shall serve him and obey him."[113] (e) "He shall speak peace to the gentiles, and his power shall be from sea to sea, and from the rivers even to the ends of the earth."[114]

Prophecies such as these find no adequate fulfillment in the conversion of a few thousand, or even a few million souls among the vast pagan populations of earth. Neither can a world largely steeped in paganism,

---

[108] "Apocalypse," xii, 14.
[109] Berry, "Apocalypse of St. John," pp. 119 sq.
[110] Ps. lxxi, 8 sq.
[111] Ps. lxxxv, 9.
[112] Is. ix, 7.
[113] Dan. vii, 26, 27.
[114] Zach. ix, 10.

torn by schism and distracted by heresy, be the only fruit of Christ's death upon the Cross. We are forced to say with St. Augustine: "Even in the islands of the sea shall be fulfilled the word of prophecy, 'He shall rule from sea to sea,' and if a prophet cannot deceive, it is necessary that all nations whatsoever He has made, shall adore Him."[115]

Even the scattered nation of the Jews shall follow the gentiles into the Church, as St. Paul plainly states: "I would not have you ignorant of this mystery . . . that a partial blindness only has befallen Israel, until the full number of the Gentiles should enter, and thus all Israel should be saved as it is written

> There will come out of Sion the deliverer
> And he will turn away impiety from Jacob.
> And this is my covenant with them
> When I shall take away their sins.[116]

Again he says of the Jewish people: "For if the rejection of them is the reconciliation of the world, what will the reception of them be but life from the dead?"[117]

After the gentile nations have entered the Church, the Jews also shall submit to the faith of Christ and the Church shall be universal indeed. Then shall begin the reign of Christ in all its fullness, "from sea to sea," and all the prophecies shall be justified. This does not mean that each and every individual of every nation and tribe shall submit to the Church; *nations* and *peoples,* not *individuals,* have been promised to the Church for her inheritance. It does mean, however, that all nations, as nations, and at least the vast majority of their subjects, shall recognize the true Church of Christ and submit to her authority.

These prophecies will not be fulfilled before the time of Antichrist, since the Apocalypse makes it certain that he will come into a world harassed by paganism, apostasy, schism, and heresy.[118] The Jews, still unconverted, will accept him as Messias and assist in his warfare against the Church. Only after the defeat of Antichrist and the conversion of the gentile nations, will the Jews accept Christ as Messias. According to the generally accepted opinion, this will take place shortly before the end of the world, since the coming of Antichrist is looked upon as a prelude to the consummation of all things earthly. If this be true, the universal reign of Christ would seem a failure in point of time. It certainly does

---

[115] "Epist. ad Hesychium," P.L., 33, 922.
[116] Rom. xi, 25.
[117] Rom. xi, 15.
[118] Apoc. ix, 20, 21.

not seem probable that thousands of years spent in preparation shall lead up to a universal reign of Christ lasting but a few short months, or at most, a few short years. It would be considered a mark of folly in a human society to labor for years building itself up to the point where it could most effectively carry out its programme, and then disband. Are we not accusing Christ of like folly if we suppose He will in like manner bring the earthly career of His Church to an end almost immediately upon attaining the state in which it can perfectly carry out its mission?

It seems far more probable that the period of fruition will at least equal, and perhaps even exceed, the period of preparation, and therefore that many centuries will intervene between the destruction of Antichrist and the end of the world. The progressive character of the Church in her extension has already been noted. Beginning at Jerusalem, she spread with miraculous rapidity, extending her limits ever farther and farther with the passing centuries, yet all the while the *gates of hell* were struggling to prevent it. The Church has been forced to wage unceasing war upon her enemies. Judaism assailed her in infancy; then followed, in succession, Arianism, Islamism, the Greek schism, the pseudo-Reformation of the sixteenth century and Rationalism in the eighteenth. Today she is warring against indifferentism and the denial of all religion. The *"mystery of iniquity,"* mentioned by St. Paul,[119] grows apace with the spread of the Church, and will culminate in the coming of Antichrist, when Satan will make a last supreme effort to prevent the universal reign of Christ in His Church. After a short but desperate struggle, the Church will emerge victorious, Antichrist will perish, and the powers of Satan will be curbed, so "That he should deceive the nations no more."[120]

After the defeat and destruction of Antichrist, all nations will flow into the Church, the Jews will enter her fold, and the universal reign of Christ will be established over all peoples, tribes, and tongues. Then shall the words of Christ be literally and completely fulfilled: "I have overcome the world."[121] After a long period of time, symbolically designated as a thousand years,[122] "Satan will be released from prison and will go forth and deceive the nations which are in the four corners of the earth, Gog and Magog, and will gather them together for the battle"[123] for a final persecution of the Church. By special intervention

---

[119] 2 Thess. ii, 7.
[120] Apoc. xx, 3.
[121] John xvi, 33.
[122] Apoc. xx, 2, 3.
[123] Apoc. xx, 7.

of God, these hostile nations shall be quickly defeated and the Church shall stand forth once more victorious. Then will the day of judgment be near at hand.[124]

Synopsis.—1. The Nature of Apostolicity.—2. The Church of Christ Apostolic.

1. The Nature of Apostolicity

Apostolicity denotes connection in some manner with the Apostles, or a likeness to them. Hence we speak of Apostolic men, i.e., men who lived in the days of the Apostles, or who are inspired with a like zeal in their ministry. In like manner the Church is said to be Apostolic because of some relation it bears to the Apostles. Historians use the term to designate the Church as it existed in the days of the Apostles; with theologians, it means that the Church is, in some manner, derived from the Apostles. In this sense the Church is Apostolic in *origin, doctrine,* and *ministry.* The Church is Apostolic in *origin,* because it is and must ever remain, the identical society founded by Christ and organized through the ministry of the Apostles; it is Apostolic in *doctrine,* because it teaches the selfsame truths that Christ committed to its custody in the persons of the Apostles. Finally, the Church is Apostolic in *ministry* (or *succession*), because the authority which Christ conferred upon the Apostles has come down through an unbroken line of legitimate successors in the ministry of the Church.

---

[124] Cf. Berry, "The Apocalypse of St. John," pp. 180 sq.—The interpretation of the prophecies regarding the time of Antichrist and subsequent events is given as an opinion to be accepted for what it is worth. So far as we know, there is no pronouncement of the Church on this question. In fact, no doctrine is involved. It is generally held by Catholic theologians that the Church will be completely Catholic after the days of Antichrist. This doctrine is not materially affected by the further consideration concerning the time of his appearance. This is merely an interesting speculation, of which the above solution seems probable to us. It might be objected that Christ Himself places the end of the world immediately after the attainment of complete Catholicity by the Church: "This gospel shall be preached in the whole world, for a testimony to all nations, and then shall the consummation come." (Matt. xxiv, 14.) And St. Paul connects the coming of Antichrist with the second coming of Christ. "And then that wicked one shall be revealed whom the Lord Jesus . . . shall destroy with the brightness of his coming." (2 Thess. ii, 8.) Neither objection has any weight; in the first Our Lord was simply assuring the Apostles that there would be sufficient time to carry the gospel to all nations, since the consummation will not come until that has been accomplished. He does not say that it will come immediately upon its accomplishment. In the other case, we see no reason why "his coming"—parousia—must be taken to mean the personal coming of Our Lord at the last day, rather than a metaphorical coming in manifest judgment against Antichrist.

SUCCESSION. Apostolicity of *origin* and of *doctrine* are easily understood without further explanation, but some knowledge of *succession* is necessary for a proper conception of apostolicity of *ministry*. Succession, as used in this connection, is the following of one person after another in an official position, and may be either *legitimate* or *illegitimate*. Theologians call the one *formal* succession; the other, *material*. A material successor is one who assumes the official position of another contrary to the laws or constitution of the society in question. He may be called a successor in as much as he actually holds the position, but he has no authority, and his acts have no official value, even though he be ignorant of the illegal tenure of his office. A formal, or legitimate, successor not only succeeds to the place of his predecessor, but also receives due authority to exercise the functions of his office with binding force in the society. It is evident that authority can be transmitted only by legitimate succession; therefore, the Church must have a legitimate, or formal, succession of pastors to transmit apostolic authority from age to age. One who intrudes himself into the ministry against the laws of the Church receives no authority, and consequently can transmit none to his successors.

TWOFOLD POWER. Succession in the Church differs from that in other societies from the fact that there is a twofold power to transmit,— the power of *Orders* and the power of *jurisdiction* or government. The power of *Orders* is purely spiritual and concerned directly with the conferring of grace; it is obtained through the Sacrament of Orders validly received and cannot be revoked by any power of the Church. For this reason, the power of Orders may be obtained by fraud or conferred against the will of the Church by anyone having valid Orders himself, and therefore does not depend upon legitimate succession.

Jurisdiction is authority to govern and must be transmitted in the Church as in any other society; it can be conferred only by a lawful superior, according to the constitution and laws of the society, and may be revoked at any time. Consequently jurisdiction in the Church can neither be obtained nor held against the will of her supreme authority; its transmission depends entirely upon legitimate succession. It is not sufficient, therefore, that a church have valid Orders; it must also have a legitimate succession of ministers, reaching back in an unbroken line to the Apostles, upon whom our Lord conferred all authority to rule His Church.

UNION WITH ROME. No one can be a legitimate successor in any society unless he receive due authority therein; it follows, therefore, that there can be no legitimate successor in the Church of Christ who has not received jurisdiction either directly or indirectly from her supreme authority. But, as will be proved elsewhere, supreme authority in the Church of Christ was committed to St. Peter and his lawful successors, the bishops of Rome: consequently all legitimate succession, or Apostolicity of ministry in the Church, depends upon communion with the chair of Peter and is lost the moment that communion is severed. Hence no particular part of the Church is indefectibly Apostolic, save the see of Peter, which is universally known by way of eminence as *the Apostolic See.*

ERRORS. Those who deny that Christ founded any visible Church must also deny the possibility of Apostolicity in the sense just explained. Practically all Protestants admit the necessity of Apostolicity of some sort in the Church, but they differ in regard to its nature according to their different conceptions of the Church itself. Anglicans maintain that the Church must be Apostolic in its ministry, but they seem to place this Apostolicity in the valid transmission of Orders alone: "The authoritative ministry (of the Apostles) was propagated by being imparted in succession to others in different degrees by the laying-on of hands."[125]

2. The Church of Christ Apostolic

Thesis.—The Church of Christ Is Necessarily Apostolic in Origin, Doctrine and Ministry

That the Church is in some sense Apostolic, is a dogma of faith as appears from the Nicene Creed: "I believe in one, holy, Catholic and *Apostolic* Church." Apostolicity of ministry and of doctrine have been defined, at least implicitly, by the Vatican Council: "If any one should say that it is not by the institution of Christ, and therefore not by divine right, that the blessed Peter has *perpetual successors in his primacy over the whole Church,* . . . let him be anathema."[126] "The Holy Spirit was not promised to the successors of Peter that He might reveal to them a new doctrine, but that He should assist *them to preserve religiously and faithfully expound the revelation, or deposit of faith, handed down by the Apostles.*"[127]

PROOFS. I. *From Reason and Scripture.* The thesis is a self-evident truth, rather than a proposition to be demonstrated.

---

[125] Bishop Gore (Anglican), "Catholicism and Roman Catholicism," Lecture I; cf. *Church Times,* Dec., 1922; also W. Palmer, "Treatise on the Church," Vol. I, p. 171 ss.
[126] Denzinger, n. 1825.
[127] Denzinger, n. 1836.

a) *Origin.* Christ instituted but one Church through the ministry of the Apostles, and to none other did He give any authority to organize a church in His name. Consequently a church existing at any time since then, is either the identical Church established by Him, and therefore Apostolic, or it is not that identical Church, and therefore in no wise the Church of Christ, but merely a false claimant having no right to exist.

b) *Doctrine.* Our Lord committed the teaching of all His doctrines to the Apostles and promised to be with them until the consummation of the world: "Teach all nations . . . teaching them to observe all that I have commanded you. . . . And behold, I am with you all days even to the consummation of the world."[128] He also promised to them the Spirit of Truth, to remain with them forever guiding them in all truth: "I will ask the Father and he will give you another Advocate to dwell with you forever, the Spirit of truth. . . . He will teach you all things, and bring to your mind whatever I have said to you."[129] Christ has either failed in His promises, or the Church must ever preserve and teach all truths committed to her through the ministry of the Apostles. In other words, the Church must be Apostolic in her doctrine even to the consummation of the world.

c) *Ministry.* It is evident that there can be no authority in the Church save that which comes directly or indirectly from her Divine Founder, Jesus Christ. But there is not the slightest intimation in Scripture or tradition that Christ ever promised to confer authority upon the ministers of the Church; consequently it can only be obtained by lawful succession from those upon whom Christ personally and directly conferred it, i.e., from the Apostles. In other words, the Church must be Apostolic in her ministry by means of a legitimate succession reaching back in an unbroken line to the Apostles.

I. *From Tradition.* In controversies with the heretics of their age, the early Fathers always appealed to Apostolic succession as a proof for the true Church of Christ, and argued that heretical sects could not be the true Church for the simple reason that they lacked this succession. In order to show that the Catholic Church actually possessed Apostolic succession, many early writers drew up lists of bishops in various churches running back to Apostolic days. Among the compilers of such catalogues of bishops may be mentioned Hegesippus, St. Irenaeus, Eusebius, and St. Optatus of Mileve. A few quotations will show the mind of the Fathers on this question.

[128] Matt. xxviii, 19-20.
[129] John xiv, 16, 26.

a) *St. Irenaeus:* "It is necessary to obey the presbyters in the Church, those who, as I have shown, possess the succession from the Apostles; those who, together with the succession of the episcopate, have received the certain gift of truth according to the good pleasure of the Father."[130]

b) *Tertullian:* "But if there be any (heresies) bold enough to plant themselves in the midst of the Apostolic age, that they may thereby seem to have been handed down by the Apostles because they existed in the time of the Apostles, we can say: Let them unfold the roll of their bishops running down in due succession from the beginning in such manner that their first bishop shall be able to show for his ordainer and predecessor some one of the Apostles, or of Apostolic men, —a man moreover who continued steadfast with the Apostles."[131]

c) *St. Cyprian:* "Novatian is not in the Church; nor can he be reckoned as a bishop who succeeding no one and despising the Evangelical and Apostolic tradition, sprang from himself. For he who has not been ordained in the Church can neither have nor hold to the Church in any way."[132]

---

[130] "Adversus Haereses," IV, 26; P.G., 7, 1053.
[131] Tertullian, "De Praescriptionibus," xxxii, P.L., 2, 44.
[132] St. Cyprian, "Epist. ad Magnum," n. 3. P.L., 3, 1140.

CHAPTER IV

MARKS OF THE CHURCH

Thus far we have considered the Church of Christ as portrayed for us on the pages of Holy Scripture and in the writings of the early Fathers. We have learned that Christ established a Church as an external visible society endowed with perpetual and indefectible unity, sanctity, Catholicity, and Apostolicity. Since the Church *is* perpetually indefectible, it must still be perpetually and indefectibly one, holy, Catholic, and Apostolic. The Church which possesses these characteristics must be the one true Church of Christ; all others, mere human inventions.

Since Christ intended His Church to be known and accepted by all, He must have endowed it with certain exterior marks, by which it may be known with certainty and clearly distinguished from all false claimants. Therefore it is necessary to consider (1) what is required for a *mark* of the Church, (2) which properties of the Church fulfill these conditions, and (3) in what church these properties are found today.

ART. I. REQUISITES FOR A MARK OF THE CHURCH

1. The Nature of a Mark

A *mark* (Latin, *nota*) may be defined as a *quality or characteristic by which the subject in which it inheres may be recognized and distinguished from every other thing.* Hence it must be a manifest and essential quality. (a) It must be manifest, i.e., it must be something that can be perceived, otherwise it cannot lead to the knowledge of the subject in which it inheres. (b) It must be an essential quality, something that must be present at all times. A mere accidental quality may be present or absent without affecting the nature of the subject; it may even be found in subjects of entirely different nature, and, therefore, can never serve as a distinguishing mark.

Marks may be either *positive* or *negative*. A *positive* mark is one whose presence is sufficient to distinguish the subject in which it inheres from all other objects; e.g., the presence of a right angle is sufficient of itself to distinguish a right-angled triangle from all other triangles. A *negative* mark is a quality that can never be absent in the thing sought, yet its presence is not sufficient to distinguish that object from all others; e.g., a square must have four straight sides. Any figure in which this quality is lacking cannot be a square, but a figure having four straight sides is not necessarily a square; many other figures have this same characteristic.

MARKS OF THE CHURCH. The requisites for a mark of the Church are easily deduced from the above considerations: (1) it must be an essential characteristic or property of the Church, (2) it must be externally manifest to all, (3) it must be suited to the capacity of all, whether learned or unlearned. All men are bound to accept the faith of Christ and submit to the authority of His Church. Therefore, the marks by which the Church is recognized must be such that the unlearned as well as the learned may know and accept it. Finally, if there is question of a *positive* mark, it must be a characteristic found nowhere save in the true Church of Christ.

The four properties,—unity, sanctity, Catholicity and Apostolicity,— fulfill these conditions, and are therefore true marks. Moreover, as they are the only characteristics of the Church that do fulfill these conditions, they must be sufficient; otherwise the Church could not be known. It follows, then, that any Church lacking a single one of these marks cannot be the Church of Christ, and any Church possessing all of them must be the true Church of Christ.

2. Marks Claimed by Non-Catholics

ORTHODOX CHURCHES. The schismatic churches of the East agree with Catholics in teaching that the Church of Christ must be one, holy, Catholic and Apostolic, but they maintain that *identity with the Church of the first centuries* is the only distinctive mark by which it may be known today. This identity is to be recognized by strict conformity with the doctrine and discipline laid down by the first seven ecumenical councils.

CRITICISM. Identity with the early Church proves nothing unless we know that the Church of those centuries was in reality the true Church of Christ. The *marks* by which the faithful of those days recognized the true Church, must still be sufficient for the people of our own day. It is true that the Church must be identical with the Church of the first centuries in all essential things, but this identity could not serve as a *mark,* even if it be granted that the early Church was true. Only the learned could make the investigation necessary to establish the fact of such identity.

PROTESTANTS. The Reformers of the sixteenth century and many of their followers claimed two marks for the Church, or rather for *a* church. Calvin wrote: "Wherever we see the word of God sincerely preached and heard, and the Sacraments administered according to the institution of Christ, there without doubt is *a* church of God."[1] The nineteenth article of the Anglican Church reads: "The visible Church of Christ is a congregation of faithful men, in which the pure word of God is preached and the Sacraments be duly administered according to Christ's ordinance in all those things that are of necessity to the same." Bullinger, an Anglican theologian, says: "There are two special and principal marks: the sincere preaching of the word of God and the lawful partaking of the Sacraments of Christ."[2]

CRITICISM. Calvin and Bullinger make *sincere* preaching of the Gospel a mark of the Church. There is a vast difference between *sincere* and *true* preaching of the Gospel. Sincerity can never make truth out of falsehood neither can sincere preaching serve as a mark for the true Church. The doctrine proclaimed by the Thirty-Nine Articles is equally foolish. The pure word of God must be preached in the true Church of Christ, and the Sacraments must be administered according to the will of Christ, but how shall we know what is the true word of God? How shall we know that the Sacraments are duly administered unless we first know what Sacraments Christ really instituted, whom He ordained to administer them, and what is essential to their right administration? These are not questions to be decided without study and investigation beyond the ability of the unlearned. Even learned Protestants do not agree on these matters.

Many Protestants of the present day are little concerned about marks of any kind; the question of deciding between true and false in religion never occurs to them. They hold that all churches are equally true, since all taken collectively constitute the Church Catholic with which a man may be united by a good life even though he belong to no particular church organization. It is a matter of supreme indifference whether a person belong to one church or another; in fact, it seems to matter little whether he belong to any church. Moreover, they hold that every man enjoys full liberty to worship God according to the dictates of his own conscience. Hence every man is free to select the church that suits his fancy or convenience, or failing that, he may establish a new one to carry out any peculiar ideas he may have about religion or divine worship. God, it seems, has no voice in the matter; He must be content to receive such worship as man sees fit to render Him. It is evident that *marks* for recognizing the true Church have no place in such a system.

[1] "Institutiones," IV, 1.
[2] W. Wilson, "The Thirty-Nine Articles," p. 168.

ART. II. THE FOUR MARKS OF THE CHURCH

1. Unity as a Mark of the Church

Several eminent theologians, such as Bellarmine, Stapleton, and Perrone, maintained that unity is a *positive* mark, sufficient of itself to identify the true Church of Christ and distinguish it from all others. In support of this opinion they appealed to the words of Christ: "I pray . . . that they may be made perfect in one; and the world may know that thou hast sent me."[3] These words leave no doubt that Christ intended the unity of His disciples to be a proof also for the Church established to carry out that same mission till the end of time. But the words of Christ do not prove that this unity is a *positive* mark, which in fact, it cannot be. Unity as a mark of the Church must be a unity of faith, worship, and government, regardless of their nature; or a unity of *true* faith, *true* worship and *legitimate* government. But as the preaching of true doctrine (the pure word of God) and the practice of true worship (due administration of the Sacraments) cannot constitute a mark of the Church, so neither can unity of true doctrine and true worship. The same reasons hold good in both cases; how are we to know what is true doctrine or true worship? How are we to know whether the government is legitimate or not? All these things must be accepted on the authority of the Church, and cannot be accepted until the Church herself has been accepted. On the other hand, if we take unity of faith, worship, and government, regardless of truth or legitimacy, we have only a *negative* mark. Any Church lacking unity in these things cannot be the true Church of Christ, but a church is not necessarily true because it has such unity, since unity of *false* faith, *false* worship, and *illegitimate* government is possible, at least for a time. Therefore unity, considered in itself, is merely a negative mark, yet it has always had the force of a positive mark due to the fact that unity in any form has always been found in one church alone.

2. Sanctity as a Mark of the Church

Sanctity, being essentially internal and invisible, can serve as a mark only in so far as it is manifested in some outward act. Hence the ontological sanctity of the Church need not be considered in this connection. The other forms,—causative, personal, and manifestative,—will be considered separately.

CAUSATIVE SANCTITY. The active or causative sanctity of the Church is manifested principally through its effects in bringing men

---

[3] John xvii, 23.

to the practice of virtue. It is also manifest in the outward means of grace,—Sacraments, doctrine, and discipline,—if they are recognized as eminently suited to produce personal holiness. In this sense causative sanctity constitutes, at least, a negative mark, because any Church lacking such means of sanctification cannot be the Church of Christ. This is especially true if the church in question not only lacks such means, but also teaches a doctrine or practice clearly opposed to right reason and morality.

In fact, causative sanctity almost amounts to a positive mark, since the presence of means *eminently* fitted to lead men to a holy life gives at least a very strong presumption in favor of the Church possessing them.

PERSONAL SANCTITY. Ordinary personal sanctity, considered in itself, is a negative mark of the Church, because, as noted above, the Church of Christ can never be without a large number of persons devoted to the practice of Christian virtues; but the value of personal sanctity as a mark is somewhat lessened by the fact that persons of virtuous life may be found in all Churches, owing to the fact that all have retained some salutary doctrine and discipline, and in many cases they retain the Sacrament of Baptism and even the Holy Eucharist, as do many schismatic Churches of the East. Nevertheless, a Church that stands out prominent for the works of piety which it inspires, and for the number of members leading holy lives, certainly has a very strong presumption in its favor,—perhaps even certain proof that it is the Church of Christ.

MANIFESTATIVE SANCTITY. Miraculous power manifested by the performance of undoubted miracles is a positive mark sufficient in itself to make known the true Church of Christ. Since miracles require the direct intervention of God, they are certain and infallible signs of divine approval for any doctrine or institution in whose favor they are wrought. Therefore, even one undoubted miracle wrought under circumstances that make it an approval of any distinctive doctrine or practice of a Church, is proof sufficient that it must be the true Church of Christ. Extraordinary or eminent sanctity must be referred to the miraculous, especially if practiced by many, because such sanctity is not acquired without special assistance from Almighty God. For this reason, personal sanctity was limited in the above paragraph to such as is practiced in the ordinary degree.

3. Catholicity as a Mark of the Church

There can be no doubt that catholicity is at least a negative mark, since a church that is not universally spread throughout the world cannot be the Church foretold by the prophets and set forth in the promises of Christ. But is catholicity also a positive mark, so that the true Church may be recognized by the mere fact of its universal diffusion throughout the world? Some theologians maintain that it is. Straub says that "Catholicity, which is both absolute and relative, can belong to the true Church alone; therefore such catholicity is a positive mark."[4] This argument presupposes that the true Church must be relatively catholic, i.e., it must be more wide-spread than any other Christian church. But the necessity for such catholicity cannot be proved from Scripture or tradition, and there seems to be no reason why a false Church might not become universal, even more universal than the true one, at least for a time.

Wilmers holds that catholicity of diffusion is a positive mark when taken in connection with the fact that this diffusion began at Jerusalem. It matters not how widely a church may be diffused, if it did not begin at Jerusalem, it cannot be the Church of Christ.[5] The fallacy of this argument is immediately apparent to any one who asks himself what Church really began its diffusion at Jerusalem. All the schismatic churches of the East can lay claim to this honor, if material succession alone be considered. Moreover, the circumstance of beginning at Jerusalem belongs to the Apostolicity of the Church rather than to its catholicity.

A third opinion was proposed by De San, who maintained that catholicity is a positive mark, because it is externally manifest in the undying zeal with which the light of the Gospel is constantly spread farther and farther throughout the world. Although a like zeal may be found in false sects, it can never be so ardent nor so fruitful as it is in the true Church, endowed with all the means of sanctification.[6] The futility of this opinion is quite evident; comparative degrees of zeal and fruitfulness are not so easily recognized by all. Moreover, zeal and fruitfulness belong not to the catholicity of the Church, but to her sanctity.

It is evident from the above considerations that catholicity in itself is merely a negative mark of the Church; practically, however, it has always been a positive mark, owing to the fact that the one Church alone has ever been truly catholic by universal diffusion throughout the world, and it is probable that this one Church has been relatively more wide-spread at all times than any other Church.

---

[4] "De Ecclesia Christi," Vol. II, n. 1443.
[5] "De Ecclesia Christi," p. 557.
[6] "Tractatus de Ecclesia," p. 123.

4. Apostolicity as a Mark of the Church

Apostolicity of *doctrine* is equivalent to "preaching the pure word of God," and, therefore, cannot be a mark of the Church; in fact, it is only through the testimony of the Church, already known and accepted, that all the doctrines taught by the Apostles may be known with certainty. Apostolicity of doctrine may serve as a mark of the true Church in individual cases. A person may know from a study of Scripture or tradition that a certain doctrine is undoubtedly Apostolic; he can then easily judge that any Church rejecting this doctrine is not the true Church of Christ, and if there be but one Church teaching and professing it, that Church must be the true one.[7]

Apostolicity of *origin,* being necessarily included in that of succession, need not be considered here. Apostolicity, as a mark, is thus restricted to succession, and that a *material* succession, since *legitimacy* is not an external quality easily recognized by all, whereas material succession, i.e., an unbroken line of pastors reaching back to the Apostles, can be known even by the unlearned as easily as the succession of civil rulers in the State. But since Apostolicity of material succession may, and probably does, exist in some schismatical churches, it constitutes a negative mark only.

5. Persecution as a Mark of the Church

Persecution may serve as a quasi-mark of the Church during the period of preparation prior to the coming of Antichrist. Christ has foretold that His Church must suffer unrelenting hatred and persecution: "If the world hates you, know that it hated me before you. . . . But because you are not of the world, but I have chosen you out of the world, therefore the world hates you. Remember the word that I have spoken to you: No servant is greater than his master. If they have persecuted me, they will persecute you also. . . . But all these things they will do to you for my name's sake." Again he said: "They will expel you from the synagogues. Yes, the hour is coming for everyone who kills you to think that he is offering worship to God. And you will be hated by all for my name's sake."[8]

As Christ was hated, despised, calumniated, and persecuted in His natural body, so also shall He be in His mystical body, the Church. Therefore a Church that is not thus despised and persecuted, can scarcely be the one which Christ had in mind when He uttered the

[7] T. W. Allies, "The See of Peter," Introd.
[8] John xvi, 2, 3; Matt. x, 22.

words quoted above. It is always consoling to realize that those who calumniate the Church and stir up persecution against her, are fulfilling the prophecies of Christ and thus they unwittingly prove her divine character. Thus does "He that dwelleth in heaven laugh at them; and the Lord deride them."[9]

Conclusion

The power of miracles (manifestative sanctity) is the only positive mark whose presence alone is sufficient to identify the true Church of Christ. The other marks, taken separately, are only negative; the presence of one or another is not sufficient proof that the true Church has been found. Taken collectively, however, they furnish infallible proof for the Church in which they are found.

Today there are hundreds of religious organizations claiming to be the Church of Christ, yet we know there can be but one true Church. Knowing the marks which this one true Church must possess, we begin our search for it by examining the different churches one by one. If we chance upon a church with the power of miracles,—the signature of God's own writing,—we look no further; God's approval is sufficient proof. But if examination shows a church to lack any one of the four marks, it must be rejected and the search continued, until a church is found possessing all four. When once this Church is found, further investigation is unnecessary; the true Church has been identified, and the others must be false. This is the investigation to be carried out in the following pages by examining (1) the Catholic Church, (2) the Protestant churches, (3) the Anglican Church, and the schismatic Churches of the East. The Anglican Church will be considered separately, not because it differs essentially from other Protestant churches, but because the High Church party makes special claims to Apostolicity.

ART. III. MARKS OF THE CHURCH APPLIED

1. The Catholic Church

A. The Catholic Church Possesses Unity of Faith, Worship, and Government

a) *Unity of Faith.* Absolute unity of faith is found in the Catholic Church. This fact is patent to any one who will examine her creeds, the decrees of her councils, her catechisms and other books of instruc-

---

[9] Ps. ii, 4.

tion, in which the same doctrines are proposed to each and every member throughout the world. It is also a well-known fact that the Catholic Church demands complete and unqualified acceptance and profession of all her teachings.

b) *Unity of Worship.* The Catholic Church maintains strict unity of worship throughout the world by administering the same Sacraments and by offering the same Sacrifice in all places and at all times. She even maintains unity in many things that are not essential, e.g., in the invocation of Saints, the veneration of relics and images, praying for the dead, and many similar devotions. These facts are obvious to all who will observe them.

c) *Unity of Government.* If there is any one characteristic of the Catholic Church more widely known than another, it is her unity of government; in fact, it is so well-known that Catholics are often unjustly accused of blind obedience to the Church even in civil matters. Unity of government is preserved by the exercise of one supreme authority, to which all Catholics give willing obedience in things spiritual; all bishops are appointed by the Roman Pontiff and rule their dioceses in subjection to him. Every priest in the Church receives authority from a bishop in communion with Rome. All laws for the universal Church are enacted by the one supreme authority, and there is but one supreme judge for the whole Church. Moreover, every part of the Church is in communion with every other part under the direction of the chief pastor, the Bishop of Rome, just as all members of the body are united under one common head. In other words, there is perfect social unity in the Catholic Church. Pere Lacordaire has eloquently portrayed the unity of the Church in these words: "I hear from far and near, from the depths of ages and of generations; I hear the voices which form but one,—the voices of infants, of virgins, of young men, of the aged; of artists, of poets, of philosophers; the voices of princes and nations; the voices of time and space: the deep musical voice of unity! It chants the canticle of the only society of minds found here below; it repeats without ceasing that declaration, the only one to be found which is stable and consolatory: *Credo in unam, sanctam, catholicam et apostolicam Ecclesiam.*"[10]

B. The Catholic Church Possesses Manifestative and Causative Sanctity

1. MANIFESTATIVE SANCTITY. a) *Miracles.* The sanctity of the Catholic Church is proved by a series of innumerable miracles

---

[10] "Conferences on the Church," Conf. 29 (Eng. tr.).

reaching back to the day when St. Peter cured the lame man at the gate of the Temple.[11] Even today miracles are frequent in the Church and performed under conditions that make them a confirmation of her doctrines and practices. The many miracles performed every year at Lourdes in France are a divine approval of the veneration which the Church gives to the Mother of God,[12] and the miracle of St. Januarius's blood that takes place at Naples several times each year is a positive approval for the veneration of relics.[13] These are only a few of the better known miracles taking place in the Church today, and they are mentioned in particular because they are well authenticated by the testimony of eminent men, both Catholic and non-Catholic.

b) *Eminent Sanctity.* The Catholic Church is justly renowned for the eminent sanctity of many of her children. Witness the glorious line of martyrs, confessors and virgins of both sexes, of every age, and from every condition of life that has spread lustre upon the Church from the days of St. Stephen, the first martyr, until the present day! How many youths and virgins, how many men and women has the Church been able to hold up as perfect examples of all virtues! Their very names fill volumes.

Eminent sanctity shines forth daily in the many religious orders of the Church, where the Evangelical Counsels are reduced to daily practice in hospitals, orphanages, and other charitable institutions that dot every country of the globe. Note, too, the many priests and religious who, from pure love of God, give themselves up to a living death in caring for lepers in different parts of the world.[14]

c) *Wonderful Fecundity.* Along with the eminent sanctity of her children, the wonderful fecundity of the Catholic Church must be classed as a moral miracle attesting her divine mission. Here should be noted her unprecedented propagation throughout the Roman Empire in the first ages of her existence, and her glorious triumph over paganism. In the centuries that followed this triumph, she tamed the fierce barbarians from the North, and reared the present structure of Christian civilization in Europe. In fact, the Catholic Church alone has succeeded in bringing barbarian tribes and nations to civilization and to the faith of Christ. Others have tried, but the only result is extermination. Witness the native tribes of America; wherever the Catholic

---

[11] Acts iii, 1 sqq.

[12] Dr. A. Marchand, "The Facts of Lourdes and the Medical Bureau"; E. Le Bec, "Medical Proof of the Miraculous."

[13] E. P. Graham, "The Mystery of Naples," Herder.

[14] Cf. Robert L. Stevenson's "Open Letter to Rev. Dr. Hyde"; Charles W. Stoddard, "The Lepers of Molokai."

Church announced the Gospel, the Indians were converted and remain today in the process of civilization. Everywhere else they have practically disappeared.

The civilizing and leavening power of the Catholic Church is evident today in the various pagan lands where converts are being made by the millions, while others are self-admitted failures. In 1897 the secretary of Protestant Missions in India wrote: "The Romanists are advancing by leaps and bounds in Tonquin. . . . Their advance is still greater at present in China and Corea where there are more than a million and half converts with one thousand priests and eight hundred schools. In India and Ceylon the strides of Romanism are startling and unprecedented."[15] Another non-Catholic wrote some years ago: "The Roman Church in India is gaining ground so rapidly that in many districts it threatens to swamp the Established missions, which it is able to outbid, while elsewhere it has the field to itself."[16] "The progress of the Catholic Church is no less remarkable in Africa where today she numbers ninety bishops, three thousand priests and over three million faithful. The native Protestants of Africa number about four hundred thousand, with little more than half that number reported as "communicants." In China the Catholic Church now has more than two million converts whereas the native Protestants scarcely amount to fifty thousand.[16a]

II. CAUSATIVE SANCTITY. It is immediately evident to any investigator of the Catholic Church that her every doctrine and precept, all her practices of devotion, and especially her sacramental system, are eminently fitted to lead men to the practice of virtue and to a life of holiness. This becomes still more evident when it is noted that her members are always holy in exact proportion to their faithfulness to her teachings and precepts. It will be sufficient to call attention to her teaching and practice in regard to marriage and divorce, to the honor she pays to the Blessed Virgin, and to the practice of confession. The Church teaches that marriage is a Sacrament of the New Law, indissoluble except by death; this sanctifies the union of husband and wife, and protects the morality of the individual, the home and society to a degree that cannot be overestimated.

Lecky, a rationalist, has eloquently set forth the influence of veneration for the Blessed Virgin: "The world is governed by its ideals, and seldom or never has there been one which has exercised a more

---

[15] Quoted in the London *Tablet*, Jan. 30, 1897.
[16] "Church Times, Jan. 28, 1910."
[16a] Cf. Encyclopedia Americana, art. "China"; Catholic Encyclopedia, art. Africa.

profound, and, on the whole, a more salutary influence than the medieval conception of the Virgin. For the first time woman was elevated to her rightful position, and the sanctity of weakness was recognized as well as the sanctity of sorrow. . . . The moral charm and beauty of female excellence was for the first time felt. A new type of character was called into being; a new kind of admiration was fostered. Into a hard and ignorant and benighted age this ideal type infused a conception of gentleness and purity unknown to the proudest civilizations of the past. . . . All that was best in Europe clustered around it, and it is the origin of many of the purest elements of our civilization."[17]

The value of confession, even apart from any question of sacramental absolution, has been recognized by many non-Catholics. Leibnitz said: "This whole institution, it cannot be denied, is worthy of divine wisdom; and if, in the Christian religion, there be any ordinance singularly excellent and worthy of admiration, it is this. . . . I believe a pious, prudent, and grave confessor to be a powerful instrument in the hands of God for the salvation of souls."[18]

C. The Catholic Church Possesses Universality of Diffusion

The universal diffusion of the Catholic Church is admitted by all. Wherever the name of Christ is heard and reverenced, there also is the Catholic Church known. There also has she her pastors with faithful subjects in communion with the See of Rome. For this reason she is known preeminently as *the* Catholic Church. Even in the beginning of the fifth century St. Augustine could say: "In the Catholic Church there are many things that justly hold me; . . . among these is the very name itself, which this Church alone among so many heresies has obtained. Even those heretics who wish to be known as Catholics, when asked by a stranger where the Catholics meet for worship, will never point out their own basilica or house of worship."[19]

The Catholic Church is not only diffused throughout the whole world, but is also more widely diffused than any other Christian denomination, and most probably has always been thus relatively universal. Many theologians insist upon the fact that the Catholic Church numbers more adherents than any other Christian Church, perhaps even more than all the others combined; but, as already noted, this has no bearing on the question of Catholicity, since it is diffusion, not numbers, that makes a Church universal. Simply as a matter of inter-

---

[17] W. E. H. Lecky, "Rationalism in Europe," Vol. I, p. 225.
[18] "Systema Theologicum."
[19] "Contra Epist. Fundament.," P.L., 42, 175.

est it may be noted that *Information Please* of the year 1951 gives the estimated Christian population of the world as follows: Catholics 421,-340,901; Protestants 193,014,595; Eastern Schismatics 127,629,985.[20] Due to the fact that few if any Eastern countries have any religious census, these figures must be accepted as merely rough estimates despite the numbers given down to the last unit.

ROMAN CATHOLIC. The Church is usually referred to as *Roman Catholic*. The title *Roman*, however, is not used in a restrictive sense, to indicate that the Church exists only in Rome; neither is it used as a distinctive term, intimating that there are other Catholic churches from which this one must be distinguished. The title *Roman* merely points out the fact that Rome is the center from which all authority in the Church radiates; it is the center whose circumference occupies the whole world.

D. The Catholic Church Possesses Apostolicity of Succession

The unbroken succession of bishops in the Roman See from the days of St. Peter to the present time, is a matter of historical knowledge, admitted by all, and since all parts of the Church are in communion with the See of Rome and derive authority from it, there can be no doubt of Apostolic succession in the whole Church.

Conclusion

The four characteristic marks of the Church founded by Christ are completely realized in the Catholic Church of today; therefore she is the one true Church of Christ, the Church commissioned to carry the Gospel and the means of salvation to all nations until the consummation of the world. She has received power and authority to carry out this mission, and all men are obliged to accept her teaching and submit to her authority under pain of eternal damnation. "If he will not hear the Church let him be as the heathen and the publican."[21]

E. Objections Answered

OBJECTION I. At the time of the Western Schism the Catholic Church lost her unity for many years by being divided into two, and even three, parties each following a pope of its own choosing.

ANSWER.—The Western Schism caused great harm to the Church in many ways, but it did not affect her unity. After the death of

---

[20] "Information Please," a yearbook edited by John Kiernan.
[21] Matt. xviii, 17.

Gregory XI, in 1378, the cardinals proceeded to elect Urban VI as his successor. Three months later, several cardinals claimed the election of Urban to be invalid and selected Robert of Geneva as Pope, under the name of Clement VII. Differences of opinion naturally arose regarding the validity of these elections; some believed Urban VI the rightful pope, while others accepted Clement VII. In 1409 an attempt was made to remedy this situation, but the result was disappointing, and matters were made worse by the election of a third claimant, who took the name of Alexander V. Thus matters continued until the Council of Constance, in 1417, when Martin V was elected and recognized by all as the lawful Pope.

At no time during these troubles did any one ever entertain the idea that there were three popes, or that the Church was divided in its government. All admitted that there could be but one legitimate pope, and each party followed the one whom they believed to be lawfully elected successor of St. Peter. The Church was no more divided by the schism than our own government would be by a disputed election to the office of presidency.

OBJECTION II. During the Arian heresy in the fourth century, the Catholic Church ceased to be Catholic or universal, for, as St. Jerome said on one occasion: "The whole world groaned and was surprised to find itself Arian."[22]

ANSWER.—These words of St. Jerome are not to be taken literally, as is evident from the circumstances. At the councils of Rimini and Seleucia, in 359, the Arians gained a victory by having a creed adopted in which their errors were not directly condemned. This aided them in the spread of their doctrines, because they could make it appear that the councils had approved them. When hearing of this, St. Jerome used the words quoted in the objection. It is true that the Arians made rapid strides, even many priests and bishops fell into their errors, but the Church never ceased to be truly universal, and most probably continued at all times more wide-spread than the Arian sect, despite the fact that the emperors did all in their power to spread the heresy. St. Athanasius and the bishops of his patriarchate wrote to the Emperor in this matter: "The churches of every nation agree with the Nicene Faith,—those in Spain, Britain, and Gaul; in Italy, Dalmatia and Mysia; in Macedonia, in all Greece and the whole of Africa; in Sardinia, Cyprus, Crete, Pamphylia, Isauria, and Lycia, and in all Egypt and Lybia, Pontus, Cappadocia, and adjacent districts, and in all the eastern churches, except a few who believe with Arius. We have

---

[22] "Contra Luciferianos"; P.L., 23, 172.

certain knowledge regarding the above-mentioned churches, because we have letters from them, and we know, most religious Emperor, how few they are who contradict this faith."[23]

Even granting that these words contain some rhetorical exaggeration, they still show that the Church had not ceased to be truly Catholic by her diffusion throughout the then known world.

OBJECTION III.—The condition of Catholic countries as compared with countries in which Protestantism prevails, clearly proves that Protestantism has far greater influence on the progress and civilization of the world than the Catholic Church, and, therefore, has greater claims to consideration as the true religion of Christ.

ANSWER.—The solution of this objection depends to a great extent upon the meaning attached to progress and civilization. Does it consist in spiritual or material progress? The Church of Christ was commissioned to preach the Gospel and save souls, not to provide material prosperity and bodily comfort. She was not established to build factories, railroads, and steamships, nor to increase the commerce of nations. That is the purpose of civil governments, and progress in these matters depends not upon religion, but upon racial genius, climate, soil, geographical position, and the nature of governments. Religion has only an indirect effect upon material progress. Many heathen nations surrounding Palestine were far more advanced materially than were the Israelites, yet no one would claim this as proof that the religion of those nations was superior to that of the Chosen People.

Nations, like individuals, are often materially prosperous precisely because they have neither religion nor conscience. A Church that makes material progress and prosperity the measure of truth cannot be the Church of Him who said: "Lay not up for yourselves treasures on earth, . . . but lay up for yourselves treasures in heaven."[24] When it is said that Protestant countries are more prosperous than Catholic countries, it is implied that the Protestant religion has produced this prosperity and, therefore, should be preferred to the Catholic religion. Prosperity and wealth are held out as the motive for accepting it. This is the argument used long ago by Satan when he said: "Behold the kingdoms of the world and the glory of them. All these will I give to thee, if falling down thou wilt adore."[25] Any church that wishes to appropriate this argument of Satan is welcome to it; the Catholic Church has no need for it.

---

[23] St. Athanasius, "Ad Jovianum," quoted in Theodoret's Church History, IV, 3; P.G., 82, 1126.
[24] Matt. vi, 19, 20.
[25] Matt. iv, 8-9.

2. Protestant Churches

Having discovered that the Catholic Church possesses all the marks of the true Church, it is unnecessary to make further investigation; the true Church has been identified and all others must be rejected as human inventions, having no claim upon our consideration. Yet, for the sake of making our investigations complete, it is well to show that no other church has any claim whatever, since they all lack every single mark of the Church as set forth in the Sacred Scriptures.

I. UNITY. It is obvious to the most casual observer that Protestant churches, whether taken collectively or singly, possess no unity of faith. Such unity is absolutely excluded by their fundamental doctrine of private interpretation in matters of faith. Each one must decide for himself what doctrines he is to believe, with the result that there are as many different faiths as there are members in the churches. They agree in one thing only,—protesting against the Catholic Church; hence the name *Protestant.* "Protestantism always bears the same name despite the great diversity of faith, and this because the name is purely negative, signifying nothing save renunciation of Catholicism. Hence the less they believe and the more they protest, the more truly do they become Protestants."[26]

The total lack of unity of faith in Protestant Churches is well illustrated by the following words of a Presbyterian author: "The catholicity of the Presbyterian Church appears in her one condition of church membership. . . . The applicant is not asked to subscribe to our standards or to assent to our theology. He is not required to be a Calvinist, but only to be a Christian. He is not examined as to his orthodoxy, but only as to his 'faith in and obedience unto Christ.' He may have imperfect notions about the Trinity and the atonement; he may question infant baptism, election, and final perseverance; but if he trusts and obeys Christ as his personal Saviour and Lord, the door of the Presbyterian Church is open to him, and all the privileges of her communion are his."[27]

As there is no unity of faith, so neither can there be unity of worship in Protestant churches. For example, some hold Baptism to be necessary and religiously look to its proper administration; others reject it as an empty ceremony, having no more value than the initiation ceremonies of a lodge. Some practice infant Baptism, while others reject it as unscriptural. These differences are found, not only among members of the different denominations, but also among the members of one and the same Church.

---

[26] J. De Maistre, "Du Pape," IV, 5.
[27] E. W. Smith, "The Creed of Presbyterians," p. 198.

The lack of unity in government is no less obvious than in faith and worship. No Protestant church even claims to be *the* Church of Christ; each is but a part of the Church universal, yet they are in no way united to form one universal, visible Church. Any attempt at union results in further division, because their fundamental doctrine of private interpretation is a principle of division that continually separates them into an ever increasing multiplicity of sects. The Methodists of this country are now divided into twenty-five distinct churches! And still the division goes on. Some years ago Dr. Stowe said: "Protestantism is a kind of modern Cerberus with a hundred and twenty-five heads, all barking discordantly, and is like the mob of Ephesus. Thoughtful Christians looking on and beholding with sadness this confusion worse confounded, cannot fail to ask: Did our Lord Jesus Christ come on this earth to establish this pitiful mob of debating societies, or a Church of the living God, capable of making itself felt as a pillar and ground of truth?"[28]

II. SANCTITY. Protestant Churches lack all manifestative sanctity; in fact they stoutly deny that the Church has any power of miracles, and they make no pretence to eminent sanctity in their members. They have never produced a saint and claim none. A non-Catholic author, writing of St. Catherine of Siena, said: "The rarity of such saints in Protestantism is probably to the devout mind the strongest argument in favor of Catholic claims."[29] Protestants have rejected the very means to produce such saints; they ridicule the practice of the Evangelical Counsels, and stigmatize works of supererogation as superstitions. Therefore, as a non-Catholic periodical admitted, "religious orders cannot flourish in Protestant countries. Those who wish to establish such orders must betake themselves to the Church of Rome."[30]

Protestant Churches also lack causative sanctity, except in so far as they have retained Catholic teaching and practices. Every distinctively Protestant doctrine tends directly to break down morality and lessen sanctity in the lives of the people. Witness, for example, the distinctively Protestant teachings on marriage and divorce. The evil results have been incalculable, as all students of social conditions admit. In rejecting confession, Protestants have removed a most powerful influence for good in restraining evil passions. Refusing honor to the Mother of God has resulted logically in a wide-spread denial of the divinity of her Son, and private interpretation of the Bible has brought about the present rejection of inspiration by an ever increasing number outside the Catholic

---

[28] Dr. Chas. E. Stowe in the *Boston Herald*, Dec. 15, 1905.
[29] T. W. Stead, in the *Review of Reviews*, Feb., 1897.
[30] *The Independent*, Nov. 28, 1895.

Church. The group of Fundamentalists, who are striving to check the spread of this evil, are acting contrary to Protestant principles. The Modernist group are correct in their contention that they are carrying the principles of the Reformation to their logical conclusions. With justice then has it been said that "the doctrines and morals of Protestantism have been placed in the balance these three hundred years, and have been found wanting."[31]

III. CATHOLICITY. Protestant churches, taken singly, are not universal in any sense of the word. For the most part they are merely national churches strictly limited in their diffusion. Even if taken together as forming one Church,—which they do not,—they can scarcely be called universal in their diffusion.

IV. APOSTOLICITY. With the exception of the Anglican Church, no Protestant church makes any claim to Apostolicity for the very good reason that it could establish no succession beyond the sixteenth century. Moreover most Protestant churches have rejected the very idea of a ministry having any authority to teach and govern other than that derived from the faithful.

3. The Anglican Church

All that has been said concerning Protestant churches in general, applies also to the Anglican Church, in particular; but we have reserved it for separate treatment because an influential party in that Church lays special claims to Catholicity and Apostolicity by what are known as the Branch Theory and the Theory of Continuity. For convenience sake we include under the term *Anglican* both the Established Church of England and the Protestant Episcopal Church in America, because the latter is a lineal descendant of the former and holds the same views on the matter in question.

Before beginning an examination of the Anglican claims, it should be noted that such an examination is really unnecessary, because the Anglican Church is notoriously deficient in another essential mark of the Church; it lacks unity of doctrine, and therefore could not be the true Church of Christ even though it possessed Catholicity and Apostolicity, as claimed.

UNITY. Lack of unity of faith in the Anglican communion is proved by the mere fact that it contains three distinct parties, teaching doctrines directly opposed one to another. The *High Church* party is strikingly Catholic in its teaching; it accepts almost every doctrine of the Catholic

---

[31] Rev. Dr. Percival in the *Nineteenth Century,* Vol. 46, p. 515.

Church except the infallibility of the Pope. The *Low Church* is thoroughly Protestant in its teachings and practices and rejects nearly all Catholic doctrine as "Romish superstition." The *Broad Church* is rationalistic and makes no definite statement of doctrine. Yet all these parties are recognized as members of the Anglican Church, teaching and professing her approved doctrines! This constitutes her "glorious comprehensiveness," by which every shade of doctrinal difference is embraced within her fold. Justly, therefore, did Macaulay say that "the religion of the Church of England . . . is in fact a jumble of religious systems without number."[32]

There can be no unity because there is no authority to enforce it. "The Church," says an Anglican vicar, "possesses no control over the conscience, mind or spiritual life of its members, save by consent; and even then can only exercise that control indirectly,—by appeal, suggestion, or influence."[33] "Bishops of the Anglican Communion," says Father Finlay, "can meet together in Lambeth or in Canterbury; and the Anglican Archbishop who holds the cathedral of Anselm and Thomas a Becket will probably be invited to preside over them. But no one has a right to convoke them; they meet because they themselves choose to meet, as the members of a Section on Religion in the British Association; and the outcome of the conference and discussions is entirely without authority. They cannot decide a doctrinal controversy. They cannot determine a point of liturgy. They cannot enact or abrogate a single detail of Church discipline. They know, they have been warned, and they profess, that even a Pan-Anglican Synod can only discuss and offer counsel; it can neither teach nor command authoritatively. There is no living principle of unity in the Anglican, as there is none in the Greek Communion."[34]

THE BRANCH THEORY. As already noted, the Branch Theory maintains that the Church of Christ consist of three parts or branches,— The Roman, the Greek, and the Anglican, and that consequently the Anglican Church is truly Catholic, since it is a part of the Church universal and a corporate continuation of the Church of England before the Reformation. The following quotation from Father Finlay will show the utter absurdity of this theory: "Though it has been prominently before the world for three-quarters of a century, it finds no one to accept and advocate it outside of the Anglican Communion. A section,— a small minority probably of the Church of England,—maintains the

---

[32] Macaulay, "Essay on Church and State."
[33] Charles A. Barry, "First Principles of the Church," p. 36.
[34] Peter Finlay, S.J., "The Church of Christ," p. 168.

theory. The large majority of Protestant Episcopalians know nothing of it; while Greeks and Roman Catholics repudiate it utterly. Is it likely that the Church of Christ is constituted on a pattern which not one in a hundred of her members will acknowledge? Are we to believe that the true constitution of the Church was hidden from mankind,—from the Church herself,—through nineteen centuries, and was only then to be made known to a little group of Anglican theologians who have failed to persuade any but a handful of their own Communion that their conception of the Church is that of Christ?"[35]

THE CONTINUITY THEORY. According to this theory the Anglican Church is a continuation of the Catholic Church which existed in England before the Reformation; thus she is an integral part of the Church universal and truly Apostolic in her succession, which reaches back in an unbroken line beyond Augustine to the first missionaries who brought the Gospel to the British Isles, perhaps even in the days of the Apostles. She differs only in a few accidental matters from the other branches of the Church. "The facts of history," says an Anglican writer, "compels us to assume the absolute identity of the Church of England after the Reformation with the Church of England before the Reformation. . . . No act was done by which legal and historical continuity was broken."[36]

This theory has as little to commend it as the Branch Theory. The facts of history compel us to assume the absolute *lack* of identity between the Church of England before the Reformation and the Church of England after the Reformation because acts were done that *did* break the legal and historical continuity. The year in which continuity was finally broken can be given, as well as the acts and the actors by which it was accomplished.

The Catholic religion had been reestablished in England by Mary, but in 1559, shortly after the accession of Elizabeth, Parliament again rejected the authority of the Pope, declared Elizabeth supreme head of the Church, and reinstated the reformed ritual of Edward VI. An oath recognizing royal supremacy in matters ecclesiastical was demanded of all the bishops. Those who refused to take it were to be deprived of their sees. As a result of this action but one bishop was left by the end of that year. The places of the others were filled by men conspicuous for their attachment to the new order of things. Matthew Parker was appointed Archbishop of Canterbury, but no Catholic bishop would consecrate him; even Kitchen of Landaff, the only one who took the oath

---

[35] "Church of Christ," p. 168.
[36] E. A. Freeman, "Disestablishment and Disendowment."

of supremacy, pleaded ill-health to escape the responsibility of consecrating the new pseudo-archbishop. Elizabeth then took matters in hand and commissioned Barlow, Scorey, Coverdale, and Hodgkins to consecrate Parker according to the Edwardine ritual. This act was undoubtedly invalid,[37] yet every bishop in the Anglican Church derives his orders and succession from Parker.

In A. D. 1560 the ritual was revised and the forty-two Articles reduced to thirty-nine, as at present accepted by the Anglican Church. These articles renounced the authority of the Pope, made Elizabeth head of the Church in England, rejected five Sacraments, the doctrine of Purgatory, the invocation of saints and the veneration of relics, and declared the Mass a blasphemous fable and a vain deceit. It is evident, then, that the faith of the Church was changed in its essential doctrines, —the supremacy of the Pope, the Mass, and the Sacraments. Elizabeth also removed every lawful bishop and filled the sees with pliant tools of her own choice, contrary to all the canons and traditions of the Church, and had them consecrated by an invalid ceremony. If the Church resulting from these acts be identical with the Church before the change, there is no possibility of destroying continuity. On the same principle the United States of America are still a part of the British Empire, because the change wrought by the American Revolution was no greater in the realm of political life than the revolution caused by Elizabeth in the Church. The American colonies rejected the authority of the English King, ousted his officials, drew up new articles of political faith, and established a supreme authority instead of the rejected authority of the king,—and the result is recognized by all as a distinct and independent government, a new nation, having no legal continuity with the British government and forming no part of it. Elizabeth and her Parliament did the same for the English Church, and the result was a new and independent Church, established, not by Christ but by Parliament,—a Church having no continuity with the ancient Church in England and forming no part of it.

SUCCESSION. The Church of England, having no valid Orders, can have no Apostolic succession in regard to the power of Orders, since this power is transmitted by valid consecration. But even granting her valid Orders, she can have nothing more than material succession, because her whole line is derived from an intruder, who obtained his position contrary to the canons of the Church and, therefore, did not receive

---

[37] Cf. Alzog, "Church History," Vol. III, p. 329, note 2 (Eng. ed.) ; Catholic Encyclopedia, art. "Anglican Orders"; H. C. Semple, S.J., "Anglican Ordinations."

the jurisdiction or authority belonging to the office. A usurper may found a new dynasty; he cannot continue the old.

But for the sake of argument, let it be supposed that all bishops of the Anglican Communion have valid Orders, and that all the bishops of Elizabeth's creation were selected according to the canons of the Church and actually confirmed by the Roman Pontiff; even then they could lay no claim to legitimate succession of jurisdiction, for the simple reason that it would have been lost by their rejection of papal supremacy. Communion with Rome, as we have seen,[38] is an essential condition for receiving or retaining jurisdiction in the Church. The situation is aptly expressed in the words of St. Optatus of Mileve to the Donatists of Africa: "You should realize, even at this late date, that you are limbs broken from the tree; branches torn from the vine; a stream separated from its source. . . . By the chair of Peter, which is ours, the other marks are proved to be in the holy Catholic Church."[39]

4. Schismatic Churches of the East

I. UNITY. The schismatic churches of the East all lack unity of government. What is known as the Orthodox Church of the East is a mere fiction; in reality it is but a number of independent, national churches, united only in their opposition to Rome. Neither have they unity of faith, since there is no supreme authority to teach or govern. Under such conditions, differences and changes in doctrine are inevitable. The rejection of the deuterocanonical books of Scripture may be cited as an example of changed teaching. The Eastern churches always numbered these among the inspired books of Scripture until Prokopovitch rejected them at the beginning of the eighteenth century. There was no authority to correct this error, and in the course of a few years it became the official doctrine of the schismatic churches. Even the official creeds, e.g., the creed of Moghila and that of Dositheus, teach contradictory doctrines on many important points,[40] and in many cases their official teaching is contradicted by their liturgies.

II. CATHOLICITY. The schismatic churches of the East, even when considered as one church, are in no sense Catholic or universal in their diffusion. They are limited almost entirely to Asia Minor, Egypt, Abyssinia, and eastern Europe.

III. APOSTOLICITY. Most of the Orthodox churches of the East

---

[38] Cf. above, p. 78.
[39] "De Schismate Donatistarum," II, 9; P.L., 11, 962.
[40] Cf. D'Ales, "Dictionnaire Apologetique," art. "Grecque, Eglise."

have valid Orders, and to that extent may be called Apostolic; they have Apostolic succession of the powers of Orders. In some cases they may also have a *material* succession of bishops from Apostolic times, but this avails them nothing, since they lack both unity and Catholicity,—two essential marks of the true Church. In no case do they have legitimate succession; there is no transmission of jurisdiction because they have withdrawn from communion with Rome, the center and source of all jurisdiction.

PART II

Dogmatic

ORGANIZATION AND POWERS OF THE CHURCH

"Behold the Tabernacle of God With Men, and He Will Dwell With Them. And They Shall Be His People."— Apocalypse XXI, 3.

INTRODUCTION

In Apologetics, the institution and nature of the Church is considered only in so far as necessary to determine which of the many Christian churches existing today is the true Church of Christ. When this Church has been identified, dogmatic theology proceeds to investigate more thoroughly its organization and powers. This investigation is most easily carried out by studying the Church as set forth on the pages of Scripture, and as she has existed through the centuries. The prophecies of old and the words of Our Lord give us the plans,—the blue-prints, as it were, according to which the Church was established and built up; the writings of the Fathers and the official acts of the Church herself show us what she has been in every age since the days of the Apostles, who actually carried out the organization according to the plans laid down for them by Christ, the Divine Architect.

Complete and systematic knowledge of a thing is best obtained by studying its various *causes,—efficient, final, material,* and *formal.* The *efficient* cause of a thing is the agent whose activity brings it into being; the *final* cause is the purpose for which it is brought into being. The *material* and *formal* causes are the constitutive elements,—the material of which a thing is made and that by which the material becomes this particular thing instead of something else. For example, the material cause of a watch is the metal from which it is made; the formal cause is the shape and arrangement of parts by which the metal becomes a watch. Applying these notions to the Church, it is evident that Christ is its efficient cause, and the salvation of souls its proximate final cause. The members of whom it is composed are the material cause, and the bonds by which they are united to form the particular society known as the Church of Christ constitute the formal cause. But since all the bonds by which men are constituted a society depend upon *authority* for their preservation, we may, for all practical purposes, consider authority as the formal cause of the Church.

Since the efficient and final causes of the Church have been sufficiently considered in the first part of our work, we may now pass on to a study of its material and formal causes, i.e., the members who constitute it and the bonds by which they are united. But no study of the Church would be complete unless it took into consideration St. Paul's conception of

107

it as the *Body of Christ*. Finally, the Church must exist in the world side by side with civil authority; therefore, it is necessary to consider their mutual relations. Hence this second part of our work will consider, (1) the Church as the mystical body of Christ, (2) its members, (3) its authority, (4) its ministry, i.e., those in whom authority resides and by whom it is exercised, (5) the relations between Church and State.

CHAPTER V

The Mystical Body of Christ*

In describing the Church as *the body of Christ,* St. Paul sets forth its real nature in a manner that could never be known from a mere study of its external organization and powers. When understood in this light, the Church stands out in all the glory of her divine majesty, and the ineffable union of her members with Christ is clearly perceived. This conception of the Church also sheds much light upon other doctrines, particularly upon the nature and operation of the Sacraments. "The Apostle surely was well aware how wonderful was the truth which he was communicating when he affirmed Christians to be members of Christ's *body from His Flesh and from His Bones;* for he himself declared it to be *a great mystery.*[1] . . . The mystical Body of Christ has an organic life like His Body natural; for Christ was personally Incarnate in that Body which was slain, but by power and presence will He be Incarnate in His Church till the end of the world. As the Gospels are the record of His Presence in the one, so is Church History that of His Presence in the other."[2]

The Church as the body of Christ must be a living *body;* therefore, it is necessary to inquire, (1) in what sense it is the *body* of Christ, and (2) what is its life-giving principle, its *soul.*

ART. I. THE CHURCH AS THE BODY OF CHRIST

We often speak of a *body* of men and we refer to societies as *bodies;* in fact, certain organizations are known officially as *corporations,* from the Latin *corpus—a body.* In the days of St. Paul such usage was unknown. The Greek *soma* (*body*) was never used in reference to a society, nor *kephale* (*head*) for its chief ruler. In Latin *corpus* (*body*)

---

*The official Catholic doctrine on the true nature of the Church was declared in:
Encyclical "Mystici Corporis" of Pius XII, on June 29, 1943;
Encyclical "Mediator Dei" of Pius XII, on November 20, 1947;
Encyclical "Humani Generis" of Pius XII, on August 12, 1950;
Letter "Suprema haec sacra" of the Holy Office to the Most Reverend Robert J. Cushing, Archbishop of Boston, dated August 8, 1949, published September 4, 1952.
The complete Latin text and the authorized English translation of this letter are in The American Ecclesiastical Review, 1952 (Oct.), pp. 307-315.
The Jurist, 1952 (Oct.), pp. 478-486.
[1] Ephes. v, 30-32.
[2] B. I. Wilberforce, "Principles of Church Authority," p. 29.

was sometimes used to designate a band of soldiers, but the modern use of the word to designate a society seems to be in imitation of St. Paul. It is evident, then, that the Apostle wished to convey some special doctrine when he called the Church a *soma;* it is no mere figure of speech. There is, of course, a striking similarity between the Church as a society and a human body; both are composed of members, each having its own peculiar duties or functions, yet all working together for the good of the whole. "Just as in one body we have many members, yet all the members have not the same function, so we, the many, are one body in Christ, but severally members one of another."[3] But St. Paul goes beyond this mere external similarity by which any society may be called a *body;* he not only compares the Church to a human body, but also calls it the *body of Christ*: "He himself gave some men as apostles and some as prophets . . . for building up the *body of Christ*."[4] Elsewhere he says: "Now you are the *Body of Christ,* member for member."[5] Again he says: "For as the body is one and has many members, and all the members of the body, many as they are, form one body, so also is it with Christ (i.e., the Church)."[6] Writing to the Colossians, he says: "He is head of this body, the Church."[7]

The mere fact that Christ is Head of the Church is not sufficient to make it His body. A king or ruler is often called the *head* of his people, but they are never referred to as his *body,* neither are they called his *members.* This proves that the bonds of union in the Church are far different from those found in mere human societies. The members of a human society are united to their head by moral bonds only, i.e., by mutual rights and duties; there is no physical connection of member with member, or of members with the head. In the Church, the members are united one with another, and all with Christ, their Head, by the real physical[8] bond of supernatural grace flowing from the Head into each and every member, thus making them partakers of His divine nature: "He hath granted us the very great and precious promises, so that through them you may become partakers of the divine nature."[9] So real is this union between Christ and His faithful that St. Paul could say: "It is now no longer I that live, but Christ lives in me."[10] For the

---

[3] Rom. xii, 4, 5.
[4] Ephes. iv, 11, 12.
[5] 1 Cor. xii, 27.
[6] 1 Cor. xii, 12.
[7] Col. i, 18.
[8] The word *physical* is here opposed to *moral,* and therefore does not imply anything material.
[9] 2 Pet. i, 4.
[10] Gal. ii, 20.

same reason he says that by Baptism we are *concorporated* with Christ, being engrafted, as it were into His Body.[11]

According to this doctrine of St. Paul, the union between Christ and the Church must be in every respect analogous to that between head and members in the human body, where the head holds the position of eminence and direction, exercises a vivifying influence, and together with the members forms one complete whole, the body:

a) *Preeminence.* In the human body the head occupies the most prominent position, being placed above all other members to guard and direct them. In like manner, Christ occupies the position of preeminence; He sits at the right hand of God the Father, whence He looks out, as it were, upon His Church, to guard and direct it: "Above every Principality and Power and Virtue and Domination—in short, above every name that is named, not only in this world, but also in that which is to come. And all things he made subject under his feet, and him he gave as head over all the Church, which is indeed his body, the completion of him who fills all with all."[12]

The head also excels all other members of the body, particularly because it contains the brain, the seat of all the senses and the intellectual faculties which direct every bodily power and all their activities. So also does Christ, in His divine perfection, excel by far every other member of His mystical Body, whose every power and activity He directs. "Our Head intercedes for us at the right hand of the Father; some He receives as members; some He punishes, others He cleanses; some He consoles, others He creates; some He calls, others He recalls; some He corrects, others He reinstates."[13] St. Paul compares Christ's fostering care for His Church to that of a bridegroom for his bride: "Christ also loved the Church, and delivered himself up for her, that he might sanctify her . . . that he might present himself the Church in all her glory, not having spot or wrinkle or any such thing, but that she might be holy and without blemish. . . . For no one ever hated his own flesh; on the contrary he nourishes and cherishes it, as Christ also does the Church (because we are members of his body, made from his flesh and from his bones)."[14]

b) *Vivifying Influence.* The vitalizing forces of the human body reside principally in the head, whence impulses go out along the tiny nerve filaments to every cell, directing its activities and thus enabling it to discharge its proper functions. In like manner, impressions received

---

[11] Rom. vi, 5 (Greek text).
[12] Ephes. i, 21-23.
[13] St. Augustine, "Enarratio in Ps.," lxxxv, 5; P.L., 37, 1085.
[14] Ephes. v, 25 sq.

in any portion of the body are carried back along the nerve fibres to
the brain. Any member cut off from this union with the head by a
severance of its nerves, soon decays and ceases to be a member of the
body. So also in the Church, the vivifying power of grace resides in
Jesus Christ, its Head, whence it flows into every member, thus uniting
him with Christ and enabling him to perform supernatural acts. "I am
the vine," says Christ, "and you the branches; he that abides in me,
and I in him, bears much fruit; for without me you can do nothing. If
any one does not abide in me, he shall be cast outside as the branch,
and wither."[15] As the branches of a vine draw from it the life-giving
sap, so do the members of Christ's mystical body draw from Him the
life-giving principle of grace. This is done principally in the Sacraments,
especially in the Holy Eucharist, where we are corporally united with
Christ, as St. Paul explains: "The cup of blessing which we bless, is it
not the partaking of the blood of Christ? And the bread which we
break, is it not the partaking of the body of the Lord?"[16]

c) *Intimate Union.* In the material body, head and members are
physiologically united to form one complete whole; neither the head
nor the trunk is complete without the other. In like manner the Church
is so united with Christ as Head that St. Paul does not hesitate to call
the resulting whole by the very name of Christ himself: "As the body
is one and hath many members; and all the members of the body,
whereas they are many, yet are one body, so also is Christ."[17] Here the
Apostle plainly applies the name *Christ* to the Church. In another place
he says that we *grow together* in Christ as the members of a natural
body with their head: "Rather are we to practice the truth in love, and
so grow up in all things in him who is the head, Christ. For from him
the whole body (being closely joined and knit together through every
joint of the system according to the functioning in due measure of each
single part) derives its increase to the building up of itself in love."[18]
These words represent Christ as dwelling within the Church, where
He operates through every joint and member, that we all may grow
together with Him (*concrescamus cum illo*), and be ever more closely
united with Him through charity. The Church, then, is not merely a
society of men instituted by Christ and subject to His authority; it is
also a society of men so intimately and physically united with Him
that it may be called the *Body of Christ* or *Christ Himself.*

THE FULLNESS OF CHRIST. St. Paul also calls the Church the

---

[15] John xv, 5-6.
[16] 1 Cor. x, 16.
[17] 1 Cor. xii, 12.
[18] Ephes. iv, 15.

fullness of Christ (plenitudo Christi) for he says: *"And all* things he made subject under his feet, and him he gave as head over all the Church, which indeed is his body, the fullness of him who is wholly fulfilled in all."[19] St. Thomas explains this as follows: "If any one should ask, why the natural body has such varied members,—hands, feet, mouth, and the like,—we reply: That they may serve the different operations proceeding from the soul as their principle and cause. . . . The body was made for the soul, not the soul for the body; therefore, the natural body is the *fullness* (or complement) of the soul. Unless the body be complete in all its members, the soul could not completely perform its varied operations. So also with Christ and the Church, which was instituted on His account and is, therefore, rightly called His *fullness*."[20] The Church is the instrument in which and through which Christ ordinarily exercises His divine power in the world.

MYSTICAL BODY. The Church is called the *mystical* body of Christ, to distinguish it from a natural physical body on the one hand, and from a mere moral body on the other. The word *mystical* shows that the Church is not a body hypostatically united to the Word after the manner of Christ's human nature. It also shows that the Church is not a merely natural society, in which the members are united to their head by the simple bonds of right and duties. The Church far surpasses such societies, because her members are actually and physically united to Christ by means of supernatural grace. The Church is called a *mystical* body also because many mysteries of faith underlie this union with Christ,—a union which "the sensual man perceiveth not";[21] it can be known by faith alone.[22]

COROLLARIES.—I. *Channels of Grace.* The natural body is equipped with various systems of organs for carrying on the processes of life. The most important of these are the circulatory system and the nervous system. The former consists of a wonderful net-work of arteries, veins, and capillaries, through which the life-bearing stream of blood flows to every cell of the body. This system is regulated in its every part by a net-work of nerves, which have their common center in the brain. In the mystical body of Christ the Sacraments are the arteries through which the life-giving streams of grace flow into each and every soul. For this reason they are often called the *channels of grace.* The nervous system of the natural body is here replaced by the ministerial power

---

[19] Ephes. i, 22-23.
[20] "In Ephes.," c. i, Lec. 8.
[21] 1 Cor. ii, 14.
[22] Cf. Dorsch, "De Ecclesia Christi," p. 364; Hurter, "Compendium Theol. Dogmat., Vol. I, n. 210; B. I. Wilberforce, "Principles of Church Authority," Ch. i.

of the Church; her priests participate in the priesthood of Christ to
direct the flow of grace through the Sacraments which they administer.

II. *The Second Adam.* St. Paul's conception of the Church as the
mystical body of Christ is intimately connected with the doctrine of
original sin, upon which he insists so strongly. Adam was endowed
with supernatural gifts, not only as an individual, but also as head of
the whole human family. Eve was formed from his side that this "bone
of his bone and flesh of his flesh" might become the mother of all
living, who would thus form one body with Adam as its head. Every
member of that body was to participate in the blessings bestowed upon
its head, but by Adam's disobedience those blessings were lost, and we
as members of his body share in his guilt as well as in his loss: Therefore as through one man sin entered into the world and through sin
death, and thus death has passed unto all men because all have sinned.
. . ."[23] We are members of a diseased body, and the history of mankind
is the history of that body reaching out through time and space, with
its deepening malady of sin in the individual and in society. This is the
mystery of original sin: without any act or will on our part we share
in the guilt of our common head. But "where the obscurity of the fall
was deepest, the light of the restoration is brightest; and where the
sentence was most severe, the grace was most wonderful."[24] The divine
Word assumed human nature in order to become a second Adam,—a
second head of the human family: "The first man, Adam, became a
living soul; the last Adam a life-giving spirit."[25]

The Church formed from the side of Christ, "bone of His bone, and
flesh of His flesh," becomes the mother of a new race, who also form
a body with Christ as Head, and "as there is a unity of the fallen Adam
. . . so much the more is there a unity of the second Adam, which is
not a collection of individuals, but a body with its Head."[26] As in the
mystical body of Adam we inherit his guilt without any fault of our
own, so likewise in the mystical body of Christ we inherit His graces
without any merits on our part. "But where the offense has abounded,
grace has abounded yet more."[27] In the history of the Church we see the
body of the second Adam reaching out into time and space with its ever
increasing blessings for the individual and for society. Eve still bears
children of men to the first Adam, but the Church bears children of Christ
to the second Adam. "These are not two mysteries, but one, unfathomable

[23] Rom. v, 12.
[24] T. W. Allies, "Formation of Christendom," Part II, p. 78.
[25] 1 Cor. xv, 45.
[26] T. W. Allies, "Formation of Christendom," Part II, p. 79.
[27] Rom. v, 20.

in both its parts of justice and mercy; but the whole history of the human race bears witness to the first, and the whole history of the Christian people, to the second. . . . Our Lord stands in the midst of His Church visibly forming from day to day and from age to age that Body of His which reaches through the ages. He takes from Himself and gives to us. He incorporated Himself in His children. He grows up in us, and by visible streams from His heart maintains the life first given."[28]

ART. II. THE SOUL OF THE CHURCH

"The Church," says Leo XIII, "is not something dead; it is the body of Christ endowed with supernatural life."[29] Therefore, the Church must possess the two elements essential to every living body,—it must have an external organism and an internal principle of life,—a body and a soul. In the Mystical Body of Christ, the external organism is the Church, considered merely as a society of faithful with Christ as their Head. It possesses all the organs necessary for the vital functions of such a body; it has Sacraments, a Sacrifice, an organized hierarchy, authority, and various institutions to promote supernatural life. But all these are as nothing unless they be animated by a life-giving principle. There must be a *soul* to vivify them with supernatural life and constitute them the Mystical Body of Christ, just as the human soul vivifies the natural body of man and constitutes it a human body.

The vital activities of the Church consist in the distribution of supernatural grace to her members and the supernatural acts performed by them through its aid. The principle or source of these activities can be none other than the Holy Spirit by whom "the charity of God is poured forth in our hearts,"[30] for to Him is appropriated the work of sanctification. Therefore the Holy Spirit is the *Soul* of the Church; the principle of supernatural life, who unites with the external organism of the Church to make it a living body, a divine body, the Body of Christ. For this reason St. Augustine says: "What the soul is to the body, that the Holy Spirit is to the body of Christ, which is the Church. What the Holy Spirit does in the whole Church, that the soul does in all the members of each body."[31] The Holy Spirit is the *informing element* in the Mystical Body of Christ, and its *vital principle.*

a) *Informing Principle.* In the language of Scholastic philosophy, the *informing principle,* or *formal cause* of a thing is that constitutive part which unites with the material body to form the one complete entity, a

[28] T. W. Allies, "Formation of Christendom," Part II, p. 107.
[29] Encyclical *"Satis cognitum,"* July 29, 1896.
[30] Rom. v, 5.
[31] "Sermon.," 267, 4; P.L., 38, 1213.

man. The soul does not act upon the body from without, but dwells within and unites with every part to vivify it and to coordinate it with every other part. The Holy Spirit *informs* the Church in a similar manner; He dwells within it by a real substantial presence and is, in a sense, substantially united with its every member. The Church, taken as a society, is the material element, the organism whose every member is vivified by the indwelling presence of the Holy Spirit and through Him united with every other member and with Christ the Head, thus constituting the Mystical Body of Christ. This is the teaching of St. Paul who says: "Do you not know that you are the temple of God and that the Spirit of God dwells in you?"[32] Again he says: "And because you are sons, God hath sent the Spirit of his Son into your hearts crying; Abba, Father."[33] Christ himself also promised that the Holy Spirit should dwell with His Church for all time: "And I will ask the Father and he will give you another Advocate to dwell with you forever . . . he will dwell with you, and be in you."[34]

The early Fathers are explicit in their teaching on this subject. *St. Gregory Nazianzen* says: "Now the Holy Spirit is given more perfectly, for He is no longer given by His (mere) operation, as of old, but is present with us, so to speak, and converses with us in a *substantial* manner."[35] *St. Cyril of Alexandria* says: "The Holy Spirit works in us by Himself, truly sanctifying us and uniting us to Himself . . . makes us partakers of the divine nature."[36] Another ancient author says: "The holy universal Church is one body constituted under Christ the Head . . . and just as the one soul quickens the various members of the body, so the Holy Spirit quickens and illuminates the whole Church. For as Christ, who is the Head of the Church, was conceived by the Holy Spirit, so the holy Church which is His Body, is filled with the same Spirit, that it may have life, and is confirmed by His power that it may subsist in the bond of one faith and charity."[37] Therefore, as Cardinal Manning says: "We are under the personal direction of the Third Person as truly as the Apostles were under the guidance of the Second. The presence of the Eternal Son by incarnation, was the center of their unity; the presence of the Eternal Spirit, by the incorporation of the mystical body, is the center of unity for us."[38]

b) *Vital Principle.* All our vital activities,—acts of intellect and will, sensation, and even the bodily functions of nourishment and growth,—

[32] 1 Cor. iii, 16.
[33] Gal. iv, 6.
[34] John xiv, 16-17.
[35] "Oratio in Pentecosten"; P.G., 36, 443.
[36] "Thesaurus de Trinitate"; P.G., 75, 593.
[37] "Expositio in P. Poenit." (author unknown); P.L., 79, 602.
[38] "Temporal Mission of the Holy Ghost," p. 68.

proceed in some way from the soul as their ultimate source. In like manner all activities in the Mystical Body of Christ proceed from the Holy Spirit: "Now there are varieties of gifts, but the same Spirit; . . . To one through the Spirit is given the utterance of wisdom and to another the utterance of knowledge, according to the same Spirit; to another faith, in the same Spirit; to another the gift of healing, in the one Spirit; to another the working of miracles; to another prophecy; to another the distinguishing of spirits; to another various kinds of tongues; to another interpretation of tongues. But all these things are the work of one and the same Spirit, who divides to everyone according as he will. For as the body is one and has many members, and all the members of the body, many as they are, form one body, so also is it with Christ."[39] In this passage St. Paul represents the Church as the body of Christ, whose members have varied functions to perform, but the Holy Spirit is the source of all power to perform them; from Him flows the diversities of graces. All our supernatural virtues find their source in the graces of the Holy Spirit: "The fruit of the Spirit is charity, joy, peace, patience, . . . mildness, faith, modesty, continency."[40] Even the simplest prayer comes only from a soul united in some manner with the Holy Spirit, for "no one can say 'Jesus is Lord,' except in the Holy Spirit,[41] who helps our weakness. For we do not know what we should pray for as we ought, but the Spirit himself pleads for us with unutterable groanings."[42]

St. Augustine aptly describes the office of the Holy Spirit in His capacity as *Soul* of the Church. He says: "The spirit by which man lives is called the soul. Now see what the soul does in the body; it gives life to all the members; it sees through the eyes, hears through the ears, smells through the nostrils; with the tongue it speaks, with the hands it works, with the feet it walks. It is present in every member to give it life; it apportions to every part its proper function. . . . What the soul is to the body, that the Holy Ghost is to the Church. . . . Through some He works miracles, in others He speaks truth, in others He perseveres virginity. In some He does one thing, in others another thing, but each has his proper task, yet all alike live by Him."[43]

A similarity between the soul of our natural body and the Soul of the Church is seen even in the bodily functions of assimilation and growth. Under the direction of the soul, food is prepared and received

---

[39] 1 Cor. xii, 4-12.
[40] Gal. v, 22, 23
[41] 1 Cor. xii, 3.
[42] Rom. viii, 26.
[43] "Sermon.," 267, 4; P.L., 38, 1231.

into the body, where it is digested and assimilated by activities which proceed likewise from the soul; the food then becomes an integral part of the body, united to the soul and vivified by it. In like manner the Holy Spirit prepares men by His graces for union with the Church; through Baptism He unites them to Himself and makes them members of Christ's Mystical body: "For in one Spirit were we all baptized into one body."[44]

COROLLARIES.—I. *Creation of the Mystical Body.* The formation of the Mystical Body of Christ bears a striking similarity to the creation of the first man. Adam's body was formed from the slime of the earth and did not become man until God breathed into it the living soul. The Church was instituted by Christ, when He sent forth the Apostles with authority to teach, govern and sanctify, but it remained a lifeless body, as it were, until Christ ascended to the Father and breathed upon it the Spirit of Life; the Holy Spirit descended upon the Church and it became a living body,—the Mystical Body of Christ. Hence the coming of the Holy Spirit on that first Pentecost was in reality the creation of the Church.

There is another noteworthy parallel between the formation of Christ's natural body and that of His Mystical Body. When the Word was about to assume human form, the angel announced to the chosen Virgin: "The Holy Spirit shall come upon thee and the power of the Most High shall overshadow thee; and therefore the Holy One to be born shall be called the Son of God."[45] Before ascending into Heaven, Our Lord makes a similar announcement to His Apostles and disciples: "You shall receive power when the Holy Spirit comes upon you, . . . I send forth upon you the promise of my Father. But wait here in the city, until you are clothed with power from on high."[46] The natural body was formed by the action of the Holy Spirit within the body of the Virgin Mary; the Mystical Body, by the same Spirit acting within the little band or body of Apostles and disciples.

II. *Indissoluble Union.* Before the coming of the Holy Spirit on Pentecost, He had been united with individual souls by His work of enlightening and sanctifying, but his union was conditioned upon the cooperation and fidelity of individuals. His union with the Church is an indissoluble union of personal and substantial indwelling. The union with individual souls is still conditional; it still depends upon fidelity to grace; but the union with the Church is unconditional and indissoluble; "The Father will give you another Advocate to dwell with you for

[44] 1 Cor. xii, 13.
[45] Luke i, 35.
[46] Acts i, 8; Luke xxiv, 49.

ever."[47] Individuals may fail; the Church cannot fail. "Individuals may fall from it, as multitudes have fallen; provinces and nations, particular churches may fall from it; but the body still remains, its unity undivided, its life indefectible. . . . The line of faith, hope and charity is never dissolved. The threefold cord cannot be broken, and the ever-blessed Trinity always inhabits His tabernacle upon earth,—the souls of the elect who "are being built together into a dwelling place for God in the Spirit."[48] From this indissoluble union of Body, Head and indwelling Spirit flow all the attributes and properties of the Church,—unity, sanctity, authority, infallibility and the like.

III. *Membership.* There is a widely accepted theory that the soul of the Church is wider in extent than the body; that many persons belong to the soul of the Church who are in no wise connected with her external organization. This theory seems to have been invented to explain the axiom "Out of the Church no salvation,"[49] but it is not tenable if we carry out the doctrine of the Mystical Body. In the natural body nothing pertains in any way to the soul unless it be physiologically connected with the body. Once a member is severed from the body, it ceases to be animated by the soul; it loses all life and immediately decays. In like manner, any part of the body that ceases to receive any life-giving influence from the soul, also decays and sloughs off; it ceases to be a part of the body. Now, since the Church is an organic body, vivified by the Holy Spirit as its life-giving principle, no person can belong to the one unless he belongs also in some degree to the other. He who belongs to the soul of the Church, must therefore also belong to her body, and he who belongs to her body, must also belong to her soul. A member may be diseased, because the life-giving influence of the soul is impeded or lessened; but once all influence ceases, the member is dead,—he is no longer a portion of Christ's Mystical Body.

The Fathers of the Church strongly insist upon this doctrine. For example, St. Augustine says: "But see what ye have to beware of, to watch over, and to fear. In the body of man it may happen that a member, the hand, the finger or foot may be cut off. Does the soul follow the severed member? While it was in the body, it was alive; cut off, its life is lost. So a man is a Christian and a Catholic while he is alive in the body; cut off, he becomes a heretic. The Holy Spirit does not follow the amputated limb."[50]

---

[47] John xiv, 16-17.
[48] Cardinal Manning, "Temporal Mission of the Holy Ghost," p. 74; Ephes. ii, 22.
[49] See below, p. 136 sq. for an explanation of this axiom.
[50] "Sermon.," 267; P.L., 38, 1321. For further information on the subject of this chapter see T. W. Allies, "Formation of Christendom," Part II, Ch. viii; Cardinal Manning, "The Temporal Mission of the Holy Ghost," Ch. I.

CHAPTER VI

MEMBERS OF THE CHURCH

In studying man, we may turn our attention to the nature and powers of the soul, or we may examine the organic structure of his body and investigate the functions of its various parts. Finally, we may investigate the manner in which body and soul are united, the action of one upon the other and the nature of the composite being resulting from their union. The striking analogy between the Mystical Body of Christ and the natural body of man suggests a similar method of treatment for both. The nature of the mystical body resulting from the union of the Church with Christ as its Head, and with the Holy Spirit as its Soul, was considered in the preceding chapter. This and the following chapters are devoted to the *anatomy* and *physiology* of the Church: the one considers its organic structure, i.e., the members who compose it and the manner in which they are united to constitute the Church of Christ; the other investigates the acts by which all conspire to a common end and the power or authority by which these acts are performed.

The members of the Church constitute its material cause; the authority by which their union into a society is preserved and directed, may be considered the formal cause. The material cause of a society is either *proximate* or *remote:* the former consists of those who actually compose the society; the latter, those who are eligible for membership. The whole human race constitutes the remote matter for the Church, since it was established for the salvation of all men, regardless of race, color, or condition. The proximate matter of the Church consists of those who fulfill the necessary conditions of membership and thereby become constituent parts of her organization.

In order to arrive at a proper conception of those matters, it is necessary (1) to consider some errors regarding the conditions of membership in the Church, (2) to establish the true conditions, (3) to point out those who certainly do not belong to the Church, (4) to consider certain classes whose membership is doubtful, and (5) to prove the necessity of membership in the Church.

ART. I. FALSE CONDITIONS OF MEMBERSHIP

Wyclif, Huss, and Calvin taught that none but the predestined[1] are members of the Church. According to Wyclif and Huss all the predestined without exception belong to the Church; according to Calvin, only such as are predestined to accept the true faith of Christ. Luther taught that all the just, and they alone, belong to the Church; he thus made the state of grace the one necessary condition for membership in the Church. This seems to be the prevailing doctrine among Protestants of the present day, at least among those who maintain that the true Church of Christ is invisible. The visible churches may contain sinners, but not the Church invisible.

1. Predestination as a Condition

Thesis.—Predestination Is Not a Condition for Membership in the Church; Much Less Is It the Only Condition

This thesis is an article of faith, as appears from the condemnation of the following propositions at the Council of Constance: "There is but one holy and universal Church, i.e., the Church which consists of all the predestined," and "The grace of predestination is the bond by which the Church and all its members are indissolubly joined to Christ the Head."[2]

PROOF. a) It has been proved that the Church is essentially an external, visible society; therefore, all members of this visible society are members of the Church. But predestination is not a condition for membership in this visible society, as Christ himself teaches by the parable of the wheat and the cockle. The field is the Church, the wheat and the cockle are the members, who will not be separated until the day of judgment. The cockle to be gathered up and burned at the harvest cannot be those who are predestined to eternal life, yet they too are represented as members of the Church, since the cockle continues to grow *in* the field together with the wheat. Likewise, in the parable of the net cast into the sea, the bad fish are as truly a part of the draught taken as the good, yet they cannot be those destined to eternal life, since they are to be separated from the good at the shore,

---

[1] God decreed from all eternity that those who, by their own free will, cooperate with His grace and keep His commandments, should be saved. In His infinite knowledge, He knew from all eternity who would thus freely cooperate and be saved. In this sense it can be said that God has predestined us to eternal life or eternal damnation. Calvin taught that every man is predestined to Heaven or hell regardless of his merits or demerits. No one is predestined in this sense.

[2] Denzinger, nn. 627, 647.

i.e., on the day of judgment. In the parable of the banquet, the man cast
forth into the darkness because he had not on a wedding garment could
not have been predestined, yet he was actually a guest and partook of the
banquet as really as those who were properly arrayed for the occasion.[3]

b) If predestination were the only condition for membership in the
Church, it would follow that all who are predestined to eternal life,
are actually members of the Church, although they may be Mahomet-
ans, pagans, or even atheists at present. It would also be useless to
send missionaries to pagan lands, since all those who are predestined
to be saved are already members of the Church.

c) The predestined are known to God alone; therefore, the Church
must be invisible if none but the predestined belong to it. Pastors could
not recognize their flock, nor the flock its pastors. St. Paul's admonition to the pastors of Ephesus would have been useless: "Take heed
to yourselves and to the whole flock in which the Holy Spirit has
placed you as bishops, to rule the Church of God."[4] All authority
would be impossible and the duty of obedience would cease. Hence
Calvin and Luther were strictly logical when they taught, contrary to
the express words of Christ, that the Church is invisible.

2. The State of Grace as a Condition

Thesis.—The State of Grace Is Not a Condition for Membership in
the Church

This also seems to be a defined doctrine of the Church, as appears
from the condemnation of several propositions that at least imply
the necessity of sanctifying grace for membership in the Church.
Among these may be mentioned the following condemned by Clement
XI: "A mark of the Christian Church is that it is Catholic, comprising,
as it does, all the angels of heaven and all the elect and just on earth
during all the centuries"; and "The Church, which is Christ entire,
has the Word Incarnate as Head and all the just as members."[5]

PROOFS. a) This theory also destroys the Church by making it
invisible, since the just as well as the predestined can be known only
to God. It seems probable that Luther and his followers adopted this
doctrine when they were forced to accept the theory of an invisible
Church, as mentioned above.[6] At any rate, the two doctrines are so
intimately related that either one logically leads to the other.

---

[3] Matt. xiii, 24 sq.; xxii, 11 sqq.
[4] Acts xx, 28.
[5] Denzinger, n. 1424.
[6] Pp. 37, 55.

b) Holy Scripture plainly teaches that sinners will always be found among the members of Christ's Church on earth. The parables of the wheat and the cockle, of the good and bad fish, and of the man without a wedding garment, show that just and unjust, saints and sinners will be found mingled together in the Church until the end of the world, for then only "The Son of Man will send forth his angels, and they will gather out of his kingdom all scandals and those who work iniquity."[6a] Those who work iniquity cannot be *gathered out* of the kingdom, unless they be *in* the kingdom.

St. Paul admonishes Timothy how to conduct himself toward the faithful. He says: "But in a great house there are vessels not only of gold and silver, but also of wood and clay; and some are for honorable uses, but some for ignoble."[6b] The vessels *unto honor* are the just; those *for ignoble* uses, the unjust, as is evident from the words which immediately follow those just quoted: "If anyone, therefore, has cleansed himself from these, he will be a vessel for honorable use, sanctified and useful to the Lord, ready for every good work." According to St. Paul, therefore, the great house of the Church contains vessels unto honor and vessels for ignoble uses, i.e., both saints and sinners.

c) The very purpose for which the Church was instituted would be in a large measure frustrated if all sinners were excluded from membership; the Sacraments, the greatest means of sanctification, would have to be denied them, and the Church's influence over them would be indirect and of slight effect. We cannot conceive that Christ founded a Church to save all men, and at the same time excluded those who stand most in need of its ministrations.

3. Objections Considered

OBJECTION I.—The Church could not be holy if sinners were numbered amongst her members.

ANSWER.—This objection has been answered in connection with the holiness of the Church.[7] It may be noted, however, that the personal sanctity of the Church need not be perfect, and may vary from time to time, but can never be entirely lost. There will always be a large number of holy persons in the Church, even though the sinners may at times outnumber them.

OBJECTION II.—No one can be a member of Christ and a mem-

[6a] Matt. xiii, 41.
[6b] 2 Tim. 11, 20-23.
[7] See above, p. 59.

ber of Satan at the same time, yet St. John says: "He who commits sin is of the devil."[8]

ANSWER.—A person cannot belong to two societies that are opposed to each other, but he may belong to a society and yet act in a manner derogatory to it. A sinner belongs to the Church, because he retains at least the supernatural gifts of faith and hope, and preserves the other bonds of union; he belongs to the devil in so far as he imitates him in his actions. A sinner does not become a member of the devil in the same sense that he is a member of Christ, because the devil has no mystical body; his imitators form no real society.

OBJECTION III.—When speaking of certain sinners, St. John says: "They have gone forth from us, but they were not of us. For if they had been of us, they would surely have continued with us."[9] These words leave no doubt that these sinners were not members of the Church; *they were not of us.*

ANSWER.—In this passage St. John is not speaking of sinners in general, but of certain men, whom he calls Antichrists, because they had "denied the Father and the Son." Consequently they were heretics and as such did not belong to the Church, as will be proved elsewhere.

OBJECTION IV.—If sinners are members of the Church here, they must also be members hereafter, since death is a mere separation of body and soul that in no way affects man's spiritual condition. But such a conclusion is manifestly absurd.

ANSWER.—The conclusion is not only absurd, but also unfounded. God, who ordained that sinners may be members of the Church in this life, also ordained that they shall not be members in the life to come. This is evident from the many passages in which Christ foretells eternal death for all sinners who die impenitent. Moreover, death severs all the bonds by which sinners are united to the body of the faithful in this life. After death there remains to them neither faith, hope, nor charity, and there is no external bond of union with the just.

OBJECTION V.—In many passages of his work on Baptism, St. Augustine teaches that sinners do not belong to the Church.

ANSWER.—These passages must be interpreted in the light of others, where St. Augustine proves at length against the Donatists that sinners may be true members of the Church. Moreover, we have the Saint's own interpretation of these passages. He says: "Wherever in those books (on Baptism) I have referred to the Church as not having

---

[8] 1 John iii, 8.
[9] 1 John ii, 19.

spot or wrinkle, I do not mean the Church as it is, but as it shall appear when glorified."[10]

Conditions for membership in the Church, as in every other society, include those things which are absolutely necessary to make one a member in the true sense of the word. There is no question about the conditions necessary to make a *perfect* member, or even a *good* member. St. Paul compares the Church to a house, in which there are *vessels for honor* and *vessels for ignoble* uses, yet all are vessels in the true sense of the term, and all belong to the house. In this connection we do not ask why they are *honorable* or *dishonorable,* but simply why they are vessels at all.

INITIATION. The first condition for membership is deduced from the social nature of the Church. No one becomes a member of any society unless he is received into it by proper authority, and made a participant in its benefits according to his capacity. The official act of receiving a person into a society must be manifested externally in some manner. This is usually done by a symbolic act, known as the rite of initiation. The initiatory rite of the Church was instituted by Christ himself, when He sent forth the Apostles to make disciples of all nations: "Go, therefore, and make disciples of all nations, baptizing them in the name of the Father, and of the Son, and of the Holy Spirit."[11] Baptism, therefore, is the rite of initiation into the Church; hence St. Paul says: "For in one Spirit we were all baptized into one body."[12] For this reason also the Council of Trent calls Baptism the *door* by which we enter the Church,[13] and Eugenius IV in his decree *pro Armenis* says: "By Baptism we are made members of Christ and of His Body, the Church."[14]

PROFESSION OF FAITH. Every member of a society must accept its end and aims according to his ability, and he must strive, at least in some degree, to realize those aims. He that rejects the purposes of a society thereby rejects the society itself; he can neither become a member, nor remain one if already received into the society.

The practice of the Christian religion, which consists in the external profession of Christian faith, is the proximate end to be obtained in

---

[10] "Liber Retractationum," II, 18; P.L., 32, 637.
[11] Matt. xxviii, 19.
[12] 1 Cor. xii, 13.
[13] Denzinger, n. 895.
[14] Denzinger, n. 696.

the Church. Therefore, external profession of faith is an essential condition for membership. Moreover, the Church must be one in the external profession of faith, consequently he that severs this bond of unity is separated from the body of the Church, i.e., he ceases to be a member.

SUBJECTION TO AUTHORITY. The very existence of a society depends upon the subjection of its members to authority; therefore he that rejects the authority of a society, rejects the society itself and ceases to be a member. Neither can the end of a society be realized unless the members be directed by its authority in their common endeavors to that end. Therefore, rejecting the authority of a society is tantamount to rejecting its end and aims, which is to reject the society itself. Consequently no one can be a member of any society unless he submits to its authority according to his ability. Furthermore, in regard to the Church, there must be unity in the external profession of the *true* faith, which Christ committed to the teaching authority of the Church.[15] Therefore, the profession of faith necessary for membership in the Church practically resolves itself into submission to her teaching authority.

SUMMARY OF CONDITIONS. I. FOR ADULTS. The above considerations show that three conditions are absolutely necessary and of themselves sufficient for membership in the Church; viz.:

a) Initiation by Baptism, which gives the right to participate in all the benefits of the Church;

b) External profession of the true faith, which is had by submission to the teaching authority of the Church;

c) Submission to the ruling authority of the Church.

These conditions may be briefly summarized in one phrase: the reception of Baptism and the preservation of the unities,—unity of faith, unity of worship, and unity of government; or in other words, the reception of Baptism and submission to the teaching and ruling authority of the Church. It should be noted, however, that *perfect* observance of the unities is not required for mere membership in the Church; a person need not make explicit profession of faith at all times, nor conform all his actions to it. He need not make *diligent* use of the Sacraments at all times, neither must he be free from all infractions of Church laws and precepts. His transgressions will not exclude from membership unless they amount to total rejection of authority.

From the principles just established it follows that the adult mem-

---

[15] See above, p. 53.

bership of the Church comprises all those who have been baptized and have not rejected her teaching or ruling authority.

II. FOR INFANTS. In the explanations given above it was stated that a member of the Church must submit to her teaching and ruling authority *according to his ability,* because infants,[16] not having the use of reason, are incapable of such submission. They become members of the Church by the valid reception of Baptism, and remain members so long as they do not violate the bonds of unity by their own free act, which, of course, cannot take place before the age of discretion. From this it follows that the validly baptized children of heretics and schismatics are true members of the Catholic Church until they attain the age of discretion and reject authority of the Church by their own free act. Benedict XIV, writing on this matter, says: "We hold it for certain that those baptized by heretics are separated from the Church and deprived of all the blessings enjoyed by her members, *if they have arrived at the age of discretion and have adhered to the errors of their sect.*"[17]

ART. III. PERSONS EXCLUDED FROM MEMBERSHIP

Only those who fulfill the three conditions mentioned above, enjoy the privilege of membership in the Church; therefore all upbaptized persons, whether infants or adults, all manifest heretics and schismatics, and those excommunicated as *vitandi* are excluded. There is one class of unbaptized persons that might seem to have some claims to membership in the Church. These are the catechumen, i.e., persons preparing to receive Baptism. They have fulfilled all the conditions necessary on their part by submitting to the authority of the Church in preparation for Baptism, but the Church has not yet accepted them; consequently they cannot be accounted members. The mind of the Church on this point is expressed in her prayer on Good Friday: "Increase the faith and understanding of our catechumens, that, being reborn in the font of Baptism, they may be associated with the children of thine adoption."[18] They are not yet *associated* with the children of adoption,—they are not yet members of the Church. In the early centuries catechumens were never numbered with the *faithful,* but formed a class apart and were not even permitted to be present at Mass.

---

[16] The term *infant* includes all persons, of whatever age, who have not attained the age of discretion, i.e., sufficient use of reason to distinguish between right and wrong.

[17] Benedict XIV, "Singulari nos," Feb. 9, 1749.

[18] Roman Missal, "Mass of the Presanctified."

1. Manifest Heretics and Schismatics

A heretic is usually defined as a Christian, i.e., a baptized person, who holds a doctrine contrary to revealed truth; but this definition is inaccurate, since it would make heretics of a large portion of the faithful. A doctrine contrary to revealed truth is usually stigmatized as heretical, but a person who professes an heretical doctrine is not necessarily a heretic. *Heresy,* from the Greek *hairesis,* signifies a *choosing;* therefore a heretic is one who chooses for himself in matters of faith, thereby rejecting the authority of the Church established by Christ to teach all men the truths of revelation. He rejects the authority of the Church by following his own judgment or by submitting to an authority other than that established by Christ. A person who submits to the authority of the Church and wishes to accept all her teachings, is not a heretic, even though he profess heretical doctrines through ignorance of what the Church really teaches; he implicitly accepts the true doctrine in his general intention to accept all that the Church teaches.

A person may reject the teaching authority of the Church knowingly and willingly, or he may do it through ignorance. In the first case he is a *formal* heretic, guilty of grievous sin; in the second case, he is a *material* heretic, free from guilt. Both formal and material heresy may be *manifest* or *occult.* Heresy is *manifest* when publicly known to such an extent that its existence could be proved in a court of law; it is *occult* if not externally manifested by word or act, or if not sufficiently public to allow proof of its existence in court.

The word *schism* is derived from the Greek *schisma* which means a *division* or *separation;* hence a schismatic is a Christian who separates from the Church by rejecting her ruling authority. He may do this by refusing submission to his bishop, no less than by rejecting the supreme authority of the Roman Pontiff. It is evident, however, that a person does not become a schismatic by a mere act of disobedience; there must be some word or act that involves rejection of authority. Schism, like heresy, may be *formal* or *material, manifest* or *occult.*

EXCLUDED FROM MEMBERSHIP. Manifest heretics and schismatics are excluded from membership in the Church. Heretics separate themselves from the unity of faith and worship; schismatics from the unity of government, and both reject the authority of the Church. So far as exclusion from the Church is concerned, it matters not whether the heresy or schism be formal or material. Those born and reared in heresy or schism may be sincere in their belief and practice, yet they publicly and willingly reject the Church and attach themselves to sects opposed to her; they are not guilty of sin in the matter, but they are not members of the Church. For this reason, the Church makes no distinction between formal and material heresy when receiving converts into her fold.

There is no need to adduce arguments from Scripture or tradition for a truth that is practically self-evident. St. Jerome says: "An adulterer, a homicide, and other sinners are driven from the Church by the priests (i.e., by excommunication); but heretics pass sentence upon themselves, leaving the Church by their own free-will."[19] St. Augustine gives expression to the same doctrine: "If you do not wish to belong to the Church, . . . separate yourselves from her members, put yourselves off from her body. But why should I now urge them to leave the Church, since they have already done this? They are heretics, and therefore already out."[20]

Objections Considered

OBJECTION I.—Heretics and schismatics retain the baptismal character, a perpetual sign of their initiation into the Church. Therefore, they also remain members of the Church, whose rite of initiation they have received.

ANSWER.—The spiritual character imprinted upon the soul in Baptism does not make one a member of the Church; it is rather a sign or badge showing that he has received the rites of initiation, but it does not prove that he retains membership. This may be illustrated by the case of a person receiving a tattoo mark as a sign of initiation into a society that uses such marking. If the person afterward leave the society, he would cease to be a member, though he still bore the indelible sign of his initiation.

OBJECTION II.—The Church claims jurisdiction over heretics and schismatics, as is evident from the fact that she formerly interpreted many of her marriage laws as binding upon them. But the Church could not thus exercise jurisdiction over persons who do not belong to her fold, for as St. Paul says: "For what have I to do with judging those outside? . . . For those outside God will judge."[21]

ANSWER.—This objection overlooks the necessary distinction between *members* and *subjects*. A person may be subject to a society even though he is not a member. This is a well-known fact in our own

---

[19] "In Titum," iii, 10; P.L., 26, 597.
[20] "Sermon.," 181; P.L., 38, 980.
[21] 1 Cor. v, 12-13.

civil life; persons coming to our shores from foreign countries are not members (citizens) of our government until they have been naturalized by legal process, yet they are subject to our State and Federal laws. Likewise, citizens by naturalization or birth, who lose their rights of citizenship for any reason, cease to be members of the State, but remain subject to its laws so long as they remain within its borders. Heretics and schismatics lose their rights of citizenship in the Church; they cease to be members, but they remain subject to her laws so long as they remain within her territory, which comprises the whole world.

2. Excommunicates

Just as a person cannot enter a society against its wishes, so neither can he retain membership therein against its expressed will. It is acknowledged by all that a society, not subject to a higher jurisdiction, has full power and authority to expel a member with or without cause. In the latter case it would act unjustly, but none the less effectively.

The Church, being a society subject to no authority save that of Christ, must also have the right to deprive members of communion with her, unless Christ has ordained otherwise, which we know He has not done. On the contrary, He gave the Church full authority in the matter when He said: "Whatever you bind on earth shall be bound also in heaven,"[22] and again when He said: "But if he refuse to hear even the Church, let him be to thee as the heathen and the publican," i.e., let him be excluded from membership. St. Paul seems to have been the first to exercise this power by excommunicating the incestuous Corinthian.[23]

A person expelled from the Church loses the benefits and privileges of membership and is deprived of communion with the faithful; for this reason he is said to be *ex-communicated*. The Church exercises this power, for the most part, by decreeing that any person guilty of certain specified sins is excommunicated by that very fact. In some cases, however, excommunication does not take place until judicial sentence has been pronounced against a person proved guilty of a crime for which such punishment has been established by law. The first is known as excommunication *latae sententiae;* the second as excommunication *ferendae sententiae.*

Excommunication, like heresy and schism, may be either *manifest* or *occult*. Manifest excommunication is incurred by judicial sentence of excommunication, or by commission of a public sin known to in-

---

[22] Matt. xviii, 17-18.
[23] 1 Cor. v, 1-5.

volve the punishment of excommunication. Occult excommunication is incurred by the secret commission of a sin to which excommunication is attached by law. Those who incur manifest excommunication are either *vitandi* or *tolerati*. The former are deprived of communication with the faithful so far as possible even in civil and social life; they are to be entirely avoided (*vitandi*). The second class are deprived of communion with the faithful in things spiritual, but may be tolerated (*tolerati*) in civil and social matters. No one incurs excommunication unless he knows before commission of the crime that it involves such punishment; consequently there can be no question of *formal* and *material* excommunication.

Since the Church may deprive a person of all the privileges and benefits of membership in punishment for sin, it follows, as a matter of course, that she may also deprive him of any part of them short of actual exclusion from membership. Consequently it depends upon the intention of the Church whether excommunication shall involve actual loss of membership or not. The new Code of Canon Law defines excommunication as "a censure by which a person *is excluded from the communion of the faithful.*"[24] This can scarcely mean anything less than complete loss of membership in the Church; at least when there is question of excommunication in all its severity. For this reason all theologians are agreed that the *vitandi* lose all membership in the Church. In regard to the *tolerati,* the answer is not so certain. Since the canon just cited makes no distinctions, it would seem that all excommunicates without exception are excluded from the Church. Another canon, however, does make a distinction between these two classes; it provides that an excommunicated person be deprived of the benefits and emoluments arising from any office or dignity that he may hold in the Church, and in case of a *vitandus,* the office or dignity itself is lost.[25] It is evident, then, that a *toleratus* does not lose his office or dignity in the Church, but it is not at all probable that the Church would exclude a person from membership and still allow him to hold an office or dignity of any kind.

COROLLARY I. A person unjustly excommunicated loses membership in the Church; he is deprived of the Sacraments and all other benefits arising from union with the Church. In this case he can only rely upon the mercy and goodness of God to compensate him in some other way for the loss unjustly sustained until such time as the excommunication is lifted.[26] It should be noted, however, that the caution

---

[24] Canon 2257.
[25] Canon 2266.
[26] Cf. Dorsch, "De Ecclesia Christi," p. 412.

exercised by the Church in such matters makes an injustice of this kind practically impossible.

COROLLARY II. Excommunication is an official juridical act; therefore, an excommunicated person, although reconciled to God by an act of perfect contrition, is not reinstated in the Church until the censure of excommunication has been lifted by another official act on the part of the Church.

An excommunicated person remains a subject of the Church, bound by all her laws, just as a person deprived of citizenship still remains a subject of the country in which he lives.

ART. IV. PERSONS OF DOUBTFUL MEMBERSHIP

1. Persons Invalidly Baptized

There is room for doubt concerning the membership of persons who have been invalidly baptized,[27] or not baptized at all, yet are publicly known as Catholics and live as such in the firm conviction that they have been baptized. Many eminent theologians, e.g., Bellarmine, Palmieri, and Straub,[28] maintain that such persons are true members of the Church because the necessary conditions are fulfilled; the persons in question submit to the teaching and ruling authority of the Church, and she, on her part, publicly recognizes them as members by admitting them to the Sacraments and other privileges of membership. Innocent II is also cited in support of this opinion because of the reply he made to inquiries concerning such a person: "I do not hesitate to assert that the person who died, as you say, without Baptism, was freed from original sin and has obtained the joys of Heaven because he persevered in the faith of holy mother, the Church, and in the confession of Christ's name."[29]

Dorsch and Wilmers[30] are of the opinion that such persons cannot be considered members of the Church because they are incapable of receiving the other Sacraments validly, and therefore, do not participate in the most essential benefits of the Church. They are publicly regarded as members, but wrongly so; being regarded a member and being a member are two different things. These authors rightly claim that the words of Innocent II prove nothing in the matter, since he does not say that the person in question was a member of the Church;

---

[27] "Invalidly baptized," i.e., an invalid ceremony of Baptism was performed.
[28] Bellarmine, "De Ecclesia Militante," iii, 10; Palmieri, "DeRomano Pontifice," Proleg., xi, 4; Straub, "De Ecclesia Christi," n. 1304-1307.
[29] Denzinger, n. 388.
[30] Wilmers, "De Ecclesia Christi," p. 627; Dorsch, "De Ecclesia Christi," p. 401.

he simply says thas he attained salvation, which, as all theologians admit, can be obtained by perfect contrition and desire for membership in the Church, if actual membership is impossible. The question is of little practical importance, since the number of such persons will always be small, and their salvation cannot be affected in the least by our opinions, one way or the other, in the matter.

2. Occult Heretics and Schismatics

The condition of occult heretics and schismatics in regard to membership in the Church has long been a matter of dispute among theologians. Many such as Bellarmine, Cornelius a Lapide, Perrone, Palmieri, Straub, and Billot, maintain that they are true, even though very imperfect, members of the Church. Suarez, Franzelin, Billuart, Dorsch,[31] and others hold that they are not members, and, therefore, belong to the Church in appearance only. Practically speaking, the question has little importance, because, as we shall see, such persons are always in bad faith; consequently membership or lack of membership makes little or no difference in their spiritual condition. The matter is considered here simply because it helps to a better understanding of the real nature of membership in the Church.

The question concerns only such as are publicly regarded as Catholics, because the moment one becomes publicly known as a heretic or a schismatic, his heresy or schism ceases to be *occult,* and there is no longer any doubt that he has lost membership in the Church. Here, then, we have to consider only such as outwardly conduct themselves as Catholics, but inwardly reject the authority of the Church; in a word, those who are hypocrites in their adherence to the Church. Since it is practically impossible for a person to act thus in good faith, *material* heresy and schism may be disregarded in this connection. The question then narrows itself down to this: Does a person who conducts himself outwardly as a Catholic while inwardly rejecting the Church, still belong to it? This is but another phase of the question referred to in connection with the unity of the Church: Is interior faith necessary for the unity of the Church, or is the mere external profession of a faith that does not inwardly exist, sufficient? The question under either form is still debated, but most of the arguments adduced by both sides are merely disguised statements asserting or denying that interior faith is necessary. Those wishing to pursue the subject further may consult the authors mentioned above.

---

[31] Consult these various authors in their respective works on the Church.

ART. V. NECESSITY OF MEMBERSHIP

KINDS OF NECESSITY. In regard to attaining salvation, theologians distinguish between those things which are necessary by a *necessity of means* and those which are necessary by a *necessity of precept.* The former are the *means* to salvation, constituted such by their nature or by divine institution; the latter are necessary simply because prescribed by law. Matters of mere precept are necessary because by omitting them we commit grievous sin, which excludes salvation; consequently whatever excuses from sin in these matters also excuses from their necessity, e.g., fasting before Communion is necessary for salvation because violating the fast constitutes a grievous sin, but any circumstance that renders this violation licit also takes away the necessity for the fast. The case is quite different with those things necessary as the *means* to salvation; they cannot be omitted without loss of salvation, even though the omission be without fault on our part. In some cases the thing is *absolutely* necessary, because it is of such nature that nothing can supply for its absence; e.g., sanctifying grace is an *absolute* necessity, whose absence cannot be supplied by anything else. Other things are necessary, not by their very nature, but by divine institution. In regard to these things God is pleased to accept substitutes when the things themselves cannot be had. Such means of salvation may be called *relatively* necessary, to distinguish them from those of *absolute* necessity. Baptism is an example of a *relative* necessity for salvation; it is a necessary *means* of salvation, because Christ has so ordained, but if for any reason it is impossible to receive Baptism, its absence can be supplied by perfect contrition and a sincere desire to receive it. The reason for this is obvious: God, being all-wise and merciful, cannot demand the impossible from His creatures.

With this brief explanation, we proceed to show that membership in the Church is necessary by the twofold necessity of precept and means, but that the necessity of means is only relative.

1. Twofold Necessity of Membership

Thesis.—Membership in the Church Is Necessary Both by
Necessity of Means and Necessity of Precept

The doctrine set forth in the thesis is a dogma of faith, since the Church has often declared membership in her fold necessary for salvation. The Fourth Lateran Council decreed: "There is one universal Church, out of which no one can be saved."[32] Even stronger are the

---

[32] Denzinger, n. 430.

words of Boniface VIII: "We declare, say, define, and pronounce that subjection to the Roman Pontiff is strictly necessary to all men for salvation."[33] Pius IX declared that "It must be held as an article of faith that out of the Apostolic Roman Church no one can be saved."[34] These declarations are sufficient to prove that the thesis is a dogma of faith, at least in regard to necessity of precept.

PROOFS. I. FROM REASON. Christ said that no one can come to the Father, except through the Son, who is the *way, the truth and the life.*"[35] But the Church bears the person of Christ to carry out His mission on earth; therefore, no one can come to the Father except through the Church. The Church is also the Mystical Body of Christ; consequently no one can receive the vivifying influence of Christ the Head, nor be animated by the Soul, which is the Holy Spirit, unless he be united as a member with the Body. Hence St. Augustine says: "A Christian man is a Catholic while he remains in the body; cut off, he becomes a heretic. The Spirit does not follow the amputated member."[36]

II. FROM SCRIPTURE. In Holy Scripture, Baptism, faith, and subjection to the authority of the Church are set forth as necessary means of salvation: "Unless a man be born again of water and the Holy Spirit, he cannot enter the kingdom of God."[36a] "He that believeth and is baptized shall be saved; but he that believeth not shall be condemned."[37] "If he will not hear the Church, let him be to thee as the heathen and publican."[38] The conditions laid down in these passages as necessary for salvation are precisely the conditions necessary for membership in the Church. Therefore, it is only by becoming a member of the Church that one can fulfill the conditions for salvation: in other words, membership in the Church is a necessary means of salvation.

God has destined all men to salvation; "who wishes all men to be saved and to come to the knowledge of the truth."[39] Therefore the means necessary for salvation must be a matter of precept. Again, Christ sent forth His Apostles with the injunction to bring all nations into the Church and to teach them all truth: "Go, therefore, and make disciples of all nations . . . teaching them to observe all things that I have commanded you."[40] Such an injunction on the part of Christ necessarily

---

[33] "Unam Sanctam," Denz., n. 469.
[34] Allocutio die 9 Dec., 1834; Denzinger, n. 1647.
[35] John xiv, 6.
[36] "Sermon.," 267; P.L., 38, 1231.
[36a] John iii, 5.
[37] Mark xvi, 15.
[38] Matt. xviii, 17.
[39] 1 Tim. ii, 4.
[40] Matt. xxviii, 19.

presupposes a corresponding command that all nations hearken to the teachings of the Apostles and become disciples by entering the Church. There are also the express words of Christ demanding this: "He who hears you, hears me and he who rejects you, rejects me; and he who rejects me, rejects him who sent me."[41] Hence union with the Church is a matter of divine command; it is a necessity of precept.

III. FROM TRADITION. The Fathers have from the very earliest ages, insisted upon the necessity of union with the Church. For example:

a) *St. Ignatius Martyr:* "Do not be deceived, brethren, if any one follows a person making a schism, he cannot obtain the inheritance of the divine kingdom."[42]

b) *Origen:* "Let no one deceive himself; outside this house, i.e., outside the Church, no one can be saved."[43]

c) *Council of Cirta* (A. D. 412): "If a person be separated from the Catholic Church, it matters not how praiseworthy his life may be otherwise, he shall not have life, but the anger God rests upon him for this one crime of separation."[44]

d) St. Cyprian: "He cannot have God for his Father who does not have the Church for his mother. If anyone escaped death outside the ark of Noah, then also may a person escape outside the Church."[45]

2. Membership a Relative Necessity

Membership in the Church is necessary for salvation not only by necessity of precept, but also by necessity of *means;* Christ *commands* all men to belong to the Church because it is the *means* which he established for salvation. Hence the well-known axiom of theologians, "Out of the Church there is no salvation." Pius IX declared this an article of faith, as already noted, but he immediately added: "It is likewise certain that those who are in ignorance of the true religion, are not accountable for any guilt in the matter before God if the ignorance be invincible."[46] On another occasion he wrote to the bishops of Italy: "It is known to us and to you that those who are in invincible ignorance concerning our most holy religion . . . can attain eternal life by the power of divine light and grace."[47] St. Augustine says: "The effects of Baptism are invisibly wrought when the ministry of Baptism is ex-

[41] Luke x, 16.
[42] "Epist. ad Philad.," 3; Funk, I, 267.
[43] "Hom. in Josue," IV, 5; P.G., 12, 841.
[44] "Epist.," 141; P.L., 33, 579.
[45] "De Unitate Ecclesiae"; P.L., 4, 503.
[46] Allocutio die 9 Dec., 1854; Denzinger, n. 1647.
[47] Pius IX, "Quanto conficiamus moerore," Aug. 10, 1863. Denz. n. 1677.

cluded, not through contempt of religion, but by force of necessity."[48] We also know that the Church numbers among her saints persons who died without the Sacrament of Baptism; v.g., St. Emerentiana, a catechumen who suffered martyrdom in the third century, is commemorated as a saint.

These facts prove that membership in the Church is a *relative necessity*, i.e., if actual membership is impossible for any reason, other means are available to supply the deficiency. This is usually explained by distinguishing between membership in the soul of the Church and membership in the external society, or body of the Church. According to this explanation, a person in ignorance of the true Church or otherwise hindered from entering it, belongs to the soul of the Church if he be in the state of sanctifying grace through perfect contrition or an act of perfect love of God. Hence it is said that membership in the soul of the Church is an absolute necessity of means for salvation, whereas membership in the body of the Church is merely a necessity of precept. But the Church herself never makes this distinction between body and soul, when there is question of membership in her fold, and it has already been noted that a person cannot belong to the soul of the Church unless he also belongs to her body.[49] Moreover, all Scriptural texts cited to prove the necessity of membership in the Church refer directly to the Church as an external organization. Therefore, union with the body of the Church is a necessity of *means*, no less than union with the soul of the Church.

"Out of the Church there is no salvation" is a dogma of faith, and membership in the Church means union with the body as well as with the soul of the Church; yet it is certain that persons who do not externally belong to the Church may be saved. How are these facts to be reconciled? Cardinal Bellarmine gives the true explanation: "When we say, *Out of the Church there is no salvation,* it must be understood of those who belong to the Church neither *in fact* nor *in desire,* as theologians commonly teach concerning Baptism."[50] The necessity of belonging to the Church,—both body and soul,—is a *relative* necessity of means; if actual membership is impossible, it can be supplied by perfect contrition, or perfect love of God, with the desire to belong to the true Church of Christ. This is evident from the fact that Baptism is the rite of initiation into the Church,—the *door* to the Church, as the Council of Trent calls it. The necessity of membership in the Church

[48] "De Baptismo," iv, 22; P.L., 43, 173
[49] See above, p. 119.
[50] "De Ecclesia," III, 9.

must be the same as the necessity for the rite by which one becomes a member. But all admit that Baptism is a relative necessity of means; when its actual reception is impossible, perfect contrition or perfect love of God, with the *desire* to receive it, will effect the same results as far as the mere attainment of salvation is concerned, but the person has not received the Sacrament of Baptism nor has the baptismal character been imprinted upon his soul.

OBJECTION. It may be objected that a person in the state of sanctifying grace is necessarily united with the Holy Spirit dwelling within him and that, therefore, he belongs to the soul of the Church, the Holy Spirit, although he does not belong to the external society or body of the Church. The conclusion does not follow. The Holy Spirit is not restricted in His operations to the limits of the Church: "The Spirit breatheth where He will."[51] He operates outside the Church, just as He operates outside the Sacraments, distributing graces as He will. But the person receiving the grace no more belongs to the Church in the one case, than he actually receives a Sacrament in the other. In neither case is the Holy Spirit acting in His capacity as soul of the Church.

COROLLARY I. A person who knowingly and willingly remains outside of the Church and dies in that condition, cannot hope for salvation; he has rejected Christ by rejecting His Church: "He who hears you, hears me."[52] But a person who is out of the Church through no fault of his own, can obtain salvation by an act of perfect contrition, or perfect love of God and, at least, an implicit desire to belong to the Church. He is then a member of the Church, both of the body and of the soul, not in fact but in desire,—*non in re sed in voto*. The desire to belong to the Church is implicitly contained in the general desire to do all that Christ commands, even though the person never heard of the Church or actually rejects it through ignorance of its real character.

COROLLARY II. All men are bound to belong to the true Church of Christ, because He has so commanded, and also because it is the means established by Him for our salvation. Therefore, it is absolutely wrong to maintain that it matters not to what Church a man belongs, provided he accept Christ as his personal Saviour and lead a virtuous life. Even those in good faith, sincerely believing that they really belong to the true Church, are far less secure of their salvation than they would be in the Church with the use of the Sacraments and other means of salvation found there.

[51] John iii, 6.
[52] Luke x, 16.

COROLLARY III. As all men are bound to belong to the true Church of Christ, so also are they bound to use all possible efforts to find and embrace it, despite any temporal losses that may ensue. The amount of effort necessary will depend upon each one's ability and the opportunity presented for study and investigation. Investigation is impossible for the person who sincerely and firmly believes that he already possesses the true Church, but the moment a doubt or suspicion arises in his mind, he is bound to use all means at his command to discover, the truth. If a sincere and serious effort fails to bring him to the truth, he is still in invincible ignorance and, therefore, guiltless of his errors before God.

CHAPTER VII

AUTHORITY OF THE CHURCH

Having considered the membership of the Church and the bonds by which the individual members are united into a visible society, we now turn our attention to the power of authority that preserves these bonds of union and enables the Church to attain the purpose of her existence by bringing the fruits of Redemption to all men. The existence and origin of authority in the Church are self-evident. Being a true society, the Church necessarily possesses authority of some sort, and since Christ is the Author and supreme Head of the Church, whatever authority she possesses must come from Him. It has also been proved that Christ conferred upon His Church the power and authority to teach, govern, and sanctity,[1] as the very nature and purpose of the Church demanded.

Every society is directed to the attainment of its purposes by the power of ruling which is more properly called *authority;* there must also be suitable means for attaining the end sought and power to use them effectively. The end to be obtained by the Church requires acceptance of certain truths as well as the observance of precepts, for "without faith it is impossible to please God,"[2] and "faith without works is dead."[3] Therefore, authority in the Church requires submission of intellect and will; in other words, the Church has authority to teach as well as authority to rule in the stricter sense of that term. And since the salvation of souls is the immediate end of the Church, she must also have the priestly power of sanctification. This power is concerned with the offering of sacrifice and the administration of Sacraments; its treatment belongs more properly to Sacramental Theology. The authority to teach is intimately connected with the infallibility of the Church and will be considered in connection with it. The present chapter, therefore, will be limited to the power of government, or authority in the strict sense of the word.

ART. I. AUTHORITY TO GOVERN

Synopsis.—1. Threefold Powers of Government.—2. Right of Temporal Punishment.—3. Right to Inflict Corporal Punishment.—4. Persons Subject to Punitive Power.

---

[1] Cf. above, pp. 10 sq.
[2] Heb. xi, 6.
[3] Jas. ii, 20.

1. Threefold Power of Government

Government implies a threefold power,—*legislative, judicial,* and *coercitive.* Government without laws is impossible but laws without interpretation and application are worthless; there must be an authority to interpret the laws officially and to judge whether they have been violated in individual cases. Both the law-making power and the judicial power presupposes coercitive power; a law without sanction, i.e., without power to enforce its observance by adequate punishment, is not a law but a mere counsel: and a judicial sentence that cannot be executed by force, if necessary, is a pure travesty.[4] It is evident, then that Christ conferred this threefold power upon His Church by the very fact that He instituted it under the form of a society. Moreover, we have the express words of Our Lord referring to each of these powers separately, and we find the Apostles exercising them from the very first days of their ministry.

I. LEGISLATIVE POWER. Christ conferred the law-making power upon His Apostles when He said to them: "Whatever you bind on earth shall be bound also in heaven, and whatever you loose on earth shall be loosed also in heaven."[5] The words *bind* and *loose* refer to bonds which, by the very nature of the case, can be none other than moral bonds, or laws, by which the faithful are obliged to do something or leave something undone. The Apostles themselves understood the words in this sense, for we find them exercising the power to make laws from the very beginning. At the Council of Jerusalem they decreed: "For the Holy Spirit and we have decided to lay no further burden upon you but this indispensable one, that you abstain from things sacrificed to idols and from immorality."[6] This decree had the force of law in all the churches, for it is said that St. Paul "traveled through Syria and Cilicia, and strengthened the churches (and commanded them to keep the precepts of the apostles and presbyters)."[7] St. Luke also says that St. Paul and Timothy "passed through the cities, they delivered to the brethren for their observance the decisions arrived at by the apostles and presbyters in Jerusalem."[8] St. Paul himself decreed that women should pray with head covered, and that no one should be bishop if married a second time.[9] He also warned the

---

[4] Cf. Murray, "De Ecclesia Christi," Disp. xv, n. 26.
[5] Matt. xviii, 18.
[6] Acts xv, 28-29.
[7] Acts xv, 41.
[8] Acts xvi, 4.
[9] 1 Cor. xi, 5 sq.; 1 Tim. iii, 1 sq.

faithful to "obey your superiors and be subject to them, for they keep watch as having to render an account of your souls."[10]

II. JUDICIAL POWER. The words of Christ presuppose judicial powers in the Church, for He said: "But if thy brother sin against thee, . . . appeal to the Church, but if he refuse to hear even the Church, let him be to thee as the heathen and the publican."[11] It is evident that our Lord does not command such a case to be brought before the Church for mere counsel or advice; it is to be a judicial proceeding, and should the guilty party refuse to comply with the sentence, he is to be excommunicated: "Let him be to thee as the heathen and publican."

The Apostles certainly knew what powers they had received from the Divine Master, and we find them exercising judicial as well as legislative power. St. Peter passed judgment upon Ananias and Saphira,[12] and St. Paul gave judgment in the case of the incestuous Corinthian: "I indeed absent in body but present in spirit, have already, as though present, passed judgment, . . . in the name of our Lord Jesus Christ on the one who has so acted."[13] He even laid down rules for the guidance of Timothy in hearing cases against priests accused of misconduct.[14] This presupposes that Timothy had power and authority to hear and judge such cases according to their merits.

III. COERCITIVE POWER. Christ plainly acknowledged coercitive, or punitive, power in the Church, when He said: "If he will not hear even the Church, let him be to thee as the heathen and publican." Excommunication is the severest form of punishment known in the Church. St. Paul exercises this power when he excommunicated the Corinthian and delivered him "to Satan for the destruction of the flesh, that his spirit may be saved in the day of our Lord Jesus Christ."[15] He also excommunicated Hymeneus and Alexander, whom he "delivered up to Satan, that they may learn not to blaspheme."[16] Now, if the Church has authority to inflict the supreme penalty of excommunication, she also has power to inflict lesser punishments.

Appeal to tradition in regard to these powers of the Church is needless, since it is well known to all that she has ever claimed and exercised legislative, judicial, and punitive powers. This is evident from the canons of councils, the decrees of popes, and the acts of individual bishops. In every age the Church has established laws, judged the

[10] Heb. xiii, 17.
[11] Matt. xviii, 15 sq.
[12] Acts v, 1 sq.
[13] 1 Cor. v, 3.
[14] 1 Tim. v, 19 sq.
[15] 1 Cor. v, 5.
[16] 1 Tim. I:20.

erring and the guilty, and punished those who refused to submit to
her authority.

2. Right of Temporal Punishment

Punishment consists in depriving a person of some good in reparation for an offense.[17] Hence there are three kinds of punishment, corresponding to the three orders of goods,—*spiritual, temporal,* and *corporal.* Spiritual punishment deprives one of some spiritual good, the
use of the Sacraments, participation in the prayers of the Church, communion with the faithful, and the like. Temporal punishment deprives
one of the goods of this world by fines, confiscation, inability to hold
office, and the like. Corporal punishment affects the very person of the
offender by depriving him of bodily comforts, freedom, and even life
itself.[18]

Thesis.—The Church Has Authority to Impose Both Temporal and Corporal Punishments

This is a defined dogma of Catholic faith, as appears from the condemnation of the following propositions; one by Pius VI, the other
by Pius IX, who stigmatized them as *heretical:* "It does not belong to
the Church to exact obedience to her decrees by external force," and
"The Church has no right to coerce the violators of her laws by temporal punishments."[19] To these proofs may be added the decrees of
several ecumenical councils; the second Council of Lyons, the fourth
Lateran Council, the Council of Vienna, and the Council of Constance
decreed fines and imprisonment for various crimes. The new Code of
Canon Law declares that the Church has an innate right, independent
of any human authority, to coerce her delinquent subjects by temporal
as well as spiritual punishment.[20]

PROOFS. The Church, being a society, even more perfect and independent than the State, must have coercive powers at least equal to
those of the State. Therefore, she has authority to inflict any just punishment which she finds necessary or useful, unless Christ has ordained
otherwise. But Christ has not forbidden the use of temporal or corporal punishment, and such punishment is often useful or even necessary.

---

[17] Suarez, "De Fide," xx, 3, 13.
[18] In connection with indulgences, *temporal* punishments are often mentioned as
distinct from *eternal.* Here the word is used in opposition to *spiritual.* As a general
term it includes corporal punishment as well as those known simply as temporal.
[19] Denzinger, n. 1504, 1697.
[20] Codex Juris Canonici, can. 2214.

I. NOT FORBIDDEN. Christ never denied the Church the use of temporal or corporal punishment; on the contrary, he implicitly granted authority to use it when He said: "Whatever you bind on earth shall be bound also in heaven."[21] These words, universal in themselves, are not limited by the context nor by any other ordinance of Christ. They refer directly and primarily to moral obligations, but these include the obligation to undergo punishment inflicted by the Church just as our moral obligations to the State include that of submitting to just punishment.

II. USEFUL. The Church is a spiritual society, because the end to be attained is spiritual; consequently the means to that end will be in large measure spiritual. On the other hand, the Church is composed of human beings, who do not always yield to purely spiritual motives. Therefore, temporal, and even corporal, punishments must be resorted to at times by the Church as well as by the State. St. Augustine recognized this fact, although he was opposed to temporal and corporal punishments except as a last resort. He says: "It is better indeed for men to be brought to the worship of God by doctrine, than to be compelled by fear and pain; but these means are not to be neglected because the other is better. Experience has proved and still proves that it is profitable to many to be forced by fear and pain that they may afterward be taught."[22]

3. Right to Inflict Corporal Punishment

Many theologians maintain that although the Church has the authority to *decree* corporal punishment, she has no authority to actually *inflict* it, but must call upon the State,—the *secular arm* as they call it,— to execute the sentence. In confirmation of this opinion they cite the words of Boniface VIII: "The Gospels teach us that there are two swords in the power of the Church,—one spiritual, the other temporal. . . . One is to be exercised *for* the Church, the other *by* the Church. One is wielded by the hand of the priest; the other by the hands of kings and soldiers, but according to the will and permission of the priest."[23] These words, however, are not to the point, because Boniface was not treating of

---

[21] Matt. xviii, 16.

[22] "Epist. ad Bonifatium," 6; P.L., 33, 802.—The so-called Reformers of the sixteenth century taught that heretics should suffer temporal and corporal punishment, but in accordance with their system they assigned the power of punishment to the State. Calvin and Beza wrote works in defense of this doctrine, and Beza quotes Luther and Melanchthon as advocates of it. Calvin was the instigator and prime mover in having Michael Servetus burned at the stake as a heretic.

[23] "Unam sanctam"; Denzinger, n. 469.

the coercive power of the Church, but of the relations between Church and State.

It seems that the Church has never inflicted corporal punishment directly, but it is certain that she has often turned persons over to the State for corporal punishment and demanded under pain of excommunication that such punishment be administered. The difference between this and direct administration of the punishment is slight indeed. Moreover, it would be strange for the Church to have authority with no inherent right to use it, yet such would be the case if she could not directly inflict corporal punishments. Prudence, of course, may often prevent the exercise of a power that is otherwise licit, for, as St. Paul says, power is "given me for upbuilding, and not for destruction."[24] There seems to be nothing but the law of prudence to prevent the Church from inflicting corporal punishment directly and in her own name whenever she deems it necessary or useful.

4. Persons Subject to Punitive Powers

It is evident that only members of the Church are subject to her spiritual punishments, since they alone enjoy spiritual benefits of which she can deprive them in punishment for crime. In regard to temporal and corporal punishments, three classes of persons must be considered,—members of the Church, baptized persons who are not members, and unbaptized persons. There is no doubt that the Church has full authority to punish her own members by spiritual, temporal, or corporal punishments, as she deems best. It is likewise certain that the Church has no authority to punish or coerce the unbaptized, since they are neither members nor subjects. The Fathers and theologians of the Church are unanimous on this point. St. Paul says: "What have I to do with judging those outside? . . . For those outside God will judge."[25] From this it follows that the Church can never use force of any kind to bring persons into her fold, nor to make them accept her doctrines; but she may use force against those who unjustly invade her rights or the spiritual rights of her members. This is merely the natural right of self-protection granted to every individual and to every lawful group of individuals.

Since all baptized persons are subjects of the Church, even though they may not be members, it follows that heretics and schismatics are subject to the coercive or punitive authority of the Church, but the exer-

---

[24] 2 Cor. xiii, 10.
[25] 1 Cor. v, 12-13.

cise of this authority would be unjust and illicit in the case of those who are out of the Church through no fault of their own. Punishment, by its very nature, presupposes guilt, but in the supposition there is no guilt, and the use of force in such cases would only result in evil for the Church and spiritual harm to those coerced. Hence the Church can exercise punitive or coercive power against none but her own members and against formal heretics or schismatics, i.e., those who are out of the Church through their own fault. The fear of the Church, entertained by many non-Catholics because of her supposed claims in this matter, is groundless. The doctrine of the Church forbids the use of force to bring any one into her fold, and history proves that she has never resorted to force for this purpose. The much dreaded Inquisition was instituted to search out and punish heretics, but only such as had fallen away from the Church through their own fault. Its purpose was to bring back such persons to a sense of the duties they had freely accepted and acknowledged. Whether this was psychologically the best means to employ for the purpose, is another question, but there can be no doubt that the Church was acting within her rights. The state resorts to the same means when it searches out and punishes traitors, and in a lesser way, when it forces persons to fulfill obligations which they have undertaken. If force was ever used to bring persons into the Church, it was without her sanction and against her will.[26]

ART. II. NATURE OF CHURCH POWERS

POWERS OF CHRIST. Our Divine Saviour possesses a twofold power, corresponding to His dual nature as God and man. As God, He possesses a power that is infinite and divine; as man, He received a finite power that is human since it proceeds from His human nature, but divine in as much as it belongs to His divine Personality. It is evident that the Apostles did not participate in the power that proceeds from the divine nature of Christ, because man, being finite, cannot become the subject of an infinite power. Hence the power conferred upon the Church in the person of the Apostles is that which flows from the human nature of Christ,—the power which He himself had received: "All power in heaven and on earth HAS BEEN GIVEN TO ME. Go, therefore, and make disciples of all nations. . . . As the Father has sent me, I also send you."[27]

---

[26] Vacandard, "L'Inquisition" (Eng. trans. by B. L. Conway, C.S.P.).
[27] Matt. xxviii, 18; John xx, 21.

But the power proper to the human nature of Christ is also two-fold, because He came in the double capacity of priest and king. A priest, says St. Paul, "is appointed for men in the things pertaining to God, that he may offer gifts and sacrifices for sins."[28] Our Lord offered Himself on the cross as a propitiation for our sins, "he should reconcile to himself all things, . . . making peace through the blood of his cross."[29] Thus was He constituted a priest forever. He also came as king, to collect all men into His spiritual kingdom and direct them to their eternal destiny: "And he shall be king over the house of Jacob forever; and of his kingdom there shall be no end."[30] But His kingdom is a kingdom of truth: "Thou sayest it; I am a king. This is why I was born, and why I have come into the world, to bear witness to the truth. Everyone who is of the truth hears my voice."[31] Therefore, the kingdom of Christ requires submission of intellect as well as submission of will: "for he was teaching them as one having authority, and not as their Scribes and Pharisees."[32]

When Christ said to His Apostles: "As the Father hath sent me, I also send you," He made them partakers of all the powers proper to His human nature,—all the powers given to Him as priest and king. They were to go forth to *offer up gifts and sacrifices for sin* and to apply the fruits of His redemption through the administration of the Sacraments. They were also to teach and govern the disciples gathered from all nations into His Church.

POWERS LIMITED. The powers conferred upon the Church through the Apostles, seem all-comprehensive; "As the Father hath sent me, I also send you," and "Whatever you bind . . . whatever you loose." Yet these powers are necessarily limited to some extent, since all derived or delegated power is limited by the nature of the purpose for which it is given and by the nature of the society in which it is to be exercised. In regard to the powers of the priesthood, the Apostles received no authority to institute new Sacraments or to change essentially those already instituted. They were commanded to baptize according to a prescribed rite, and to offer a sacrifice instituted by Christ himself. They were simply agents to administer the Sacraments and to offer Sacrifice in the name of Christ and by His power.

In regard to governing power, the Apostles were constituted superiors to rule the Church already established by Christ; they received

---

[28] Heb. v, 1.
[29] Coloss. i, 20.
[30] Luke i, 32-33.
[31] John xviii, 37.
[32] Matt. vii, 29.

no authority to change or abolish it, much less to establish another.
Hence St. Paul speaks of the "power that the Lord has given me for
upbuilding, and not for destruction."[33] This is clearly implied in the
words addressed to St. Peter: "I will give thee the keys of the kingdom of heaven."[34] He that receives the keys of the house from the
master, receives power and authority to care for the house and to preserve it, not to destroy or change it. Hence the Apostles and their successors are the custodians who preside over the house of the Lord,
to guard and preserve both the house and the treasures which it contains. For this reason the rulers of the Church are called *bishops*, from
the Greek word *episkopein*, which means *to superintend* or *oversee*.

In regard to doctrine, the Apostles were commissioned to teach only
those things which Christ commanded: "Teach them to observe all
that I have commanded."[35] They could neither add to nor subtract
from the truths taught them by their Divine Master; they were but
the dispensers of His mysteries: "Let a man so account us, as servants
of Christ and stewards of the mysteries of God."[36]

MINISTERIAL POWER. When a person acts in the name and
by the authority of another, he is a mere instrument in the hands of
the one whom he represents; he is an agent or minister, and the power
or authority by which he acts is *ministerial*. The power of conferring
grace and forgiving sins in the Church is purely ministerial, because
the human agent is merely an instrument in the hands of Christ. For
this reason the one who confers a Sacrament is rightly called the minister of that Sacrament. It is Christ himself who confers the grace
through the instrumentality of the Sacrament and its minister. Hence
the Apostles always refer to themselves as *ministers of Christ* when
there is question of conferring grace or forgiving sins. St. Paul says:
"(Christ) by entrusting to us the message of reconciliation. On behalf
of Christ, therefore, we are acting as ambassadors, God, as it were,
appealing through us."[37] Again he says: "Was Paul then crucified for
you? Or were you baptized in the name of Paul?"[38] St. Augustine
explains this matter in regard to Baptism in particular. He says: "Lest
as many baptisms should be spoken of as there are servants who received power from the Lord to baptize, the Lord kept to Himself the
power of baptizing, and gave to His servants the ministry. The serv-

---

[33] 2 Cor. xiii, 10.
[34] Matt. xvi, 19.
[35] Matt. xxviii, 20.
[36] 1 Cor. iv, 1.
[37] 2 Cor. v, 19-20.
[38] 1 Cor. i, 13.

ant says that he baptizes; he says so rightly, as the Apostle says, 'And I baptized also the household of Stephanas,' but as a servant."[39] The Council of Florence has confirmed the teaching of St. Augustine by defining that "The Holy Trinity is the principal cause whence Baptism derives its efficacy, but the minister who confers the Sacrament externally is the instrumental cause."[40]

Since the minister of the Sacraments is only an instrument in the hands of God, the efficacy of a Sacrament does not depend upon the worthiness of the one who administers it, for, as St. Augustine says, "the special virtue of the Sacrament is like the light; it is received pure by those to be enlightened, and if it pass through the impure, it is not stained."[41]

In regard to priestly power, Christ is the supreme and only Head of the Church. No bishop or pope can confer this power, except in so far as he is an instrument in the hands of Christ to administer the Sacrament of Holy Orders, and in this matter the pope has no more power than any other bishop. When Orders are once validly conferred, no power on earth can revoke or annul them; therefore, even an excommunicated bishop can ordain a priest, consecrate a bishop, celebrate Mass, or confer any other Sacrament that does not require jurisdiction, just as validly as the Pope.

PRINCIPAL POWER. A person who acts in his own name and by his own power is a principal cause, and the power by which he acts is a *principal* power. If the power be that of commanding others, it is thereby constituted a superior. Authority may be obtained by virtue of an office, or it may be delegated by another; in either case it is a principal power if it is exercised in the name of the person who possesses it.

In regard to jurisdiction or power of ruling, the Apostles were constituted true superiors with authority to enact laws in their own name: "For the Holy Spirit and we have decided to lay no burden upon you."[42] The enactments of this first council are known as the decrees, not of Christ but of the Apostles and ancients: "He (Paul) travelled through Syria . . . and commanded them to keep the precepts of the apostles and presbyters."[43] When writing to the Corinthians, St. Paul lays down certain precepts in his own name and carefully distinguishes them from the precepts of Christ: "But to those who are married, not

---

[39] Augustine, "On the Gospel of St. John," v. 7; P.L., 35, 1417.
[40] Denzinger, n. 696.
[41] "On the Gospel of St. John," v. 15; P.L., 35, 1422.
[42] Acts xv, 28.
[43] Acts xv, 41.

I, but the Lord commands . . . for to the rest I say, not the Lord."[44] It is evident therefore that jurisdiction, or the power to rule, is a principal power conferred by Christ, but exercised by the Church in her own name. He who holds supreme jurisdiction in the Church is as truly head of the Church as a king is of his kingdom; no jurisdiction in the Church can be obtained or held against his will. Since the Church exercises a principal power in ruling, it also follows that she has full authority to abrogate or dispense from her laws at any time.

PROTESTANT TEACHING. Protestants in general seem to hold that all power in the Church is purely ministerial and consists in authority to preach the Gospel and administer the Sacraments. Stahl, a German Protestant, says: "With Protestants the Church is an electric conductor that conveys the divine spark to men. With Catholics it is a glowing iron having in itself the power of burning."[45] The simile is good, but wrongly applied. According to Protestant theology, the faith of the individual is the sole cause of justification; neither the Church nor the Sacraments have any intrinsic efficacy. Consequently faith, not the Church, should be compared to an electric conductor. According to Catholic teaching, the Church is both an electric conductor and a glowing iron;—an electric conductor in the power of Orders, where it acts merely as the agent of Christ; a glowing iron in the power of jurisdiction, which the Church exercises in her own name.

CHURCH POWERS PERPETUAL. Perpetuity of the powers of the Church is a necessary consequence of her perpetual indefectibility. It follows also from the very purpose for which the Church was instituted, namely, the glory of God and the salvation of souls. The power of Orders is directly concerned with both; therefore, it must exist so long as there are men on earth to attain salvation through the proper worship of God. The power of jurisdiction is ordained for the government of the Church, a visible society that must endure until the end of time; therefore, this power itself must be perpetual. Finally Christ has promised perpetual powers to His Church: "And behold, I am with you all days, even unto the consummation of the world."[46]

---

[44] 1 Cor. vii, 10 sq.
[45] Fr. J. Stahl, "Gegenwartige Parteien in Staat und Kirche," p. 373.
[46] Matt. xxviii, 20.

CHAPTER VIII

RULERS OF THE CHURCH

The nature of the powers conferred upon the Church being determined, the further question arises: To whom were these powers committed? To the whole body of the faithful, or to superiors divinely commissioned to teach, govern, and sanctify? The answer to this question demands (1) a notice of the principal errors in the matter; (2) proof that Christ himself instituted a ruling body in the Church by conferring all power and authority upon the Apostles and their successors, to the exclusion of all others; (3) an inquiry to establish the identity of these successors to the Apostles; (4) consideration of the prerogatives proper to the Apostles and therefore not transmitted to their successors.

ART. I. ERRONEOUS DOCTRINES

MARSILIUS OF PADUA (A. D. 1270-1342). During the troubles between Louis of Bavaria and Pope John XXII, Marsilius of Padua and Jean de Jandun sided with the Emperor and defended his position in a work entitled *Defensor Pacis* (*Defender of Peace*). In this work they maintained that all power of government in the Church rests with the faithful, who exercise it through their chosen representatives, the secular rulers. Consequently the Church is subject to the State, and neither bishops nor Pope can make any laws or regulations for Church government without the consent of the State, for whom they are mere agents. These authors admitted that the power of Orders is conferred independently of the faithful, but they denied any distinction between priests and bishops.

PROTESTANTS. With the exception of a party in the Anglican Church, Protestants follow the teaching of Luther and Calvin, that whatever powers the Church possesses, resides in the body of the faithful, but since it is impossible for all to exercise authority, certain ones are chosen to act as delegates in the matter. They maintain that "every believer is a priest of God. Every believer has as much right as anybody else to pray, to preach, to baptize, to administer communion. . . . But it does not follow that therefore the clergy are superfluous. Experience has shown that certain persons are by natural endowment better fitted for spiritual functions than others, and also that in the Christian communities there will be leaders to whom will gravitate the major part of the work. The clerical order took its rise therefore in the

151

very necessity of the case. . . . If everybody discharged the spiritual functions of which they are capable, then confusion and anarchy would result. . . . The office is only necessary to the orderly progress of the Church. But the means of grace gain not a whit of efficiency from their administration. Baptism, the Lord's Supper, preaching and praying, like singing and taking up a collection; reading the Scriptures, like reading of notices,—may be performed by laymen with precisely the same spiritual effect as if the highest or the most godly minister in the land had been the administrator."[1]

According to this doctrine, Protestant clergymen are mere agents or representatives of their people, and are therefore rightly called *ministers,* —ministers, not of God, but of the people, from whom they receive their *call,* and by whom they are hired and discharged, much the same as an ordinary servant. Ordination is not a Sacrament, but a mere external ceremony by which a person is constituted a minister of the people to preach the Gospel and administer what few sacred rites they have. This is a logical deduction from the Protestant viewpoint that the real Church of Christ is invisible. The various external organizations known as churches are merely human societies, differing from hundreds of other private societies only in this, that they are religious. They were organized without any special authority from Christ, and there is no reason why one person should have any special power not possessed by every other. A person becomes a leader or minister because he is selected by the society for that purpose.

FEBRONIUS. Nicholas von Hontheim, auxiliary bishop of Treves, conceived the idea of effecting a union between Catholics and Protestants by paring down the teaching of the Church to such an extent that Protestants might be induced to accept them. With this purpose in view, he wrote a work under the fictitious name of Justin Febronius. The work, edited in 1763, was entitled *De Statu Ecclesiae (On the State of the Church).* The doctrine which it sets forth differs little from that of Protestants. All power in the Church belongs to the faithful; the bishops, including even the Roman Pontiff, are merely representatives delegated by the people to act in their name in the government of the Church, especially in ecumenical councils.[2]

ART. II. A RULING BODY OF DIVINE INSTITUTION

It is a defined doctrine of Catholic faith that the pastors of the Church are constituted a ruling body by divine appointment, and receive their

[1] Burger in Schaff-Herzog, art. "Clergy, Biblical."
[2] Cf. Catholic Encyclopedia, art. "Febronianism."

power and authority, not from the faithful, but from Christ, through succession from the Apostles, upon whom He conferred all power in the Church. The Council of Trent decreed: "If anyone should say that all Christians have equal powers to preach and to administer the Sacraments let him be anathema."[3] Pius VI condemned as heretical the "Proposition which states that all power was given by God to the Church to be communicated to the pastors, who are her ministers for the salvation of souls; if the proposition be understood to mean that the power of ministry and government is communicated to the pastors by the faithful."[4] The Vatican Council declared that, as Christ "sent the Apostles . . . as He himself had been sent by the Father, so He willed that there should ever be pastors and teachers in His Church to the end of the world."[5] This doctrine of the Church presupposes (1) that Christ conferred all authority in the Church upon the Apostles exclusively, and (2) that this authority descends to their legitimate successors for all time.

1. Apostles Alone Receive All Authority

Thesis.—All Power in the Church, Whether of Orders or Jurisdiction, Was Immediately Conferred Upon the Apostles Alone

PROOF. a) *From the Words of Christ.* Whenever there is question of conferring power or authority, Christ addresses none but the twelve chosen disciples, whom He calls Apostles: "He summoned his disciples; and from these he chose twelve (whom he also named apostles)[6] . . . then having summoned his twelve disciples, he gave them power over unclean spirits."[7] It was to the twelve alone that Christ said: "Amen I say to you, whatever you bind on earth shall be bound also in heaven; and whatever you loose on earth shall be loosed also in heaven."[8] It is certain that the twelve alone are meant for, as a non-Catholic author says, "The word *disciple* is applied most especially to the twelve in all four Gospels, sometimes with *dodeka*[9] and sometimes without; they are *the* disciples. Matthew seems indeed to confine the plural to them, unless v, 1 and viii, 21 be exceptions."[10]

After the Resurrection Jesus appeared to the eleven in Galilee and "spoke to them saying, 'All power in heaven and on earth has been

---

[3] Denzinger, n. 853.
[4] Denzinger, n. 1502.
[5] Denzinger, n. 1821.
[6] Luke vi, 13.
[7] Matt. x, 1.
[8] Matt xviii, 16-20
[9] The Greek word for *twelve.*
[10] Hasting's Bible Dictionary, art. "Disciples."

given to me. Go, therefore, and make disciples of all nations."[11] In these words He gave full power to the Apostles, and to them alone. On the very day of the Resurrection, "When it was late that same day, . . . though the doors where the disciples gathered had been closed, . . . Jesus came and stood in the midst, . . . He breathed upon them, and said to them, 'Receive the Holy Spirit; whose sins you shall forgive, they are forgiven them; and whose sins you shall retain, they are retained. Now Thomas, one of the Twelve, called the Twin, was not with them when Jesus came."[12] Here again Power is conferred, and the Apostles alone are mentioned; they are even called the *twelve,* although at that time there were only eleven. This indicates that the Apostles formed an official body known as *The Twelve.*

b) *From the Practice of the Apostles.* The Apostles always proclaimed by word and act that all their powers came immediately from Christ. In His name they spoke, in His name they taught, in His name they ruled. St. Paul distinctly says that he is "an apostle, sent not from men nor by man, but by Jesus Christ and God the Father."[13] To the Romans he writes: "by resurrection from the dead, Jesus Christ our Lord, through whom we have received grace and apostleship to bring about obedience to faith among all the nations for his name's sake."[14] In the Epistle to the Galatians he proves at length that he is the equal of the other Apostles, for the simple reason that he received authority, not from man, but from Christ himself. St. Peter likewise claims authority from God and a divine command to teach: "But God raised him on the third day and caused him to be plainly seen, not by all people, but by witnesses designated beforehand by God, that is, by us, who ate and drank with him after he had risen from the dead. And he charged us to preach to the people."[15]

The Apostles placed bishops and other ministers over the various Churches without the advice or consent of the faithful. St. Paul leaves Titus as bishop of Crete, with orders to constitute other pastors in every city, but there is no mention that the faithful have any voice in the matter.[16] It is God, not the people, who "has placed some in the Church, first apostles, secondly prophets, thirdly teachers."[17]

These few references are sufficient to show that the Apostles never recognized any power or authority in the people; in fact, St. Paul tells

---

[11] Matt. xxviii, 16-20.
[12] John xx, 19-24.
[13] Gal. i, 1.
[14] Rom. i, 4-5.
[15] Acts x, 41-43.
[16] Titus i, 5.
[17] 1 Cor. xii, 28.

the Corinthians plainly that the Apostles, as ministers of Christ, are independent of the faithful, and therefore have no fear of any criticisms: "Let a man so account us, as servants of Christ and stewards of the mysteries of God. Now here it is required in stewards that a man be found trustworthy. But with me it is a very small matter to be judged by you or by man's tribunal."[18]

COROLLARY. AN OBJECTION. St. Peter calls the faithful "a chosen race, a royal priesthood, a holy nation, a purchased people."[19] Therefore, the faithful are both rulers and priests,—a kingly priesthood; all have equal powers and rights to rule and to perform spiritual functions as Protestants maintain.

ANSWER. In this passage St. Peter applies to the faithful of the New Law words addressed to the chosen people of the Old: "You shall be to me a priestly kingdom, and a holy nation."[20] These words did not constitute all the people rulers in Israel, neither did they give to all the power of the priesthood, as Core, Dathan, and Abiron learned to their sorrow.[21] In both passages the words are used in a spiritual sense. The faithful of the Old Law as well as those of the New, are in a sense priests, they are consecrated to God and offer to Him the spiritual sacrifice of praise and thanksgiving according to the admonition of St. Paul: "Let us offer the sacrifice of praise always to God, that is to say, the fruit of lips confessing his name."[22] In this sense St. Jerome calls Baptism the priesthood of the laity, which he contrasts with the true priesthood of Orders.[23] In the same spiritual sense the faithful may be called kings, because by Baptism they become co-heirs with Christ, the King of kings, destined to reign with him: "They who have received the abundance of the grace, and of the gift and of justice, reign in life through one, Jesus Christ."[24]

2. Apostolic Power Descends by Succession

Thesis.—The Power of Orders and Jurisdiction, Conferred Upon the Apostles, Is Perpetuated in Their Successors According to the Institution of Christ

PROOF. All power in the Church was originally conferred upon the Apostles, to the exclusion of all others, and there is not the slightest

---

[18] 1 Cor. iv, 1-3.
[19] 1 Pet. ii, 9.
[20] Ex. xix, 6.
[21] Num. xvii, 1 sq.
[22] Hev. xiii, 15.
[23] "Dialog. adversus Luciferianos," 4; P.L., 23, 158.
[24] Rom. v, 17.

intimation in Scripture or tradition that Christ promised to confer a similar power upon others at any time in the future. It follows, then, that all power, whether of Orders or jurisdiction, must be perpetuated by an unbroken line of succession, reaching back to the Apostles, who received it directly from Christ Himself. This is clearly intimated in the words of Christ to the Apostles: "Behold, I am with you all days, even unto the consummation of the world."[25] Christ was with His Apostles during their life on earth; He remains with them in their successors through all the centuries. Therefore, succession is a matter of divine institution, and those who occupy the place of the Apostles in the Church, obtain also their power and authority; they obtain it independently of any action on the part of the faithful, and exercise it by divine right.

The practice of the Apostles shows how their power was to be transmitted to others. Matthias, elected to succeed Judas, was immediately "numbered with the eleven apostles" and exercised equal authority with them.[26] A little later, Paul and Barnabas were also numbered with the Apostles and, in turn, appointed others to teach and govern the faithful: "And when they had appointed presbyters for them in each church, with prayer and fasting, they commended them to the Lord."[27] St. Paul left Titus in Crete with authority over the church there, and commanded him to ordain others for the various cities: "I left thee in Crete, that thou shouldst set right anything that is defective and shouldst appoint presbyters in every city, as I myself directed thee to do."[28]

The teaching of the Fathers on this question will be given in the following article on the successors of the Apostles. It will be sufficient here to record the words of St. Clement of Rome, a friend and disciple of St. Peter, and the third to occupy his throne as Supreme Pontiff. In his Letter to the Corinthians, St. Clement says: "Our Apostles also through our Lord Jesus Christ . . . appointed the first rulers in the church at Corinth, and ordained that after their death other approved men should succeed to the ministry."[29] Here we find a complete description of the manner in which power and authority are transmitted in the Church. By the authority of Christ, SS. Peter and Paul appoint the first ministers at Corinth and ordain that the line of succession be continued by other approved men at the death of those whom they had appointed.

[25] Matt. xxviii, 20.
[26] Acts i, 20 sq.
[27] Acts xiv, 22.
[28] Titus i, 5 sq.
[29] "Epist. ad corinth.," 44; Funk, Vol. I, p. 155.

ART. III. THE SUCCESSORS OF THE APOSTLES

In the strict sense of the term, the successors of the Apostles are those in the Church who obtain by *right of succession* the *full* powers of Orders and jurisdiction enjoyed by the Apostles. Other ministers of the Church, who participate more or less in the power of Orders and exercise a delegated jurisdiction, may also be called successors in a less proper sense of the term.

1. *True Successors of the Apostles*

Thesis.—The Bishops of the Church Are the True Successors of the Apostles

It is a doctrine of faith, defined by the Council of Trent, that the bishops of the Church are the true and legitimate successors of the Apostles: "Wherefore the holy Synod declares that besides the other ecclesiastical grades, bishops in particular belong to the hierarchical order, since they succeed to the place of the Apostles and were placed, as the Apostle says, by the Holy Spirit to rule the Church of God."[30]

PROOFS. It has just been proved that the Apostles must have successors to perpetuate their powers of teaching, governing, and sanctifying until the end of time; but it is a well-known fact that the bishops, and the bishops alone, have ever claimed and exercised these powers in their fullness, and they alone have ever been recognized as the legitimate successors to these powers. Before the so-called Reformation of the sixteenth century, the right of the bishops to rule as successors of the Apostles was never questioned, except by a few individuals swayed by political or private interests. Even today, all parties admit that the bishops were the recognized successors of the Apostles, at least from the second century until the time of the pseudo-Reformation. Testimony from the Apostles and early Fathers prove that they were recognized as such from the earliest years of the Church. Now, it is manifestly impossible for any body of men to obtain recognition as successors of the Apostles from the very beginning of the Church, and maintain that position undisputed for sixteen centuries, unless they were in fact what they claimed to be,—true successors. Any other hypothesis would mean that the Church, as Christ founded it, ceased to exist with the death of the Apostles, and that the world has since been without the means of salvation; it would mean that Christ failed in His promise to be with the Church all days, even to the consumma-

---

[30] Denzinger, n. 960.

tion of the world. If the bishops of the Church are not the successors of the Apostles, then there are no successors, for no one else has even claimed this distinction; in that case the power and authority committed to the Apostles have lapsed, and cannot be renewed, except by a direct intervention of Christ in conferring them anew and re-establishing His Church. Such an act on the part of Christ would have to be confirmed by the performance of miracles as the only means by which we could be assured of its reality.

The following testimonies are sufficient to prove that bishops were recognized as the successors of the Apostles from the very beginning of the Church:

a) ST. PAUL plainly intimates that Timothy was to carry forward the work which he himself had begun: "But do thou be watchful in all things, bear with tribulation patiently, work as a preacher of the gospel, fulfill thy ministry. As for me, I am already being poured out in sacrifice, and the time of my deliverance is at hand."[31] When addressing the leaders of the church of Ephesus, he says: "Take heed to yourselves and the whole flock in which the Holy Spirit hath placed you bishops to rule the Church of God."[32] These words of the Apostle show that St. Timothy and the other ministers of Ephesus, known as *bishops,* ruled the Church there, and were expected to continue in that work after the death of St. Paul. In a word, they were his successors in the Church.

b) ST. JOHN THE APOSTLE. In the Apocalypse St. John narrates that he was ordered to write to the *angels* of the seven churches in Asia. In each church there is a single minister (*angel*) held responsible for doctrine and morals. This presupposes that he was also charged with the government of that particular church.[33] From other sources we know that ministers thus charged with the care and government of a church were called *bishops,* and held precisely the same position as bishops in every age of the Church.[34] This is evident from the following testimonies of the Fathers.

c) ST. IGNATIUS MARTYR. In his letter to the Christians of Smyrna, St. Ignatius says: "Let all be subject to the bishop, as Jesus Christ was to the Father; . . . apart from the bishop let no one do any of those things which pertain to the Church. . . . It is not lawful without

[31] 2 Tim. iv, 5-6.
[32] Acts xx, 28.
[33] Apoc. ii, 1 sq.
[34] Cf. Testimony of St. Clement, above, p. 156.

the bishop either to baptize or celebrate a lovefeast; but whatsoever he shall approve, that is also pleasing to God."[35]

d) ST. IRENAEUS. The testimony of St. Irenaeus is especially valuable, because he was a disciple of St. Polycarp, who in turn had been a disciple of St. John the Apostle. He says that he had heard Polycarp tell of his relations with John the Apostle and with others who had seen the Lord, and that he had learned much from them concerning the Lord, His miracles and teachings.[36] With such opportunities for knowing the teachings of Christ and the Apostles, St. Irenaeus wrote: "We are in position to reckon up those who were by the Apostles instituted bishops in the churches, and to demonstrate the succession of these men to our own times. . . . The Apostles were desirous that these men should be very perfect and blameless in all things, whom also they were leaving behind as their successors, delivering up their own place of government to them."[37]

e) TERTULLIAN. A few years after St. Irenaeus wrote the above words, Tertullian challenged the heretics of his day to prove the soundness of their position by tracing their succession back to an Apostle: "Let them unfold the roll of their bishops, running back in due succession from the beginning in such manner that their first bishop shall be able to show for his ordainer and predecessor some one of the Apostles or of Apostolic men; . . . as the Church of Smyrna, which records that Polycarp was placed therein by John; as also the church of Rome, which makes Clement to have been ordained in like manner by Peter. In exactly the same way the other churches likewise exhibit those whom they regard as transmitters of the Apostolic seed, having been appointed to their episcopal places by the Apostles."[38]

2. Other Ministers of the Church

Several orders of ministers are mentioned in Holy Scripture, especially by St. Paul, who enumerates apostles, prophets, doctors, evangelists, deacons, presbyters, bishops, and several others, whose duties are little understood. Most of these orders served a temporary need in the Church and then disappeared. The most important of these seem to have been the evangelists, doctors, and prophets. The evangelists most probably assisted in spreading the Gospel among unbelievers, much the same as catechists do today in missionary countries. The doctors and prophets

[35] "Epist. ad Smyrneos," viii, 9; Funk, Vol. I, p. 283.
[36] "Epist. ad Florin.," in Eusebius, "Church History," P.G., V, 20.
[37] "Adversus Haereses," III, 3; P.G., 7, 848.
[38] "De Praescriptione," n. 32; P.L., 2, 44.

seem to have been charged with further instruction for those who had been received into the Church; the doctors being permanently attached to particular churches, whereas the prophets travelled from place to place. St. Paul intimates that the members of these various orders were endowed with special miraculous gifts (charismata),[39] but they exercised no jurisdiction in the Church and, therefore, did not belong to the hierarchy. They were subject to the Apostles even in the exercise of their miraculous powers.[40]

Deacons, presbyters, and bishops constituted the ruling body or hierarchy. They are the permanent orders of the Church, constituted to teach and govern, and to perform the offices of the priesthood. The powers and duties of bishops will be considered elsewhere,[41] but some consideration of deacons and priests is necessary, since they participate more or less in the powers of the priesthood and exercise a delegated jurisdiction in the Church; to this extent they also are successors of the Apostles.

DEACONS. Shortly after the ascension of Our Lord, the Apostles associated with themselves a number of assistants, known as *deacons,* a Greek word signifying *ministers.* A temporal need in the Church at Jerusalem gave occasion for the introduction of deacons,[42] but they also exercised certain spiritual functions, such as preaching the Gospel, baptizing and assisting other ministers in their sacred functions; e.g., Philip preached the Gospel in Samaria and baptized many: "And Philip went down to the city of Samaria and preached the Christ to them . . . but when they believed Philip as he preached the kingdom of God and the name of Jesus Christ, they were baptized, both men and women."[43] St. Ignatius distinctly mentions deacons as of divine institution: "Reverence the deacons as being the institution of God."[44]

In the first centuries, the deacons administered the temporalities of the Church, cared for the cemeteries, and directed the various works of charity. These duties were gradually taken over by other agencies in the Church, and the deacons then gave themselves entirely to the spiritual work of baptizing and assisting at divine services. Even these duties were finally performed by other ministers, and the order of deacons ceased to have any utility. Today the order scarcely exists in the Church except as a preparatory step to the priesthood.

PRIESTS. From the very earliest times priests have formed an

[39] 1 Cor. xii, 28; Eph. iv, 11.
[40] 1 Cor. xiii, xiv.
[41] Cf. below, Ch. XII, Art. II.
[42] Acts vi, 1 sq.
[43] Acts viii, 5, 12.
[44] "Epist. ad Smyrneos," viii; Funk, Vol. I, 283.

important part of the ministry of the Church, and since they share in large measure the power of Orders conferred upon the Apostles, they constitute an order of divine institution, as the Council of Trent solemnly declared: "If anyone says that there is no hierarchy in the Catholic Church of divine institution, consisting of bishops, priests, and ministers, let him be anathema."[45] Yet it is a matter of dispute whether simple priests, i.e., priests as distinguished from bishops, existed in the days of the Apostles, or whether they were introduced later, as the needs of the Church demanded. Sacred Scripture mentions both bishops (*episcopi*) and priests (*presbyteri*), but it seems that these terms were not used in the same distinctive sense in which we use them today.

The word *presbyter* is simply the Greek *presbyteros* (an elderly man) used in a special sense. It is rendered *an ancient* in the Douay version and *an elder* in the King James. *Episcopus* is also a Greek word meaning *overseer* and is so translated in the King James version. It is practically certain that in the first years of the Church, all ministers above the order of deacon were known indiscriminately as *presbyteri* or *episcopi*. St. Paul commands Titus to "ordain *presbyters* in every city." He then enumerates the qualities necessary in the candidates for, as he says, "*a bishop* (*episcopus*) must be without crime."[46] When at Miletus, the same Apostle, sending to Ephesus, "called the *presbyters* of the Church," but in his address to them he calls them *episcopi:* "Take heed to the whole flock in which the Holy Spirit hath placed you bishops (episcopos)."[47] In his letter to the Philippians, St. Paul enumerates *bishops* and *deacons,* but makes no mention of presbyters.[48] On the other hand, St. Peter mentions *presbyters* without any reference to *bishops.*[49] The *Didache,* a work written toward the end of the first century, says: "Elect to yourselves *bishops* and *deacons* worthy of God."[50] St. Clement of Rome likewise says: "The Apostles constituted *bishops* and *deacons* for those who were to believe."[51] If the words *episcopus* and *presbyter* were used as they are today, to denote two separate orders, no reason can be assigned why St. Peter should omit the bishops, or why St. Paul and the other writers mentioned should omit the presbyters.

The above considerations leave no room for doubt that *presbyter* and *episcopus* were used as synonymous terms and the reason for this is

[45] Denzinger, n. 966.
[46] Titus i, 5-7.
[47] Acts xx, 28.
[48] Phil. i, 1.
[49] 1 Pet. v, 1.
[50] *Didache,* ch. xv; Funk, Vol. 1, 33.
[51] "Epist. ad Corinth.," 42; Funk, Vol. I, 153.

not far to seek. Among the Jews every synagogue was ruled by a committee composed originally of the older men of the congregation. For this reason they soon came to be known officially as *elders* (*presbyteri*),—a name applied even to those who were not advanced in years. Christian converts from Judaism would naturally employ the same terms of respect to designate the rulers in the Church. On the other hand, converts coming from paganism would use the term *episcopus,* which they had been accustomed to apply to anyone holding authority. In a short time both terms were used indiscriminately by all, whether of Jewish or pagan origin.

MATTER IN DISPUTE. It seems that in the earliest years particular churches were ruled by a council of ministers variously known as *bishops* or *presbyters,* but the exact status of these ministers is a matter of dispute. Some maintain that all were priests in the present meaning of the term, but those acting as chairmen or presidents of these committees, soon acquired greater power and influence and thus became what we know as *bishops.* This opinion is rejected by practically all Catholic scholars, and rightly so, since it can scarcely be reconciled with the divine origin of the episcopate. Others hold that each church was ruled by a bishop, assisted by a number of priests, who, with the bishop, constituted the *presbyterium* in much the same way as a bishop and his *canons* now form a *cathedral chapter* for the government of the diocese. This opinion fits in well with the fact that a monarchical form of government for each church is known to have prevailed from very early times. Nevertheless, several eminent Catholic scholars believe that all ministers above the grade of deacons were originally bishops, strictly so-called, and that simple priests were not introduced until some years later. In favor of this opinion they cite the fact that in the Church of Alexandria, and perhaps in other churches also, those known as *presbyters,* not only elected the bishops, but also consecrated them. This, of course, presupposes that the presbyters were really bishops.[52]

MONARCHICAL GOVERNMENT. Whatever may be said of the Government of the various churches in the first years of Christianity, it is certain that the monarchical form of government, i.e., the rule of one bishop in each church, is of Apostolic origin. It is evident from the first chapters of the Apocalypse that in the days of St. John the Apostle the churches of Asia were each ruled by a single bishop. St. Ignatius also speaks of a single bishop in each church. He says: "There is one flesh of our Lord Jesus Christ, and there is one chalice in the unity of His

---

[52] Cf. Duchesne, "Histoire ancienne de l'Eglise," Vol. I, c. 8; Cabrol, "Dictionnaire d'Archeologie," t. I, col. 1204.

blood; there is one altar, as there is one bishop with the presbyter and the deacons my fellow-servants."[53] In almost every epistle he warns the faithful to obey the bishop and the deacons. St. Paul likewise intimates that there should be but one bishop in charge of each church; he always speaks of the bishop in the singular and of the deasons in the plural, e.g., "A bishop then, must be blameless . . . deacons also must be honorable."[54] The Council of Nicaea (325) mentions it as a well recognized axiom that there should be but one bishop in each city: "In one church there shall not be two bishops."[55] There is also the testimony of several early writers, such as Hegesippus, St. Irenaeus, and Eusebius, who drew up lists of bishops for various churches. In each case these lists show a line of single bishops reaching back in unbroken succession to one who had received the ministry directly from the Apostles.

ART. IV. APOSTOLIC PREROGATIVES

1. The Apostolic Office

The name *Apostle,* from the Greek *apostellein,* to *send,* signifies *one sent,* a messenger who is also commissioned to act as legate for the one sending. An Apostle, therefore, differs from an angel because the latter acts merely as a messenger. The word *Apostle* occurs but once in the Septuagint version of the Old Testament,[56] but its use in the New Testament is frequent, especially in the writings of St. Paul. In a few instances St. Paul uses the word in its original meaning of a messenger; for example, he calls Epaphroditus an *apostle* of the Philippians because he had acted as their messenger in carrying a letter.[57] He also mentions *apostles of the churches,* i.e., messengers sent to him from the various churches which he had founded.[58] But he always speaks of himself as an *apostle* in a peculiar, or technical, sense: "Paul an apostle of Jesus Christ by the will of God."[59] He carefully distinguishes himself as an Apostle from his co-laborers, who did not enjoy that dignity: "Paul an apostle . . . Timothy our brother."[60]

CONDITIONS REQUIRED. According to St. Paul, a mission from Christ is the first and most important condition for the Apostolic office.

---

[53] "Epist. ad Philadelp.," 4; Funk, Vol. I, 267.
[54] 1 Tim. iii, 2, 8.
[55] Council of Nicaea, canon viii.
[56] 3 Kings xiv, 6.
[57] Phil. ii, 25.
[58] 2 Cor. viii, 23.
[59] 1 Cor. i, 1; Rom. i, 1.
[60] 2 Cor. i, 1.

An Apostle must be sent, "not of men, neither by man, but by Jesus Christ and God the Father."[61] Throughout the whole Epistle to the Galatians, St. Paul insists that he is truly an Apostle, equal to the others, because he had received his mission directly from Christ: "The Gospel which was preached by me is not of man. For neither did I receive it of man; but by the revelation of Jesus Christ."[62] He then proves that he had received neither his mission nor his knowledge of the Gospel from the other Apostles: "When it pleased him who from my mother's womb set me apart and called me by his grace, to reveal his Son in me, that I might preach Him among the Gentiles, immediately, without taking counsel with flesh and blood, and without going up to Jerusalem to those who were appointed Apostles before me, I retired into Arabia."[63] These arguments put forth by St. Paul in defense of his Apostleship presuppose that a personal mission from Christ is a necessary condition.

St. Peter set forth the second condition necessary in an Apostle when he proposed the election of a successor to Judas: "Therefore, of these men who have been in our company all the time that the Lord Jesus moved among us, from John's baptism until the day that He was taken up from us, of these one must become a witness with us of His resurrection."[64] It is necessary for an Apostle to have been a witness of the entire public Life of Our Lord, i.e., from His Baptism in the Jordan to His ascension into Heaven it is especially necessary that he be able to bear witness to the Resurrection, because, as St. Paul says, "If Christ has not risen, vain then is our preaching, vain also is your faith."[65]

Our Lord first selected twelve from among His disciples, "whom he also named apostles."[66] After the Ascension, Matthias succeeded to the place left vacant by the defection and death of Judas. Matthias had been a constant companion of the Lord and His little band of Apostles; he also received a commission directly by means of lots. Paul and Barnabas were afterward numbered with the twelve,[67] and St. Paul seems to account Andronicus and Junias as Apostles, but his meaning is not certain.[68] St. Paul had not been an eye witness of Our Lord's life on earth; in fact it seems that he had never seen Christ during His earthly life, but he was made a witness by means of direct revelation. Hence he

---

[61] Gal. i, 1.
[62] Gal. i, 11-12.
[63] Gal. i, 15-16.
[64] Acts i, 21-22.
[65] 1 Cor. xv, 14.
[66] Luke vi, 13.
[67] Acts xiv, 13.
[68] Rom. xvi, 7.

appeals to these visions and revelations in proof of his apostleship: "Am I not an apostle? Have not I seen Christ Our Lord?"[69] We have no record of the calling of St. Barnabas as an Apostle, unless it be that mentioned in the Acts: "The Holy Spirit said, Set apart for me Saul and Barnabas unto the work to which I have called them."[70] This seems to be a call to a particular work of the Apostolate, rather than to the Apostolate itself, since St. Paul considered himself a true Apostle before this time. It is certain, however, that Barnabas did receive a divine call and became a witness of the life, death, and Resurrection of Our Lord in some manner, because St. Luke calls him an Apostle along with St. Paul: "When the apostles Barnabas and Paul had heard, . . . they leaped out among the people."[71]

2. Special Prerogatives

The first ministers of the Church were not only bishops endowed with full power and authority to teach, govern, and sanctify; they were also Apostles, i.e., witnesses of Our Lord's life, death, and Resurrection, whom He personally commissioned to carry out the organization of the Church which He had established. For this purpose they were endowed with special prerogatives; they were personally infallible, exercised universal jurisdiction, were confirmed in grace, and possessed the power of working miracles. As bishops, they were to have true successors, with equal powers to teach, govern, and sanctify; as Apostles they could have no successors, as is evident from the nature of the Apostolic office. Hence the prerogatives peculiar to the Apostles as such, are not perpetuated in their successors.

a) INFALLIBILITY. The mission entrusted to the Apostles, and the conditions under which they labored, made the gift of personal infallibility a practical necessity. They were sent forth to become the foundation stones for the churches which they were to establish among the nations; the faithful, as St. Paul says, being "built upon the foundation of the Apostles and prophets,"[72] i.e., upon the doctrines preached by them concerning Christ, the chief cornerstone. Hence the Apostles, being the foundation stones of doctrine for the churches, must have been enabled to announce the true doctrines of Christ without any admixture of error; they must have been infallible. But the infallibility granted to them as a body was of little use. Circumstances made it im-

---

[69] 1 Cor. ix, 1.
[70] Acts xiii, 2.
[71] Acts xiv, 13.
[72] Eph. ii, 19-20.

possible for them to meet, except on rare occasions; in consequence each one was left almost entirely to his own resources in the matter of doctrine and discipline. Yet each must preach the true doctrines of Christ if he would be a foundation stone instead of shifting sand. Moreover, all men were obliged under pain of eternal damnation to hear and accept their teaching: "He that believeth not shall be condemned,"[73] and "He that rejects you rejects me."[74] Such a demand on the part of Christ presupposes that He had provided against the possibility of error by endowing His Apostles with personal infallibility.

Another argument is found in the words of St. Paul: "Even if we or an angel from heaven should preach a gospel to you other than that which we have preached to you, let him be anathema."[75] These words prove that the great Apostle was confident of his own infallibility in regard to the truths of the Gospel; not even an angel from heaven could convict him of error. On several occasions he appeals to his Apostolic office as sufficient proof for his teachings, fully confident that no further proof would be demanded.[76] This proves that St. Paul considered infallibility a prerogative attached to the office itself and therefore common to all his brethren in the apostolic college.

The Fathers of the Church show their belief in the personal infallibility of the Apostles when they appeal to the Apostolicity of a doctrine as a certain and undeniable proof that it is a doctrine of Christ Himself. It is a well-known fact that they constantly make this appeal.

b) UNIVERSAL JURISDICTION. Because of the monarchical form of government that prevails in all dioceses throughout the Church, each bishop is limited to a particular territory or diocese. He is known as the bishop of that particular diocese and is forbidden to exercise jurisdiction outside its limits. The Apostles, on the contrary, exercised universal jurisdiction. Each and all were sent to teach all nations. Like St. Paul, they were "set apart for the gospel of God, . . . received grace and apostleship to bring about obedience to faith among all nations."[77] They are not known as Apostles of this or that place, of this or that particular nation or people; they are simply *the Apostles of Jesus Christ,* commissioned to carry the Gospel to every creature.[78]

c) CONFIRMED IN GRACE. Catholic theologians hold that the

---

[73] Mark xvi, 16.
[74] Luke x, 16.
[75] Gal. i, 8.
[76] Rom. xv, 15 ss; 2 Cor. xii, 12 sq.
[77] Rom. i, 1, 5.
[78] See above, Ch. I, Art. ii.

Apostles were confirmed in grace and therefore preserved from all sin, or at least from grievous sin. St. Thomas does not hesitate to say that "the Apostles, even in their mortal life, could not sin grievously, although they could be guilty of venial sin."[79] This opinion prevailed widely in the sixteenth century and is still the common opinion, yet it would be difficult to offer any positive proof other than that of fitness. It was eminently fitting that the Apostles should be preserved at least from all grievous sin.

d) GIFT OF MIRACLES. As legates of Christ to all nations, the Apostles needed some means to prove their mission no less than Christ himself. For this reason they received the power to perform miracles as is evident from many passages of Holy Scripture; e.g., "But they (the Apostles) went forth and preached everywhere, while the Lord worked with them and confirmed the preaching by the signs that followed."[80] Again: "By the hands of the apostles were many signs and wonders wrought among the people."[81]

The power of miracles, however, was not a prerogative peculiar to the Apostles alone; many of the faithful were endowed with like powers, as is evident from the words of St. Paul to the Corinthians.[82] This power always remains in the Church, as was proved elsewhere,[83] but it does not descend by right of succession, and as it was not limited to the Apostles in the beginning, so neither is it limited now to their successors. It is a power residing in the Church, to be exercised at such times and by such persons as God in His wisdom determines, because, unlike the power of Orders or jurisdiction, it is needed only for extraordinary occasions.

GLOSSOLALIA. Among the miraculous powers shared by the Apostles and many of the faithful was the gift of tongues, technically known as *glossolalia*, a Greek word, which means *speaking with tongues*. In narrating the events of Pentecost St. Luke says: "And they were all filled with the Holy Spirit, and they began to speak with divers tongues according as the Holy Spirit gave them to speak."[84] St. Paul mentions speaking in tongues as one of the gifts enjoyed by many at Corinth, and also states that he himself possessed it: "I thank my God that I speak with all your tongues."[85]

---

[79] "Comment in Sent.," II, dist. 12, qu. 2, ad 1.
[80] Mark xvi, 20.
[81] Acts v, 12; xix, 11 sq.; Rom. xv, 18 sq.
[82] 1 Cor. xiv, 22 sq.
[83] See above, Ch. II, Art. ii.
[84] Acts ii, 4.
[85] 1 Cor. xiv, 18.

No doubt the Apostles were able to preach the Gospel in any language, if need be, just as St. Francis Xavier is said to have done, but there is no proof for this in Scripture. The gift of tongues mentioned there was not for the purpose of preaching, but for prayer and praising God. This may be gathered from the words of St. Paul: "He who speaks in a tongue does not speak to men, but to God; for no one understands, though he is speaking mysteries by the Spirit. But he who prophesies speaks to men for edification. . . . I had rather speak five words with my understanding, that I may also instruct others, than ten thousand words in a tongue."[86]

---

[86] 1 Cor. xiv, 2-19; cf. Semeria, "Venticinque Anni di Storia," Lect. II, n. 12; Catholic Encyclopedia, art. "Tongues, Gift of"; *Ecclesiastical Review,* May and June, 1910.

CHAPTER IX

The Primacy Promised

As a physical body cannot live and function without a head, so neither can a moral body. Every society must have a head, i.e., a person or group of persons in whom supreme authority resides and by whom it is exercised. Without such a head a society speedily dissolves and passes out of existence. Hence the Church, being a true society, must have a head invested with the supreme authority to teach, govern, and sanctify the faithful. Therefore, after examining the body of the Church, its organization and powers, it is necessary to investigate the nature and person of its head. Is it a single person or group of persons? What powers does it possess, and what relation does it bear to the rest of the body? Christ Himself is the supreme and only Head of the Church, considered as His Mystical Body; the question here regards the Church simply as an external organization or society of men, and as such it must have a human head.

It has been proved that all power in the Church was conferred upon the Apostles to be transmitted to their lawful successors, the bishops, who constitute the ruling body in the Church. Consequently the Church is neither a democracy nor a republic in her form of government; she is governed by a divinely constituted body of rulers, but do they rule as a body whose members have equal power and authority, or are they subject to one who exercises supreme authority over the whole Church? In other words, is the Church a monarchy or an oligarchy? These questions are answered by proving that St. Peter was given the primacy of jurisdiction over the universal Church, and that this primacy descends to his successors.

ART. I. THE PREEMINENCE OF PETER

THE TWELVE. The New Testament constantly represents the Apostles as members of a ruling body in the Church. They are referred to as *The Twelve,* even when their number was more or less.

a) He summoned his disciples; and from these he chose twelve (whom he also named apostles)."[1]

---

[1] Luke vi, 13.

b) "And having summoned his twelve disciples . . . now these are names of the twelve apostles . . . these twelve Jesus sent forth."[2]

c) "And he appointed twelve that they might be with him and that he might send them forth to preach."[3]

d) "Now when evening arrived, he came with the twelve."[4]

e) "Jesus answered them, Have I not chosen you, the Twelve? Yet one of you is a devil. Now he was speaking of Judas Iscariot . . . for he it was, though one of the Twelve, who was to betray him."[5]

St. Paul also mentions *the twelve* although at the time of which he was writing, there were only eleven: "He was seen by Cephas; and after that by the twelve."[6]

"It is true," says Batiffol, "that at a very early date *The Twelve* are spoken of; the Apocalypse, for instance, reckons only *twelve Apostles of the Lamb.* The title chosen by the *Didache* is: *The Lord's Teaching through the Twelve Apostles to the Nations.* The expression, *The Twelve Apostles,* is synthetic rather than enumerative; writers speak of the *Twelve* . . . regardless of the fact that the *Twelve* were actually fourteen."[8] This manner of referring to the Apostles as *The Twelve* in the Scriptures and in the earliest Christian writings, presupposes that they formed a body or corporation, as it were, to rule the Church. This fact is intimated by Christ himself, for He always addresses them collectively when there is a question of conferring power or authority upon them: "Whatever you bind (alligaveritis) . . . Go, therefore, teach (docete) all nations. . . . Do this (Hoc facite) in remembrance of me. . . . Receive the Holy Spirit; whose sins you shall forgive (remiseritis)."[9] His words are always in the plural, always addressed to the whole body of the Apostles.

ST. PETER THE HEAD. Since the Apostles constituted a ruling body in the Church, it is natural to expect a head or leader for the little band, and this expectation is realized; St. Peter is everywhere set forth as first among the Apostles, both before and after the Ascension of Our Lord.

a) BEFORE THE ASCENSION. Even while Our Lord was personally present among the Apostles, St. Peter enjoyed a certain preeminence. Wherever two or more of them are named, St. Peter always

[2] Matt. x, 1, 2, 5.
[3] Mark iii, 14.
[4] Mark xiv, 17; Matt. xxvi, 20.
[5] John vi, 71, 72.
[6] 1 Cor. xv, 5 (Greek text).
[7] Apoc. xxi, 14.
[8] P. Batiffol, "Primitive Catholicism," p. 52 (Eng. tr.).
[9] Matt. xviii, 18; xxviii, 20; Luke xxii, 19; John xx, 23; Luke x, 16.

heads the list, but the order of the others varies.[10] In fact, St. Matthew distinctly calls St. Peter the *first*, without assigning any order for the others: "Now these are the names of the twelve apostles: first Simon, who is called Peter, and his brother Andrew; James etc."[11] There are many other indications of this preeminence; v.g., "But as all were denying it, Peter and those who were with him said etc. . . . Mary Magdalen ran therefore and came to Simon Peter and to the other disciples whom Jesus loved."[12] St. Peter was also the first to confess the divinity of our Lord,[13] and when Christ "said to the twelve: Will you also go away?" Peter answering for all said: "Lord to whom shall we go? Thou hast the words of eternal life."[14]

b) AFTER THE ASCENSION. Immediately after the Ascension, St. Peter assumed the role of leader among the Apostles. He proposed the election of a successor to Judas, and preached the first sermon to the people;[15] he performed the first miracle and was the first to receive gentiles into the Church.[16] Being filled with the Holy Spirit, he defended the other Apostles before Annas and Caiphas,[17] and at the Council of Jerusalem, when he spoke, the matter was settled, and the people immediately turned to hear Paul and Barnabas relate their experiences among the gentiles: "Then after a long debate, Peter got up and said to them, etc. . . . then the whole meeting quieted down and listened while Barnabas and Paul told of the great signs and wonders that God had done among the Gentiles through them."[18] St. Paul also hints at the preeminence of Peter, when he says that he went up to Jerusalem for the express purpose of seeing him: "But I saw none of the other Apostles, except James, the brother of the Lord."[19]

WHENCE THE PREEMINENCE. There can be no doubt that St. Peter held a position of honor among the Apostles and even exercised some authority over them, but whence did he derive this preeminence, and what was its nature? Did his impetuous nature lead him boldly to assume an attitude of superiority, or was he, perhaps, elected to this position by the other Apostles on account of some special fitness for the office? Many non-Catholics give such explanations,[20] and they

[10] Mark iii, 16; Luke vi, 14 sq.; Acts i, 13 sq.
[11] Matt. x, 2.
[12] Luke viii, 45; John xx, 2, 3.
[13] Matt. xvi, 16.
[14] John vi, 69.
[15] Acts i, 15 ss; ii, 14 sq.
[16] Acts iii, 1 ss; x, 44-48.
[17] Acts iv, 8 sq.
[18] Acts xv, 7, 12.
[19] Gal. i, 18, 19.
[20] Cf. Palmer, "Treatise on the Church," Vol. II, p. 478; Schaff-Herzog, art. "Peter."

might seem plausible if we had nothing but the foregoing indications to guide us. Fortunately, we have the very words of Christ promising to Peter the primacy, which He afterward conferred upon him in most explicit terms. Before entering further into this question, it is well to consider the nature of primacy in general and its various kinds.

PRIMACY. Etymologically the word *primacy*, from the Latin *Primus* —*first*, signifies the state of being first among others for any reason whatsoever. Hence there are many kinds of primacy, the most important being those of *honor, excellence, order,* and *jurisdiction.* Primacy of *honor* consists in holding the first place among equals; it confers no privilege other than that of being accorded certain marks of respect, such as the place of honor at table or in assemblies. The primacy of excellence is a certain preeminence due to some personal merit or accomplishment. In this sense Demosthenes is known as the prince of orators, Homer as the prince of poets; they hold the first rank of excellence in their respective arts. The primacy of *order* consists in the directive authority necessary to carry out some business with order and promptness. The chairman of an assembly exercises such primacy in directing its deliberations and other proceedings according to recognized rules of order. The primacy of *jurisdiction* consists in holding the supreme powers of government in a society,—the supreme legislative, judicial, and coercive powers.

Such is the primacy claimed for St. Peter over the universal Church, and the Vatican Council declares it an article of faith that this primacy was conferred upon him by Our Lord: "If any one says that Christ the Lord did not constitute the blessed Peter prince of all the Apostles and head of the whole Church militant; or if he says that this primacy is one of mere honor and not of real jurisdiction received directly and immediately from Our Lord Jesus, let him be anathema."[21]

ERRONEOUS TEACHINGS. Today most non-Catholic scholars admit that St. Peter held a certain preeminence among the Apostles, but they maintain that it was a mere primacy of honor. Their doctrine that all power in the Church comes from the body of the faithful necessarily excludes a primacy of jurisdiction by divine institution; even the primacy of honor was due to accidental circumstances. The extraordinary zeal of St. Peter, his love for Christ, his impetuous nature, or perhaps his more advanced age, caused him to be more highly honored than the others.

The schismatic churches of the East and many Anglicans concede the primacy of honor by divine institution, but they hold that power in the

[21] Denzinger, n. 1823.

Church was conferred equally upon all the Apostles to be exercised by them as a body. "The special dealing with Peter and the promises to Peter are connected with our Lord's personal dealings with him; and though he appears as leader of the Apostles, it does not appear that any office or authority is given to him which is not shared equally with all the Apostles."[22]

These errors are refuted and the true position of St. Peter established by proving that Christ promised him the primacy of jurisdiction over the whole Church, and afterwards conferred it upon him. The primacy was promised when Christ foretold that Peter was to be (1) the foundation rock of the Church, (2) the key-bearer of the kingdom, (3) its law giver, and (4) the confirmer of his brethren.

ART. II. PETER THE ROCK FOUNDATION

Thesis.—The Primacy of Jurisdiction Over the Universal Church Was Promised to Peter Under the Figure of a Rock Foundation

PROOF. The proof of this thesis is found in the words of Christ addressed to St. Peter on the way to Caesarea Philippi: "Jesus saith to them (the Apostles): But who do you say that I am? Simon Peter answered and said: Thou art the Christ, the Son of the living God. And Jesus answered and said to him: Blessed art thou Simon Bar-Jona; because flesh and blood has not revealed this to thee, but my Father who is in heaven. And I say to thee: Thou art Peter and upon this rock I will build my church and the gates of hell shall not prevail against it."[23]

In these words Christ promised to St. Peter a real primacy of jurisdiction, (1) if the Church mentioned in the text is the universal Church of Christ, (2) if St. Peter is the rock upon which the Church is to be founded, and (3) if this rock foundation symbolizes the power of jurisdiction. There can be no doubt in regard to the first condition; any one who admits that Christ founded a church at all, must admit that it is the Church mentioned in the text quoted. Christ simply says "My Church," without restriction or qualification. It is the Church which He is about to establish upon a rock, and the rock is Peter.

1. St. Peter the Rock

The following considerations show conclusively that St. Peter is the rock designated by Christ as the foundation upon which He will build His Church:

a) The Greek *Petros* (Peter) is simply a masculine form of *petra*

---

[22] Bishop Gore (Anglican), "Catholicism and Roman Catholicism." I.
[23] Matt. xvi, 15-18.

(*a rock*), adopted for use as a proper name. This is evident from the fact that in Aramaic, the language spoken by Christ, the one word *Kepha* was used. This originally Aramaic word has been retained in the name *Cephas,* given to St. Peter in several passages of S. Scripture;[24] in one instance St. John explicitly says that it signifies the same as *Petras:* "But Jesus looking upon him said: Thou art Simon the son of Jona; thou shalt be called Cephas, which is interpreted Peter."[25]

In his commentary, St. Ephrem of Syria uses the word (*kipho, a rock*) for *Petros* and *petra,* just as the French use the one word *pierre:* "Tu es Pierre et sur cette pierre, etc." The proper English translation would be "Thou art Rock, and upon this rock I will build my Church."

b) The context demands that *Petros* and *petra* refer to the same subject. Our Lord has given His Apostle a new name: "Thou art Simon the Son of Jona; thou shalt be called Cephas, which is interpreted Peter." But we know that new names are never given in Scripture without some special reason. The name of Abram was changed to *Abraham,* and that of Sarai to *Sara;* Jacob received the name *Israel,* and the Blessed Virgin was directed to call her child *Jesus.*[26] In every case the name given by God foreshadowed an important office or dignity. The new name given to Simon must likewise portend some important office or dignity to be conferred upon him. On this occasion Our Lord reveals to him the nature of this office as a reward for his open confession of faith. Thou hast confessed that I am the Son of God; thou hast acknowledged my divinity. I in return shall reveal to thee who and what thou art: Thou art the son of Jona. I have called thee Peter (a rock), because upon thee shall I build my Church.

The sense of the passage is so evident that all interpreters of any note, whether Catholic or Protestant, agree that St. Peter is the *rock* upon which Christ founded His Church; the only disagreement is in regard to the office or dignity symbolized. Siefert, a non-Catholic, says: "By *rock* Jesus meant the person of the Apostle addressed, as is proved by the fact that in Aramaic, which He spoke, *rock* and *man of rock* would both be expressed by the same word, *kepha.*"[27] Weiss, a rationalist, says: "The emphasis lies on *this,* pointing to Peter; on no other than upon this rock, i.e., upon this rock nature . . . I will build my Church."[28]

[24] Cf. 1 Cor. i, 12; iii, 22; ix, 5; xv, 5; Gal. ii, 9.
[25] John i, 42.
[26] Gen. xvii, 5; xvii, 15; Matt. i, 21.
[27] F. Siefert in Schaff-Herzog, art. "Peter the Apostle."
[28] B. Weiss, "Matthaus-Evangelium," t. I, p. 334.

The testimony of tradition is unnecessary in a matter so evident, yet a few witnesses may be quoted: (a) TERTULLIAN: "Could any of these things be hidden from Peter who was called the rock, on which the Church was to be built?"[29] (b) ORIGEN. "See what the Lord said to that great foundation of the Church; that most solid rock upon which Christ founded His Church."[30] (c) JAMES OF SARUG (451-521) in a Syriac hymn to St. Peter: "Thou art *Kipho*;[31] down in the foundations of the great house I set thee. Upon thee will I build my elected Church. I will place thee first in my building, thou being hardy. Be thou basis to the Holy Temple which I am to inhabit. On thee will I expand all the superstructures of the Daughter of day."[32]

d) THE GREEK LITURGY calls St. Peter "the foundation of the Church and the rock of faith."[33]

2. Primacy of Jurisdiction Symbolized

PROOFS. St. Peter is not represented as the cornerstone of the Church, nor even as its superstructure; he is the immovable rock upon which the whole building is securely raised. Therefore the relation of St. Peter to the Church must be that of a foundation rock to the structure built upon it; he is to give the Church strength and solidity, and preserve the unity of its parts against all destructive forces, whether they come from within or without. In a society such strength and union of parts is secured and preserved by means of authority; therefore, in calling St. Peter the rock foundation of His Church, Christ promised him the primacy of power and jurisdiction over it.

Christ himself assigns the reason for founding His Church upon a rock; namely, that "the gates of hell shall not prevail against it." The whole passage is an evident allusion to the parable of the wise man who built his house upon a rock. "The rain fell, and the floods came, and the winds blew, and they beat against that house but it did not fall because it was founded upon a rock."[34] All down the centuries the forces of evil,—the powers of earth and hell,—will beat upon the Church, but it shall not fall, for it is founded upon a rock, and that rock is Peter. Weiss, a rationalist, commenting on this passage says: "On no other than upon this rock, i.e., upon this rock nature which,

---

[29] "De Praescript," xxii; P.L., 2, 34.
[30] "Homil. in Exodum," v, 4; P.G., 12, 329.
[31] The Syriac word for *rock*.
[32] James of Sarug, Homily xxiv, quoted in "Traditions of the Syriac Church of Antioch," by most Rev. Cyril Benham Benni, p. 21.
[33] Nilles, "Kalendarium Manuale," I, 72.
[34] Matt. vii, 25.

as the rock in the parable, could ensure the existence of the house, the continuance and cohesion of the new community, I will build my Church. The primacy among the Apostles is here undoubtedly awarded to Peter."[35]

The Church is here depicted as an impregnable fortress, secure against every foe, because founded upon Peter, the rock. The interpretation of this symbolism is evident: the fortress is the Church and the rock is St. Peter, who renders the Church secure against her every foe. This implies that St. Peter is in supreme command of all her forces with authority to make ordinances, to appoint or remove subordinate officers and to provide everything necessary for all operations both defensive and offensive.

The voice of tradition is in complete accord with the above interpretation of the *rock* as a symbol of supreme authority in the Church, as the following passages show:

e) ST. AMBROSE: "It was this Peter to whom Christ said: Thou art Peter, and upon this rock I will build My Church. Therefore where Peter is, there also is the Church."[36]

b) ST. EPHREM OF SYRIA introduces Christ speaking to St. Peter in these words: "Simon, I have made thee foundation of My holy Church; I have called thee Peter, because thou shalt sustain the whole edifice. Thou shalt be overseer of those who build up for Me the Church on earth, . . . if they select faulty material, thou the foundation, shalt restrain them. . . . Behold I have made thee master of all my treasures."[37]

c) GREEK LITURGY. In the office for the 29 June, St. Peter is called "the leader and ruler of the Church."[38]

d) SYRIAC LITURGY. In the Syriac Liturgy for the 29 June, St. Peter is thus addressed: "Thou, O Simon, who duly wast named *Kipho* when Our Lord established the true and immaculate faith of the Church which He had redeemed by Christ, thou wert made and authorized head shepherd of rational sheep."[39]

e) SYRO-CHALDAIC LITURGY: "He is Simon, the head of the Apostles, the foundation, the ruler, the pastor and the governor of the Church of Christ, to whom his Lord bore witness saying: Thou art a rock (*kipho*), and upon this rock I will build my Church."[40]

---

[35] B. Weiss, "Matthaus-Evang.," Vol. I, p. 334.
[36] "In Ps." xl, n. 30; P.L., 14, 1082.
[37] "De Passione et Ressur. Salvatoris," R. 1. (Lamy, I, 412).
[38] Nilles, "Kalendarium Manuale," I, 194.
[39] Benni, "Traditions of the Syriac Church of Antioch," p. 57.
[40] Benni, "Traditions of the Syriac Church of Antioch," p. 55.

3. *Objections Answered*

OBJECTION I.—St. Paul says that the Israelites in their wanderings "drank from the spiritual rock which followed them, but the rock was Christ."[41] The rock is a symbol of Christ; therefore, Christ himself and not Peter is the rock upon which the Church is founded.

ANSWER.—The application of a symbol is not always the same; the meaning it is intended to convey must be determined from the context in which it is found. Because *rock* is a symbol for Christ in one passage, does not prove that it must be in another. Christ himself said: "I am the light of the world,"[42] yet this did not prevent Him from saying to the Apostles: "You are the light of the world."[43] They were truly the light of the world, because they participated in and reflected "that true light which enlighteneth every man who comes into the world."[44] In like manner both Christ and His Apostle, St. Peter, are the rock upon which the Church is built; Christ primarily and by nature, St. Peter secondarily and by participation as an ancient author explains: "Peter indeed is a rock, but not in the same manner as Christ, who is the immovable rock. Peter is rock because of that other Rock, for Jesus can share His dignities without exhausting them. . . . He is a Priest, yet He constitutes others priests . . . He is a Rock, yet He fashions a rock and gives to His servant His own dignities."[45]

OBJECTION II.—In his first Epistle to the Corinthians St. Paul says: "Other foundation no man can lay, but that which has been laid, which is Christ Jesus."[46] How, then, can St. Peter be called a foundation?

ANSWER.—In this passage the Apostle makes no reference whatever to the *foundation* of the Church; he is speaking of the *foundation* of doctrine, or faith. Rival parties had sprung up at Corinth and were causing much strife. Some claimed to be the followers of Paul; others of Apollo, whom they praised as a more eloquent preacher and a better teacher of doctrine. St. Paul rebukes them for such folly; he and Apollo taught them the same doctrine, although he had been unable to use the eloquence of Apollo or to expound the more sublime doctrines of Christ: "I, brethren, could not speak to you as to spiritual men, but only as carnal, as to little ones in Christ. I fed you with milk, not with solid food, for you were not ready for it. Nor are you now ready

---

[41] 1 Corinth. x, 4.
[42] St. John viii, 12.
[43] St. Matt. v, 14.
[44] St. John i, 19.
[45] "Homily on Penance," a work formerly attributed to St. Basil, P.G., 31, 1483.
[46] 1 Cor. iii, 11.

for it, for you are still carnal,"[47] as your conduct shows. The Corin thians, being babes in Christ, St. Paul was forced to omit all attempts at eloquence and to teach them the mere rudiments of doctrine. He taught them nothing "except Jesus Christ, and Him crucified."[48] This is the foundation of all faith and any one who gives them further instruction must build upon it, for "other foundation no one can lay."

Even though St. Paul were speaking of Christ as the foundation of the Church, it would offer no difficulty; what was said above concerning Christ as the *Rock* of the Church would be sufficient to explain it.

OBJECTION III.—St. Paul writes to the Ephesians: "Therefore, you are no longer strangers and foreigners, but you are citizens with the saints and members of God's household; you are built upon the foundation of the apostles and prophets with Christ Jesus himself as the cornerstone."[49] Here all the Apostles are mentioned equally as the foundation stones of the Church in dependence upon our Lord as the chief cornerstone.

ANSWER.—This passage also has reference to doctrine, as is evident from the context, in which the prophets are associated with the Apostles as foundation stones of the Church. Yet the prophets were certainly not foundations of the Church in the same sense that Christ calls St. Peter the foundation rock. St. Paul teaches that the faithful are built upon the foundation of the prophets and Apostles by being instructed concerning Christ crucified, whom the prophets had foretold, and whom the Apostles now preach to them. Christ Himself is the chief cornerstone, i.e., the One foretold and now announced to the people.

Although St. Paul does not refer to the Apostles as the foundation of the Church, he could have done so with perfect truth; all were in a true sense foundation stones. They were the first members of the Church and its first ministers; through them Our Lord effected the actual organization of His Church, and by them it was extended far and wide to Jew and Gentile. For this reason it is often said that Christ instituted the Church in and through the Apostles, and St. John describes the Church triumphant as a city, "and the wall of the city has twelve foundation stones, and on them twelve names of the twelve apostles of the Lamb."[50] The twelve Apostles were the twelve foundation stones; St. Peter was even more than this. He was also the solid rock upon which stood both foundation and superstructure.

---

[47] 1 Cor. iii, 1 sq.
[48] 1 Cor. ii, 2.
[49] Eph. ii, 19-20.
[50] Apoc. xxi, 14.

OBJECTION IV.—The Fathers frequently speak of Christ as the rock of the Church; they also mention Peter's faith as the rock. Hence they did not recognize St. Peter himself as the rock.

ANSWER.—The Fathers frequently speak of Christ as the Rock of the Church, and rightly so, for, as noted above, Christ was primarily and by nature the *Rock* or *Foundation* of the Church, St. Peter only secondarily and by participation. In this sense the Fathers call him the rock upon which the Church is built, as the quotations given above amply prove. Innocent III says: "Although the first and principal foundation of the Church is Jesus Christ, the only begotten Son of God, . . . the second and subordinate foundation is Peter who . . . by authority was chief among the others."[51]

The faith of St. Peter and his open confession may also be called the rock or foundation of the Church, as is done at times by the Fathers. It was through his faith that St. Peter merited the honor of becoming the foundation; it was through his faith that he participated in the nature of the principal *Rock* and thus himself became a *rock*.

ART. III. PETER THE KEY-BEARER

Thesis.—Primacy of Jurisdiction Over the Universal Church Was Promised to St. Peter Under the Symbol of Keys

PROOF. When Christ had designated St. Peter as the rock upon which He would build His Church, He immediately added: "And I will give thee the keys of the kingdom of heaven."[52] In these words Christ promised to St. Peter the primacy of universal jurisdiction, (1) if St. Peter was the person addressed, (2) if the *Kingdom of Heaven* meant the Church which Christ was about to establish, and (3) if the *keys* are a symbol of supreme power in the Church. There can be no doubt in regard to the first two conditions. It is evident from the whole context that St. Peter and he alone was addressed by Our Lord, and all interpreters concede that the *Kingdom of Heaven* is here the same as the Church to be established on Peter the rock. It is the kingdom in which St. Peter shall exercise the power of the keys; therefore, it must be a visible society existing among men, which can be no other than the Church militant. It is also evident that *keys* are here taken symbolically and, since no explanation is given, Our Lord must have intended the symbolism then in common use, for otherwise His words could not have been understood.

[51] "Epist. ad Patriarch. Constantinop"; P.L., 214, 758.
[52] Matt. xvi, 19.

SIGNIFICANCE OF KEYS. Among all ancient peoples, especially those of the East, keys were a symbol of power and authority, and the giving of keys indicated a transfer of authority. Henderson, a non-Catholic, says: "In the East the key is the symbol of power and authority, with special reference to palaces, treasures, stores, etc. It resembles a sickle with a long handle, and the crooked part is so formed as to allow of its being suspended on the shoulder or around the neck. That it actually formed part of the insignia of office, and that the language is not to be taken figuratively, is unquestionable. Among the Greeks it was worn as a badge of sacerdotal dignity."[53]

The use of symbols was much more common among Eastern peoples of antiquity than with us, yet we still preserve traces of this use of the key as a symbol of authority. When cities were protected by walls and the only entrance was by means of gates, possession of the keys to these gates gave full authority, because a city was in the power of him who controlled its entrances. City walls long since disappeared as a means of protection, but the ancient custom of giving a king, or other ruler, the keys of the city upon his solemn entry, still obtains. Even in our country, a person of distinction is honored by giving him the "keys of the city." A similar use of keys also obtains in the transfer of a house or other building; a person leasing or purchasing a building does not get full possession or control until the keys have been delivered to him.

Outside of the passage under consideration, keys are mentioned but six times in Scripture.[54] In five of these passages, the key is used as a symbol of power or authority; three times the power of Christ is directly signified, and once a power typifying that of Christ. The latter is found in Isaias: "I will call my servant Eliacim the son of Helcias and I will clothe him with thy robe . . . and will give thy power into his hand . . . and I will lay the key of the house of David upon his shoulder; and he shall open and none shall shut; and he shall shut and none shall open."[55] Our Lord applies these same words to Himself in the Apocalypse: "Thus says the holy one, the true one, he who has the key of David he who opens and no one shuts, and who shuts and no one opens."[56] "And behold, I am living forevermore; and I have the keys of death and hell."[57]

This Scriptural use of the key as a symbol of power, together with

---

[53] E. Henderson, "Commentary on St. Matthew."
[54] Judges iii, 25; Is. xxii, 22; Luke xi, 52; Apoc. i, 18; iii, 7; ix, 1.
[55] Is. xxii, 19-22.
[56] Apoc. iii, 7.
[57] Apoc. i, 18.

its use in the same sense by all nations of antiquity, proves beyond a doubt that Our Lord promised some special and extraordinary power to St. Peter when He promised him "the keys of the kingdom of heaven."

SYMBOL OF JURISDICTION. The words of Christ, considered in their context and compared with other passages of Scripture, leave no doubt that real jurisdiction over the universal Church militant was promised to St. Peter. Christ had just compared His Church to a house; He now promises the keys to St. Peter, thus constituting him administrator and sole custodian during the Master's absence. Knabenbauer aptly notes that the keys of a house belong to the master and that, by giving them to another, the master thereby entrusts to him the care and administration of the whole house and all that it contains. Therefore, in promising to St. Peter the keys of the kingdom, Christ promised him a power in the Church, subject only to His own.[58]

Mason, a non-Catholic, gives a similar interpretation: "The kingdom of heaven, here to be understood of the Messianic theocracy about to be established, is likened to a house or palace of which Our Lord promises that St. Peter shall be the chief steward or major-domo, who is entrusted with full authority over everything which the house contains. The keys are not merely those of the outer doors of the house, which give the holder power to admit or reject; the porter's office is only part of the authority committed to St. Peter. They are the keys of the inner chambers also, giving command, for example, of the treasures from which it will be his duty to feed the household. As the house is at the same time *the Kingdom,* it is evident that the authority is of very wide range."[59]

AN OBJECTION.—On one occasion Christ said to the Pharisees: "Woe to you lawyers! because you have taken the keys of knowledge; you have not entered yourselves and those who were entering you have hindered."[60] By their false teachings and unwarranted interpretations of Scripture, these Pharisees were preventing the people from accepting Christ as the Messias; thus they "shut the kingdom of heaven against them."[61] The power of the keys, therefore, is the power or authority to teach. Hence the keys promised to St. Peter symbolizes a mission to preach the gospel,—a primacy in evangelizing, which he exercised by preaching the first sermon to the people on Pentecost and by admitting the first gentiles into the Church.

---

[58] Knabenbauer, "Commentarium in Matthaeum," Vol. II, p. 66.
[59] A. J. Mason in Hasting's "Dictionary of the Bible," art. "Power of Keys."
[60] Luke xi, 52.
[61] Matt. xxiii, 13.

ANSWER.—The objection strengthens the arguments for Peter's supremacy rather than refuting or weakening them. Christ promised to Peter not the *key of knowledge,* but the *keys of the kingdom.* The objection admits that the *key of knowledge* symbolizes some power or authority over doctrine; therefore the *keys of the kingdom* must signify power and authority over the Church, which is the Kingdom of Heaven on earth,—a power that includes authority to teach as proved elsewhere.[62] The keys of the kingdom are promised to Peter alone; therefore, he alone shall receive supreme power or primacy of jurisdiction over the kingdom.

ART. IV. PETER THE LAW-GIVER

Thesis.—Primacy of Universal Jurisdiction Over the Church Was Promised to St. Peter Under the Symbol of Binding and Loosing

PROOF. Having promised the keys of the kingdom, Our Lord continued to address St. Peter with these words: "And whatever thou shalt bind on earth, it shall be bound in heaven; and whatever thou shalt loose on earth, shall be loosed also in heaven."[63]

It cannot be denied that Christ was directly addressing St. Peter in these words; neither can there be any doubt that some extraordinary power was promised to him. Our Lord seems to be fairly struggling, as it were, to convey in human language an adequate idea of the unprecedented powers to be conferred upon St. Peter. He is to be the rock foundation, upon which the Church will stand secure against the natural forces of decay and all the power of evil; he shall be its supreme ruler, subject to Christ alone. Now he is told that these powers shall be limited in extent only by the confines of the earth: "Whatever thou shalt bind on earth, . . . whatever thou shalt loose on earth." Nay more, his every official act on earth shall be ratified in Heaven!

What can be the nature of this most extraordinary power? What must St. Peter and the other Apostles have understood by the words *bind* and *loose?* These words are often taken as a continuation of the preceding symbol of the keys, with special reference to the power of forgiving sins. But it must be evident to all that keys are for *opening* and *closing,* not for *binding* and *loosing.* In Sacred Scripture keys are never mentioned in connection with *binding* or *loosing,* but in five of the seven passages in which keys are mentioned, they are connected with *opening* and *closing.* Consequently there is a new and distinct

---

[62] See below, Ch. ix, Art. v.
[63] Matt. xvi, 19.

symbol presenting the powers of Peter under a different aspect. It refers directly and primarily to the power of jurisdiction; it makes St. Peter the law-giver in the Church as was Moses in the Synagogue. This supreme power of jurisdiction includes the power to forgive sins, but only implicitly.

POWER OF LEGISLATION. Since Christ evidently used the words *bind* and *loose* in a figurative sense, He must have intended them to be accepted according to the meaning current at the time; otherwise neither St. Peter nor the other Apostles could have understood their meaning without explanations, which were not given. Hence the words must be interpreted according to their acceptation in the time of Christ, with only such changes as the context demands. They are found in hundreds of passages in the Talmud, and in almost every case *to bind* means to declare unlawful, while *to loose* is to pronounce lawful. In the Jerusalem Talmud, for instance, we read: "They do not begin a sea voyage on the eve of the Sabbath nor on the fifth day of the week. The school of Shammai *binds* it even on the fourth day, but the school of Hillel *looses*,"[64] i.e., the followers of Shammai declare it unlawful to undertake a sea voyage on the fourth day of the week, whereas the followers of Hillel maintain that it is lawful.

If the person who declares a thing lawful or unlawful, does so officially, he thereby imposes an obligation in conscience, i.e., he commands or forbids, makes laws or abrogates them. Consequently, the terms *to bind* and *to loose* assumed by natural transition the sense of making and unmaking laws. There can be little or no doubt that the terms were used in this sense by the rabbis in the days of Our Lord. In fact, Christ himself used the words in this sense: "Do not think that I am come to destroy (Greek, to loose) the law or the prophets."[65] In this passage the word *to loose* evidently means to repeal or abrogate. Again He said of the Pharisees: "They bind heavy and oppressive burdens and lay them on men's shoulders."[66] The context shows clearly that the *insupportable burdens* were foolish laws and precepts which the Pharisees imposed (*bound*) upon the people.

"The doctors of the Mosaic Law interpreted it and accordingly determined what was lawful and what was unlawful. In like manner Peter is to interpret the Law of Christ; he is to determine and prescribe what is licit and what is not licit according to the mind and doctrine of Christ. . . . This he shall do by the promulgation of laws,

---

[64] J. Lightfoot, "Horae Hebraicae in Evang. Matt.," xvi, 19.
[65] Matt. v, 17.
[66] Matt. xxii, 4.

precepts, and prohibitions. Hence no one can rightly deny that these words of Christ confer a law-giving power."[67] Mason, a non-Catholic, gives the same interpretation: "Authority is given to St. Peter to say what the law of God allows and what it forbids; and the promise is added that his ruling shall be upheld in Heaven,—and is consequently to be regarded as binding upon the conscience of Christians. The power of binding and loosing is in fact the power of legislation for the Church."[68]

JUDICIAL AND COERCIVE POWERS. The legislative power explicitly promised to St. Peter necessarily implies the judicial and coercitive powers without which laws would be useless. The very words of Our Lord also imply these powers, since no restrictions or limitations of any sort are added: *whatever* Peter prohibits, *whatever* he permits by legislative, judicial, or coercive power, shall be prohibited or permitted by Christ in Heaven. Thomas Arnold, a non-Catholic, makes some pointed observations on this matter. He says: "To bind and to loose are metaphors certainly, but metaphors easy to be understood. They express a legislative and judicial power. To bind legislatively is to impose a general obligation; to say that a thing ought to be done, or ought not to be done; to bind men's consciences either to the doing of it, or to the abstaining from it. . . . Again, to bind judicially is to impose a particular obligation on an individual, to oblige him to do or to suffer certain things for the sake of justice, which, if left to himself, he would not choose to do or suffer. Again to loose judicially is to pronounce a man free of any such obligation. . . . But such legislative and judicial power is the power of government; government, in fact, consisting mainly of these two great powers."[69]

PRIMACY OF POWER. The power of government promised to St. Peter under the figure of *binding* and *loosing,* extends to the whole Church and to everything subject to the Church. It is a power to be exercised *on earth* without restrictions as to time or place, and includes within its scope all persons or things subject to the Church,—"Whatever thou shalt bind . . . whatever thou shalt loose." In a word, the power here promised to St. Peter is the supreme power of jurisdiction over the universal Church,—the primacy of jurisdiction.

The fact that Christ afterward addresses these same words to all the Apostles.[70] does not militate against the primacy of Peter. On that

[67] Knabenbauer, "Commentarium in Matt.," Vol. II, p. 68.
[68] A. J. Mason in Hasting's "Dictionary of the Bible," art. "Power of Keys."
[69] Thomas Arnold, "Fragment on the Church," pp. 35-36.
[70] Matt. xviii, 18.

occasion Our Lord addressed the Apostles collectively; He conferred upon them as a body complete authority to rule, but in subjection to St. Peter, their head, to whom alone the words of Christ were addressed individually: "Whatever thou shalt bind . . . whatever thou shalt loose."[71]

LIMITATIONS. The words of Christ to St. Peter are absolutely universal and contain no restricting clause. Therefore, the power promised to him is subject to no limitations save those incidental to all authority, i.e., it must be subject to the divine law and be conformed to the nature of the society in which it is exercised. Consequently the power of binding and loosing extends to every bond or obligation that may be imposed or removed by divine law, but since it is to be exercised in the Church, it extends only to persons and things subject to her authority. The power of Peter is measured by the power of the Church. The Church has no authority to change the teachings of Christ, to increase or diminish the number of Sacraments or to sever the bonds of a consummated marriage; neither was such authority promised to Peter. The Church has authority to define doctrines, to make or repeal laws, to inflict punishment, to constitute or remove pastors; the same authority was promised to Peter when Christ said: "Whatever thou shalt bind, . . . whatever thou shalt loose." In fact, the Church has authority only in so far as it was conferred upon the Apostolic college, of which St. Peter was the head.

ART. V. PETER CONFIRMER OF THE BRETHREN

Thesis.—Primacy of Universal Jurisdiction in Teaching and Governing Was Promised to St. Peter as the One Appointed to Confirm His Brethren

PROOF. On the night of the Last Supper Christ said to Peter: "Simon, Simon, behold, Satan has desired to have you (plural), that he may sift you as wheat. But I have prayed for thee (singular), that thy faith may not fail; and do thou, when once thou hast turned again, strengthen thy brethren."[72] On this occasion Our Lord was admonishing the Apostles that eternal happiness in Heaven is to be obtained only after many labors, sorrows, and temptations. Unceasing vigilance and special help from God are necessary, because Satan never wearies in his efforts to lead souls astray; in fact, he was even then seeking to try the Apostles, as he had long before sought to try the Constancy of Job:[73]

---

[71] See below, Ch. x, Art. iii.
[72] Luke xxii, 28-32.
[73] Job i, 9-12.

"Behold Satan has desired to have you, that he may sift you as wheat." As he had tempted the Lord, so now he would tempt the Apostles, and through them the whole Church;[74] he would seek especially to weaken and destroy their faith, the very foundation of all spiritual life, but Christ has provided for this danger: "Satan hath desired you all, but I have prayed for thee, Simon, that thy faith fail not."

PRIMACY IN TEACHING. The unconditional prayer of Christ for unfailing faith in His Apostle must produce the effect desired; the faith of Peter shall ever remain immune to all error. This is nothing less than a promise of infallibility made in the clearest terms. Satan seeks to tempt all the Apostles,—"Satan hath desired you (the plural, Vos),"—But Christ prays for Peter alone,—"I have prayed for thee, that thy faith may not fail." Peter is then constituted the future guide for all in matters of faith, the supreme teacher in the Church: "And thou being once converted, confirm thy brethren."[75] It shall be the duty of St. Peter to confirm the other Apostles in the faith, and through them all the faithful for all time; but this constitutes the primacy of teaching authority for the whole Church.

The other Apostles, being themselves infallible, stood in no need of Peter's confirming power, but Christ was providing for His Church in later ages. The bishops of the Church were not to succeed the Apostles in their special prerogatives; they were not to enjoy the privilege of personal infallibility and would, therefore, need the strengthening power of Peter's faith handed down through his successors.

PRIMACY OF GOVERNMENT. The primacy of teaching authority in the Church necessitates the primacy of government. The Church founded by Christ is a kingdom of truth, in which unity of true faith must be preserved at all times until the end of the world; but such unity cannot be had nor preserved without proper laws and precepts binding on all. Therefore, he who holds the supreme authority as teacher, must also have the supreme power of ruling, i.e., he must have the primacy of government over the universal Church.[76]

---

[74] Temptation is aptly compared to the sifting of wheat. As the wheat is tossed and shaken in the sieve, the light particles of straw and chaff are caught up by the wind and carried away, while the heavier grains remain behind. In like manner, those who are truly virtuous and sound in faith remain unmoved by temptation, whereas the weak and vacillating fall away and are lost. Cf. Cornelius a Lapide, "Commentarium in Lucam," xxii, 31.

[75] Interpreters do not agree in explaining the words "thou being once converted." Some take them to mean, "thou being converted to Me again after thy denial and fall." Others interpret them "and thou in turn confirm thy brethren." But this question has no bearing on our matter, for in either case St. Peter is the one appointed to confirm his brethren.

[76] For the testimony of tradition in this matter, see Ch. x, Art. ii.

COROLLARY. The parallelism between the words of Our Lord as recorded in Matthew xvi, 18, 19 and those recorded in Luke xxii, 31, 32 is immediately evident upon comparison. In St. Matthew the primacy of government over the whole Church is promised explicitly but in symbolic language. The primacy of teaching authority is implicitly contained in that of government. In St. Luke the primacy of teaching authority is explicitly promised and in plain language, while the primacy of government is only implied.

Objections Answered

OBJECTION I.—The temptations of Satan mentioned by Our Lord in the passage from St. Luke have reference to the time of the Passion, when as Christ foretold, "You will all be scandalized this night because of me."[77] Hence there is no promise of infallibility or primacy of teaching authority.

Answer.—In the passage quoted there is question of temptations to which all the Apostles succumbed, and the fall of St. Peter was especially grievous. In the text from St. Luke it is distinctly foretold that St. Peter shall not only remain steadfast, but also confirm his brethren. Consequently there is no reference here to the time of the Passion, as the facts plainly show.

OBJECTION II.—St. Peter not only deserted Our Lord during His Passion, but even denied Him with an oath. How, then, can he be called the *rock* of the Church and the *confirmer* of his brethren?

ANSWER.—It is a disputed question whether St. Peter actually denied his faith in Christ on that occasion, or simply sinned against it by denying that he knew Our Lord.[78] But even granting that he actually denied his faith, there is no difficulty to be explained, because at that time, he was neither the *rock* of the Church nor the *confirmer* of his brethren. As yet these powers and dignities had only been promised to him. It was not until after the Resurrection of Christ that he was actually constituted head of the Church with universal power to rule and infallible authority to teach.

---

[77] Matt. xxvi, 31.
[78] Cf. Cornelius a Lapide, "Commentarium in Lucam," xxii, 31.

CHAPTER X

The mere promises of Christ are amply sufficient to establish the fact of St. Peter's primacy over the Church, but we also have the words of Our Lord actually conferring this dignity and power upon him. Then we have the teaching of the Fathers to prove that our interpretation of these words is correct. These facts being established, two other questions call for consideration; viz., the relation of St. Peter to the other Apostles, and the perpetuity of the primacy in the Church.

ART. I. INSTITUTION OF THE PRIMACY

1. Peter Constituted Chief Pastor

Thesis.—The Primacy of Universal Jurisdiction Was Conferred Upon St. Peter When He Was Constituted Supreme Pastor in the Church

PROOF. After the Resurrection Our Lord appeared to His disciples on the shore of Lake Tiberias, and the following dialogue with St. Peter ensued: "Simon, son of John, dost thou love me more than these do? He said to him, Yes, Lord, thou knowest that I love thee. He said to him, Feed my lambs. He said to him a second time, Simon, Son of John, dost thou love me? He said to him, Yes, Lord, thou knowest that I love thee. He said to him, Feed my lambs. A third time he said to him, Simon, son of John, does thou love me? Peter was grieved because he said to him the third time, Dost thou love me? And he said to him, Lord, thou knowest all things, thou knowest that I love thee. He said to him, Feed my sheep."[1]

With this threefold charge, Our Lord solemnly entrusted the care of His flock to St. Peter and thereby conferred upon him the primacy of universal jurisdiction in the Church (a) if the *lambs* and *sheep* represent the whole body of the faithful, and (b) if the pastoral office signifies the power of jurisdiction.

a) There can be no doubt that here, as elsewhere, the *sheep* are Christ's faithful,—those for whom the Good Shepherd gave His life: "I am the good Shepherd. The good shepherd giveth his life for his

---

[1] John xxi, 15-17.

sheep. . . . I am the good Shepherd . . . and I lay down my life for my sheep. And other sheep I have that are not of this fold: them also I must bring, and they shall hear my voice and there shall be one fold and one shepherd."[2] When about to leave this *one fold* by ascending into heaven, Christ constituted Peter supreme pastor in His stead to care for the whole flock: "Feed my lambs; feed my sheep." No exceptions are made; Christ says *My lambs, My sheep,* and it matters not whether *lambs* and *sheep* represent the young and the old in years, the weak and the strong in faith, or laity and clergy; in any case the whole flock of Christ, including even the other Apostles, is clearly meant.

b) In depicting St. Peter as chief shepherd of the flock, Christ teaches that his powers and duties in regard to the faithful shall be those of a shepherd for the sheep committed to his care. He shall guide them into suitable pastures and restrain them from things hurtful; he shall protect them from ravening wolves, from savage dogs, and lurking thieves; he shall care for the weak and bring back those strayed from the fold. If need be, he shall appoint other pastors subject to his own authority, or remove them when the good of the flock demands it.[3]

What more picturesque symbol could be found for the supreme ruling authority in the Church? Translating the imagery into plain language shows St. Peter endowed with supreme power to rule and guide the faithful in all things pertaining to their eternal salvation. He has authority to teach the universal Church, to define doctrines to be accepted as true and wholesome or rejected as false and injurious. He has the power to make laws for the whole Church, or for any part of it, and to dispense or repeal them. He has authority to take cognizance of all things pertaining to faith and morals at any time and throughout the entire Church. He has universal power to judge, absolve, punish, reprove, and correct. He has authority to constitute pastors for any and all parts of the Church, and to limit their jurisdiction in regard to persons, places, and things, or, if need be, to remove them from office. The words are few, "Feed my lambs, feed my sheep," but they are the words of God; their power is divine.[4]

2. Objections Considered

OBJECTION I.—Feeding is simply providing food; hence when Christ said, "Feed my sheep," He meant that St. Peter should provide the faithful with the spiritual food of doctrine by preaching the Gospel

---

[2] John x, 11-16; cf. Jer. xxiii, 1 sq.; Zach. xiii, 7.
[3] Cf. Jer. xxiii, 1 sq.; Ezech. xxiv, 1 sq.; 2 Kings v, 1 sq.; John x, 11 sq.
[4] Murray, "De Ecclesia Christi," Disp. xviii, n. 69.

to them,—a mission given equally to all the Apostles: "Go, therefore, and make disciples of all nations."[5] There is no proof for a primacy of jurisdiction conferred upon St. Peter in this passage.

ANSWER.—Neither the English nor the Latin version brings out the full meaning of our Lord in this passage. The Greek text has *boske* (feed) and *poimane* (shepherd). Hence Moffatt, a non-Catholic, correctly translates: "Feed my lambs, . . . be shepherd to my sheep, . . . feed my sheep."[6] Feeding the flock is only part of St. Peter's duty; he must fulfill all the duties of a shepherd toward his flock: "Shepherd my sheep." In all ancient literature, whether sacred or profane, *poimainein* taken figuratively means to rule as king, i.e., with supreme authority. Homer often calls kings *poimenes laon* (pastors of the people). The Psalmist says: "The Lord ruleth me (*poimaine me*),[7] and in the Apocalypse it is said that Christ shall rule (*poimanei*) with a rod of iron.[8] Arnold, a non-Catholic, says: "This term of feeding as a shepherd feeds his flock, is one of the oldest and most universal metaphors to express a supreme and at the same time a beneficent government."[9]

OBJECTION II.—On this occasion Our Lord was simply restoring to St. Peter the Apostolic dignity and office lost by his denial on the eve of the Passion. The triple profession of love was to atone for the threefold denial.

ANSWER.—There is not the slightest indication anywhere in Scripture that St. Peter lost the Apostolic office on account of his denial, and even had he lost it, he must have received it anew on the very day of the Resurrection, when Our Lord said to him as to the other Apostles: "As the Father hath sent me I also send you."[10] The threefold profession of love was evidently intended to remind St. Peter of his fall and give him the opportunity to make public reparation. St. Peter must have understood it in this light, because he was grieved when Christ asked him the third time: "Lovest thou me?" But this fact has no bearing on the nature of the powers conferred; it would serve to warn him of the manner in which they should be exercised, for as St. Augustine remarks: "What else mean the words, 'Lovest thou me? Feed my sheep,' than if it were said, If thou lovest me, think not of feeding thyself, but feed my sheep as mine, and not as thine own; seek my glory in them, and not thine own; my dominion, and not thine; my gain, not thine."[11]

[5] Matt. xxviii, 19.
[6] James Moffatt, "Translation of the New Testament."
[7] Ps. xxii, 1.
[8] Apoc. xix, 15.
[9] Thomas Arnold, "Fragment on the Church," p. 26.
[10] John xx, 21.
[11] "Tractatus in S. Joannem," cxxiii, 5; P.L., 35, 1967.

OBJECTION III.—St. Paul evidently did not recognize in St. Peter any superiority, such as the primacy of jurisdiction would have conferred upon him, otherwise he would not have rebuked him as he did at Antioch: "But when Cephas was come to Antioch, I withstood him to the face, because he was deserving of blame."[12]

ANSWER.—The same argument would force us to deny that Herod was king for we read that John the Baptist rebuked him to his face. Superiors can claim no exemption from just reproof on the part of a subject, provided that due respect be observed. Hence St. Paul's rebuke to St. Peter at Antioch proves nothing against the primacy; in fact, it proves rather that St. Paul did recognize some sort of superiority in St. Peter. Some false brethren of Jewish origin had been trying to force all Christians to observe the Mosaic Law. St. Paul was their great opponent in this matter, and for this reason they wished to minimize his authority. It seems that they had even denied that he was an Apostle of equal standing with the rest. St. Paul wrote to the Galatians to warn them against these Judaizers and proves that he is a true Apostle and recognized as such by Peter, James, and John, whom the Judaizers were holding up as pillars of the Church. He then goes on to show how he had constantly opposed those "who slipped in to spy upon our liberty which we have in Christ Jesus, that they might bring us into slavery" (to the Mosaic Law). He had even gone so far as to withstand Peter to his face when he was acting imprudently in this matter at Antioch. St. Paul's whole line of argument indicates that his rebuke to St. Peter was something out of the ordinary and therefore presupposed some sort of superiority on the part of St. Peter. This superiority, as just proved, consisted in his primacy of jurisdiction over the whole Church.

ART. II. THE TESTIMONY OF TRADITION

It is to be expected that a doctrine so clearly set forth in S. Scripture as that of St. Peter's primacy will find frequent mention in the writings of the Fathers. This expectation is fully justified by facts. Implicit references are innumerable, since all the Fathers and Councils of the Church from the very earliest times teach that the Roman Pontiff holds supreme jurisdiction in the Church, because he is the legitimate successor of St. Peter. Such implicit testimony usually has more weight that direct statements, because only doctrines admitted as certain by all can be adduced in proof of other doctrines without the formality of proof for their own truth. Many such implicit arguments will be found in the

---

[12] Gal. ii, 11.

The Church of Christ

chapter on the Roman Pontiff.[13] For the sake of brevity only a few of the more explicit testimonies from the Eastern and Western Churches will be cited here.

I. EASTERN CHURCH. a) ORIGEN: "When the chief care of the sheep was being committed to Peter, and the Church was being founded upon him as the foundation, the profession of no other virtue than charity was demanded of him."[14]

b) ST. JOHN CHRYSOSTOM: "He said unto him; *Feed my sheep*. And why, having passed by the others, doth He speak with Peter on these matters? He was the chosen one of the Apostles, the mouth-piece of the disciples, the leader of the band; on this account also Paul went up upon a time to inquire of him rather than the others. And at the same time to show him that he must now be of good cheer, since the denial was done away, Jesus putteth into his hands the chief authority among the brethren. . . . He said: If thou lovest Me, preside over My brethren. . . . And if any one should say: How then did James receive the chair at Jerusalem?—I would make reply, that He appointed Peter teacher, not of the chair but of the world. . . . He was entrusted with the chief authority over the brethren."[15]

c) ST. EPHREM SYRUS: "Our Lord selected Simon Peter, con-stituted him prince of the Apostles, the foundation of His holy Church and her firm support. He made him head of the Apostles and com-manded him to feed His flock and teach laws for the preservation of pure doctrine."[16]

d) GREEK LITURGY. In the Greek Liturgy St. Peter is often referred to as *occupying the chief throne* among the Apostles, the *supreme head* of the Apostles and the one *presiding over* them.[17]

e) SYRIAC LITURGY: "Christ, the Head-Shepherd, stayed thee up, O Peter, as ruler of the faithful, and entrusted thee with the man-agement of His flock."[18]

f) SYRO-CHALDAIC LITURGY: "Here is Simon, whom the Lord thrice called upon, saying, Feed my rams and my gentle sheep. I en-trust thee with the keys of my spiritual treasury, that thou mayest bind and loose on earth and in Heaven. I will install thee vicar of the Heavenly Kingdom; rule justly and govern the children of thy house-hold the Church."[19]

---

[13] See below, Ch. xi, Art. ii.
[14] "In Epist. ad Romanos," i, 5; P.G., 14, 1053.
[15] "Hom., in Joannem," lxxxviii, I, 2; P.G., 59, 478.*
[16] "De Abraham Kidnuaia," Hymn, v (Lamy, I, 75).
[17] Nilles, "Kalendarium Manuale," I, 72, 194.
[18] Benni, "Tradition of the Syriac Church of Antioch," p. 57.
[19] *Op. cit.*, Ch. i.

II. WESTERN CHURCH. a) ST. CYPRIAN: "Peter, whom the Lord chose first and upon whom He built His Church, when Paul disputed with him about circumcision, did not claim anything insolently, nor did he arrogantly assume anything so as to say that he held the primacy and ought to be obeyed by novices."[20] In this St. Cyprian praises St. Peter for his humility and meekness in not *arrogantly* asserting his power of primacy, as he might have done.

b) MARIUS VICTORINUS: "After three years, says Paul, I came to Jerusalem. He then gives the reason: To see Peter! For if the foundation of the Church was placed in Peter, as the Gospel says, and this was known to Paul by revelation, he realized that he ought to visit the one to whom Christ had given such great authority."[21]

c) AMBROSIASTER: "Paul's desire to see Peter was praiseworthy because Peter was the first among the Apostles and the one to whom the Saviour had committed the care of the churches."[22]

d) ST. LEO THE GREAT: "Peter alone, out of the whole world, was selected to preside over the calling of all nations, and was placed over all the Apostles and all parts of the Church, so that, although there are many priests and pastors among the people of God, Peter really rules those whom Christ primarily rules."[23]

ART. III. ST. PETER AND THE OTHER APOSTLES

APOSTLES SUBJECT TO PETER. St. Peter alone was constituted the foundation of the Church and supreme pastor of the flock. He alone was appointed to confirm the brethren, and to him alone were given the keys to the kingdom. He was therefore constituted supreme ruler of the whole Church and of its every part; all the faithful, individually and collectively, were subjected to his authority. Consequently St. Peter possessed real power of jurisdiction over the other Apostles, both as individuals and as members of the Apostolic college.

When speaking to all the Apostles as a body, Christ said: "All power in heaven and on earth has been given to me. Go, therefore, and make disciples of all nations. . . . As the Father has sent me, I also send you. . . . Whatever you bind on earth shall be bound also in heaven; and whatever you loose on earth shall be loosed also in heaven."[24] These words, taken by themselves, would indicate that equal powers

---

[20] "Epis. ad Quintum," 3; P.L., 4, 410.
[21] "In Galatas," I, 18; P.L., 8, 1155.
[22] An ancient commentary formerly attributed to St. Ambrose, hence the unknown author is designated "Ambrosiaster." (P.L., 17, 344.)
[23] "Sermon," IV: P.L., 54, 149.
[24] Matt. xxviii, 18, 19; John xx, 21; Matt. xviii, 18.

were given to all the Apostles, and that in consequence St. Peter enjoyed no preeminence of authority over the rest. But, as noted before, all authority must be exercised according to the constitution of the society for which it is given. The power conferred upon the Apostles was to be exercised in the Church instituted by Christ as a kingdom with St. Peter as supreme ruler. It is evident, then, that all power received by the other Apostles was subject to the authority of St. Peter and to be exercised under his direction, i.e., St. Peter had real jurisdiction, both direct and indirect, over the other Apostles.

DIRECT JURISDICTION. All the faithful were committed to the teaching and governing power of St. Peter, when Christ said to him: "Feed my lambs; feed my sheep." The Apostles were included with the rest of the faithful, since Christ made no exception; in fact, an exception for the Apostles is precluded by the very nature of their office. The Apostles constituted an organized governing body, of which St. Peter was the divinely appointed head; consequently they were directly subject to him as members of the Church and also as members of the Apostolic body. But the Apostles, being personally infallible, confirmed in grace and endowed with special knowledge by the Holy Spirit, could neither err against faith nor fail seriously in regard to charity or prudence; hence there was but little need for the exercise of any authority over them on the part of St. Peter. Such authority was needed only for extraordinary affairs such as, for instance, the election of St. Matthias, the calling of a council or the enactment of disciplinary regulations for the whole Church.

INDIRECT JURISDICTION. The Apostles were also indirectly subject to St. Peter because of his direct jurisdiction over those immediately subject to them. In virtue of their office, received directly from Christ, the Apostles had equal authority to preach the Gospel and to establish churches in any part of the world, but orderly progress and discipline in the Church demanded that no Apostle should interfere with, or exercise jurisdiction over, a church established by another Apostle. For this reason St. Paul writes to the Romans that he had long desired to preach the Gospel to them as to other nations, but that he had been restrained hitherto because it was his custom not to preach "where Christ has already been named, lest I might build on another man's foundation."[25] Peter alone, as supreme pastor, was privileged to exercise jurisdiction over all churches throughout the world. It was his special prerogative to make laws for all the faithful, even against the will of the Apostle who labored among them. He could also annul

---

[25] Rom. I, 11 sq.; xv, 20.

any law or regulation made by the other Apostles for their respective churches.

COROLLARY. St. Peter, as an Apostle, was in no way superior to the other Apostles. In virtue of the Apostolic office, all possessed the same power of Orders and the same authority to teach and govern. For this reason the Fathers often say that the Apostles enjoyed equal powers; e.g., St. Cyprian says: "Assuredly the rest of the Apostles were also the same as Peter, endowed with a like partnership both of honor and power."[26] St. Peter exercised supreme jursidiction because he was more than an Apostle; he was also the head of the Church, as St. Cyprian explains in the passage from which the above words are quoted: "Although to all the Apostles, after the Resurrection, Christ gives an equal power, . . . yet that He might set forth unity, He arranges by His authority the origin of that unity as beginning from one (St. Peter)."

ART. IV. THE PRIMACY A PERMANENT INSTITUTION

Protestant scholars today generally admit that St. Peter enjoyed a certain preeminence of honor; some even admit a primacy of jurisdiction; but practically all agree that whatever privileges or powers he possessed were strictly personal and, therefore, not to be perpetuated by a line of succession. "Protestants generally," says a non-Catholic author, "even when they have admitted the individual primacy of Peter, have denied that these powers and privilege have been continued in his successors, the Bishops of Rome. The usual assertion and favorite contention of Protestants is that the papacy originated in the Middle Ages and was the result of the worldly ambition and love of power on the part of certain designing popes. When the stern light of history, thrown upon the medieval period, has forced these controversialists to seek a more distant beginning for the papacy, they have hit upon some earlier Pope, as Gregory the Great, Leo I, or Victor, as the originator of the Roman supremacy."[27]

Lightfoot even admits that the first steps toward papal domination are found in the Epistle of Clement of Rome to the Corinthians, towards the end of the first century.[28] But whatever the date of its origin, the primacy found in the Church today, in the opinion of Protestants, is a mere human institution that owes its existence chiefly to the importance

---

[26] "De Unitate Ecclesiae," 4; P.L., 4, 449.
[27] Edmund S. Middleton, "Unity and Rome," p. 62.
[28] J. B. Lightfoot, "St. Clement of Rome," Vol. I, p. 70.

which attached to the Church of Rome on account of its location in the capital of the Empire.

Eastern schismatics admit a primacy of honor transmitted to the successors of St. Peter, but they seem to hold that this primacy was transferred to Constantinople when that city became the capital of the Roman empire.[29] Anglicans of the High Church party also admit a primacy of honor perpetuated to an extent in the successors of St. Peter; a few of the more advanced High Churchmen even admit a primacy of jurisdiction. Opposed to these theories is the doctrine of the Catholic Church, expressed in the following thesis:

Thesis.—St. Peter's Primacy of Universal Jurisdiction Over the Church Is Perpetuated in His Successors According to Divine Institution

This doctrine is a dogma of faith, defined by the Vatican Council in the following words: "If any one should deny that it is by the institution of Christ the Lord, or by divine right, that blessed Peter should have a perpetual line of successors in the primacy over the universal Church, . . . let him be anathema."[30]

It is here maintained that the primacy of universal jurisdiction conferred upon St. Peter was not a personal privilege, such as the power of working miracles, or freedom from sin, but a permanent institution, necessary for the very existence of the Church. Therefore, the primacy with all its powers and privileges is transmitted to the successors of St. Peter, who form an unbroken line of supreme pastors to rule the Church in its continued existence as the *one, holy, Catholic,* and *Apostolic* Church founded by Christ.

PROOF. The various symbols used by Our Lord to designate the powers conferred upon St. Peter, clearly indicate their nature and the purpose for which they were conferred, thus proving also that their continued existence in the Church is a necessity.

a) St. Peter was constituted the rock foundation of the Church in order to give it unity and strength, and to secure it against the powers of darkness and the gates of hell in all ages, "even to the consummation of the world." Therefore, the power and authority that made St. Peter the *rock* of the Church must remain intact for all time; his primacy of jurisdiction must be perpetuated in the only possible way, i.e., by transmission through a continuous line of successors. No doubt, Our Lord could have provided some other means to preserve the unity of

---

[29] D'Ales, "Dictionnaire Apologetique," Vol. II, Col. 365.
[30] Denzinger, n. 1825.

His Church and secure it against all foes, but we are not concerned with what He *could* have done; we wish to know what He *actually did*, and the only answer is that He provided for the continued existence of the Church by establishing a primacy of jurisdiction. Therefore, such a primacy is necessary by divine institution.

b) Through the power of the keys, St. Peter became custodian of the Church and all its spiritual treasures; the power to bind and loose constituted him supreme law-giver and judge in the Church. Such powers are never given for the benefit of him who exercises them, but for those over whom he rules; therefore, the duration of Peter's primacy is to be measured, not by the brief span of his mortal life, but by the ever lengthening centuries of the Church's existence. The Church must ever have a custodian, a supreme law-giver and judge, if she is to continue as Christ founded her.

The primacy was not a personal privilege granted to St. Peter as a reward for his outspoken professions of faith and love, as some would have it. To institute an office is one thing; to confer that office upon one person rather than another is quite a different thing. St. Peter's faith and love, no doubt, merited for him the honor of being chosen supreme pastor of the Church, but they contributed nothing to the institution of the office itself.

c) The permanent character of the primacy is also deduced from the teaching authority committed to St. Peter with the injunction to *confirm* his brethren. In conferring this power, Christ was undoubtedly looking to the future, when the successors of the Apostles, lacking the gift of personal infallibility, would stand in need of such a guiding power in the Church to prevent their being "carried about by every wind of doctrine; ever learning but never attaining knowledge of the truth."[31] The wisdom of Christ in establishing such an authority is readily seen by comparing the unity of faith in the Church with the Babel of confusion that reigns outside.

---

[31] Eph. iv, 14; 2 Tim. iii, 7

CHAPTER XI

Successors to St. Peter

Since the primacy of St. Peter is a permanent institution, perpetuated in the Church by a line of legitimate successors, the question naturally arises: Who are those successors? The answer is stated in the form of a thesis.

ART. I. THE DOCTRINE AND ITS PROOFS

Thesis.—The Roman Pontiff Is the Legitimate Successor of St. Peter in His Primacy of Universal Jurisdiction Over the Church

DOCTRINE DEFINED. The doctrine set forth in the thesis has been defined as a dogma of faith by the Vatican Council: "If any one should deny . . . that the Roman Pontiff is the successor of the blessed Peter in his primacy; let him be anathema."[1] And again: "Peter the Prince and Chief of the Apostles . . . lives, presides, and judges to this day and always in his successors, the bishops of the Holy See of Rome, which was founded by him and consecrated by his blood. Hence, whosoever, succeeds to Peter in this See, does by the institution of Christ himself obtain the Primacy of Peter over the whole Church."[2]

Fifteen hundred years before this, Pope Damasus I had defined the same doctrine. In the year 382 he solemnly decreed that "the holy Roman Church obtained the primacy, not by decrees of councils, but by the words of the Lord and Saviour: *Thou art Peter and upon this rock I will build my Church.*"[3]

NATURE OF PROOFS. Whether or not the bishop of Rome is the legitimate successor of St. Peter is a purely historical question that must be established in the same manner as every other historical fact, i.e., by the testimony of competent witnesses and by a critical examination of everything connected with it. Therefore it is necessary (1) to adduce competent witnesses sufficient to establish the fact, and (2) to consider the objections urged against it.

It is taken for granted that St. Peter came to Rome, where he established his episcopal see and gave his life for the faith. These facts

---

[1] Denzinger, n. 1825.
[2] Denzinger, n. 1824.
[3] This decree, first made by Damasus I, was afterwards repeated by Gelasius I, in 495. (See Denzinger, n. 163; P.L., 59, 159.)

are now admitted by all, but the truth of our thesis does not depend upon them. Christ could have personally designated the bishop of Rome as the successor of St. Peter, or He could have left it to St. Peter to designate a line of succession. In either case the bishop of Rome, being designated as such, would have become the lawful successor of St. Peter with all his powers of jurisdiction, even though St. Peter had never set foot within the Eternal City.

As a matter of interest, however, it may be mentioned that all scholars of reputation, both Catholic and non-Catholic, admit that St. Peter came to Rome and died there about the year 67. It will be sufficient to quote the eminent archeologist, Rodolfo Lanciani: "For the archeologist the presence of SS. Peter and Paul in Rome are facts established beyond the shadow of doubt by purely monumental evidence. There was a time when persons belonging to different creeds made it almost a case of conscience to affirm or deny *a priori* these facts according to their acceptance or rejection of the tradition of any particular church. This state of feeling is a matter of the past, at least for those who have followed the progress of recent discoveries and of critical literature."[4]

THE ARGUMENT STATED. Since the successors of St. Peter are the supreme pastors in the Church with jurisdiction over bishops, priests, and people in every part of the world, their identity must have been a matter of common knowledge to all in every age. No organized society, at least none publicly known and operating in the light of day, can be ignorant of its own organization and of the official who exercises its supreme power. Therefore, whoever has been recognized at all times by the whole Church as supreme pastor, must be the legitimate successor of that first pastor, St. Peter. But the bishop of Rome, and he alone, has been recognized at all times by the universal Church as its supreme head on earth. Therefore the bishop of Rome is the legitimate and only successor of St. Peter and rules the Church by divine authority.

In order to substantiate the fact of universal recognition of the bishop of Rome as supreme head of the Church, it is necessary to consider the first five or six centuries only. Even the most pronounced enemies of the Roman Primacy freely admit that the bishop of Rome has been universally recognized as head of the Church in the West since the sixth century, and perhaps even since the fifth. They also admit that the idea of the Primacy was forming in the Church even before that date, but maintain that it was entirely unknown in the first

---

[4] Rodolfo Lanciani, "Pagan and Christian Rome," p. 123.

centuries and was never accepted in the East, except, perhaps, as a primacy of mere honor.

It will be sufficient, then, to cite a few of the innumerable witnesses at hand to prove that both East and West recognized in the bishop of Rome a primacy of real jurisdiction over the whole Church, and this not from the third or fourth century only, but from the very days of SS. Peter and Paul in Rome. These witnesses will be arranged by centuries, beginning with the fifth and going back to the first. Brevity is sacrificed for accuracy by quoting more at length than is customary in order to show that the sense of a writer has not been perverted by taking his words out of their context. Brief notices of councils and other historical events are added to bring out the exact values of the testimony cited.

The wealth of material in this matter and its evidential value can be appreciated only by an extended study of the literature of those ages. No amount of quoting from authors can do justice to the question. The voluminous correspondence that passed between the bishops of Rome on the one hand, and the bishops and emperors of the East on the other, seldom mentions the primacy of Rome directly; this fact was admitted by all, and other questions are discussed on that basis. Even a casual perusal of the varied correspondence brings this fact home with striking force; but from the nature of the case, it is often impossible to select any single passage that will even partially reveal this constantly underlying faith in the primacy of the Roman Pontiff.

Witnesses are selected largely from the Eastern Church, and for two reasons: first, because of the persistent claim that the Eastern Church never recognized a primacy of jurisdiction in the Church of Rome, and secondly, because any authority exercised over the Eastern Church by the Roman Pontiff must be ascribed to his primacy over the universal Church. The Pope, as is well known, exercises a multiple authority in his various capacities as bishop of Rome, primate of Italy, patriarch of the West, and supreme pastor of the whole Church. Authority exercised over a church of the West might, at times, be ascribed to his power as patriarch, but this cannot be the case in the East, where he possesses no authority except that of supreme pastor of the universal Church.

ART. II. THE TESTIMONY OF HISTORY

1. Witnesses From the Fifth Century

I. FLAVIAN OF CONSTANTINOPLE. Eutyches, archimandrite of a monastery outside the walls of Constantinople, was excommunicated and deposed by Flavian. He appealed to Rome and accused

Flavian of condemning him after he had made an appeal. Flavian also wrote the Pope, Leo the Great, as follows: "Deign to confirm by your letters the deposition canonically made. . . . The affair needs only aid and pressure on your part to bring peace and tranquillity at once through your prudence. By the help of God, through your letters, the heresy which has arisen and the tumult which it has caused will be easily ended. The council, which reports say is to be called, will also be forestalled and disturbance to all churches throughout the world prevented."[4a]

The fact that Eutyches appealed to Rome proves that the Pope had an acknowledged right to interfere in matters pertaining to the Eastern Church. When Leo rebuked Flavian for condemning Eutyches after he had appealed his case to Rome, Flavian did not exculpate himself by saying that Leo had no authority to interpose in the matter, but simply explained that Eutyches had misrepresented the case by stating that his condemnation had taken place after appeal to Rome, which was not true. It was on this occasion that Flavian wrote the words quoted above, openly acknowledging supreme power of jurisdiction in the bishop of Rome, because without such power letters from him could not have ended the heresy and even forestalled a council.

II. COUNCIL OF CHALCEDON. Eutyches having lost his case in Rome, now turned to the civil power for assistance. The Emperor Theodosius yielded to his entreaties and called a council to meet at Ephesus in 449. By command of the Emperor, Dioscorus, patriarch of Alexandria, presided, but Leo's letter to the council was not read, the canons of the Church were disregarded, and the whole proceedings were carried out in such a high-handed manner that the Pope dubbed it the *Robber Council,* and annulled all its acts. This fact alone proves the recognized power of the Pope over the Eastern Church, but the sequel is still more convincing.

In 451 another council of about six hundred Eastern bishops convened at Chalcedon, to correct the evils caused by the Robber Council of Ephesus. When the legates sent by Pope Leo saw Dioscorus sitting in the council, one of them, Paschasinus by name, arose and addressed the bishops in these words: "We hold in our hands letters from that most blessed and Apostolic man, the Pope of Rome, who is head of all the churches. His Apostolic Excellency commands by these letters that Dioscorus shall not have a seat in the council and shall only be admitted for a hearing. It is necessary that these instructions be carried out." Then turning to the imperial officers, he continued: "Your

---

[4a] "Epist. ad Leonem"; P.L., 54, 747.

Excellencies will order this man to leave, or we go out." When asked for the reason of this action, Lucentius, another legate, replied: "Because he has dared to hold a council without authority from the Apostolic See, a thing that was never done before, and is not lawful to be done."[5]

Dioscorus was ejected from the council, his case was heard, and sentence pronounced against him in these words: "Leo, the most holy and blessed Archbishop of the great and elder Rome, through us and through this holy Synod, together with the thrice blessed and most praiseworthy Apostle Peter, who is the rock and support of the Catholic Church and the foundation of true faith, has stripped Dioscorus of his episcopal dignity, and also removed him from all priestly ministration."[6]

At the close of the council, the bishops sent the *Acts* to Pope Leo for confirmation. In the accompanying letter they said: "If Christ promised to be in the midst of two or three gathered together in His name, what should we not expect when five hundred and twenty bishops are assembled, . . . especially when thou didst preside as head over its members. This thou didst in those who represented thee. . . . We have brought the whole contents of what we have done to thy knowledge, and have communicated it to thee for confirmation and assent."[7]

Comments on the transactions just described are superfluous; they speak for themselves, explicitly acknowledging supreme power of jurisdiction in the bishop of Rome. Words could not be plainer, and they express the unanimous belief of more than five hundred Eastern bishops!

III. THE COUNCIL OF EPHESUS. Pope Celestine condemned the heretic Nestorius and deposed him from the See of Constantinople. Execution of the sentence was entrusted to St. Cyril of Alexandria in these words: "Taking to yourself the authority of our See, and acting in our stead, you will execute the sentence strictly according to its provisions; viz., He shall condemn his evil teachings in writing within ten days, . . . or failing in this, Your Holiness will immediately look to the good of his church and let it know that he must be entirely removed from our body."[8]

Nestorius, after the usual manner of heretics, appealed to the civil authorities, and Theodosius, wishing to favor him, called a council, which met at Ephesus in 431. St. Cyril presided. After the council had

---

[5] Mansi, t. vi, coll. 579-582.
[6] Mansi, t. vi, col. 1047.
[7] Migne, P.L., 54, 959 sq.
[8] "Epist. ad Cyrillum Alexand."; P.L., 50, 463.

opened, legates arrived from Rome with a letter from Pope Celestine, saying: "In our solicitude we have sent the holy brethren, our fellow-ministers, . . . Bishop Arcadius, Bishop Projectus and the Presbyter Philip, to take part in the proceedings and to carry out what we have already decreed. We do not doubt that Your Holiness will give assent thereunto."[9]

In the second session of the council Philip addressed the bishops as follows: "No one doubts, in fact it has never been known in all ages, that the most holy and most blessed Peter, Prince of the Apostles, the pillar of faith and foundation of the Catholic Church, received the keys to the kingdom from Our Lord Jesus Christ, the Saviour and Redeemer of mankind. The power of binding and loosing sins was also given to him, who even today and ever lives and judges in his successors. Our holy and most blessed Pope, Bishop Celestine, holding the place of this Peter in due order of succession, has sent us to represent him in this holy synod."[10]

After the three citations demanded by canon law, the council proceeded to pass sentence of deposition against Nestorius: "We come to the sorrowful sentence against him in accordance with the sacred canons, being constrained of necessity by the letter of the most holy Father and fellow minister Celestine, bishop of the Roman Church. . . . Wherefore, let Nestorius understand that he is separated from communion in the priesthood of the Catholic Church."[11]

Here again two hundred bishops of the Eastern Church acknowledge by word and act the supreme jurisdiction of Rome. Pope Celestine excommunicated and deposed Nestorius, bishop of Constantinople, at that time capital of the Empire; he commissioned St. Cyril, patriarch of Alexandria, to execute the sentence. He sent legates to the council with letters directing the bishops to confirm what he had decreed, yet there was not a word of protest voiced in the council. On the contrary, the bishops acknowledged his rights and powers in the matter; they openly stated that they were constrained,—*necessarily* constrained,—by Celestine's letter to proceed against Nestorius. In the second session of the council, the Pope's legate stated that St. Peter's position as head of the Church was known to all, and that Celestine, being his legitimate successor, occupied the same position, yet no one denied or questioned the statement. A more explicit acknowledgment of Rome's Supremacy could not be made.

[9] "Epist. ad Synodum Ephesinam"; P.L., 50, 511.
[10] Mansi, t. iv, col. 1295.
[11] Mansi, t. iv, coll. 1211, 1295.

2. Witnesses From the Fourth Century

I. POPE DAMASUS 1 (366-384). The convictions of Pope Damasus in this matter are evident from his decree of 382: "The Church of Rome was not raised above the other churches by any synodical decree, but received the primacy by virtue of the words of Our Lord and Saviour recorded in the Gospel: 'Thou art Peter, etc.' "[12] He exercised this supremacy over East and West alike. He condemned Eustatius and Apollinaris, both heretics of the East; he deposed Maximus the Cynic from the See of Constantinople and confirmed the election of Nectarius in his stead.[13] When a number of Eastern bishops petitioned him to depose Timothy, also an Eastern bishop, he replied: "It is indeed a great honor to yourselves that you give due reverence to the Apostolic See. . . I wish to inform you, brethren, that we have already deposed Timothy, the profane disciple of Apollinaris, and condemned his impious doctrine."[14] St. Jerome also informs us that matters from every part of the Church were brought to Pope Damasus for adjudication. He says: "Several years ago, while I was assisting Damasus, bishop of the City of Rome, in the office of the Church archives, I used to reply to synodical matters referred both from the East and from the West."[15]

II. ST. JEROME. In 376 St. Jerome himself consulted Pope Damasus concerning a matter pertaining to the church in Antioch, where a schism was in progress, with three claimants for the episcopal throne. He says: "The church here is divided into three parties, each trying to draw me to its side. . . . But I cry out: I hold with the one who is in union with the chair of Peter. Melitius, Vitalis, and Paulinus all claim to be in union with you. If only one of them claimed this, I could believe him, but as it is, two at least, and perhaps all of them, are lying. Therefore, I beseech Your Blessedness . . . to inform me by letter with whom I am to communicate here in Syria."[16]

These words of St. Jerome leave no doubt that union with the See of Rome and approbation by the Roman Pontiff were considered necessary at Antioch, itself a patriarchal see that claimed St. Peter as its founder. If the primacy of Rome be denied, there is no reason why Antioch should have considered union with her any more important than union with the other patriarchal sees.

---

[12] Denzinger, n. 163; P.L., 59, 159.
[13] Jaffe, "Regist. Episcoporum," 237, 238.
[14] Pope Damasus, "Epist. ad Episcopos Orientis"; P.L., 13, 370.
[15] "Epist. ad Ageruchiam"; P.L., 22, 1952.
[16] "Epist. ad Damasum"; P.L., 22, 359.

III. ST. BASIL THE GREAT. Appeal was also made to Pope Damasus from the East by St. Basil the Great of Cappadocia. In 371 he wrote to Damasus describing the sad condition of the Church in those parts, and implored his assistance: "I have looked upon the visit of Your Mercifulness as the only possible solution of our difficulties. Ever in the past have I been consoled by your extraordinary affection; and for a short time my heart was cheered by the gratifying report that we shall be visited by you. But as I was disappointed, I have been constrained to beseech you by letter to be moved to help us. . . . In this I am by no means making any novel request, but am only asking what has been customary."[17]

In another letter on the same subject, St. Basil says: "Of these things I implore you to take due heed. This will be the case if you will consent to write to all the churches of the East, that those who have perverted these doctrines are in communion with you if they amend, but that if they contentiously determine to abide by their innovations, you are separated from them."[18] Even stronger words are found in a letter to St. Athanasius: "It has seemed to me to be desirable to send a letter to the Bishop of Rome, begging him to examine our condition, and since there are difficulties in the way of representatives being sent from the West by a general synodical decree, to advise him to exercise his own personal authority in the matter by choosing suitable persons to sustain the labors of a journey,—suitable too, by gentleness and firmness of character to correct the unruly amongst us."[19]

IV. THE CASE OF EUSTATIUS. The history of this case proves the authority of the Roman Pontiff over the Eastern Churches. Eustatius, bishop of Sebaste in Asia Minor, was deposed by the Synod of Melitene. Thereupon he appealed to Pope Liberius, who reversed the decision and ordered his reinstatement. When he appeared with the Pope's letter at the Synod of Tyana, he was restored to his see without further question. This is evident from a letter of St. Basil written to Liberius's successor, Pope Damasus, regarding Eustatius: "What propositions were made to him by Liberius, and to what he agreed, I am ignorant. I only know that he brought a letter restoring him, which he showed to the synod of Tyana and was restored to his see."[20]

V. COUNCIL OF SARDICA (343 or 344). Among the decrees passed at Sardica in Moesia, several deal with the trial and deposition

---

[17] "Epist. ad Damasum"; P.G., 32, 434.*
[18] "Epist. ad Damasum"; P.G., 32, 982.*
[19] St. Basil the Great, "Epist. ad Athanasium"; P.G., 32, 431.*
[20] St. Basil the Great, "Epist. ad Damasum"; P.G., 32, 979.*

of bishops and with the procedure in case of appeal to the Bishop of Rome. One of these reads: "If judgment has gone against a bishop in any case, and he thinks that he has a good case, in order that the question may be reopened, let us, if it be your pleasure, honor the memory of St. Peter, the Apostle, and let those who tried the case write to Julius, the Bishop of Rome, and if he shall judge that the case should be retried, let that be done, and let him appoint judges."[21]

Another decree provides that in case a bishop, condemned in this second trial, should appeal to Rome, no one shall be consecrated in his stead, until the bishop of Rome has decided the case: "When any bishop has been deposed by the judgment of those bishops who have sees in neighboring places, and he shall announce that his case is to be examined in the city of Rome,—no other bishop shall in any wise be ordained to his see after the appeal of him who is apparently deposed, unless the case shall have been determined in the judgment of the Roman bishop."[22]

These decrees explicitly acknowledge the right of any bishop to appeal his case to the supreme tribunal of the Roman Pontiff, and in case he does so, any sentence of deposition pronounced against him shall be held in abeyance,—he is only *apparently deposed,*—until the sentence has been ratified in Rome. For this reason no one is to be ordained to his see in the meantime.

VI. POPE JULIUS I (337-352). The Eusebian party of Arians unjustly brought about the deposition and exile of St. Athanasius and Marcellus in 336. They then met at Antioch and passed decrees to prevent their return. Pope Julius severely condemned this action and wrote as follows: "Even if they were guilty of crime, as you say, judgment should have been given according to the canons of the Church, not in the manner in which you acted. You should have written to us first of all, that we might decide what was just. . . . Above all, why was nothing written to us from the church at Alexandria? Do you not know that it is the custom to write us first of all, so that justice may be dispensed from here? If any suspicion attached to the bishop of that city, it should have been notified to this church. But they have proceeded in the matter without notifying us; . . . but that was a strange procedure, a novel invention."[23]

The Pope's action in this matter, and even the tone of his letter, shows that the bishop of Rome possessed a recognized authority of

[21] Mansi, t. iii, col. 32.*
[22] Mansi, t. iii, col. 32.*
[23] Pope Julius I, "Epist. ad Antiochenos"; P.L., 8, 906.

long standing in the Eastern Church; acting without his authority was a strange and novel proceeding. Nor was this a mere assumption on the part of Julius, as is evident from the fact that St. Athanasius journeyed to Rome to lay the matter before him,—a useless undertaking if the Pope's authority was not recognized in the East.

3. Witnesses From the Third Century

The incessant persecutions that harassed the Church during the first three centuries made it difficult, and often impossible, for the Roman Pontiff to exercise jurisdiction over distant churches; nevertheless, several incidents are recorded which prove that the Pope was recognized as chief pastor in the Church, and that he actually exercised authority as such, when occasion demanded and circumstances permitted.

I. TERTULLIAN. After Tertullian fell away from the Church, he became very bitter toward the bishops of Rome, as heretics are wont to do. In his work *De Pudicitia* he inveighs against a certain edict published by Zephyrinus or Callistus. He says: "I even hear that an edict has been published,—a peremptory edict, which the supreme pontiff, that bishop of bishops, has put forth."[24] The titles here used in derision by Tertullian evidently presuppose a claim to supreme jurisdiction on the part of the Pope; no other meaning could be attached to the phrase "bishop of bishops." This is also true of the other title, "supreme pontiff." The Pontifex Maximus (supreme pontiff) was the highest in authority among the pagan priests of Rome, with jurisdiction over all religious matters. The office had been held by the emperors themselves since the year 13 B. C. Hence, when Tertullian applies the term to the bishop of Rome, he clearly intimates the position claimed for the pope in the Church.

II. DIONYSIUS OF ALEXANDRIA (d. 264). St. Athanasius says that when Dionysius, patriarch of Alexandria, was accused of heresy by some of his people, the Pope, who happened to bear the same name, immediately asked for an explanation and a profession of faith. The patriarch at once complied by composing two works concerning the faith which he submitted to the Pope: "When Dionysius the bishop, . . . moved by zeal for religion, had written to Ammonius and Euphranor against the Sabellian heresy, some of the brethren . . . betook themselves to Rome and accused him before his namesake, Dionysius, bishop of Rome. When he had heard these things, he sent

---

[24] "De Pudicitia," c. I; P.L., 2, 980.

a letter to Dionysius to acquaint him of the things of which he was
accused by these men. In order to prove his innocence, Dionysius set
about at once to edit the books which he entitled *Elenchus* and
Apologia."²⁵

The very fact that these men went to Rome to accuse their bishop,
proves that they recognized some superior authority in the bishop
of that city, and Dionysius' solicitude to refute their charges shows
that he also acknowledged this superiority.

III. ST. CYPRIAN (200-258). Felicissimus and Fortunatus rejected the authority of St. Cyprian in Carthage and started an open
schism by setting up a bishop of their own. They then sent emissaries
to Rome, in order to stir up like troubles there. St. Cyprian, apprised
of this project, writes to Pope Cornelius. He describes their actions in
Carthage and then adds: "After such things as these they still dare
. . . to set sail and to bear letters from schismatic and profane persons
to the throne of Peter, and to the chief Church, whence priestly unity
takes its source."²⁶

On another occasion, when St. Cyprian had heard that Marcian,
bishop of Arles, had fallen into heresy, he wrote to Pope Stephen,
asking him to excommunicate Marcian and have another bishop installed in his place. He says: "It behooves you to write a very copious
letter to our fellow bishops appointed in Gaul, not to suffer any longer
that Marcian . . . should insult our assembly, because he does not yet
seem to be excommunicated by us. . . . Let letters be directed by you
into the province and to the people abiding at Arles, by which Marcian
being excommunicated, another may be substituted in his place."²⁷

St. Cyprian takes for granted that Pope Stephen has the necessary
authority to excommunicate a bishop in Gaul and to see to it that
another is consecrated in his stead; it is only necessary to remind him
of the need for taking such action.²⁸ No doubt is entertained that such
action will be taken; in fact, it is so certain that St. Cyprian speaks
as if the matter were already settled, for he says: "Inform us who
has been substituted at Arles in the place of Marcian, that we may
know to whom to direct our brethren, and to whom we ought to write."

IV. EMPEROR AURELIAN (270-275). The supreme authority
of the Roman Pontiff was known even to the pagans of Rome, as is
evident from an incident that happened in the reign of Aurelian. Paul
of Samosata, bishop of Antioch, had been deposed by his fellow-bish-

²⁵ St. Athanasius, "In Sententiam Dionysii"; P.G., 25, 499.
²⁶ "Epist. ad Cornelium," xiv; P.L., 3, 818.*
²⁷ St. Cyprian, "Epist. ad Stephanum Papam"; P.L., 3, 993-994.
²⁸ See Ch. xi, objection ix, regarding St. Cyprian's controversy with Pope Stephen.

ops, but refused to give up possession of the episcopal residence. He was protected in this matter by Zenobia, queen of Palmyra. When Aurelian came to Antioch after his victory over Zenobia, the case was brought before him for settlement; "and he decided it most equitably, ordering the building to be given to those whom the bishops of Italy and of the city of Rome should adjudge it."[29]

The mention of *bishops of Italy* in connection with the bishop of Rome does not weaken the testimony in the least, since it is well-known that the Pope did not decide important questions without first seeking counsel of others. It was customary to convoke a synod composed of the bishops in the vicinity of Rome, and those who happened to be visiting there at the time. The titular priests and regional deacons also took part in the deliberations. The decisions arrived at were embodied in the form of synodal decrees. For this reason the Pope generally employed the plural *we* when communicating with other churches. The Pope still has his advisers; the bishops in the vicinity of Rome, the titular priests of the City, and the regional deacons form the college of cardinals,—the Pope's cabinet of official counselors.

4. Witnesses From the Second Century

I. ST. IRENAEUS (d. about 200). The testimony of St. Irenaeus is especially valuable, because it gives the faith of the Church in the East and West alike. He was born and grew to manhood in Asia Minor, where he heard the teaching of St. Polycarp, a disciple of St. John the Evangelist. He then came to Rome and was finally made bishop of Lyons in Gaul.

In his work *Against Heresies,* St. Irenaeus appeals to the doctrines handed down by lawful succession from the Apostles as proof against the heretics of his day. He then says: "It would be very tedious, in such a volume as this, to reckon up the successions in all the churches," it will be sufficient "to indicate that tradition derived from the Apostles of the very great, the very ancient and universally known Church founded and organized at Rome by the two most glorious Apostles, Peter and Paul, . . . for it is a matter of necessity that every Church should agree with this Church on account of its preeminent authority, that is, the faithful everywhere, inasmuch as the Apostolic tradition has been preserved by those who exist everywhere."[30]

It is evident that St. Irenaeus attributes some special preeminence to the Roman Church whose bishops are the lawful successors of

---

[29] Eusebius, "Hist. Ecclesiastica," vii, 30, xix; P.G., 20, 719.*
[30] "Adversus Haereses," iii, 2, 2; P.G., 7, 848.

SS. Peter and Paul: "The blessed Apostles, then having founded and built up the Church, committed into the hands of Linus the office of the episcopate . . . to him succeeded Anacletus, and after him in the third place form the Apostles, Clement was allotted the bishopric." Consequently the Roman Church is eminent, not because it was located at Rome, but because it was founded by the Apostles and derives its authority from them. St. Irenaeus indicates the nature of this pre-eminence in his account of St. Clement's Letter to the Corinthians: "In the time of this Clement, no small dissension having occurred among the brethren at Corinth, the Church in Rome despatched a most powerful letter to the Corinthians exhorting them to peace, renewing their faith and declaring the tradition which it had lately received from the Apostles."[31] In other words, the Church at Rome, under the guidance of St. Clement, exercised a preeminence of real jurisdiction over the Church at Corinth.

Some non-Catholic scholars seek to evade the force of the passage from St. Irenaeus by claiming that the *preeminent authority* was that of the city, to which people flocked from all parts of the Empire, bringing with them the traditions of their own churches. "Everybody visits Rome," says one author, "hence you find there faithful from every side; and their united testimony it is which preserves in Rome the pure Apostolic tradition. The faith is preserved by those who come to Rome, not by the Bishop who presides there."[32] In this interpretation the Latin *convenire* is taken to mean *assemble* or *resort,* instead of *agree;* "Every church most *resort* to the Church of Rome because of the fact that it is located in the capital of the Empire." But this does not suit the context; the *principality* is that of the Church in Rome, not of the city itself, which is mentioned only incidentally. Furthermore, why was it *necessary* for every church to *resort* to the church at Rome, if it possessed no special authority? St. Irenaeus plainly states that Apostolic traditions are preserved in the Roman Church, not by the faithful who flock there, but by the lawful succession of pastors in that church. He says: "To this Clement there succeeded Evaristus . . . Soter having succeeded Anicetus, Eleutherius does now in the twelfth place from the Apostles, hold the inheritance of the episcopate. In this order, *and by this succession,* the ecclesiastical tradition from the Apostles, and the preaching of the truth have come done to us."[33]

---

[31] "Adversus Haereses," iii, 3, 3; P.G., 7, 849.*
[32] Roberts-Donaldson, "Ante-Nicene Fathers," Vol. I, p. 460.
[33] "Adversus Haereses," iii, 3, 3; P.G., 7, 8.*

II. POPE VICTOR I (189-198). The Churches of Asia Minor celebrated Easter on the day of the Jewish Pasch, regardless of the day of the week on which it might fall. The Western Church had always celebrated the feast on a Sunday. Several years before the time of Victor, this difference in rite had been discussed by Pope Anicetus and St. Polycarp but nothing was done in the matter. Pope Victor now decided to bring about uniformity by having the churches of Asia follow the practice of the West; he therefore asked the bishops of those parts to hold conferences to consider the matter and report to him. This is evident from the letter of Polycrates, bishop of Ephesus, informing Pope Victor of their decision. He says: "I could mention the bishops who were present, whom I summoned at your request." He then continues to inform the Pope that the bishops had decided to continue the old custom, because it had been handed down from the days of St. John the Apostle, and had been hallowed by the approval of many saintly bishops.[34]

This decision did not please the Pope; he condemned their custom and threatened to excommunicate all who refused to conform with the practice of the West in this matter. At this juncture, St. Irenaeus wrote to Pope Victor, with due reverence, as Eusebius informs us, but more sharply than was necessary. He did not accuse the Pope of exceeding his authority by threatening excommunication, but simply advised moderation in a matter that was purely disciplinary. He cited the example of Victor's predecessors, who were content to tolerate a custom of such antiquity. The whole tenor of the letter, as preserved by Eusebius, recognizes full authority in the Pope to proceed with the threatened excommunication, but questions the prudence of such action.[35]

It is not certain whether Victor actually excommunicated the refractory bishops of the East; but the western custom of celebrating Easter on Sunday soon became the practice of the universal Church, despite the Apostolic origin claimed for the practice of the Asiatic churches. This in itself shows the influence which Rome exercised over the whole Church in those early days.

III. ST. ABERCIUS. In the epitaph which Abercius, bishop of Hieropolis in Phrygia, composed for his own tomb, he says that he had travelled to Rome at the command of Christ, "to contemplate the royal city, and to behold a queen in vestments of gold, and golden sandals on her feet. There I saw a people having a gleaming seal."

---

[34] Eusebius, "Hist. Eccles.," v. 24 (Greek text) ; P.G., 20, 495.
[35] Eusebius, "Hist. Eccles.," v. 24; P.G., 20, 494 sq.

Abercius uses symbolic language throughout the inscription. For example, he calls Christ "the Fish which the chaste virgin drew from the fountain." In like manner he refers to the church in Rome as "a queen in vestments of gold." Lowrie, a non-Catholic scholar, says: "Under the figure of the queen clad in gold, he refers to the Roman Church. The Christian people of Rome had the *gleaming seal*. It is well known that baptism was commonly spoken of under the figure of a seal."[36]

Now, since Abercius undertook the long and difficult journey to Rome at the command of Christ to see the church there, he must have recognized some special importance attached to that church. The epitaph does not state the nature of that preeminence, but it may easily be conjectured, if we remember that only a few years later St. Irenaeus calls it the very great and very ancient church founded by the two great Apostles Peter and Paul; the church with which all others must agree, or to which all others must resort, on account of its preeminent authority.

5. Witnesses From the First Century

I. ST. IGNATIUS MARTYR.[37] About 107 St. Ignatius, bishop of Antioch in Syria, was sent to Rome to be cast to the wild beasts in the amphitheatre. While on his journey he wrote to several churches in Asia and also the Church at Rome. Each letter begins with epithets in praise of the church addressed; those in praise of the Roman Church are far more numerous and more significant than any other. It is the church "which has obtained mercy through the majesty of the Most High Father, and Jesus Christ, His only-begotten Son; the Church which is beloved and enlightened by the will of Him that willeth all things which are according to the love of Jesus Christ, our God; which presides in the place of the region of the Romans, worthy of God, worthy of honor, worthy of the highest happiness, worthy of praise, worthy of obtaining her every desire, worthy of being deemed holy and which presides over love."[38]

Such praise bestowed upon the Church of Rome certainly bespeaks some preeminence, as the Anglican Bishop Lightfoot concedes.[39] The

---

[36] Walter Lowrie, "Monuments of the Early Church," p. 236; cf. Leclerq in "Dictionnaire d'Archeologie," Vol. I, col. 66, sqq.

[37] The letters of St. Ignatius were written in the first years of the second century, but his testimony is placed in the first, because practically his whole life belonged to that century.

[38] Funk, "Patres Apostolici," Vol. I, p. 253.*

[39] J. B. Lightfoot, "St. Clement of Rome," Vol. I, p. 71.

Roman Church presides in the country of the Romans; she presides over the love-feasts or as some scholars render it: "presiding over the society of charity, i.e., the Church." Duchesne remarks that "if the martyr had been writing to the bishop of Rome, these presidencies might be considered local in character, because in his own diocese the bishop always presides. But here there is no question of the bishop, but of the Church. Over what did the Roman Church preside? Was it merely over some other churches or dioceses within a limited area? Ignatius had no idea of a limitation of that kind. Besides, were there in Italy any Christian communities distinct in organization from the community of Rome? The most natural meaning of such language is that the Roman Church presides over all the churches."[40]

St. Ignatius also refers to a teaching authority exercised by the church at Rome over other churches. He says: "Ye have never envied any one; ye have taught others. Now I desire that those things may be confirmed (by your conduct) which in your instructions ye enjoin (on others)."[41]

II. ST. CLEMENT OF ROME (91-100). About ten years before St. Ignatius addressed his letter to the Romans, St. Clement had occasion to use the teaching authority referred to in that letter. He also interposed in the government of another church, thus showing his primacy of jurisdiction. "In the time of this Clement," says St. Irenaeus, "no small dissension having occurred at Corinth, the Church in Rome dispatched a most powerful letter to the Corinthians, bringing them to peace, renewing their faith, and declaring the tradition which it had lately received from the Apostles."[42] This letter mentioned by St. Irenaeus is still extant, and all scholars admit that it was written by St. Clement of Rome, the third successor of St. Peter.

It is not certain whether the Corinthians had appealed to St. Clement, or whether he intervened of his own accord, but it *is* certain that he acted with full authority, as Lightfoot candidly admits. He says: "It may perhaps seem strange to describe this noble remonstrance as the first step toward papal domination; and yet undoubtedly this is the case."[43] If this be the first step toward papal domination, then such domination must have been of Apostolic origin, for, as St. Irenaeus says, "this man (Clement), as he had seen the blessed Apostles, and had been

---

[40] Duchesne, "Eglises Separees," Engl. Tr. by A. H. Mathew, pp. 85-86.
[41] Funk, "Patres Apostolici," Vol. I, p. 255.*
[42] St. Irenaeus, "Adversus Haereses," III, 3, 3; P.G., 7, 850.
[43] J. B. Lightfoot, "St. Clement of Rome," Vol. I, p. 70.

conversant with them, might be said to have the preaching of the Apostles still ringing in his ears, and their traditions before his eyes."[41]

One passage will be sufficient to show the tone of authority used by St. Clement: "But if any will not obey these things which He (Christ) has spoken through us, let them know that they will be implicating themselves in no small danger and offense."[45] This passage alone amply justifies the statement of Bishop Lightfoot. St. Clement claims divine authority; it is Christ who has spoken through him, and those who do not obey, will be guilty of grievous sin. Yet despite this imperious tone and the claim to divine authority, there was not the slightest protest on the part of the Corinthians. For many years the letter was read at Corinth during divine services and even numbered among the inspired works of Scripture, as Eusebius informs us.[46] The Corinthians must have accepted this "first step toward papal domination" as in full accord with the teaching of Christ and His Apostles!

Conclusion

The testimony of Christian antiquity proves beyond doubt that the bishop of Rome was universally recognized as head of the Church by East and West alike. The witnesses for the third, fourth, and fifth centuries are numerous; those from the first and second are necessarily few in number, because very few documents have come down to us from those times. Only three extra-scriptural documents by Christian authors can be ascribed to the first century, yet one of these shows the bishop of Rome exercising undisputed supremacy in the Church. A recent author has said: "Instead of being distressed at the small amount of evidence for the papal claims in the earliest times, I stand amazed at the celerity with which the papal idea came to maturity. . . . The most eminent Protestant scholars in Germany take a view of the development of the Roman Church which in some cases, I think, exaggerates its rapidity and import. But when all allowances are made, the facts as they are, present us with a surprising development in an age when the relation of the Son of God to the Father, and the Divinity of the Holy Spirit . . . were ill understood, or incorrectly stated, by Catholic writers."[47]

The actual exercise of papal powers gradually increased with the growth of the Church. Many powers, latent in the primacy of Peter,

[41] "Adversus Haereses," III, 3, 3; P.G., 7, 850.*
[45] Funk, "Patres Apostolici," Vol. I, p. 175.
[46] "Hist. Eccles.," iv, 23; P.G., 30, 390.
[47] Dom Chapman, "Bishop Gore and Catholic Claims," p. 62.

were not exercised or fully realized until circumstances demanded it. This is true of all governmental powers, and was therefore to be expected in the Church. Christ instituted the primacy to meet conditions as they arose in the Church; it must be sufficiently elastic to accommodate itself to the ever-growing needs of the Church as she increases in numbers and extent. It must also be able to meet the problems presented by the advancing stages of civilization among the various peoples and nations. There must be a gradual unfolding of latent powers to make it possible for the Church to keep her identity without losing her life, and keep her life without losing her identity; to enlarge her teachings without changing them, and to remain ever the same, yet always developing."[48]

God summed up His revelations to man when He promised that the seed of the woman should one day bruise the serpent's head; all subsequent prophecy was but the unfolding of this one promise. So likewise in the creation of His Church, Christ set forth in a word the person of its ruler and the nature of its perpetual government. He spoke to Peter once in promise and once in fulfillment. It was the voice of the Creator summing up his work in a word. Age after age brings to light more and more the force of that word. Time has not yet exhausted that first prophecy made to Adam, neither has it revealed all contained in those words addressed to Peter on the shores of Lake Tiberias some nineteen hundred years ago.[49]

ART. III. OBJECTIONS CONSIDERED

OBJECTION I.—The Roman primacy is excluded by the fact that Christ alone is Head over all the Church: "The Church, being to abide through all generations of time, needs also an ever-abiding head; and such is Jesus Christ alone. Wherefore the Apostles take no higher title than that of ministers of the Church."[50]

ANSWER.—This is the stock argument of the Eastern schismatics, who do not seem to realize that it would also exclude the authority of their own patriarchs, since Christ is Head of each and every part of the Church in the same sense in which He is Head of whole Church. Only Protestants who maintain that the Church is essentially invisible can logically bring such an objection against the primacy. But it has already been proved against them that the Church is an external visible society,

---

[48] W. H. Mallock, "Is Life Worth Living?" p. 313.
[49] T. W. Allies, "The See of Peter," pp. 167-168.
[50] Philaret's "Longer Catechism of the Eastern Church"; cf. Schaff, Vol. ii, p. 485.

and as such must have a visible head. The Roman Primacy does not exclude or deny the headship of Christ, since the Roman Pontiff is head of the Church in his capacity as Vicar of Christ. Our Lord said to Peter: "Feed my lambs; feed My sheep." The chief shepherd of a flock need not be the owner of it.

The fact that the Apostles called themselves ministers is no objection; they were ministers of Christ and as such exercised jurisdiction over His Church with St. Peter at their head. Their position in the Church is determined from the authority they exercised, rather than from the title they assumed. The Pope frequently signs himself, "the servant of servants," but he does not thereby intend to renounce his supreme authority in the Church.

OBJECTION II.—The primacy of the Roman Pontiff is due entirely to human causes. The bishop of Rome, living in the capital of the Empire, soon came to be regarded as having some preeminence over other bishops. This gradually developed into a preeminence of power and jurisdiction, which ambition gladly seized upon for its own aggrandizement.[51]

ANSWER.—No hypothesis, however plausible it may seem, can be accepted in explanation of a fact whose true explanation we *know* to be different. We know why the bishop of Rome was accepted as supreme pastor in all ages, because we have the testimony of those who so accepted him. The Fathers of the Church and the bishops assembled in councils have always proclaimed the Roman Pontiff supreme pastor, because he holds the place of Peter, prince of the Apostles and foundation of the Church. They never connected the primacy with Rome because Rome was the capital of the Empire. Moreover, the bishop of Rome did not lose his preeminence when the imperial power was transferred to Constantinople, which was never recognized as anything more than a patriarchal see, and that only after long and persistent efforts on the part of bishops and emperors.

There is no doubt that God, in His wisdom, selected Rome as the seat of primacy in the Church, because external circumstances made the exercise of universal jurisdiction easier there than elsewhere. The imperial preeminence of Rome was not the cause of the primacy, but the reason why it was located there instead of elsewhere, for, as Leo the Great says, "The most blessed Peter, prince of the Apostle band, was appointed to the citadel of the Roman Empire, that the light of truth, which was being displayed for the salvation of all the nations, might

---

[51] Cf. W. Palmer, "Treatise on the Church," Vol. ii, p. 547 sqq.

spread itself more effectively throughout the body of the world from the head itself."[52]

OBJECTION III.—The first Council of Constantinople (381) issued a decree to the effect that "the bishop of Constantinople shall have the prerogative of honor after the bishop of Rome, because Constantinople is New Rome."[53] Therefore, the Roman Pontiff owes his preeminence to the fact that he is bishop of "Old Rome," as the Council of Chalcedon explicitly stated in its twenty-eighth canon (451): "We also enact and decree the same things concerning the privileges of the most holy Church of Constantinople, which is New Rome. For the Fathers rightly granted privileges to the throne of Old Rome, because it was the royal city. And the hundred and fifty most religious bishops,[54] actuated by the same consideration, gave equal privileges to the most holy throne of New Rome, justly judging that the city which is honored with the Sovereignty and the Senate, and enjoys equal privileges with the old imperial Rome, should in ecclesiastical matters also be magnified as she is, and rank next after her, so that in the Pontic, the Asian and the Thracian dioceses, the metropolitans only and such bishops also of the aforesaid as are among the barbarians, should be ordained by the aforesaid most holy throne of the most holy Church of Constantinople."[55]

ANSWER.—The two canons quoted are a proof for the divine origin of the Roman primacy rather than an objection against it. If the bishop of Rome obtained preeminence because of the imperial dignity of the city, the bishop of Constantinople, now become the capital of the Empire, should have received this preeminence instead of ranking *next after* Rome. The Fathers of two great councils would certainly not have committed such a blunder.

As a matter of fact, neither of these two canons is concerned with the primacy of Rome; they refer to patriarchal rights and privileges, as the latter part of the canon of Chalcedon explicitly states. From the earliest times, the Church had been divided into three patriarchates,—Rome, Alexandria, and Antioch,—with precedence of honor in the order named. In each case the patriarch had certain rights and privileges in regard to consecrating bishops and archbishops in his territory. The Nicene Council (325) had recognized these ancient rights and ordered them to be respected.

The Emperors and bishops of Constantinople constantly strove to have their own church raised to patriarchal dignity next to that of

---

[52] Leo the Great, "Sermon," 82, 3; P.L., 54, 424.*
[53] Mansi, T. III, col. 573.
[54] The bishops attending the first Council of Constantinople.
[55] Mansi, t. vii, col. 370.*

Rome, and therefore, with precedence over Alexandria and Antioch. But the ancient arrangement sanctioned by the sixth canon of Nicaea stood in their way; they could offer but one reason for changing the established order,—because Constantinople is New Rome, i.e., the new capital of the Empire. They would have it raised to patriarchal dignity with jurisdiction over the churches of Pontus, Asia Minor, and Thrace. Leo the Great, who was pope at the time of the Council of Chalcedon, rejected the canon on the ground that it violated the sixth canon of Nicaea, but he made no reference to any violation of his own rights as supreme pastor. Consequently he failed to see any denial of the Roman Supremacy involved although his legates were present at the council and must have known the sentiments of its Fathers.

In regard to this matter, a non-Catholic scholar says: "It should be remembered that the change effected by this canon did not affect Rome directly in any way, but did seriously affect Alexandria and Antioch, which till then had ranked next after the See of Rome. When the Pope refused to acknowledge the authority of this canon, he was in reality defending the principle laid down in the canon of Nicaea that in such matters the ancient customs should continue. Even the last clause, it would seem, could give no offence to the most sensitive on the papal claims, for it implies a wonderful power in the rank of Old Rome, if a See is to rank next to it because it happens to be "New Rome."[56]

OBJECTION IV.—The sixth canon of Nicaea makes the Church of Alexandria equal in power with that of Rome: "Let the ancient customs in Egypt, Libya, and the Pentapolis prevail, that the bishop of Alexandria have jurisdiction in all these, since this is also the custom for the bishop of Rome."

ANSWER.—This canon was evidently intended to confirm some rights of jurisdiction which the church of Alexandria had been exercising over other churches in Egypt, Libya and the Pentapolis. What these rights were is uncertain, but the reasons for their official recognition are given; viz., their antiquity ("let the ancient customs prevail") and the authority, or perhaps the example, of the Roman Church ("this is also the custom for the bishop of Rome"). The meaning of this last phrase is very obscure. Some take it to mean that the ancient customs should prevail because approved of by the bishop of Rome. The more probable meaning is that the ancient customs should prevail because a like custom obtains at Rome, i.e., the bishop of Rome exercises like jurisdiction over the churches of his patriarchate. The first interpretation explicitly recog-

---

[56] Henry R. Percival in "Nicene and Post-Nicene Fathers," Vol. xiv, p. 178.

nizes that supremacy of Rome,—customs are to prevail because approved by Rome. The second implicitly recognizes that supremacy by making the Roman Church the model for all others. But in any case the council is concerned only with patriarchal rights, as a non-Catholic author freely admits: "It is evident that the Council has not in view here the primacy of the Bishop of Rome over the whole Church, but simply his power as patriarch."[57]

OBJECTION V.—The Church in Africa did not recognize any primacy in the Roman Church, as is evident from the action taken at the provincial council held at Mileve in 416. It decreed that "Presbyters, deacons, and lower clerics, who are dissatisfied with the judgments of their bishops in any case, may be heard by neighboring bishops; . . . but if they wish to appeal from their decision, such appeal shall be made to an African council or to the primates of their provinces. Any one presuming to appeal *beyond the seas,* shall be excommunicated in Africa."[58] The phrase, *beyond the seas,* evidently refers to Rome. Consequently any appeal to Rome from Africa was punished by excommunication, according to this canon, which was approved by a synod held at Carthage in 418 and by another at Mileve in 419.

ANSWER.—The right of appeal *beyond the seas* was denied priests and lower clerics only; bishops were not included in the provisions of this canon, and the case of Apiarius proves that appeal to Rome on the part of priests was not so strictly forbidden as the canon would indicate. Apiarius, a priest in Africa, was excommunicated and deposed shortly after this decree had been passed but he went to Rome and presented his case to Pope Zosimus, who decided that he should have a rehearing. As a result, the African bishops absolved and reinstated him. Four years later he was again deposed, and again appealed to Rome. Celestine, who was then Pope, ordered him reinstated and sent a legate into Africa to see that the order was carried out. In the meantime, Apiarius had confessed to the crimes of which he was accused, and the legate's mission came to nought, because it was evident that the Pope had acted without due knowledge of the case. The bishops of Africa then wrote to Celestine: "We beseech you that hereafter you will not give ear too readily to persons coming from Africa, nor receive into communion those whom we have excommunicated, lest it appear that persons excommunicated in their own provinces have been too hastily restored to communion by Your Holiness without due consideration."[59]

[57] Henry R. Percival in "Nicene and Post-Nicene Fathers," Vol. xiv, p. 16.
[58] Canon xxii; Labbe-Consart, t. ii, col. 1542.
[59] "Epist. ad Caelestinum"; P.L., 50, 424.

These words contain a sharp but well-deserved rebuke, yet they plainly recognize the primacy of Rome. There is no denial of the pope's authority; neither is there any complaint that Apiarius had violated the canon against appeals beyond the seas,—a canon made, not to deny the supremacy of Rome, but to prevent just such mistakes as Celestine had made in the case of Apiarius.

OBJECTION VI.—St. Jerome, writing to Evangelus, says: "If you ask for authority, the world outweighs its Capital. Wherever there is a bishop, whether it be at Rome or at Eugubium, whether it be at Constantinople or at Rhegium, whether it be at Alexandria or at Zaon, his dignity is one and his priesthood is one."[60]

ANSWER.—The words quoted from St. Jerome's letter have no reference whatever to the primacy of the Roman Pontiff, but are directed against an abuse then prevalent at Rome. This abuse consisted in an assumption of superiority over the priests on the part of the deacons. St. Jerome says: "Bad habits have by degrees so far crept in that I have seen a deacon, in the absence of the bishop, seat himself among the presbyters and at social gatherings give his blessing to them. Those who act thus must learn that they are wrong and must give heed to the Apostles' words. . . . They must consider the reasons which led to the appointment of deacons in the beginning."

When it was objected that this was the custom at Rome, St. Jerome replied: "Why do you bring forward a custom which exists in one city only? Why do you oppose to the laws of the Church a paltry exception which has given rise to arrogance and pride? . . . If you ask for authority, the world outweighs its capital, i.e., if you seek to justify your actions by appealing to custom, you should appeal to the customs of the Church in general, not to the abuse of your own city. Why should deacons be set above priests in your city, if they are not so exalted in the rest of the world, since priests are of equal dignity wherever they are found? In fact, priests differ from bishops only in the power of giving Orders, yet all bishops have the same priesthood and are entitled to the same honor. If deacons are not exalted above bishops in any part of the world, why should they be exalted above priests in Rome or elsewhere?

There is not a single word in the whole letter that refers even remotely to the primacy of the Roman Pontiff.

OBJECTION VII.—St. Gregory the Great severely rebuked John the Faster, bishop of Constantinople, for assuming the title of *"universal bishop."* He says: "None of the Roman Pontiffs ever wished to be

---

[60] "Epist. ad Evangelum"; P.L., 22, 1194.*

known by such a title; no one was ever so foolhardy as to assume such a name."[61] Here, then, is an explicit repudiation of the primacy; before Gregory's day no bishop of Rome was so foolhardy as to assume the title of *universal bishop,* as the Popes now do.

ANSWER.—In reply to this objection it may be asked, why St. Gregory dared to reprove the bishop of an eastern Church if he had no authority to do so? It was not a case of fraternal correction; he sent Sabinianus as legate to Constantinople and wrote to John saying: "In case of your refusing to amend, I forbade him to celebrate Mass with you, that so I might first appeal to Your Holiness through a sense of shame, to the end that, if the execrable and profane assumption could not be corrected through shame, strict canonical measures might be resorted to."[62] In another letter to John, bishop of Syracuse, he says: "Who doubts that the Church of Constantinople is subject to the Apostolic See, as the most pious Emperor and our brother, the bishop of the same city, constantly profess?"[63]

Why, then, did Gregory say that no bishop of Rome had ever assumed such a title as that of *universal bishop?* The solution of this question is very simple when it is known that John the Faster used the title to signify that he was the only bishop properly so-called; all others were merely his vicars or agents. That, at least, is the sense in which St. Gregory understood it, for he wrote to Empress Constantia: "It is sad to see how my brother and fellow-bishop is patiently borne with when he rejects all others and wishes to be called the only bishop."[64] He uses the same words in his letter to John himself: "Having rejected your brethren, you desire to be known as the only bishop."[65] It is perfectly true that no bishop of Rome ever assumed the title of *universal bishop* in that sense.

OBJECTION VIII.—There is not a single word concerning the primacy of the Roman Pontiff in St. Cyprian's treatise on the unity of the Church, yet in a work of that nature he could scarcely have failed to mention the primacy if it had been known to him.

ANSWER.—St. Cyprian wrote this treatise on unity for the purpose of combating a schism then ravaging the Church at Carthage. His sole intention was to prove that, according to the institution of Christ, there can be but one lawful bishop in each church, and that, as a consequence, whoever withdraws from the authority of that one bishop, ceases to be

---

[61] "Epist. ad Eulogium"; P.L., 77, 771.
[62] St. Gregory the Great, "Epist. ad Joannem Constant."; P.L., 77, 738.*
[63] St. Gregory the Great, "Epist. ad Joannem Syracusanum"; P.L., 77, 957.
[64] "Epist. ad Constantiam"; P.L., 77, 749.*
[65] "Epist. ad Joannem Constant."; P.L., 77, 738.

a member of the Catholic Church. He was concerned with the unity, not of the whole Church, but of each particular church or diocese. For this reason he had no occasion to treat of the Roman primacy. He mentions the See of Peter merely as an example of what Christ intended each particular church to be in regard to unity.

OBJECTION IX.—St. Cyprian and his friend Firmilian of Caesarea stoutly resisted the decree of Pope Stephen concerning Baptism and declared that, in ruling their dioceses, bishops are accountable to no one except God. They also referred to Pope Stephen as proud, ignorant, contumacious, and the friend of heretics. This proves that neither St. Cyprian nor Firmilian recognized any superior authority in the Roman pontiff.

ANSWER.—In the heat of controversy St. Cyprian acted against his better judgment and thus involved himself in many errors and inconsistencies. The best answer to the objection will be found in a short history of the controversy itself.

St. Cyprian had been teaching that Baptism administered by anyone outside the Church must be invalid, and consquently heretics and schismatics coming into the Church must be re-baptized, or rather baptized, since the former ceremony was no Baptism at all. This doctrine, which he explains at length in a letter to Magnus, was approved by a synod of African bishops at Carthage in 255. A letter to this effect was sent to the bishops of Mauretania, but they rejected the doctrine as opposed to the tradition of the Church. When St. Cyprian heard of this, he rejected the authority of tradition, saying: "The matter is to be settled by reason, not tradition."[66] In this he contradicted himself, because tradition was the principal argument he adduced in his letter to the bishops of Numidia: "We set forth no new doctrine, but one already established by our predecessors."[67]

A second synod of sixty bishops held at Carthage in the beginning of 256 reaffirmed the doctrine of St. Cyprian and sent a synodical letter to St. Stephen, in which they openly declared that bishops are free in the administration of their respective dioceses, having to render account to God alone. Consequently each bishop was free to act as he thought proper in the matter of re-baptizing: "In this matter we constrain no one, nor make laws for anyone, since each bishop is free in the administration of his own church and must render an account to God for his Acts."[68] Here, again, St. Cyprian contradicted himself. He

[66] "Epist. ad Quintum"; P.L., 3, 1106.
[67] "Epist. ad Januarium"; P.L., 3, 1038.*
[68] St. Cyprian, "Epist. ad Stephanum"; P.L., 3, 1050.

had been teaching that this question of Baptism, was a matter of faith; now it is a mere matter of discipline, in which each bishop may act as he thinks best.

St. Stephen's reply to this letter has not been preserved, but it is evident from St. Cyprian's letter to Jubaianus that he severely reprehended the bishops for their action and called them perverters of the truth. The bishops had written: "We constrain no one, nor do we make laws for anyone." St. Stephen did both by issuing a peremptory decree and threatening excommunication for those who violated it. The decree read: "Therefore, if a person comes to you from any heresy whatsoever, nothing shall be done except what has been handed down by tradition; viz., that hands be imposed upon him in penance."[69]

These facts and the nature of the decree are gathered from St. Cyprian's letter to Pompey and from Firmilian's letter to St. Cyprian. Firmilian plainly indicates that St. Stephen had threatened excommunication and based his authority for so doing upon the fact of his being the successor of St. Peter; "Stephen dares to break the peace with you, which his predecessors have always kept. . . . And in this I am justly indignant at this so open and manifest folly of Stephen, that he who so boasts of the place of his espiscopate, and contends that he holds the succession from Peter, on whom the foundations of the Church were laid, should introduce many other rocks. . . . He is not ashamed to divide the brotherhood for the sake of maintaining heretics; and in addition calls Cyprian a false Christ, a false prophet, and a deceitful worker."[70]

In September 256 another synod was held in Carthage. Various letters were read to the assembled bishops, but St. Stephen's letter was not among them; neither does his name seem to have been mentiond during the session, yet the address of St. Cyprian shows that the Pope's authority was strongly felt in that meeting. After the letters had been read, St. Cyprian urged the bishops to express their sentiments freely and without fear: "It is now time for every one to express his opinions in this matter of Baptism without judging any one or depriving him of communion if he happens to differ from us. None of us have constituted ourselves a bishop of bishops, neither do we wish to restrain our colleagues by tyrannical fear."[71]

What was the necessity for such admonition if every bishop was

---

[69] St. Cyprian, "Epist. ad Pompeium"; P.L., 3, 1123.
[70] Firmilian, "Epist. ad Cyprianum"; P.L., 3, 1169 sq.*
[71] St. Cyprian, "Epist. ad Jovianum"; P.L., 3, 1086.

free in the government of his own church, having to give an account to God alone? Why the mention of a *bishop of bishops*,[72] if no one claimed that position? Why the reminder that no one was to be excommunicated or constrained by tyrannical fear for holding dissenting views? Almost every word of St. Cyprian manifests a fear of superior authority resting in some *bishop of bishops,* who could be none other than St. Stephen, Bishop of Rome. Furthermore, if St. Cyprian and the other bishops did not recognize the primacy of Rome, why were they so solicitous to gain the approval of St. Stephen? The bishops of Mauretania had rejected their doctrine, but no further attempts were made to win them over. The bishop of Rome,—one single bishop, —rejects the doctrine and strenuous efforts are made to secure his approval; synods are held, letters are dispatched, and at least two delegations are sent to Rome.

Persecution put an end to the controversy, but the decree of St. Stephen was finally accepted throughout the whole Church. Rome had spoken, the case was ended. This is the best proof we could have for the primacy of the Roman Pontiff. St. Cyprian, bishop of the important see of Carthage, with many bishops of Africa and Asia Minor, were arrayed on one side; St. Stephen, bishop of Rome, on the other; acting as successor to St. Peter, he issued a decree of some dozen words, and that decree becomes the law of the universal Church! Rivington well says: "If there be in this an argument against the supremacy of the pope, we can desire nothing better than that our opponents should discover many similar ones in their historical studies."[73]

This brief account makes it evident that St. Cyprian really resisted the authority of Pope Stephen, and even denied his primacy, but in words only. In the heat of controversy, he was carried away and would have rejected the authority of Rome, but his inner self would not permit. He struggled against his own convictions and lost the fight. His every action proves that his heart would not consent to what his head contrived. Hence we may say with St. Augustine: "If any cloud of human frailty crossed his mind, it was dispelled by the glorious light of his blood."[74] He suffered martyrdom for the faith in 258.

---

[72] This phrase seems to be an echo of Tertullian, whose works greatly influenced St. Cyprian. Cf. above, Ch. xi, Art. ii, 3.

[73] "The Primitive Church and the See of Peter," p. 116.

[74] St. Augustine, "Contra Donatistas," I, 18; P.L., 43, 125.

CHAPTER XII

Primacy and Episcopate

The supreme power of the Roman pontiff brings him into certain necessary relations with the other bishops of the Church: (1) in the government of their respective dioceses, and (2) when assembled in council for the government of the universal Church. The nature of these relations is determined by the nature and extent of the powers exercised by the Roman Pontiff in the discharge of his duties as supreme pastor and to some extent also by the manner in which he obtains these powers.

ART. I. NATURE OF POWERS AND TENURE OF OFFICE

1. Nature of the Powers Exercised by the Roman Pontiff

The Roman Pontiff is the lawful successor of St. Peter in his supreme power to teach and govern the whole Church and all its parts. To him belongs the power and authority to define doctrines and to condemn errors, to make and repeal laws, to act as judge in all matters of faith and morals, to decree and inflict punishment, to appoint and, if need be, to remove pastors. This supreme power to shepherd the whole flock of Christ is truly *episcopal, ordinary,* and *immediate,* as the Vatican Council has declared: "We teach and declare that by the ordinance of the Lord, the Roman Church holds the primacy of *ordinary* power over all others, and that this truly *episcopal* power of jurisdiction, which belongs to the Roman Pontiff, is also *immediate.*"[1]

a) EPISCOPAL. De Dominis and Febronius taught that the power of the Roman Pontiff is that of a mere inspector or supervisor, and consequently he can do no more than watch over the other bishops so that they may discharge their duties faithfully. This doctrine gives the Roman Pontiff a sort of jurisdiction over the bishops, but no direct power over the faithful. The Vatican Council rejected this doctrine when it declared the power of the Roman Pontiff to be truly episcopal, i.e., he has the same power over all the faithful that the bishop has over those of his diocese,—a power that is exercised directly, without any intervention on the part of the bishops.

When Christ said, "Feed My lambs; feed My sheep," He gave to

---

[1] Denzinger, n. 1827.

St. Peter, and through him to his successors, direct jurisdiction over all the faithful,—a jurisdiction that does not have to be exercised through the bishops, but reaches the faithful directly in every part of the world, as is evident from those other words, likewise addressed to St. Peter: "Whatever thou shalt bind on earth, it shall be bound also in heaven; and whatever thou shalt loose upon earth, it shall be loosed also in heaven." Hence the Roman Pontiff, as successor to St. Peter, has power and authority to impose laws upon the faithful without the consent of their bishop, and even against his wishes. He can also annul any law or obligation imposed by a bishop upon his people. In other words, all the faithful, individually and collectively, are directly subject to the authority of the Roman Pontiff, which is therefore truly episcopal.

b) ORDINARY. The term *ordinary* is here opposed to *extraordinary*. Febronius, Eybel, and others taught that the Roman Pontiff can exercise his supreme authority for extraordinary cases only; e.g., when a bishop fails to perform his duties, or when some unusual danger threatens the Church. The Vatican Council condemned this doctrine in express terms: "If any one should say . . . that this power (of the Roman Pontiff) is not ordinary and immediate, . . . let him be anathema."[2]

Our Lord did not say to St. Peter, "Feed My sheep if others fail to do so, or if some special danger threatens"; He said simply: "Feed My lambs, feed My sheep." The pastoral office thus committed to St. Peter is lawfully and validly exercised at any time, in any place, and for any cause whatever pertaining to the good of the flock. Ordinarily, however, the Roman Pontiff acts only in matters of general interest to the Church, or in matters of local interest that have been referred to him for adjudication. When affairs in a diocese are proceeding in an orderly manner and religion is prospering under the direction of the bishop, there is little necessity for the Pope to interpose the exercise of his supreme authority.

c) IMMEDIATE. The power and authority of the Roman Pontiff is immediate in the sense that it is received immediately from Christ and not through the agency of another person or groups of persons. It has been proved that power and authority in the Church do not come to her ministers through the faithful, but were conferred directly upon the Apostles and descend to their successors by divine institution. In like manner the supreme power of jurisdiction was conferred directly and immediately upon St. Peter, to the exclusion even of the

---

[2] Denzinger, n. 1831.

other Apostles. Therefore, neither the faithful nor the bishops of the Church can confer the powers of the primacy upon the successors of St. Peter, for, as the axiom says, "Nemo dat quod non habet."[3]

Christ ordained that St. Peter should have successors in his primacy of jurisdiction over the Church, but He did not designate the person of the successor. It is left to the Church to elect, or otherwise designate, the person who then obtains the power of universal jurisdiction by virtue of divine institution, i.e., immediately from Christ, not from those who have elected him. When the Apostolic See is vacant, there is no supreme authority in the Church; the bishops retain power to rule their respective dioceses, but no laws can be made for the universal Church, no dogmas of faith can be defined, no legitimate council convened. In place of this supreme authority, the Church has the right and the duty of selecting someone upon whom Christ will again bestow it. It is evident, then, that the Apostolic succession cannot fail in the Apostolic See so long as the Church herself continues to exist, for although the see be vacant for many years, the Church always retains the right to elect a legitimate successor, who then obtains supreme authority according to the institution of Christ.

2. Tenure of the Supreme Pastoral Office

ELIGIBILITY. Any person of the male sex having the use of reason can be elected Supreme Pontiff, provided he be a member of the Church and not excluded from the office by ecclesiastical law. It is absolutely necessary that the Roman Pontiff be of the male sex, for to such only has Christ committed the government of His Church and the power of Orders.[4] He must also be a member of the Church since no one can be the head of any society unless he also be a member of that society. Finally, he must have the use of reason because the primacy consists essentially in the exercise of jurisdiction and this in itself is an act of reason. Consequently a person who is permanently insane, or a person who has not yet attained the age of discretion, cannot be validly elected to the supreme pontificate.

A layman can be validly elected to the office, since the power of jurisdiction can be exercised without the power of Orders. In such a case, the person elected would receive the power of jurisdiction immediately upon his election, but the power of Orders would come only through the Sacrament of Orders, which he would be obliged to

---

[3] No one can give what he does not possess.
[4] This is proved in any dogmatic treatise on Holy Orders; e.g., MacGuinness, "Commentarii Theologici," Vol. III, p. 506.

receive, since Christ evidently intended that His Church be governed by bishops,—bishops by the power of Orders as well as by the power of jurisdiction.

The very nature of the office makes it necessary that the Supreme Pontiff be a member of the Church and have the use of reason; the will of Christ demands that he be of the male sex. Other conditions may be required by the Church, since the Pope, having full authority in the government of the Church, may establish laws that would render a papal election null and void unless the prescribed conditions be fulfilled. It is true that the laws made by one pope do not bind his successors, but they can and do bind the one to be elected.

ELECTION. Since Christ left to His Church the right to select the person of St. Peter's successor, she has authority to make such regulations in the matter as she deems proper. But as the Roman Pontiff holds supreme authority in the Church, the right and duty of making such regulations devolves upon him alone; he alone has authority to designate the electors and the manner of election. In the earlier ages the clergy and people of Rome elected the Pope. St. Cyprian, referring to the election of Pope Cornelius, says: "He was made bishop by the testimony of almost all the clergy, by the suffrage of the people who were present, and by the assembly of the ancient priests and good men."[5] Since the middle of the twelfth century the right of electing the pope has been restricted to the cardinals.

It is a disputed question whether the pope has authority to appoint his successor, but the common opinion is that he has not. A few popes did name their successors, but this seems to have amounted to nothing more than a nomination, since "none of the persons thus named ever presumed to declare themselves popes before the ratification of the legal electors had been obtained."[6]

LOSS OF THE PRIMACY. The power of the primacy may be lost by voluntary resignation. Pope Pontian is said to have resigned when sent into exile, in 235. This he did to allow another to be elected in his stead and thus save the Church the inconveniences that would arise from his enforced absence. Pope Celestine V also resigned, in 1294, after he had consulted the cardinals and with their unanimous consent officially declared that a pope may validly and licitly resign his office.

Perpetual or long continued insanity would deprive a pope of his office as supreme pastor, because, without the use of reason, he could

[5] "Epist. ad Antonianum"; P.L., iii, 770.*
[6] Catholic Encyclopedia, Art. "Papal Elections."

not perform the duties essential to that office. A temporary attack, however, would not deprive him of jurisdiction, but should there be frequently recurring attacks, he would probably be obliged in conscience to resign, since there would always be reason to doubt the validity of his acts and, as a result, the whole Church would suffer. As a matter of fact, no pope has ever been afflicted with insanity, and it is probable that God in His providence will never permit such an unfortunate circumstance to arise. But should the condition arise, it would devolve upon the bishops of the Church to establish and declare the fact officially; the cardinals would then proceed to the election of a successor.

Finally, if a pope, in his private capacity as an individual, should fall into manifest heresy, he would cease to be a member of the Church, and consequence would also cease to be her supreme pastor. But this is another purely theoretical hypothesis, since no Pope is known to have fallen into heresy, and it is most probable that the vicar of Christ is divinely protected from such a misfortune, although the Church has never defined anything in the matter.

In case a Pope becomes a scandal to the Church on account of a sinful life, he can and ought to be admonished by the bishops, singly or in council, but they have no authority to depose him. "It would be unlawful to go beyond admonition; a change of heart must be left to the Providence of God and sought only by prayer and supplication."[7]

A DOUBTFUL POPE. When there is a prudent doubt about the validity of an election to any official position, there is also a similar doubt whether the person so elected really has authority or not. In such a case no one is bound to obey him, for it is an axiom that a doubtful law begets no obligation—*lex dubia nom obligat*. But a superior whom no one is bound to obey is in reality no superior at all. Hence the saying of Bellarmine: a doubtful pope is no pope. "Therefore," continues the Cardinal, "if a papal election is really doubtful for any reason, the one elected should resign, so that a new election may be held. But if he refuses to resign, it becomes the duty of the bishops to adjust the matter, for although the bishops without the pope cannot define dogmas nor make laws for the universal Church, they can and ought to decide, when occasion demands, who is the legitimate pope; and if the matter be doubtful, they should provide for the Church by having a legitimate and undoubted pastor elected. That is what the Council of Constance rightly did."[8]

ROME AND THE PAPACY. It is an article of faith that the

---

[7] Perrone, "Praelect. Theolog.," n. 633; cf. Suarez, "De Fide," X, 6.
[8] Bellarmine, "De Concilio," ii, 19.

successor of St. Peter holds supreme jurisdiction in the Church, and that by divine institution. It is also a matter of faith that according to the present order of things the bishop of Rome is that successor. Theologians, going further, inquire by what right the primacy is connected with the Roman See, and whether it could be transferred to another. The solution of these questions depends upon the manner in which Rome was selected as the see of St. Peter's successors. There are only three ways in which this could have been done: (a) Our Lord could have personally designated Rome as the see of St. Peter and his successors, or (b) St. Peter could have been left free to select his own see, to which Christ would then attach the primacy for him and his successors. In either case, the primacy would be attached to the chosen see by divine institution and could be changed only by divine intervention. Finally, (c) Christ could have left the selection of a suitable see entirely in the hands of St. Peter and his successors. In this case the primacy would be connected with Rome by purely ecclesiastical law and could be changed at any time by papal authority.

Arguments can be adduced on either side, but the Church, it seems, has never defined the question. The majority of theologians hold that the primacy is attached to the Roman See by divine institution and, therefore, cannot be changed under any circumstances.

Straub even maintains that this is an article of faith. He appeals to three documents in particular to support this opinion: (a) A letter of Nicholas I to the Emperor Michael, in which he says: "The privileges of the Roman Church . . . cannot be lessened in the least nor infringed upon, nor changed, because no human power can remove the foundation which God has laid."[9] (b) The letter of Clement VI to the Catholics of the Armenians, stating the conditions for reunion with Rome: "If you are ready to believe that all the Roman pontiffs canonically succeeding the blessed Peter, have succeeded and will succeed him in the same plenitude and jurisdiction of power."[10] (c) A decree of the Council of Florence: "We define that the holy Apostolic See and the Roman Pontiff holds the primacy over the whole world, and that the same Roman Pontiff is the successor of St. Peter."[11]

These documents have considerable weight, but they are not entirely convincing. The first two may easily be interpreted without any reference to the question under discussion, and the third, the decree of the Council of Florence, was repeated almost verbatim by the Vatican Council with-

---

[9] Denzinger, n. 332.
[10] Denzinger, n. 3011.
[11] Denzinger, n. 694.

out any intention of deciding this matter, as is evident from the acts: "The questions and hypotheses, more or less freely debated, concerning the perpetuity of the city of Rome and the union of the Primacy with the Roman See were passed by, they did not wish at this time to stigmatize the opinion which holds that Peter's fixing his see at Rome was of human authority."[12]

COROLLARY. The Roman Pontiff does not cease to be bishop of Rome by the mere fact of taking up his residence elsewhere. For many years the popes lived at Avignon in France, yet they remained the true and legitimate bishops of Rome. Even granting, then, that the primacy is attached to the Roman See by divine institution, there is nothing to prevent the pope taking up his residence in Jerusalem, as some think he will from the days of Antichrist until the end of the world. He could simply change his residence while still remaining bishop of Rome, or the papacy itself might be removed by divine intervention at the time of Antichrist. The necessity for a change of residence is indicated in the Apocalypse, where the complete destruction of Rome is prophesied,—a destruction that shall continue for all time: "That great city, will be overthrown, and will not be found anymore."[13] On the other hand, a future greatness is promised to Jerusalem that would be fittingly fulfilled by the pope's residing there to rule the Church, then completely universal by the submission of all nations and the conversion of the Jews. "And there shall be one day," says the prophet, "which is known to the Lord. . . . And it shall come to pass in that day that living waters shall go out from Jerusalem; half of them to the east sea, and half of them to the last sea; they shall be in summer and winter. And the Lord shall be King over all the earth; in that day there shall be one Lord, and His name shall be one. . . . And there shall be no more anathema; but Jerusalem shall sit secure. . . . And many nations shall be joined to the Lord in that day, and they shall be my people, and I will dwell in the midst of them."[14]

ART. II. THE POPE AND THE BISHOPS SEVERALLY

THE EPISCOPATE OF DIVINE ORIGIN. The Apostles personally received from Christ a real power of jurisdiction to be exercised in subjection to St. Peter, their divinely constituted head. Christ also ordained that the Apostles should have successors in the Church for all time. He said to them: "Go, therefore, and make disciples of all

---

[12] Coll. I, vii, 293, 364 sq.
[13] Apoc. xviii, 21 sq.
[14] Zach. xiv, 7-11; ii, 10-12; cf. Berry, "The Apocalypse of St. John," pp. 193 sqq.

nations, . . . and behold, I am with you all days, even unto the consummation of the world."[15] Consequently the bishops of the Church, as successors of the Apostles, constitute an order of divine institution. It is the will of Christ that there should always be bishops to teach and govern the particular portions of the Church committed to their care. The pope, then, is not free to govern the Church alone without the assistance of bishops, for, as Leo XIII says, "although the power of Peter and his successors is complete and supreme, it is not an only power. He who made Peter the foundation of the Church, also selected the twelve, whom He called Apostles. Just as the authority of Peter must be perpetuated in the Roman Pontiff, so also the ordinary power of the Apostles must be inherited by their successors, the bishops. Hence the order of bishops pertains of necessity to the very constitution of the Church."[16]

THE APOSTOLIC SUCCESSION. Every lawfully constituted bishop is a true successor of the Apostles, taken collectively. The Apostles, with St. Peter at their head, formed a ruling body that must be perpetuated for all time, and enlarged, as the Church increases in numbers and extent. In this respect the Apostolic body is like a legal corporation,—it must be perpetuated and enlarged by the admission, from time to time, of new members, who participate in the powers originally conferred upon its first members, the Apostles. A bishop, then, is a new member incorporated into the Apostolic body perpetuated in the Church; he succeeds the Apostles in the same sense that a new member of a corporation succeeds its charter members. The presidency, or supreme power, over the Apostolic body is held *ex officio* by the Roman Pontiff, in virtue of the fact that he is the direct and only successor of St. Peter, whom Christ personally constituted its first head, ordaining that his successors should hold the same position.

Every episcopal see in the Church is truly Apostolic, because its bishop is a true successor of the Apostles and inherits their episcopal powers and authority to teach and govern, although he does not inherit the prerogatives peculiar to them as Apostles. The Roman See is preeminently Apostolic, because its bishop succeeds one particular Apostle, St. Peter, not only in his episcopal power, but also in his power as supreme head of the apostolic body. For this reason the term *Apostolic See* has been applied exclusively to Rome for many centuries. St. Vincent of Lerins, in the beginning of the fifth century, deemed it unnecessary to use any other title to distinguish the Roman See from all others.

---

[15] Matt. xxviii, 19-20.
[16] "De Unitate Ecclesiae," June 29, 1896.

THE APPOINTMENT OF BISHOPS. Christ personally selected the first members of the Apostolic body: "He called to him men of his own choosing, and they came to him. And he appointed twelve that they might be with him and that he might send them forth to preach."[17] None but those chosen by Christ Himself could be numbered with the Apostles, for He said to them: "You have not chosen me, but I have chosen you, and have appointed you that you should go forth and bear fruit."[18] St. Paul also says: "And no man takes the honor to himself; he takes it who is called by God, as Aaron was."[19]

After the Ascension St. Peter and his successors take the place of Christ as visible head of the Apostolic body, with full authority to carry out His will: "Whatever thou shalt bind on earth, it shall be bound also in heaven."[20] Consequently the Roman Pontiff, as successor of St. Peter, has sole authority to accept new members into the Apostolic body, i.e., he alone has authority to constitute bishops, since authority to teach and govern the faithful was conferred upon the Apostles as a body and can be obtained only by incorporation into that body.

The very nature of the episcopal office and of the primacy proves that the Roman Pontiff has exclusive authority to constitute bishops for every part of the Church. Bishops are shepherds for portions of the flock that was committed in its entirety to the pastoral care of St. Peter and his successors; but no one becomes a shepherd of any portion of a flock unless he be made such by the chief pastor of the whole flock. It is also evident that the chief purpose of the primacy,—the preservation of unity,—could not be realized if the bishops of the Church were not subject in all things to her supreme pastor.

The authority of the Roman Pontiff to constitute bishops for all parts of the Church may be exercised directly by personal appointments, or indirectly by delegating others, either by law or by approved custom, to elect persons to the episcopal office. The former method is in general use today, at least in the Western Church; the latter was common in the earlier ages and is practiced to some extent even today.[21]

EPISCOPAL JURISDICTION. Since the episcopate is a divine institution, bishops receive the power of jurisdiction from Christ; but whether this power comes directly from Christ, or through the agency of the Roman Pontiff, is a disputed question. The opinion that jurisdiction is conferred by episcopal consecration is made untenable by the

[17] Mark iii, 13-14.
[18] John xv, 16.
[19] Heb. v, 4.
[20] Matt. xvi, 19.
[21] Cf. Catholic Encyclopedia, art. "Bishop."

fact that a bishop-elect may exercise jurisdiction even before his consecration, whereas a consecrated bishop loses jurisdiction by deposition;
schismatic bishops, though validly consecrated, have no jurisdiction in
the Church. Valid episcopal consecration can be given without the consent of the Roman Pontiff, or even against his will, and when once
given, cannot be revoked. Consequently, if jurisdiction were given by
episcopal consecration, the Pope could not prevent the installation of a
bishop, nor depose one already installed; the bishops would be independent of his authority, and the unity of the Church at end.

Since jurisdiction does not come through the reception of Orders,
it must be conferred upon appointment to the episcopal office by the
Roman Pontiff; but the question still remains whether he simply designates the person upon whom Christ himself confers it. This question
was discussed at the Council of Trent, but no decision was given, probably because it has no practical bearing. If the Pope confers the jurisdiction, he may validly withdraw it by deposing a bishop at any time, with
or without cause; if he simply designates the person to receive jurisdiction from Christ, he cannot validly withdraw it without sufficient
reason.[22]

NOT MERE VICARS. Even though bishops receive all jurisdiction
immediately from the Roman Pontiff, they are not mere agents acting
in his name; they are veritable rulers in their respective dioceses, for
which they make laws in their own name and act as judges in all matters
pertaining to their jurisdiction. Hence Leo XIII says: "Although
bishops do not exercise complete and universal power, nor hold supreme
authority, they must not be considered mere vicars of the Roman
Pontiff. They are, in the truest sense of the word, rulers of their people,
because they exercise a power proper to them."[23]

ECCLESIASTICAL DIGNITIES. The Roman Pontiff and the
bishops exercise jurisdiction by divine institution; all other offices in
the Church are of ecclesiastical origin and their incumbents exercise a
delegated jurisdiction. Cardinals, patriarchs, primates, and metropolitans
(archbishops) hold jurisdiction from the Roman Pontiff; pastors, from
their bishops. The cardinals are official advisers of the pope and assist
him in the government of the Church. Upon the death of the pope
it is their privilege and duty to elect a successor. Patriarchs were originally the bishops of the three patriarchal sees of Rome, Alexandria, and
Antioch. Jerusalem and Constantinople were afterward added to the
list. At present several uniat bishoprics of the East enjoy patriarchal

[22] Cf. Straub, "De Ecclesia Christi," n. 767 sqq.
[23] "De Unitate Ecclesiae," June 29, 1896.

privileges, which consist in certain rights of jurisdiction over other bishops within a prescribed district known as the patriarchate.[24] An archbishop (metropolitan) presides over a number of dioceses united to form an ecclesiastical province, whereas a primate unites under his jurisdiction all the provinces of a country or nation.

In former time, when communication with Rome was slow and difficult, the organization of dioceses into provinces, and provinces into patriarchates, was almost a necessity for the orderly government of the Church. The primates and metropolitans then exercised far greater authority over their suffragan bishops than at present.[25]

In each diocese the bishop is the divinely constituted teacher and governor of the faithful, but since he cannot personally care for all the souls committed to his charge, he constitutes pastors, who act as his representatives and hold jurisdiction from him in the government of particular portions of the diocese, known as parishes. The doctrine of *Parochialism*, which arose in the thirteenth century, maintained that the division of a diocese into parishes under the care of pastors is a matter of divine institution, and therefore pastors exercise jurisdiction by divine right. This theory is refuted by the fact that the parish system was not generally adopted until the eleventh century, and did not become universal until the Council of Trent in the sixteenth.[26]

ART. III. THE POPE AND THE BISHOPS IN COUNCIL

Ordinarily the bishops of the Church are dispersed throughout the world, each engaged in the government of his own diocese, but at times they assemble in council, where, in union with the Roman Pontiff, they define dogmas of faith or legislate for the universal church. The relation of the Pope to the bishops thus assembled in council is easily determined by considering (1) the nature of councils in general and of ecumenical councils in particular, (2) the rights and powers of the Roman Pontiff in regard to councils, and (3) the objections urged against these rights and powers.

1. Nature and Various Kinds of Councils

The word *council* is probably derived from the Latin *conciere—to call* or *bring together*. It signifies an assembly, especially an assembly held for deliberation and consultation. In ecclesiastical language, it

---

[24] Cf. Catholic Encyclopedia, art. "Patriarch."
[25] Cf. Catholic Encyclopedia, art. "Metropolitan."
[26] Cf. Straub, "De Ecclesia Christi," n. 793.

signifies a lawful assemblage of bishops to decide questions of faith or morals and to legislate for the good of the faithful. Therefore, a Church council is similar to the legislative body in a civil government, yet they differ in certain important features. The bishops assembled in council represent their respective churches, but they are not elected by the people, neither are they delegates of the people, as are the members of our legislative bodies. Again, our legislative bodies have authority to make laws independently of the executive power of the State, whereas a council has no authority to act independently of the Roman Pontiff. This difference arises from the fact that in our government the supreme legislative, executive and judicial powers are vested in separate and distinct persons or bodies, whereas in the Church they are all vested in one person, the Roman Pontiff. Hence the bishops in union with the Roman Pontiff constitute one law-making body, but separated from him they have no authority whatever.

Councils may be *provincial, national, general* or *ecumenical.* A provincial council consists of the bishops of a province convoked and presided over by their metropolitan. Their acts have legal force for the faithful of that province, but not until they have been approved and sanctioned in some way by the Roman Pontiff. A national council is an assemblage of the bishops of a nation or partiarchate convoked and presided over by their primate or patriarch, as the case may be. A council is general when it represents the entire Eastern or Western Church. When *both* the Eastern *and* the Western Churches are represented, the council is ecumenical.

In the earlier centuries all councils exceeding the limits of a single province were known indiscriminately as *universal, plenary,* or *general,* and for many centuries all councils were called *synods.* Today this term is usually restricted to an assembly of diocesan priests presided over by their bishop or archbishop, as the case may be.

ECUMENICAL COUNCILS. For the present purpose it will be sufficient to consider ecumenical councils only, since they alone have jurisdiction over the universal Church, and what is true of them is also true of the others in their respective spheres. In order to be completely ecumenical, a council must be universal by *convocation, celebration,* and *confirmation.*

a) BY CONVOCATION. A council that is truly ecumenical must represent the whole church—*ten oikoumenen,* whence the name *ecumenical.* Consequently all the bishops of the Church must be notified and summoned to attend. It is understood, of course, that *all* is not to be interpreted mathematically to mean each and every bishop without a single exception. It means that practically *all* must be summoned. And none but bishops need be summoned, for to them alone was the government of the Church committed. Neither laymen nor priests, and perhaps not even titular bishops, have any right to sit in councils, unless this has been provided for by the law of the Church or by special act of the Roman Pontiff. The Code of Canon Law provides that the following persons be summoned in addition to the bishops: all cardinals, whether bishops or not, abbots and prelates *nullius,* abbots primate and abbots Superiors of monastic congregations, the supreme moderators of exempt religious clerics, and titular bishops.[27]

b) BY CELEBRATION. A council is ecumenical by celebration when the universal Church is represented by its bishops. Such representation does not require the presence of all the bishops of the whole world, which would be a practical impossibility; neither does it require a majority of them. It does require, however, that sufficient number be present to represent practically all parts of the Church. It would be difficult to assign any definite number. Cardinal Bellarmine says that "the number cannot be defined accurately, but that it should be sufficient to constitute a moral representation of the whole Church. There should be at least some bishops from the majority of provinces."[28] Bishops who were summoned but fail to attend thereby renounce their rights and consent beforehand to all decrees enacted by their brethren.

c) BY CONFIRMATION. A Council becomes ecumenical, i.e., its decrees obtain the force of law for the universal Church, when confirmed by the Roman Pontiff, even though it had not been ecumenical either in its convocation or in its celebration. Papal confirmation may be given either *post factum* or *ante factum,* i.e., the pope may give his approval after the council has taken action, just as the president of the United States signs bills that have been passed by Congress, or he may request certain action to be taken by the council, somewhat in the same manner as the president manages to have measures presented to Congress. In this case, the requested action is approved *ante factum* and needs no further confirmation.

2. *Rights of the Roman Pontiff in Regard to Ecumenical Councils*

I. THE RIGHT OF CONVOCATION. "No council is ecumenical unless convoked by the Roman Pontiff."[29] The Roman Pontiff alone

---

[27] Canon 223.

[28] "De Conciliis," I, 17.

[29] "Codex Juris Canonici," Can. 222, 1: "Dari nequit Oecumenicum Concilium quod a Romano Pontifice non fuerit convocatum."

has authority to convoke an ecumenical council, since he alone, as head
of the Apostolic body of bishops, has authority over all its members;
even the very calling of a council is an act of jurisdiction affecting the
whole Church, and therefore to be exercised only by her supreme pastor. Bishops, as such, have no authority outside the limits of their own
dioceses; consequently they can take no action, separately or collectively, that will have the force of law for the universal Church, unless
authority to do so be given them by the Roman Pontiff, who alone possesses it. A meeting of bishops without authority of the Roman Pontiff
would be similar in every respect to a convention of the State governors in this country; they could pass resolutions and recommend needed
legislation, but their action would have no legal force. Hence Straub
remarks that he who convokes an ecumenical council must be able to
confer upon its members authority to enact laws binding upon the
whole Church. But since the Roman Pontiff alone possesses such power,
it is evident that the bishops assembled in council receive from the
Roman Pontiff authority to unite with him in making laws for the
universal Church. This authority is conferred by the very act of convocation.[30]

THE RIGHT TO PRESIDE. "The Roman Pontiff presides over
an ecumenical council either in person or by delegates; he also designates the matters to be considered and the order to be observed."[31] It
is not only a matter of *right* that the Pope, as supreme pastor of the
Church, preside at all ecumenical councils; it is also a matter of *necessity*, since the bishops receive from him all authority to legislate for the
Church and in union with him constitute one supreme source of teaching and governing power. The moment the pope withdraws his authority, the council ceases to exist; it becomes a mere convention of bishops
without authority to legislate, to sit in judgment, or to define doctrines.

Since the Roman Pontiff confers all authority upon the bishops to
legislate and define matters for the universal Church, he is free to re-
strict this authority within certain limits; in other words, he has the
right to designate the matter to be discussed and the order to be followed. This also follows from his duty as supreme pastor of the flock,
which he has been charged to feed. He has the right as well as the duty
to determine what shall be given the sheep at any and all times.

THE RIGHT OF CONFIRMATION. "The decrees of councils

---

[30] Straub, "De Ecclesia Christi," n. 806; cf. Palmieri, "De Romano Pontifice,"
p. 671 sqq.; Wernz, "Jus Decretalium," Vol. II, n. 844.
[31] "Codex Juris Canonici," can. 222, 2: "Romani Pontificis est Oecumenico
Concilio per se vel per alios praeesse, res in eo tractandas ordinemque servandum
constituere ac designare."

have no binding force unless confirmed by the Roman Pontiff and promulgated by his authority."[32] The doctrine expressed in this canon is simply a corollary to what has been said regarding the authority of bishops assembled in council. Their authority comes from the Roman Pontiff and they hold it only while in union with him; hence no decree can have binding force unless accepted and approved by him. "The final sentence remains with the pope. He it is that *ratifies* the decrees either at the council itself, if he is personally present, or when they are submitted to him, generally by the secretary of the council."[33] The necessity for such ratification has always been recognized by the councils themselves; every ecumenical council without exception presented its acts to the pope for confirmation. The decrees ratified by him obtained the force of law, whereas those rejected were considered null and void. Pope Gelasius I (492-496) said of the Council of Chalcedon: "Everything, as we have said, remains with the Apostolic See. Whatever the Apostolic See confirmed in this synod, obtained the force of law; whatever it rejected, could have no effect."[34] Hence Leo XIII justly remarked: "The acts and decrees of councils have ever been ratified or rejected by the Roman Pontiffs. Leo the Great annulled all the acts of the conciliabulum of Ephesus; Damasus rejected those of Arimini, and Hadrian I, those of Constantinople.[35] The twenty-eighth canon of Constantinople, which lacked the consent and authority of the Apostolic See, remained a dead letter."[36]

The necessity for papal confirmation extends to all councils, whether ecumenical, national or provincial, because without authority from the Apostolic See, bishops can make no laws binding outside the limits of their respective dioceses. They might meet and agree on certain measures, which each bishop could give the force of law for his own diocese, but such agreement would not be legislative action, and the assembly would not constitute a council.

THE CONCILIAR THEORY. At the time of the Western Schism, in the fourteenth and fifteenth centuries, there were two and even three claimants for the throne of Peter, and the faithful were divided in their allegiance, since it was not clear who was the legitimate pope, yet none of the claimants was willing to abandon his position. This produced an intolerable state of affairs that all parties were anxious to

---

[32] "Codex Juris Canonici," can. 227: "Concilii decreta vim definitivam obligandi non habent, nisi a Romano Pontifice fuerint confirmata et eius iussu promulgata."
[33] Chas. Augustine, O.S.B., "Commentary on Canon Law," Vol. ii, p. 225.
[34] Gelasius I, "De Anathematis Vinculo"; P.L., 59, 107.
[35] This refers to a pseudo-synod held in 753 or 754.
[36] Leo XIII, "De Unitate Ecclesiae," June 29, 1896.

remove, but the great question was how to go about the matter, since there was no authority to depose a Roman Pontiff. Finally Peter D'Ailly, Gerson and others hit upon the doctrine of Marsilius of Padua, who had maintained that an ecumenical council is superior to the pope and therefore could depose him.[37] Since the position of all three claimants was doubtful, there was really no legitimate pope, for, as Cardinal Bellarmine says, a doubtful pope is no pope. Consequently the proper proceeding was for the bishops to declare this fact and authorize the cardinals to elect a legitimate pope. This was finally done at the Council of Constance, when Martin V was elected.

The doctrine of Marsilius, afterward espoused by the Gallicans and Febronians, was condemned by the Vatican Council in these words: "None may re-open the judgment of the Apostolic See, than whose authority there is no greater, nor can any lawfully review its judgments. Wherefore they err from the right course who assert that it is lawful to appeal from the judgments of the Roman Pontiff to an ecumenical council, as to an authority higher than that of the Roman Pontiff."[38] Pope Gelasius I, at the end of the fifth century, had stated the same doctrine: "We state only what is known by the whole Church throughout the world, viz., that the See of blessed Peter the Apostle has authority to loose what has been bound by sentence of any bishops whatsoever, because it has authority to judge all churches, but can be judged by none. Appeals may be made to it from all parts of the world, but no one may appeal from it."[39] Almost a hundred years before this, Pope Zosimus wrote to Aurelius of Carthage: "It is not unknown to you that we rule the Roman Church and hold its power. This you know, my brethren, and as priests you ought to know it. Such is our authority, that no one dare revise our judgment."[40]

The very nature of a council proves the absurdity of the theory which would make it superior to the Roman Pontiff, from whom it holds all authority. It is simply asserting in different words that the pope is superior to himself. There is only one supreme authority in the Church, and this was committed to St. Peter and his successors. The pope united with the bishops in council has no greater authority than when acting alone. The pope acting alone can legislate, define doctrine, and judge matters for the whole Church; he can also dispense or abrogate any law or disciplinary decree enacted by an ecclesiastical authority whatsoever, including even ecumenical councils.

---

[37] Cf. L. Salembier, "The Great Schism of the West," pp. 109 sqq. (Eng. Tr.)
[38] Denzinger, n. 1830.
[39] Gelasius I, "Epist. ad Episcopos Dardaniae"; P.L., 59, 66.
[40] Zosimus, "Epist. ad Aurelium"; P.L., 20, 676.

3. Objections Considered

OBJECTION I. The first eight general councils were called not by the Pope, but by the emperors; yet they were all accepted as legitimate and truly ecumenical. Consequently the calling of councils was not recognized as an exclusive right of the Roman Pontiff until later centuries.

ANSWER.—A council convoked without authority of the Roman Pontiff is not ecumenical by convocation; in fact, it is not even a council in the strict sense of the word, and its decrees have no binding force on anyone, unless accepted and confirmed by the Roman Pontiff. When thus approved, the council becomes ecumenical by confirmation. If those first councils were convened by sole authority of the emperors, they were not ecumenical until accepted and ratified by the pope. It is certain, however, that some of them were convoked by the emperor with the consent, and even at the instigation, of the pope. For instance, Leo the Great earnestly begged Theodosius to convoke a council in Italy, but finally consented to have it meet in Chalcedon,[41] where Dioscorus was deposed, because "he had dared to hold a synod without authority from the Apostolic See,—a thing which was never done before, and is not lawful to be done."[42] In view of this statement it seems very probable that the emperors in every case acted with the knowledge and consent of the Roman Pontiff in summoning councils.

OBJECTION II.—The emperors not only summoned the councils, but also presided over their deliberations, Constantine, for instance, presided at the Nicene Council.

ANSWER.—It is historically certain that the Roman Pontiffs, through their legates, really presided at all ecumenical councils except the first and second of Constantinople, which were not originally intended to be ecumenical, but became such afterwards by papal confirmation. Although the papal legates directed and dominated the councils, the emperors or their representatives were at times, given an honorary presidency. This was perfectly legitimate and, under the circumstances, a becoming recognition of the emperor's interest and good will. Without his aid the council could not have been held; he provided a suitable place for its meetings, supplied the bishops with the means of travel, and protected them with his soldiers from the attacks of heretics and other enemies.

OBJECTION III.—If the Roman Pontiff can take all necessary measures for the government of the Church without a council, and

---

[41] Leo Great, "Epist. ad Pulcheriam Augustam"; P.L., 54, 873 sq; "Epist. ad Theodoium Augustum"; P.L., 54, 890.
[42] See above, Ch. xi, Art. ii.

can even nullify its actions by refusing to ratify them, there can be no reason for its existence. The bishops can only discuss and approve what the pope can do without their approval, and even despite their disapproval.

ANSWER.—The Roman Pontiff has power and authority sufficient to rule and guide the Church at all times and under all circumstances, and this he usually does. Ecumenical councils are confessedly an extraordinary means for the governance of the Church. This is evident from the fact that only twenty such councils have been held in the course of nineteen centuries. Councils are not necessary because of any lack of authority on the part of the Roman Pontiff, yet they may be necessary at times to obtain results more effectively and with greater promptness than would otherwise be possible. The knowledge that matters of great importance have been decided after mature deliberation by the bishops of the whole church, cannot fail to have a wholesome effect upon the minds of the faithful. Even the bishops themselves will feel an increased responsibility and greater readiness to put into effect laws and regulations which they have helped to formulate.

A council can also be of great assistance to the Pope in framing suitable laws for the Church. He cannot use his supreme authority for the best interests of the Church unless he knows her various needs, and the circumstances under which she labors in the different parts of the world. There are many ways to obtain this knowledge, but an ecumenical council may, at times, be the easiest and most effective. When bishops from all parts of the world assemble, the needs of all are made known, and the united counsel of many can scarcely fail to discover the most effective and salutary course to follow.

CHAPTER XIII

The Infallible Teaching Authority

The Church received from her Divine Founder the solemn commission to teach all nations whatsoever He had commanded. With this commission she received authority to demand acceptance of her doctrines and the promise of immunity from error in discharging her duty as teacher of the nations.

ART. I. THE TEACHING AUTHORITY OF THE CHURCH

THE TEACHING OFFICE. Teaching must be numbered among the principal duties of the Church. Christ himself constituted the Apostles teachers for all nations: "Go, therefore, and make disciples of all nation, . . . teaching them to observe all that I have commanded you."[1] Again He said to them: "Go into the whole world and preach the gospel to every creature."[2] Because of these commands St. Paul says: "If I preach the gospel, I have therein no ground for boasting, since I am under constraint. For woe to me if I do not preach the gospel!"[3] The other Apostles also proclaimed that their teaching was by command of God, for when the high priests Annas and Caiphas "charged them not to speak or to teach at all in the name of Jesus. But Peter and John said to them, 'Whether it is right in the sight of God to listen to you rather than to God, decide for yourselves.'"[4] St. Paul even intimates that his principal duty as an Apostle was that of preaching: "For Christ did not send me to baptize, but to preach the gospel."[5]

AUTHORITY IN TEACHING. The Apostles were not only commissioned to teach, but were also endowed with authority, such that all who heard their teaching were obliged, under pain of eternal damnation to accept it: "He who does not believe shall be condemned,"[6] and "he who hears you, hears me; and he who rejects you, rejects me."[7] St. Paul says that he received the grace of the Apostolate "to bring about obedience to faith among all the nations, . . . bringing every mind

---

[1] Matt. xxviii, 18-19.
[2] Mark xvi, 15.
[3] 1 Cor. ix, 16.
[4] Acts iv, 18-20.
[5] 1 Cor. i, 17.
[6] Mark xvi, 16.
[7] Luke x, 16; Matt. x, 14.

243

into captivity to the obedience of Christ, and being prepared to take vengeance on all disobedience."[8] He admonished Titus: "Thus speak, and exhort, and rebuke, with all authority. Let no one despise thee."[9]

These few references prove that the teaching office, or *magisterium*, of the Church belongs to her power of jurisdiction, which, therefore, includes authority both to rule and to teach and likewise demands submission of intellect and will.

BISHOPS, THE TEACHERS. The very purpose of the teaching office in the Church demands that it be perpetual, for, as St. Paul says, "God wishes all men to be saved and to come to the knowledge of the truth."[10] And Christ not only promised that He Himself would be with the Apostles for all time in the discharge of their duty as teacher; He also promised them the Holy Spirit to assist them in this same work forever: "I will ask the Father and he will give you another Advocate to dwell with you forever, . . . he will teach you all things, and bring to your mind whatever I have said to you."[11]

Since the teaching authority conferred upon the Apostles is a permanent institution in the Church, it must descend to their lawful successors, the bishops, who thereby become the divinely appointed teachers to preserve the doctrines of Christ and bring them to the knowledge of men in all ages until the consummation of the world. For this reason St. Paul was careful to mention ability to teach as a necessary qualification in bishops: "A bishop then, must be blameless, . . . hospitable, a teacher."[12] And to Titus he writes: "A bishop must be blameless, . . . holding fast the faithful word which is in accordance with the teaching, that he may be able both to exhort in sound doctrine and to confute opponents."[13]

The bishops of the Church are the only divinely authorized teachers, since teaching with authority is an act of jurisdiction, which they alone possess by divine right. From this it follows that the Roman Pontiff, holding the supreme power of jurisdiction, also holds the supreme teaching authority in the Church. In each diocese the bishop is the divinely constituted teacher and judge in matters of faith, but he exercises this office in subjection to the supreme teaching authority of the Roman Pontiff.

EXTENT OF TEACHING AUTHORITY. Christ himself deter-

---

[8] Rom., i, 5; 2 Cor. x, 4 sq.
[9] Titus ii, 15.
[10] 1 Tim. ii, 4.
[11] John xiv, 16, 26.
[12] 1 Tim. iii, 2.
[13] Titus i, 7-8.

mined the extent of the Church's teaching authority when He said: "Make disciples of all nations, . . . teaching them to observe all that I have commanded you."[14] The whole body of revealed truth,—whatsoever Christ has taught,—is committed to the Church for the enlightenment of nations. It is her duty, then, to preserve, interpret, and proclaim these truths of revelation, and whatever is necessary for this purpose falls within the scope of her teaching authority. Since this question comes up again in connection with infallibility,[15] it will be enough to mention here only a few practical conclusions that follow from the Church's duty of preserving and teaching the truths of revelation.

I. REPRESSION OF HERESY. It is the duty of the Church to see to it that the faithful receive the true doctrines of Christ and to this end she may use adequate means to protect them from the contaminating influence of those who seek to spread false doctrines. She has not only the right, but also the duty, to take all necessary measures to protect the spiritual health of her members, just as the State protects the physical health of its citizens by various regulations, even excluding diseased aliens from its borders. Hence the Church is obliged to condemn and proscribe every doctrine at variance with the teachings of Christ. For this reason St. Paul warned Titus of certain persons in Crete "These must be rebuked for they upset whole households, teaching things that they ought not, . . . Hence rebuke them sharply that they may be sound in faith."[16] Our Lord also commanded St. John to write to certain bishops of Asia Minor, severely reproving them because they had not condemned and rooted out false teachings.[17]

II. PROHIBITION OF BOOKS. The duty of preserving the truths of revelation and of protecting the spiritual life of the faithful makes it necessary for the Church to point out and condemn books and periodicals dangerous to the faith and morals of her subjects. The State claims the same right in regard to writings considered dangerous to civil order and to the good of the community. For this reason it forbids the publication and sale of works advocating treason, anarchy, or the commission of crime; it also forbids the use of the mails for any scheme to defraud the unsuspecting. If the State may prohibit books dangerous to the temporal welfare of its citizens, the Church certainly has like authority to protect the eternal welfare of her members.

Many persons ridicule the Church for her practice of condemning

---

[14] Matt. xxviii, 19-20.
[15] See below, Ch. 16 sq.
[16] Titus i, 11-13.
[17] Apoc. ii, 14 sq.

books and forbidding their use to the faithful. They claim it is a suppression of the freedom of thought and a tyrannical use of power in favor of ignorance. But very often these same persons clamor for state and national censorship of theatres, and the suppression of immoral literature, and by so doing prove the wisdom of the Church in her censorship of books.

St. Paul was the first to use this power of the Church by condemning evil books, which he even committed to the flames: "And many who had practiced magical arts collected their books and burnt them publicly ; and they reckoned up the price of them, and found the sum to be fifty thousand pieces of silver. Thus mightily did the word of the Lord spread and prevail."[18] The Church follows the example set by St. Paul. In the sixth century Pope Leo the Great said : "He that uses books condemned by the Catholic Church, cannot be considered a Catholic."[19]

III. IMPRIMATUR. The Church has long recognized the importance of *prophylaxis,* or prevention of disease. She not only forbids the use of literature dangerous to faith and morals, but also prevents the publication of such literature by demanding that all books dealing with matters of faith and morals be submitted to her inspection before publication. In this matter, of course, the Church can exercise authority over her own subjects only. The bishops, as divinely constituted teachers in their dioceses, are charged with the duty of inspecting all books on matters of faith and morals before granting permission for publication in places under their jurisdiction. Needless to say, the Roman Pontiff holds supreme authority in this matter for all parts of the world.

If the bishop, upon examining a work, finds nothing in it contrary or injurious to faith or morals, he gives permission for its publication by the Latin formula, *Imprimatur,* or *Imprimi potest,* i.e., it may be published. Hence the permission itself has come to be known as *Imprimatur.*

IV. APPROBATION FOR PREACHING. The duty of preserving purity of doctrine in regard to faith and morals extends to the spoken as well as to the written word. Consequently the Church forbids any one to preach or publicly teach such doctrines without her consent and approval. Here again, the bishops are charged with the duty of guarding the deposit of faith in their several dioceses. They cannot be expected to examine all sermons and religious discourses to be delivered under their jurisdiction, but they are expected and commanded to select and

---

[18] Acts xix, 19.
[19] "Epist. ad Turribium"; P.L., 54, 688.

approve only such persons as they know to be qualified for the office of preacher or teacher.

The necessity for episcopal approval in these matters also follows from the fact that the bishop is the only divinely constituted teacher in the diocese. All others act as mere agents to assist him in the work of teaching, but no one can act as agent for another unless he has been selected and commissioned for that express purpose. Consequently no one dares to assume the office of preaching in a diocese without due permission and approval from the bishop: "No one may exercise the ministry of preaching unless he has received due permission from a lawful superior."[20]

ART. II. INFALLIBILITY OF THE CHURCH

The Church not only teaches and interprets the doctrines of Christ with divine authority, but also possesses the gift of infallibility, by which these doctrines are proposed and accepted without the possibility of error. Therefore, it is necessary to consider (1) the nature of infallibility, (2) infallibility in teaching, (3) infallibility in believing, and (4) the objections urged against this prerogative of the Church.

1. Nature of Infallibility

Infallibility, from the Latin *in—not* and *falli—to be deceived,* signifies inability to err, and therefore differs from *inerrancy.* A person is *inerrant* when free from error; he is *infallible* when free from the possibility of error. Infallibility must also be distinguished from *revelation* and *inspiration. Revelation* is a manifestation or making known of truths; *inspiration* is a divine impulse to commit certain truths to writing, and a positive assistance of the Holy Spirit to direct the writer in recording precisely those truths which God wishes to have recorded and in the particular way that He wishes them recorded. Infallibility is merely a divine protection by which a person is unfailingly preserved from error in declaring and interpreting truths already revealed. Consequently, infallibility does not bring to light any new truths; it simply provides that revealed truths be proposed and interpreted without the possibility of error.

Infallibility does not require special divine influence at all times. The interposition of such influence is necessary only when the person, left to his own natural powers, is about to fall into error. The difference between inspiration and infallibility may be illustrated by the assistance

---

[20] "Codex Juris Canonici," can. 1328.

given a child in writing. The teacher may grasp the hand of the child and direct it in writing such words as the teacher wishes and in the way he wishes, or he may simply hold his hand in readiness to prevent the child from making any errors in writing the words to be copied. The first case illustrates the action of the Holy Spirit in inspiration; the second, His action in preserving a person from error by the gift of infallibility.

The above explanation makes it evident that infallibility does not exclude, but rather presupposes, the use of natural means to avoid error. The divine protection is only to supply the deficiency of natural means and thereby preclude the possibility of error, but since the exclusion of error is the end to be obtained without fail, neglect on the part of the human agent will not prevent the Holy Spirit from realizing that end. Hence if the person endowed with infallibility fails to use the natural means at hand for discovering the truth, he commits sin, but will be protected from error none the less, because infallibility is a *gratia gratis data*,—a gift freely bestowed for the good of others.

Infallibility, as a property of the Church, is an ever-present right to be divinely preserved from error whenever such divine assistance is needed.

DEGREES OF INFALLIBILITY. Perfect infallibility belongs to God, the Eternal Truth, but rational creatures may enjoy a certain immunity from error,—an immunity which they hold as a gift from God. This communicated infallibility is either *natural* or *supernatural*. *Natural infallibility* is the immunity from error which all men possess in regard to certain self-evident truths. We know from experience that there are certain truths so evident that no one having the use of reason can mistake or misunderstand them. *Supernatural infallibility* is an immunity from error maintained by special assistance of the Holy Spirit. This special gift may concern the teaching of truths without error, and is then known as *active* infallibility, or *infallibility in teaching*. When its purpose is to prevent error in the acceptance of truths taught, it is called *passive infallibility*, or *infallibility in believing*. The Church possesses both active and passive infallibility.

2. Active Infallibility of the Church

Thesis.—The Church of Christ Is Infallible in Teaching
Revealed Truths

DE FIDE. The Vatican Council indirectly proclaimed the Church infallible in teaching when it declared that "the Roman Pontiff possesses that infallibility with which the Divine Redeemer willed that His Church should be endowed for defining doctrine regarding faith or morals."[21] Even before this declaration the doctrine was rightly considered a dogma of faith for, as Fenelon had said, "the Church always takes for granted that she possesses this fundamental authority and exercises it against those who dare call it in question. This constant practice of the Church is a continual declaration of her infallible authority."[22]

OPPONENTS OF INFALLIBILITY. a) PROTESTANTS. All Protestants without exception reject the very idea of infallibility as an absurdity. For them it is quite sufficient if a church have authority to declare what doctrines it teaches and to demand their profession by all who wish to become members. No society, it seems, could be denied such authority, yet the fundamental Protestant doctrine of private interpretation renders even this modicum of authority impossible. In order to become a member of a Protestant church, it is not necessary to accept its doctrinal standards, because all are free to take their faith from the Bible according to their own interpretation of it. In such a system there is no place for a teaching authority, fallible or infallible. No minister can logically claim to present anything more than his own private opinion, which others are, therefore, free to accept or reject. According to this theory, the faithful must be, as St. Paul says, "ever learning yet never attaining knowledge of the truth."[23]

b) EASTERN SCHISMATICS. The position of the schismatic churches of the East on this question is difficult to determine. They teach that the first seven ecumenical councils were infallible, or at least free from error, in proclaiming the doctrines of Christ. They also maintain that these doctrines have been preserved intact by all so-called Orthodox churches, but whether the Church still possesses an infallible teaching authority seems to be a disputed question. Among the Orthodox theologians of the present day, Androutsos teaches that the Church is infallible, while Kyriakos is said to deny it.[24]

THE QUESTION. It is evident that the infallibility of the Church in teaching can be nothing else than the infallibility of those who exercise the teaching authority in the Church. Hence, to prove the Church infallible in teaching is to prove that the bishops, as successors of the Apostles, are infallible in teaching the truths of Revelation. This must be established by proving that the gift of infallibility was bestowed

---

[21] Denzinger, n. 1839.

[22] "Instructio Pastoralis," iii, 57.

[23] 2 Tim. iii, 7.

[24] Androutsos, "Dogmatics of the Orthodox Church," p. 265; D'ales, "Dictionnaire Apologetique," Art. "Grecque, Eglise."

upon the Apostles, not only as individuals, but also as members of the Apostolic body, of which St. Peter was the head.

Infallibility granted to the Apostles as individuals was a personal prerogative, and consequently did not descend to their successors. But if infallibility was also granted to them as a body, then the bishops, who perpetuate that body in the Church, must possess the same prerogative and in the same manner, i.e., not as individuals, but as a body.

PROOFS. I. From Reason. a) The Church, as the mystical body of Christ, is animated and vivified by the Holy Ghost, much the same as the natural body is informed and vivified by the soul; and as in the natural body, all vital activities proceed from the soul, so likewise those of the Church must proceed from the Holy Spirit. Therefore, if the Church as a whole falls into error through her official teaching body, that error must be ascribed to the Holy Spirit, the Spirit of Truth, which is manifestly impossible. Consequently, the bishops, as the teaching body in the Church, must be infallible.

b) Christ ordained that all men must accept the teachings of the Church under pain of eternal damnation: "He who does not believe shall be condemned."[25] Therefore, He is bound in justice to provide against the possibility of our being led into error by following this precept of obedience to the teaching authority of the Church. Besides, it is inconceivable that Christ, the eternal Truth, could allow a single error to be proclaimed to the world in His name; yet this would be the case if the Church, teaching in His name and by His authority, were not infallible.

II. *From Scripture.* a) Our Lord proclaimed His Church infallible when He said: "The gates of hell shall not prevail against it."[26] If *gates of hell* means the powers of darkness, then Christ directly promised His Church infallibility, because the moment she would fall into error, she would succumb to the powers of darkness, and the promise of Christ would be made void. On the other hand, if the *gates of hell* is merely a synonym for death or destruction, Christ has promised that His Church will endure for all time, unchanged in any essential feature, because the moment it would lose a single essential feature, it would cease to be the Church established by Christ. Therefore Christ has implicitly promised the gift of infallibility, without which unity of faith could not be preserved through all the centuries among peoples of every nation, tribe, and tongue, especially since many of the truths to be preserved transcend the powers of human understanding. "The Church of Christ would fail

---

[25] Mark xvi, 16.
[26] Matt. xvi, 18.

in her immutability, fall from her dignity, and cease to be the necessary means of salvation, if she could wander from the saving truths of faith and morals, or if she could either deceive or be deceived in expounding or proclaiming them."[27]

b) "And Jesus drew near and spoke to them saying, 'All power in heaven and on earth has been given to me. Go, therefore, and make disciples of all nations . . . teaching them to observe all that I have commanded you; and behold, I am with you all days, even unto the consummation of the world."[28] With these words Our Lord conferred upon His Disciples unlimited authority to teach: Teach all nations, teach all truths; and behold I am with you—not for a month, or a year, or a life-time, but all days, even to the consummation of the world. The mission is for all time; for the Apostles and their successors down through the ages.

It is evident from the very words of Our Lord that He was conferring a most extraordinary power. He appeals to His own divine power to prove, as it were, His authority for the commission He is conferring: "All Power is given to me in heaven and in earth; going therefore, teach with all my divine power and authority." Only a few days before, Our Lord had made a similar appeal as a prelude to the conferring of another extraordinary power: "As the Father has sent me, I also send you. . . . Receive the Holy Spirit; whose sins you shall forgive, they are forgiven them; and whose sins you shall retain, they are retained." Hence, divine power must be as necessary in one case is in the other, but the mere office of preaching the Gospel would not require such extraordinary power; the ordinary assistance of God's grace would be amply sufficient for that. What, then, was the purpose of this unusual power and the solemn manner in which it was conferred? There can be but one answer to this question: "Our Lord was conferring upon His Apostles and their successors an infallible authority to teach all nations whatsoever He had commanded them; He constituted them teachers, whom all must accept under pain of eternal damnation; therefore, He made them infallible.

Christ not only conferred a divine prerogative upon the Apostles as teachers of the nations, but He also promised to be with them in this work until the end of time: "Behold I am with you all days even to the consummation of the world." But why this special and constant presence of Christ with His Apostles and their successors down through the ages? Evidently, that they might teach aright the truths of Revelation to all

---

[27] Canon 9 of the schema proposed at the Vatican Council.
[28] Matt. xxviii, 16-18.

nations until the consummation of time. Here, then, is a promise of complete and perpetual infallibility. Wherever God is said to *be with* a person, it is a promise of special divine assistance that never fails in its purpose. For example, when Moses was sent to lead the Israelites out of Egypt, he hesitated to accept the difficult mission, but God assured him of His assistance and success: "I will be with thee."[29] In like manner God said to Josue: "As I have been with Moses, so will I be with thee: I will not leave thee nor forsake thee."[30] It is also said of the Apostles: "And the hand of the Lord was with them, and great number believed and turned to the Lord."[31] Hence when Christ promised to *be with* the Apostles and their successors, He promised them an assistance that cannot fail in its purpose; they shall infallibly teach aright the truths committed to them for the enlightenment of all nations.

c) On the night of the Last Supper Our Lord promised His Apostles the guiding presence of the Holy Spirit, and He promised this not once, but many times: "And I will ask the Father and he will give you another Advocate to dwell with you forever. . . . But the Advocate the Holy Spirit, whom the Father will send in my name, he will teach you all things, and bring to your mind whatever I have said to you. . . . But when the Advocate has come, whom I will send you from the Father, the Spirit of truth who proceeds from the Father, he will bear witness concerning me. . . . But I speak the truth to you; it is expedient for you that I depart. For if I do not go, the Advocate will not come to you. . . . Many things yet I have to say to you, but you cannot bear them now. But when he, the Spirit of truth, has come, he will teach you all the truth."[32]

Throughout this whole discourse, Our Lord refers to the Holy Spirit as the *Paracelete*, i.e., the Helper or Advocate. Christ himself was the *Paraclete* or Helper of the Apostles during His life on earth, and promised to be with them for all time. He now promises *another* Paraclete to assist and guide them during His bodily absence after the Ascension. The coming of this second Paraclete is even more important for the Apostles than the continuation of Our Lord's personal presence among them: "It is expedient for you that I go, for if I go not, the Paraclete will not come to you." The mission of this second Paraclete is clearly marked out. He is the Spirit of truth, who is to keep clearly before the minds of the Apostles all things taught them by

---

[29] Ex. iii, 11-12.
[30] Jos. i, 5.
[31] Acts xi, 21.
[32] John xiv, 16-17; xiv, 26; xv, 26-27; xvi, 7; xvi, 12-13.

Christ: "He will teach you all truth," or as the Greek text has it, "He will lead you into all truth."

The Holy Spirit is to abide forever with the Apostles and their successors, and His guidance shall be effective; he shall lead them into all truth and preserve them therein. In a word, the Holy Spirit shall preserve the Apostles and their successors free from every error. He shall render them infallible. Christ had commissioned the Apostles to teach "all things whatsoever I have commanded." He now promises them the Holy Spirit to keep these same truths ever before their minds, that they may teach them without the fear or possibility of error; "He will bring all things to your mind whatsoever I shall have said to you." Could Our Lord have promised infallibility in more explicit or more emphatic language?

d) St. Paul explicitly appeals to the infallibility of the Church in his first Epistle to Timothy. He admonishes Timothy that sound doctrine must be carefully guarded and preached, and all Jewish fables avoided, as becomes a bishop of the Church: "I write these things to thee . . . in order that thou mayest know, if I am delayed, how to conduct thyself in the house of God." He then adds the reason: "Because the Church of the living God is the pillar and mainstay of the truth."[33]

The Church is the *pillar* of truth because, like the pillar of a material building, it sustains and strengthens the whole structure of divine Revelation. It is the *foundation* upon which revealed truths are based and made secure for all time. In a word, the Church is the firm foundation and the secure guardian of the truth which she teaches with infallible security from all error.[34]

III. *From Tradition.* The infallible teaching authority of the Church has been recognized in all ages, as is evident from the fact that any one who denied or questioned a single dogma of her teaching was promptly condemned as a heretic and cut off from communion with the faithful. There was never the least question that her teachings might be false. The Fathers also manifest their faith in the infallible authority of the Church by appealing to her teachings as the standard of truth. A few examples will illustrate this belief:

a) *St. Irenaeus:* "It is incumbent to obey the presbyters who are in the Church,—those who, as I have shown, possess the succession from the Apostles; those who, together with the succession of the episcopate, have received *the certain gift of truth* according to the good pleasure of the Father."[35]

---

[33] 1 Tim. iii, 15.
[34] Knabenbauer, Commentarius in 1 Tim., iii, 15.
[35] "Adversus Haereses," iv, 26; P.G., 7, 1053.*

b) *St. Cyril of Jerusalem:* "The Church is called Catholic, because it extends all over the world . . . and because it teaches *universally and completely one and all the doctrines which ought to come to man's knowledge,* concerning things both visible and invisible, heavenly and earthly."[36]

c) *St. Athanasius:* After enumerating a number of errors, St. Athanasius says: "It is enough merely to answer such things as follows: 'We are content with the fact that this is not the teaching of the Catholic Church, nor did the fathers hold this.' "[37]

d) St. Augustine. "Many tongues contradict the true doctrine; hasten thou to the tabernacle of God, cling to the Catholic Church, be not separated from the *standard of truth,* and thou shalt be protected in the tabernacle from the contradiction of tongues."[38]

3. Passive Infallibility of the Church

Thesis.—The Body of the Faithful Infallibly Accept the Truths of Revelation Proposed to Them by the Teaching Authority of the Church

The Church is *infallible in believing,* i.e., the faithful *as a body,* are preserved from error in accepting and professing the doctrines taught by the Church. Individuals may err; whole provinces, and even nations may fall away from the faith, as history testifies; but those professing the true faith must always remain sufficient in number and in distribution throughout the world to preserve the Church truly Catholic in the unity of faith and worship.

PROOFS. I. *From Reason.* Passive infallibility, in the sense just explained, is a necessary consequence of the indefectible unity of faith and the perpetual Catholicity of the Church. Since the Church is immutably one in the profession of faith, the faithful as a body must be free from error, otherwise the faith would not be one, but many. Moreover, the profession of a false faith constitutes manifest heresy and excludes one from membership in the Church. Consequently, if the faithful as a body could fall into error in the profession of faith, the Church would immediately cease to be Catholic and would therefore cease to be the Church of Christ. It is evident, then, that the faithful as a body must be infallible or free from error, at least in the profession of faith.

II. *From Scripture.* a) The Church is the mystical Body and the

---

[31] "Catecheses," xviii, n. 23; P.G., 33, 1043.*
[37] "Epist. ad Epictetum"; P.G., 26, 1055.*
[38] "Ennaration. in Ps.," xxx, Sermo. 3; P.L., 36, 2533.

Spouse of Christ, for which He "delivered himself up for her, that he might sanctify her, cleansing her in the bath of water by means of the word; in order that he might present to himself the Church in all her glory, not having spot or wrinkle or any such thing, but that she might be holy and without blemish."[39] But a Church tainted with error and the profession of falsehood would be neither glorious nor without spot; neither would it be a spouse worthy of Christ. If the faithful as a body could fall into error, would not Christ have delivered Himself in vain to cleanse and sanctify the Church which they constitute? And would not the error of the mystical Body be justly imputable to its Head and to the Holy Spirit who animates it?

b) St. Paul describes the Church as the pillar and ground of truth, but this she cannot be, unless the body of the faithful be preserved free from error in accepting and professing the truths of faith. She is the pillar and ground of truth, because the gates of hell cannot prevail against her. In the words of St. Augustine, "the Church is true, the Church is Catholic, fighting against all heresies. She may fight, but she cannot be overcome. All heresies have gone out from her, like useless brambles pruned from the vine. She herself remains firmly rooted. . . . The gates of hell shall never conquer her."[40]

III. *From Tradition.* The Fathers constantly appeal to the faith professed, as well as to that taught, by the universal Church as an unfailing norm of truth. Hence, the famous axiom of ST. VINCENT OF LERINS in the fifth century: "We confess that one faith to be true which the whole Church throughout the world confesses."[41] ST. AUGUSTINE expresses the same thought in almost identical terms: "What is held by the whole Church, and that not as instituted by councils, but as a matter of invariable custom, is rightly held to have been handed down by Apostolic authority."[42] TERTULLIAN expressly states that the Church is preserved from error in the profession of faith by the action of the Holy Spirit: "The Holy Spirit was sent with this in view by Christ, and for this asked of the Father that He might be the teacher of truth. . . . Has He neglected His office, permitting the churches for a time to understand differently, and to believe differently what He himself was preaching by the Apostles?"[43] He uses this argument to prove that the faith professed in the Cath-

---

[39] Eph. v, 25-27.
[40] "Sermon. de Symbolo," c. 6; P.L., 40, 635.
[41] "Commonitorium," cf. 2; P.L., 50, 640.*
[42] "De Baptismo," iv, 24; P.L., 43, 174.
[43] "De Praescrip. Haer.," 28; P.L., 2, 40.

olic Church had not varied from that taught by the Apostles, as the heretics claimed.

COROLLARY. Since the faithful as body are infallible in accepting and professing the faith proposed to them, it follows that any doctrine professed by the whole Church as a matter of revelation is infallibly true and may be defined as an article of faith by the teaching authority of the Church. A mere opinion or pious belief accepted by the whole Church is not necessarily true, but should not be rejected lightly, because such universal acceptance gives strong presumption in favor of its being a doctrine handed down from the Apostles.

Passive infallibility, bestowed upon the Church primarily for the purpose of preserving unity of faith, also furnishes a rule of faith, since any doctrine professed by the whole Church must be a revealed truth. Practically, however, such a rule of faith is not sufficient for the needs of the faithful, because it requires long and diligent research to discover whether any particular doctrine is held by the universal Church, and also whether it is held as a revealed truth or merely as a pious belief.

4. Objections Answered

OBJECTION I.—Infallibility cannot be inferred from the necessity of preserving the true faith, nor from the command of Christ that all must accept the teachings of the Church. In the Old Law there were revealed doctrines to be conserved, and the people were commanded to accept the teachings of their superiors under pain of death: "He that shall be proud and refuse to obey the commandment of the priest . . . and the decree of the judge, that man shall die."[44] Yet, despite these facts the Synagogue, the Church of the Old Law, was not infallible.

ANSWER.—Whether the Synagogue was infallible or not is a disputed question, but granting that it was not, this proves nothing against the necessity of infallibility in the Church. In the Old Law there were but few supernatural truths to be conserved, and those only in one nation, among a people of one language. Yet, even under these conditions, it was necessary for God to send prophets at frequent intervals to recall the people to a knowledge of the truth and to a sense of their duty. In the New Law there are many truths transcending the powers of the human intellect, and these must be preserved intact among peoples of all nations, tribes, and tongues, not for a few cen-

---

[44] Deut. xviii, 12.

turies only, but for all time. Because of these different conditions under the New Law, God substituted an infallible teaching authority for the prophetic ministry of the Old Law.

OBJECTION II.—Catholics claim to prove the infallibility of the Church from the authority of Scripture, and then, in open violation of all logic, they proceed to establish the authority of Scripture from the infallible authority of the Church.

ANSWER.—Catholics prove the infallibility of the Church from the Scriptures taken as purely historical documents. The historical reliability of the Scriptures must be established the same as that of any other document. Catholic and non-Catholic scholars have done this to the satisfaction of all reasonable men. Taking the Scriptures as genuine historical documents, Catholics prove that Christ was a divine legate, that He established a Church, and endowed it with infallibility. Having thus established the infallibility of the Church by purely historical arguments, Catholics then appeal to it in proof of the inspired character of those same Scriptures. The whole process is perfectly logical, since the historical accuracy of a work is quite different from its inspiration; many human works are historically accurate, but not divinely inspired.

OBJECTION III.—Even granting the infallibility of the Church, we must still have recourse to the Protestant principle of private judgment. Infallibility is known only by an act of our own reason, but if we must rely on private judgment in this most important matter, why not also in other matters of faith? Again, the knowledge of infallibility rests upon an act of our own judgment. Consequently, an infallible authority can never give any greater certainty than that of the judgment accepting it; a chain is never stronger than its weakest link, which in this case is an act of our own private judgment. Therefore, infallibility is useless.[45]

ANSWER.—The objection is refuted by the old axiom that "who proves too much, proves nothing." The same argument would destroy the infallible authority of God and make divine Revelation useless. The existence of God and His infallible authority are known only by an act of our own reason, but if we exercise our judgment in regard to these truths, why not in other matters as well? Therefore, Revelation is useless and does not exist since God can do nothing useless. The absurdity of this conclusion proves the absurdity of the argument from which it is deduced.

We exercise our own reason and judgment to establish the exist-

---

[45] Cf. G. Salmon, "Infallibility of the Church," pp. 47 sq.

ence of God, His infinite knowledge and truthfulness, and the fact
that He has made a Revelation. Then, as becomes rational beings, we
accept the infallible authority of God for the knowledge of truths beyond our own powers of intellect, and also for truths which we could
know by our own reason, but not so easily nor so securely. In like
manner, we establish the existence of infallible authority in the Church
by the use of reason, and then rely upon that authority for truths
which we cannot know by reason, or which we cannot know with ease
and security. Even supposing that all men could attain knowledge of
all revealed truths by their own private judgment, an infallible authority would not be useless by any means. Any mathematician can
construct a table of logarithms, yet he finds it very useful to have
one at hand which he knows to be perfectly accurate.

Finally, if infallible authority in the Church could give no certainty
of faith, because that authority itself must be established by reason,
then all faith, both human and divine, would become impossible. Divine faith rests upon the testimony of God; human faith, upon the
testimony of man; but in either case we must use our reason to establish the existence and trustworthiness of the testimony.

OBJECTION IV.—An infallible teaching authority in the Church
is useless unless every member of the Church can be infallibly certain
what that authority teaches. But for this knowledge, the members of
the Church must depend upon priests, catechists, or parents, none of
whom are infallible. Consequently, they believe upon the fallible authority of their teachers instead of the infallible authority of the
Church. In other words, they have only human faith.

ANSWER.—This objection also proves too much. It proves that
divine Revelation is useless and divine faith impossible. Many persons
learn the truths of Revelation from parents, catechists, or pastors, who
are neither infallible nor inspired. Therefore, they cannot be infallibly
certain what truths have been revealed. Even if these truths be learned
directly from Holy Scripture, the person accepting them must rely
upon the fallible and uninspired testimony of others for the fact that
the books of Scripture are genuine and have come down through the
centuries uncorrupted. Consequently, they believe upon the fallible
authority of man instead of the infallible authority of God; their faith
is human, not divine. The absurdity of the conclusion proves the absurdity
of the argument.

Priests, catechists, parents, and others are simply witnesses to the
teachings of the Church. They are human witnesses, it is true, but
their testimony can give absolute certainty when the proper conditions

are verified, i.e., when we know the witnesses have sufficient knowledge of the matter and are truthful. These two facts are easily established beyond the possibility of doubt when there are many independent witnesses testifying to the same thing. Who, for instance, could force himself to doubt the existence of the city of Paris, although his only knowledge of the fact has been derived from the testimony of others? The witnesses for the teachings of the Church are just as numerous and just as reliable as those for the existence of Paris, and the certainty they beget is no less absolute. Bishops, priests, catechists, parents, learned friends and companions, official creeds and catechisms, books, pamphlets, and periodicals all agree in their testimony regarding the teachings of the Church. From this human testimony we know with absolute certainty what the Church teaches, and knowing this, we believe it, because of her infallible authority.

OBJECTION V.—The infallibility of the Church cannot be a dogma of faith. The Church would have to use her infallible authority to define her own infallibility which is manifestly begging the question, —taking for granted the very thing to be proved. Therefore, since the infallibility of the Church cannot be a dogma of faith, we are not obliged to believe it.

ANSWER.—If we need not accept the testimony of the Church defining her own infallibility, neither are we obliged to accept the testimony of God revealing His authority, since in both cases the existence of the authority must be established by reason before its testimony can be accepted. The falsity of the conclusion proves the falsity of the argument. As a matter of fact, we arrive at a knowledge of God and His divine authority by the use of reason. Then, relying upon that authority, we accept the testimony of God revealing it to us. In like manner, we prove the infallible authority of the Church from Revelation and then rely upon that authority of the Church when she defines it as an article of faith. What we know by reason, we also accept by faith.

CHAPTER XIV

Infallibility of the Bishops

The infallibility of the Church in teaching can be none other than that of her divinely constituted teachers, who, as successors of the Apostles, perpetuate the Apostolic body with all its powers and prerogatives for teaching and governing the faithful. The bishops, then, as successors of the Apostles, enjoy the gift of infallibility, not as individuals, but as a body in union with the Roman Pontiff, their divinely constituted head. But since the bishops exercise their teaching authority when assembled in council to define doctrines of faith or morals for the whole Church, and also when instructing the people of their own dioceses in these same doctrines, it is necessary to consider (1) the infallibility of ecumenical councils, and (2) the infallibility of the episcopal body in its ordinary work of teaching the faithful in the various parts of the Church.

ART. 1. INFALLIBILITY OF ECUMENICAL COUNCILS

Thesis.—The Bishops Assembled in Ecumenical Council Are Infallible When Exercising Their Supreme Authority to Define Questions of Faith or Morals for the Universal Church

1. Preliminary Explanations

CONDITIONS. Certain conditions are necessary for the exercise of infallible teaching authority by bishops assembled in council, namely: a) the council must be summoned by the Roman Pontiff, or at least with his consent and approval, because all power in the Church, whether of teaching or governing, is subject to the supreme authority of the pope. Again, since the bishops enjoy infallibility in their corporate capacity only, they cannot exercise it independently of the Roman Pontiff, their divinely constituted head. From this it also follows that all definitions must have the approval and confirmation of the Roman Pontiff, for without such confirmation the bishops are acting independently of their head and, therefore, without any authority.

b) The council must be truly ecumenical by celebration, i.e., the whole body of bishops must be represented. This, of course, does not require the presence of each and every bishop of the whole Church, for if such were the case, the willful or enforced absence of one bishop would frustrate the will of the entire body. Neither is it necessary that every bishop present should consent to the definition proposed, for since the bishops individually are fallible, false opinions will almost invariably find some supporters among them. On this account it would be practically impossible to define any doctrine if unanimous consent were necessary, yet at times a definition is imperative, because some fundamental doctrine of Christianity is at stake, as happened during the Arian and Nestorian heresies. Hence a lawful and infallible definition may be made without the unanimous consent of the Fathers present. In case of a real division in a council, truth must lie with the party whom the Roman Pontiff supports, since no definitions have any force unless confirmed by him.

Definitions of faith may also be made by councils that are not truly ecumenical in their celebration, but in that case the infallible authority is not that of the bishops, but that of the Roman Pontiff, who approves the decrees and thus makes them his own.

c) Bishops assembled in council are infallible only when exercising their supreme authority as teachers of faith or morals by a definite and irrevocable decree that a doctrine is revealed and, therefore, to be accepted by every member of the Church.[1] But since the bishops need not intend such an irrevocable decision at all times, it is necessary that an infallible definition be so worded as to indicate clearly its definitive character. For this purpose no set formula is necessary; it is sufficient to mention the doctrine as *an article of faith, a dogma of faith, a Catholic dogma, a doctrine always believed in the Church, or a doctrine handed down by the Fathers.* Anathema pronounced against those who deny a doctrine is also sufficient evidence of a dogmatic definition.

A large majority of the acts of councils are not infallible definitions, because they are not intended as such. "Neither the discussions which precede a dogmatic decree, nor the reasons alleged to prove and explain it, are to be accepted as infallibly true. Nothing but the actual decrees are of faith, and these only if they are intended as such."[2]

d) Since infallibility is due to mere *assistance* of the Holy Spirit, human agencies should be employed to discover and understand the truth to be defined, but the certitude of the definition does not depend upon the previous investigation made by the bishops of the council,

---

[1] Other matters falling under the infallible authority of the Church will be considered elsewhere. Cf. pp. 288 sq.

[2] Cardinal Bellarmine, "De Conciliis," I, 17.

nor upon their skill and learning. Failure to make proper investigation would be sinful on the part of the bishops, but the Holy Spirit can and does prevent all error in the actual definition, even though all investigation has been neglected, or false reasons adduced to prove the doctrine.

ADVERSARIES. Protestants, of course, deny the infallibility of ecumenical councils, since they reject the very idea of infallibility in any form. One of the Thirty-nine articles of the Anglican Church reads: "General councils . . . may err and sometimes have erred even in things pertaining to God."[3] The Gallicans and Jansenists of the seventeenth and eighteenth centuries professed to accept the infallibility of ecumenical councils, but actually denied it by teaching that their decrees and definitions are not irreformable unless accepted by all the faithful. The Modernists hold practically the same doctrine, as is evident from the proposition condemned by Pius X: "In the definition of truths the Church teaching and the Church taught work together in such wise that nothing remains for the Church teaching except to sanction the common opinions of the Church taught."[4]

2. Infallibility of Councils Demonstrated

PROOFS. I. *From Reason.* a) If the bishops are free from error at any time, they certainly must be when assembled in council by the supreme head of the Church to exercise their authority as teachers in the most solemn manner by defining matters of faith and morals for the universal Church.

b) If the bishops assembled in council to define questions of faith or morals for the whole Church should fall into error, the Church herself would inevitably fall into the same error, since the faithful are obliged to accept their teachings. Then would the gates of hell prevail against the Church, the Holy Spirit, the Spirit of truth, would fail in His mission; the indefectibility and Apostolicity of the Church would be destroyed; the Church would cease to be the pillar and ground of truth established by Christ upon the rock.

II. *From Scripture.* "For where two or three are gathered together for my sake, there am I in the midst of them."[5] On the occasion when Our Lord uttered these words He was speaking to His Apostles of the man who proves incorrigible under fraternal correction. He is to be denounced to the Church for official correction, but "if he will

---

[3] Art. XXI. Cf. Schaff, Vol. III, p. 500.
[4] Pius X, "Decree Lamentabili," July 3, 1907; Denzinger, n. 2006.
[5] Matt. xviii, 20.

not hear the Church, let him be to thee as the heathen and publican."
Then, to show that the ministers of the Church have authority to handle such cases, He added: "Whatsoever you shall bind upon earth, shall be bound also in heaven." Christ then continues to tell the Apostles that, whenever they meet to consider a case of this kind, or, in fact, any matter of interest to the Church, they shall have special assistance and shall obtain whatever they ask of the Father: "I say to you further, that if two of you shall agree on earth about anything at all for which they ask, it shall be done for them by my Father in heaven. For where two or three are gathered together for my sake, there am I in the midst of them."

Now, if two or three gathered together to decide matters of such minor importance, are promised special assistance and shall obtain whatever they ask of the Father, what must be expected when the bishops of the whole world are called together by the supreme head of the Church to define questions of faith or morals for all the faithful? Will not the promise of Christ be fulfilled when they ask the Father for wisdom and light to know the truth and to define it unerringly for the faithful?

III. *From Tradition.* In refuting heretics, the Fathers of the Church constantly appeal to the definitions of ecumenical councils as to a secure standard of faith. For example:

a) *St. Gregory the Great says:* "I confess that I accept and venerate the four councils even as the four books of the Gospel."[6] At that time there had been but four ecumenical councils, and St. Gregory accepts them as of equal authority with the Gospels.

b) *St. Cyril of Alexandria:* "When the Fathers (of the council) issued canons of sincere and irreproachable faith, they were directed by the Holy Spirit, that they might not depart from the truth. In fact, as Christ the Saviour testifies, it was not they who spoke, but the Spirit of God the Father who spoke in them."[7]

c) *St. Athanasius:* "The word of the Lord, which came through the ecumenical Synod of Nicaea, abides forever."[8]

d) *Pope Hormisdas:* "Those who hold to the constitutions of the Fathers and cherish those foundations of faith, do not depart from the things which they defined by the impelling power of the Holy Spirit."[9]

The Fathers of the councils always looked upon their definitions as infallibly true and, therefore, excommunicated all who dared deny or

---

[6] "Epist. ad Joannem Constantinop."; P.L., 77, 478.
[7] "Epist. ad Monachos Aegypti"; P.G., 77, 15.
[8] "Epist. ad Episcopos Afros"; P.G., 26, 1031.*
[9] "Epist. ad Epiphanium Hierosol."; P.L., 53, 519.

question them. The Council of Chalcedon distinctly asserted the fact of divine assistance: "We seemed to see the heavenly Bridegroom present with us. For if where two or three are gathered together in His name, He has said that there He is in the midst of them, must He not have been much more particularly present with five hundred and twenty bishops who preferred the spread of knowledge concerning Him to their country and their ease?"[10]

3. Objections Answered

OBJECTION I.—St. Gregory of Nazianzen certainly did not believe councils infallible, for he says: "If I am to write the truth, I keep as far as possible from any meeting of bishops, because I never knew a council with a happy ending, nor one that did not do more harm than good."[11]

ANSWER.—In this passage St. Gregory refers to the numerous local councils, in which Arian bishops under the protection of the emperor, sought to pervert the Catholic faith. Only one ecumenical council,—that of Nicaea in 325,—had been held up to the time of St. Gregory, and he speaks of it with the greatest respect. He says: "In the holy Synod held at Nicaea, the Holy Spirit brought together three hundred and eighteen most chosen men."[12]

OBJECTION II.—St. Augustine expressly declares that ecumenical councils are fallible, for he says: "Councils which are held in the several districts and provinces must yield, beyond all possibility of doubt, to the authority of plenary councils, which are formed for the whole Christian world; and even of the plenary councils, the earlier are often corrected by those which follow them."[13] Councils thus subject to correction cannot be infallible.

ANSWER.—When St. Augustine wrote these words, only two ecumenical councils had been held,—one at Nicaea in 325, and one at Constantinople in 381. Consequently, he was not referring to ecumenical councils when he said that "the earlier are *often* corrected by those which follow them." *Plenary* councils are evidently those which represent more than one province or district of the Church, but not the *whole Christian world* in the literal sense. But even granting that ecumenical councils are meant, there is nothing to indicate that St. Augustine

[10] "Epistola Synodica ad Leonem"; P.L., 54, 951.*
[11] "Epist. ad Procop."; P.G., 37, 226.
[12] St. Gregory Nazianzen, "Oratio in Laudem Athanas"; P.G., 35, 1095.
[13] "De Baptismo," ii. 3; P.L., 43, 128.*

denied them infallibility. He says: "The earlier are often corrected by those which follow them, when, by some actual experiment, things are brought to light which were before concealed, and that is known which previously lay hid." A doctrine defined by one council in its more general aspects may be taken up by another council and defined more in detail, because further study or controversy has made such action necessary or advisable. The doctrine of transubstantiation, for instance, was defined by the Fourth Lateran Council, but was afterward defined in more definite terms by the Council of Trent, because the controversies on this subject in the sixteenth century made such action necessary. The words of St. Augustine naturally suggest just this sort of correction.

OBJECTION III.—In 431 the Council of Ephesus reaffirmed the Nicene Creed and anathematized any one who should dare write or compose any other. Yet many other creeds have been composed by subsequent councils.

ANSWER.—This objection has reference to the seventh canon of Ephesus, which reads: "The holy Synod decreed that it is unlawful for any man to bring forward, or to write or compose, a different faith as a rival to that established by the holy Fathers assembled with the Holy Spirit in Nicaea."[14] If "to compose a different faith" simply means to express in different words, or with fuller explanation, the faith defined at Nicaea, the canon is merely disciplinary and might be changed by a subsequent council. On the other hand, if the phrase refers to *a faith* inconsistent with that defined at Nicaea, it is an evident acknowledgment of infallibility in the Council of Nicaea, whose dogmatic decrees cannot be changed by any authority in the Church. That this is the true meaning is evident from the words of St. Cyril of Alexandria, who presided at the Council of Ephesus and seems to have been the author of the canon in question. He says: "The holy Ecumenical Synod gathered at Ephesus provided, *of necessity*, that no other exposition of faith besides that which existed, which the most blessed Fathers, *speaking in the Holy Spirit,* defined, should be brought into the Churches of God." Then he answers those who accused him of violating this canon by his own explanations of the faith: "The divine disciple wrote, 'Be ready always to give answer to every one who asketh you an account of the hope which is in you.' But he who willeth to do this, innovates nothing, nor doth he frame any new exposition of faith, but rather maketh plain to those who ask him, what faith he hath concerning Christ."[15]

---

[14] Labbe-Gossart, T. III, col. 689.*
[15] St. Cyril of Alexand., "Epist. ad Acacium"; P.G., 77, 190.*

ART. II. INFALLIBILITY OF THE BISHOPS IN THEIR ORDINARY
TEACHING CAPACITY

*Thesis.—The Bishops of the Church, Taken as a Body in Union With the
Roman Pontiff, Are Infallible in the Ordinary Exercise of
Their Universal Teaching Authority*

1. Explanation and Proof

EXPLANATION. The *ordinary* teaching authority of the bishops is
that which they exercise in teaching the faithful of their respective
dioceses by pastoral letters, by sermons delivered by themselves or by
others approved for that purpose, and by catechisms or other books of
instruction edited or approved by them.[16] When the bishops of the
Church, thus engaged in the duty of instructing their people, are
practically unanimous in proclaiming a doctrine of faith or morals, they
are said to exercise a *universal* teaching authority, and are then infallible in regard to that doctrine. In other words, a doctrine of faith
or morals in which practically all the bishops of the Church agree, is
infallibly true.

Taken in the sense just explained, the thesis is a dogma of faith,
defined by the Vatican Council in the following words: "All things are
to be accepted by divine and Catholic faith, which are contained in the
written or traditional word of God and set forth by the Church as
divinely revealed, whether this be done by solemn decree or by the
ordinary and universal teaching authority."[17]

PROOFS. I. *From Reason*. The faith of the Church believing must
correspond to the faith proposed by the bishops who constitute the teaching body in the Church. Therefore, if the bishops as a body were not
infallible, the whole Church might be led into error at any time, and
thereby cease to be the Church of Christ, the pillar and ground of truth.
The faithful, it is true, have often refused to accept false teaching from
bishops and priests, but they refused precisely because the doctrines were
recognized as differing from those commonly taught in the Church. In
such cases particular churches were saved from error by the recognized
infallible authority of the episcopal body as a whole.

II. *From Scripture*. Christ promised special assistance to His Apostles
and their successors in the discharge of their duty as teachers. He
promised that He himself would be with them all days even to the
consummation of the world, and that the Holy Spirit abiding with them

---

[16] Wilmers, "De Ecclesia Christi," n. 226.
[17] Denzinger, n. 1792.

forever would lead them into all truth. Neither of these promises was limited to the rare occasions of ecumenical councils; such limitation would nullify the words of Christ, "I am with you all days."

III. *From Tradition.* The Fathers often appeal to the universal teaching of the Church as to an undoubted norm of divine truth. For example, St. Vincent of Lerins says: "Whatever a man shall ascertain to have been held, written, or taught, not by one or two, but by all equally with one consent, openly, frequently, and persistently, that, he must understand, he himself also is to believe without any doubt or hesitation."[18]

Many heresies in the Church were overcome by the unanimous teaching of the bishops, without the intervention of ecumenical councils. When heretics urged that councils be called to pass judgment on their doctrines, the Fathers often objected that the universal teaching of the Church was sufficient to condemn them. St. Augustine, for instance, said of the Pelagian heresy: "Indeed was there need of the congregation of a synod to condemn this open pest, as if no heresy could at any time be condemned except by a synodical congregation? On the contrary, very few heresies can be found for the sake of condemning which any such necessity has arisen."[19]

2. Practical Conclusions

MAJORITY INFALLIBLE. Since the bishops are infallible in their corporate capacity only, individual bishops may err at any time in regard to faith and morals, but all cannot fall into the *same* error at the *same* time. The further question now arises: Can a majority of the bishops fall into error at one and the same time regarding a matter of faith or morals? Or, to state the opposite side of the question: Is the agreement of a majority of the bishops of the world sufficient to establish the infallible truth of a doctrine, or must there be a practically unanimous agreement? It seems most probable that the agreement of a majority is sufficient to insure the truth of any doctrine, for it would certainly be a great evil for the Church if the greater part of her teaching body could fall into error at any time. It is true that in such a crisis the infallible authority of the Roman Pontiff would be sufficient to preserve the faith, but the Catholicity of the Church would be seriously affected, if not destroyed. Besides, it can scarcely be admitted that Christ, in His wisdom would allow such a calamity to befall His Church. But it may be objected that this very thing did happen at the councils of Arimini

---

[18] "Commonitorium," 3; P.L., 50, 641.*
[19] "Contra Epistolas Pelagianorum," iv, 34; P.L., 44, 638.*

and Seleucia, in 359, when practically all the bishops of the West and many from the East signed an heretical formula of faith. An examination of the facts show that no defection from faith really took place.

The Arian party gained a victory at the double council of Arimini and Seleucia by skillfully managing to avoid any direct condemnation of their doctrines. They succeeded in having a creed signed that practically ignored the questions at issue, but the creed itself was not heretical. It clearly taught the equality of the Father and the Son, who was "born before all ages, . . . who is similar to the Father in all things as the Scriptures say and teach."[20] The bishops also condemned in express terms all those who taught that the Son is unlike the Father, but the words *substance, person, consubstantial,* around which the whole controversy raged, were entirely omitted. Hence the bishops did not err in regard to faith, but simply failed to meet the occasion, as they should have done, by a direct and decisive condemnation.

CUSTODIANS OF FAITH. Even though not infallible as an individual, each bishop is the divinely constituted teacher and judge of the faith in his diocese. He is the custodian of the faith for those committed to his care; his duty is to teach and interpret the truths of revelations and to decide controverted points, when necessity requires. Consequently, his teaching and his declarations on matters of faith and morals are to be accepted, unless they are opposed to the universal teachings of the Church. Should any doubts arise on this point, it must be decided by superior authority, not by the faithful. The bishop is neither the supreme teacher nor the supreme judge in matters of faith or morals; hence, appeal may always be made to a higher tribunal; but order and unity in the Church demand that the bishop's judgment be respected until final decision has been made.

VALUE OF TRADITION. The value of Tradition as proof for revealed doctrine rests principally upon the active and passive infallibility of the Church. Whenever there are sufficient witnesses to prove that a certain doctrine is accepted by the whole Church as a revealed truth, or that it is taught as such by a majority of the bishops, it is immediately evident that the doctrine is infallibly true and could be defined as a dogma of faith, if not already so defined. When appealing to tradition in this sense, it matters not what age of the Church be selected, since truth does not change with the centuries. The truth of a doctrine is established just as securely by proving its universal acceptance today, as by showing that it was universally accepted in any past age of the Church.

---

[20] Socrates, "Hist. Eccles.," ii, 27; P.G., 67, 306. Sozomen, "Hist. Eccles.," iv, 17; P.G., 67, 1162.

But when tradition is used simply for its historical value, as a witness to what Christ or His Apostles did or taught, then the earlier the witness, the more valuable his testimony, because he approaches nearer to those who actually saw and heard the things related.[21]

---

[21] So far we have used tradition simply for its historical value. Now that the infallibility of the Church has been established, we may use tradition as a witness to prove that a doctrine is infallibly true because taught or professed by the universal Church.

CHAPTER XV

Since the Roman Pontiff holds supreme power in the Church, the infallible teaching authority of the bishops must be exercised in complete subjection to him. This fact alone is sufficient proof that he himself must be preeminently infallible, for otherwise the infallible authority of the bishops would be thwarted by subjection to their fallible head; but the doctrine is so often misunderstood and so strenuously opposed by non-Catholics that it is necessary to treat it more in detail. This is most conveniently done (1) by giving an accurate statement of the doctrine with proofs drawn from Scripture and Tradition, (2) by answering the principal objections urged against it.

ART. I. THE DOCTRINE OF PAPAL INFALLIBILITY

Thesis.—The Roman Pontiff Is Infallible When He Speaks ex Cathedra, Defining a Doctrine of Faith or Morals for the Universal Church

1. The Doctrine Explained

DOGMA OF FAITH. The doctrine of papal infallibility was defined by the Vatican Council in the following words: "Faithfully adhering to the tradition received from the beginning of the Christian faith, for the glory of God our Saviour, the exaltation of the Catholic religion, and the salvation of the Christian people, the Sacred Council approving, we teach and define that it is a dogma divinely revealed that the Roman Pontiff, when he speaks *ex cathedra,* that is, when in the discharge of the office of pastor and teacher of all Christians, by virtue of his supreme Apostolic authority, he defines a doctrine regarding faith or morals to be held by the universal Church, by the divine assistance promised him in the blessed Peter, is possessed of that infallibility with which the Divine Redeemer willed that His Church should be endowed for defining doctrine regarding faith or morals; and that, therefore, such definitions of the Roman Pontiff are irreformable of themselves, and not from the consent of the Church."[1]

CONDITIONS OF INFALLIBILITY. The Council carefully

---

[1] Denzinger, n. 1839.

states the conditions under which the Roman Pontiff enjoys the gift of infallibility; viz., that he speak (a) *ex cathedra,* (b) for the universal Church, (c) with supreme authority, (d) on matters of faith or morals.

a) EX CATHEDRA. The Greek word *cathedra* (seat) is here used to designate office or authority, just as Our Lord used it when He said: "The Scribes and the Pharisees have sat on the chair of Moses. All things, therefore, that they command you, observe and do."[2] The English equivalents for this word are used in the same sense when we say that a judge occupies the *bench,* or a professor, the *chair* of philosophy. In fact, *chair* is as widely recognized as a symbol of teaching authority as *throne* is for ruling authority. In Church usage *cathedra* unites both ideas and designates, in particular, the authority of a bishop to teach and govern, since his throne is known as a *cathedra,* whence the name *cathedral,* i.e., the church containing the bishop's *cathedra.* It is evident, then, that when the Pope speaks *ex cathedra,* he is speaking officially as supreme pastor of the universal Church, and it is then only that the Council declared him infallible. There is nothing to indicate that he is infallible in his private capacity as a theologian or as teacher instructing others in the faith.

b) FOR THE UNIVERSAL CHURCH. As noted above, the Pope is not only supreme head of the Church, but also bishop of Rome, Primate of Italy, and patriarch of the West. The Council declared him infallible only in his capacity as supreme pastor,—"when discharging the office of pastor and teacher of all Christians." Consequently decisions rendered in particular cases, or decrees issued for particular churches, are not considered infallible; but it is not necessary that the Pope directly address all the faithful, or even all the bishops, when defining a doctrine *ex cathedra.* Theologians commonly hold that such a decree might be issued directly to one bishop only, provided it is evidently intended for the whole Church. Hence, as Cardinal Mazzella observes, "it should be noted *for* whom, rather than *to* whom the Pope speaks. If it is evident from the nature of the matter treated, from the manner of treatment, or from any other circumstance, that he speaks for all, there seems to be nothing lacking for an *ex cathedra* pronouncement."[3]

c) WITH SUPREME AUTHORITY. A definition of faith or morals is not infallible unless intended to be such, for the Pope acting as supreme pastor may issue decrees for the whole Church and still

---

[2] Matt. xxiii, 2-3.
[3] Mazzella, "De Religione et Ecclesia," n. 1052.

not intend them to be definite and irrevocable pronouncements on the matter treated. Hence the Council says: "When, by virtue of his supreme Apostolic authority, he defines a doctrine," i.e., when he uses his supreme authority, to give a final and irrevocable decision. This does not require the use of a set formula; any words may be used that will sufficiently indicate the definitive nature of the decree.

d) FAITH OR MORALS. Infallibility is given as a means to preserve the truths committed to the custody of the Church,—truths concerning faith and morals, which alone pertain to the matter of salvation. Consequently, the very purpose of infallibility restricts it to these same truths.

SOURCE OF INFALLIBILITY. The Council expressly stated that the infallibility of the Roman Pontiff is due to divine *assistance;* both *revelation* and *inspiration* are thus excluded, and the use of natural means of knowledge presupposed. Before issuing a definition of faith, the Pope must diligently inquire into the matter to be defined, for otherwise he would be forcing God, as it were, to give supernatural assistance where natural means are sufficient. Should the Pope neglect to make due investigation, he would be guilty of sin, but his decree would be protected from error, because infallibility would be utterly useless if definitions could not be accepted with certainty until it were known that sufficient investigation and study of the matter had been made.

PERSONALLY INFALLIBLE. The advocates of Gallicanism in the seventeenth century taught that the decrees of the Roman Pontiff are not infallible unless accepted by the whole Church. "His judgment is not irreformable or exempt from revision unless accepted by the Church." Some tried to maintain a sort of papal infallibility by making a distinction between the See of Rome and its occupant. They held that the See itself is infallible, although individual Popes may err; if one Pope falls into error, his mistake will be corrected without fail by some successor, thus preserving the See from error.[4]

The Council rejected this doctrine by declaring that "definitions of the Roman Pontiff are irreformable of themselves, and not from the consent of the Church." To make infallibility depend upon acceptance by the Church is to subvert the very constitution of the Church and make the faithful judges of their divinely constituted rulers and teachers. Power and authority in the Church was given to the Apostles and their successors independently of the consent of the faithful, and the Church never sought such consent to make laws or to define doctrines

---

[4] Cf. Catholic Encyclopedia, art. "Gallicanism."

of faith. The supreme power in the Church was conferred directly upon St. Peter, and through him upon his successors, independently even of the other Apostles; consequently, whatever power and prerogatives the Roman Pontiff holds as successor of St. Peter, he holds and exercises independent of all others, and neither his decrees nor his definitions of faith receive any binding force or infallible authority from the consent of bishops or faithful.

The absurd distinction made by the Gallicans between the See and its occupant would frustrate the very purposes of papal infallibility. If individual popes may err, their definitions could not be accepted as infallible until tested by time, but who is to decide what length of time is necessary? And if one pope reverses the definition of a predecessor, who is to decide which definition is to be accepted as true?

IN PRIVATE CAPACITY. The Council declared the Roman Pontiff personally infallible when speaking officially as head of the universal Church, but left untouched the question whether the Pope in his private capacity, or in his official capacity as bishop, primate or patriarch, can fall into heresy or teach heresy. Some theologians maintain that he can. Straub cites Hadrian II and Innocent III as favoring this opinion. Cardinal Bellarmine, Suarez, and many other eminent theologians consider the opposite opinion more probable. Suarez says: "God could provide that no injury would accrue to the Church from an heretical pope, but it seems more in accord with His divine providence to preserve the pope from heresy in consequence of the promise that he shall never err in defining faith. Furthermore, as such a thing has never happened in the Church, we may conclude that, in the providence of God, it cannot happen."[5]

2. The Doctrine Proved From Scripture

The passages of Scripture having direct reference to this subject are found in Matthew xvi, 18, 19; Luke xxii, 31, 32 and John xxi, 16, 17. In the text from Matthew infallibility is implicitly promised to St. Peter in symbolic language. In Luke it is again promised, but this time explicitly and in plain language. Finally, in John the promise is fulfilled when the primacy of teaching and governing authority is conferred upon St. Peter under the symbol of pastoral care for the flock of Christ. In every case St. Peter is addressed as head of the Apostolic body, and the power conferred upon him is to endure until the end of time; it is a power to be perpetuated in his successors, the bishops of

---

[5] Straub, "De Ecclesia Christi," n. 1068; cf. Card. Ballarmine, "De Romano Pontifice," iv, 6; Suarez, "De Fide," Disp. x, 6, n. 11.

Rome. These texts have been considered in their relation to Peter's primacy of jurisdiction; we shall now examine them briefly in their bearing upon the question of infallibility.

a) MATTHEW XVI, 18-19: "Thou art Peter, and upon this rock I will build my Church; and the gates of hell shall not prevail against it." In these words Our Lord promised that St. Peter and his successors should be the rock-foundation, to render His Church firm and impregnable for all time, even to the consummation of the world. It is to be the *pillar and ground of truth,* and therefore impregnable against the assaults of error. Should the Church fall into error, it would cease to be the Church of Christ and the gates of hell would prevail against it. Therefore, the Church is rendered infallible and preserved infallible by that rock-foundation which secures it against the gates of hell and constitutes it the pillar and ground of truth: and since the Church derives her infallibility from this rock-foundation, i.e., from St. Peter and his successors, the latter must also be infallible, and their infallibility is even prior to that of the Church.

On this same occasion Christ promised that whatever St. Peter would bind or loose on earth, should be bound or loosed also in Heaven. On another occasion the same words were addressed to all the Apostles collectively; but here they are addressed to St. Peter alone, thus promising him a supreme power of binding and loosing that is unlimited in its extent and application; it applies to teaching as well as to governing authority. In fact, most Protestant interpreters claim that it refers to teaching authority alone. Consequently, whatever St. Peter or his successors teach on earth shall be ratified in Heaven, and that without fail since the promise is unconditional. Could such a promise be made by Our Lord if there were any possibility of error in the teaching which He assures us will be ratified in Heaven?

b) LUKE xxii, 31-32: "Simon, Simon, behold, Satan has desired to have you, that he may sift you as wheat. But I have prayed for thee, that thy faith may not fail; and do thou, when once thou hast turned again, strengthen thy brethren." These words from part of the last will and testament of Our Lord, made but a few hours before His death on the cross. Looking out upon the centuries, He saw the trials and temptations prepared for His faithful by Satan; He foresaw the many heresies that would arise to lead astray the unwary and the unsuspecting. He provides against these dangers by conferring a special grace,—the gift of infallibility,—upon the chief pastor of His flock, and charges him to confirm his brethren: "I have prayed for thee, that thy faith may not fail. Strengthen thy brethren." Plainer or more emphatic words could not have been uttered by Him who came as the Teacher of mankind.

c) JOHN XXI, 16-17: "Feed my lambs . . . feed my sheep." These solemn words of Our Lord, uttered shortly before His Ascension, conferred upon St. Peter and his successors the promised primacy of jurisdiction with its grace of infallibility. The entire flock of Christ was committed to the care of their supreme pastor; the lambs and the sheep were subjected to his authority in all things. But if the pastor, whom the sheep must obey, should fall into error, they would inevitably be led into the same error; he would feed them poison instead of the wholesome food of revealed truth and the promises of Christ would be void, for the Spirit of truth would desert the Church. Our Lord must have provided against such an eventuality in the only way possible, i.e., by making the chief pastor of the flock infallible.

3. Doctrine Proved From Testimony of Councils

The doctrine of papal infallibility is established beyond the possibility of doubt by the fact that it is accepted throughout the entire Church as a revealed doctrine and taught as such by the bishops of the whole world in their ordinary teaching capacity. It was also defined by an almost unanimous vote of more than eight hundred bishops assembled in ecumenical council from every part of the world. No one can deny these facts today, and it has been proved in the preceding chapters that the believing Church (*ecclesia discens*) is infallible in accepting truths of revelation, and that the bishops as a body are infallible in their ordinary teaching capacity, no less than when assembled in ecumenical council. Again, the fact that a doctrine is now believed and taught by the whole Church as a revealed truth, is positive proof that it has been so believed and taught in all ages, since the Church must proclaim and profess the entire deposit of faith at all times. Hence, in defining the doctrine of papal infallibility, the Vatican Council professed to "adhere faithfully to the tradition received from the beginning of the Christian faith." Just how faithfully the Fathers of the Vatican Council adhered to tradition may be gathered from a study of other councils celebrated at various times. For this purpose we select five ecumenical councils, ranging over a period of almost ten centuries. With one exception, they were all celebrated in the East and attended almost exclusively by bishops from the Eastern Church which, it is now claimed, never recognized the Roman Primacy, much less the doctrine of papal infallibility.

(A) COUNCIL OF LYONS (1274). The infallibility of the

Roman Pontiff is clearly implied in the following words: "The holy Roman Church also holds supreme and complete primacy and domination over the universal Catholic Church, which primacy and domination she truthfully and humbly recognizes as coming from Our Lord himself through the blessed Peter, prince and head of the Apostles, and whose successor is the Roman Pontiff. Wherefore, *as he is obliged above others to defend the truth of faith, it follows that when any questions concerning faith arise, they are to be decided by his judgment.*"[6]

This decree was reaffirmed by bishops from the East and the West assembled at the ecumenical Council of Florence during the years 1439-1445.

(B) FOURTH COUNCIL OF CONSTANTINOPLE (869). All the Fathers attending this council signed a formula of faith, in which the following significant words occur: "The first requisite of salvation is to cling to the rule of right faith, and to depart in nothing from the constitutions of the Fathers. Neither can those words of Our Lord Jesus Christ be neglected: 'Thou art Peter, and upon this rock I will build my Church.' The words have been proved by their effects, *for in the Apostolic See the Catholic religion has ever been preserved from stain. . . . Therefore I hope to be worthy to remain with you*[7] *in that communion preached by the Apostolic See, in which the true Christian religion is preserved entire and in perfect solidity.*"[8]

This formula, signed by the bishops of Constantinople in the ninth century, is also a witness to the faith of the Eastern Church in the sixth century, since it was originally drawn up by Pope Hormisdas, about the year 516 and submitted to a number of eastern bishops, who wished to abandon the Acacian schism and return to the Church.[9]

(C) THIRD COUNCIL OF CONSTANTINOPLE (680). The letter of Pope Agatho, read before the Fathers of the council and approved by them, contains the following words, setting forth the doctrine of papal infallibility in unmistakable terms: "Through the protection of Peter, who was pronounced blessed, this his Apostolic church has never departed from the way of truth into any error whatsoever. . . . In prosperity and in adversity, the rule of true faith is held and defended by this spiritual mother, . . . who, by the grace of God, shall never be known to have erred nor succumbed to heretical novelties. From the beginning of the Christian faith even unto the end, she re-

---

[6] Denzinger, n. 466.
[7] These words were addressed to Pope Hadrian II.
[8] Denzinger, n. 171-172.
[9] Hormisdas, "Epist. ad Joannem Nicopolitanum"; P.L., 63, 393.

mains unsullied, according to the divine promise made by the Saviour himself to the prince of His disciples: 'Peter, Peter, behold Satan hath desired to have you, etc.' Let your clemency[10] consider, therefore, that the Lord and Saviour of all, who promised unfailing faith to Peter, admonished him to confirm his brethren. This the Apostolic pontiffs, predecessors of my unworthiness, have ever done, as is known to all."[11]

At the close of the council the acts were sent to Pope Agatho for his approval and confirmation. The accompanying letter contained these words: "We leave to your judgment what should be done, since as bishop of the first See in the universal Church you *stand upon the firm rock of faith.* We willingly agree with the letters of true confession sent to the most pious Emperor by your fatherly Beatitude; we acknowledge them *as divinely prescribed by the chief head of the Apostles.* . . . By means of them we have put down the heretical sect lately arisen . . . and we have cut off the heretics by anathemas, according to the sentence already decreed against them by your sacred letters."[12]

It would be difficult to find a more explicit acknowledgment of papal infallibility, even today, after its definition by the Vatican Council.

(D) COUNCIL OF CHALCEDON (451). Leo the Great sent representatives to this council, with the instruction that the bishops gathered there should subscribe to the faith as formulated in his letter to Flavian, archbishop of Constantinople. He wrote: "Most dear brethren, let all attempts at disputing against the divinely inspired faith, and the vain unbelief of heretics be laid to rest, and let not that be defended which may not be believed; since in accordance with the authoritative statements of the Gospel, in accordance with the utterances of the prophets and the teaching of the Apostles, with the greatest fullness and clearness *in the letter which we sent to Bishop Flavian of happy memory, it has been laid down what is the loyal and pure confession upon the mystery of Our Lord Jesus Christ's Incarnation.*"[13]

It is evident from these words that Pope Leo formulated the doctrine to which all were to subscribe without *any attempts at disputing against the divinely inspired faith,* yet no one raised his voice in protest against this manifest assumption of infallible authority. When the Pope's letter to Flavian was read, the bishops cried out with one voice: "This is the faith of the Fathers. . . . Anathema to him who believes

---

[10] The letter was addressed to the Emperor.
[11] St. Agatho, "Epist. ad Augustos"; P.L., 87, 1169.
[12] "Epist. ad Agathonem"; P.L., 87, 1248-1249.
[13] Pope Leo, "Epist. ad Synodum"; P.L., 54, 937, 939.*

differently. Peter hath spoken thus by the mouth of Leo."[11] The sentence of deposition against Dioscorus was also passed in the name of Leo, the successor of St. Peter and the *foundation of true faith*. It reads: "Leo through us and through this holy synod, in union with the thrice blessed and most holy Apostolic Peter, the rock and support of the Catholic Church and the foundation of the true faith, hath stripped Dioscorus of his episcopal dignity."[15]

(E) COUNCIL OF EPHESUS (431). Pope Celestine wrote the Fathers at Ephesus, directing them to "carry out what things have been already decreed by us." When the letter was read, "all the most reverend bishops cried out at the same time: 'To Celestine the guardian of the faith! To Celestine of one mind with the Synod! To Celestine the whole Synod offers its thanks!'" Philip, one of the papal legates, then said: "We offer our thanks that when the writings of our holy and blessed Pope had been read to you, . . . ye joined yourselves to the most holy head by your holy acclamations. For Your Blessedness is not ignorant that *the head of the whole faith, the head of the Apostles, is blessed Peter the Apostle. . . .* We ask that ye give order that there be laid before us what things were done in this holy Synod before our arrival, in order that, according to the opinion of our blessed Pope, . . . we may likewise ratify their determination."[16]

In the bishops' letter to Pope Celestine these words occur: "The zeal of Your Holiness for piety, and your care for the right faith, so grateful and highly pleasing to God, the Saviour of us all, are worthy of all admiration. For it is your custom in such great matters to make trial of all things and the confirmation of the Churches you have made your own care."[17]

These various references to the position and authority of the Roman Pontiff do not explicitly mention the doctrine of infallibility, but they certainly presuppose it. The Pope is the *guardian of the faith,* the successor of St. Peter, *head of the whole faith;* he *cares for the right faith,* makes trial of all things, and *confirms* the Churches. Duties such as these demand infallibility for their proper performance, yet the Fathers of the council express no misgivings on that point. These expressions of the Fathers at Ephesus leave no doubt as to their import when they are considered in the light of the more explicit testimony of later councils and of the Fathers who wrote before and after that time.

REMARK. Very little has come down to us from the first council

[11] Mansi, VI, col. 971.*
[15] Mansi, VI, col. 1047.
[16] Labb-Cossart, III, 617.*
[17] "Epist. ad Coelestinum"; P.L., 50, 511.*

held at Nicaea in 325, or of the first council of Constantinople, in 381. Consequently we have no record of their belief in regard to papal infallibility, but we do have the testimony of the Fathers who lived and wrote in that century. It proves that the doctrine was recognized by the whole Church then as now.

4. The Doctrine Proved From the Testimony of the Fathers

The testimony of the councils proves that the infallibility of the Roman Pontiff was officially recognized in every age of which we have a record. It also gives us the united testimony of the hundreds of bishops and Fathers who attended these councils, thus making it really unnecessary to quote from any individual Father or writer of those ages, yet for the sake of completeness, a few private witnesses may be added (a) from the West, and (b) from the East.

I. FROM THE WEST. (a) FULGENTIUS FERRANDUS (died 533). Severus, a scholastic of Constantinople, wrote to Fulgentius, a deacon of Carthage, for instructions concerning the Blessed Trinity, and received the following reply: "Let those speak and preach who have received authority to teach along with the honor of the priesthood. We are ever ready to learn, but do not presume to teach others. Therefore, most prudent man, if you wish to learn the truth, address first of all the bishop of the Apostolic See, *whose doctrine is preserved sound by the judgment of truth and is supported by the strength of authority.*"[18]

b) ASCANIUS OF TARRAGONA. About the year 465, Ascanius of Tarragona in Spain and the bishops of his province wrote to Pope Hilary concerning a bishop who had been consecrated contrary to the canons of the Church. They said: "Even though we were not compelled by ecclesiastical discipline, it would still be our duty to have recourse to that privilege of your See by which the preaching of the most blessed Peter sufficed for the illumination of all throughout the whole world. . . . Therefore, we have recourse to that faith praised by the Apostle, and *seek a reply where nothing is given out in error or presumption.*"[19]

c) ST. LEO THE GREAT (440-461). "The solidity of the faith which was praised in the chief of the Apostles is perpetual; and as that remains which Peter believed in Christ, so that remains which Christ instituted in Peter. . . . The blessed Peter, persevering in the strength of the rock which he received, has not abandoned the helm of the

---

[18] "Epist. ad Severum"; P.L., 67, 914.
[19] "Epist. ad Hilarium"; P.L., 58, 14-15.

Church . . . and still today he more fully and effectually performs what is entrusted to him. And so if anything is rightly done and rightly decreed by us, it is his work and merits, whose power lives and whose authority prevails in his See. . . . With such solidity is it endued by God that the depravity of heretics cannot mar it nor the unbelief of the heathen overcome it."[20]

d) ST. AUGUSTINE (died 430). In speaking of the Pelagian heresy, St. Augustine says: "Two councils sent reports of this matter to the Apostolic See, and the decision has come back. The case is finished. Would that the error also were ended."[21] These few words, clearly recognizing the decision of Rome as final, and therefore infallible, have been crystallized into the well-known saying, "Rome has spoken, the case is ended."

e) ST. JEROME (died 420). When St. Jerome was in Syria, a great controversy was going on concerning the use of the Greek word *hypostasis* in reference to the persons of the Trinity. Although one of the greatest scholars of his age, Jerome turned to Rome for authoritative information. He wrote to Pope Damasus: "I think it my duty to consult the chair of Peter, and to turn to a church whose faith has been praised by Paul. . . . You alone keep the heritage of the fathers intact. . . . You are the light of the world. . . . Let the state of Roman majesty withdraw; my words are addressed to the successor of the fisherman, to the disciple of the Cross. As I follow no leader save Christ, so I communicate with none but Your Blessedness. For this, I know, is the rock on which the Church is built. . . . I implore Your Blessedness, therefore, to authorize me by letter, either to use or to refuse this formula of the *three hypostases*."[22]

f) ST. AMBROSE (died 397). Satyr, a brother of St. Ambrose, suffered shipwreck on a voyage to Africa. He was a catechumen at the time, and in thanksgiving for his deliverance, immediately sought baptism; "but he was not so eager as to lay aside caution. He called the bishop to him, and esteeming that there can be no true thanksgiving except it spring from true faith, he enquired whether he (the bishop) agreed with the Catholic bishops, that is with the Roman Church."[23] There were heretical bishops in Africa at the time, but Satyr makes sure to receive Baptism from none of them; he applies the test of true faith,—agreement with the Catholic bishops, which is established by agreement with the bishop of Rome, for, as St. Irenaeus had written

[20] "Sermon.," iii; P.L., 54, 146.
[21] "Sermon.," cxxxi, n. 10; P.L., 38, 734.
[22] St. Jerome, "Epist. ad Damasum Papam"; P.L., 22, 356-358.*
[23] St. Ambrose, "De Excessu Fratis sui Satyri," i, 47; P.L., 16, 1306.*

two hundred years before, "it is a matter of necessity that every church should agree with this Church, on account of its preeminent authority."[24]

II. FROM THE EAST. (a) ST. THEODORE OF STUDIUM (died 826). When the iconoclast heresy was raging in the East, Theodore, the learned abbot of a monastery at Constantinople, wrote to Pope Paschal for assistance. He said: "Give ear, O Apostolic head, whom God hath constituted shepherd of Christ's sheep, doorkeeper of the kingdom of Heaven, and the rock of faith upon which the Catholic Church is built. Thou art Peter, adorning and guiding the See of Peter. Ravening wolves have broken into the house of the Lord; the gates of hell are loosed against it as of old. Come forth from the West, O follower of Christ. Arise and do not cast us off forever! Christ hath said to thee, 'Confirm thy brethren.' Behold, now is the time, and here is the place. Come to our assistance, thou whom God hath raised up for that purpose! . . . Thou hast the power since thou art head over all! . . . Strike terror, we beseech thee, into these fierce heretics by the pen of thy divine word."[25]

b) MAXIMUS THE CONFESSOR was born at Constantinople about 580; died in exile in 662. He wrote: "It is not lawful to praise a man who has been condemned and cast out by the Apostolic See of Rome, until he has been reconciled and received back by it. . . . Therefore, if one does not wish to be a heretic and be known as such, let him not seek reconciliation with this or that see; such action is unnecessary and unreasonable. Let him seek peace with the See of Rome above all others, because he will then be recognized everywhere and by all as orthodox. . . . In vain does he seek recognition elsewhere, if he has not recourse to the blessed Pope of the most holy Church of the Romans, i.e., the Apostolic See, which holds from the Incarnate Word of God Himself the power of government and the authority to bind and loose all things for all men."[26]

c) JOHN, BISHOP OF JERUSALEM (572-592). In a letter to an Albanian bishop, John of Jerusalem mentions the infallibility of the Roman Pontiff in express terms: "We, that is, the Catholic Church, have the words of Our Lord addressed to Peter, head of the Apostles, giving him the *primacy of firm faith for the Churches.* . . . To Peter also he gave the keys of the kingdom of heaven and earth, hence . . . the successors in his holy and venerable See remain *sound in faith and infallible* according to the promise of the Lord."[27]

---

[24] St. Irenaeus, "Adversus Haereses," iii, 3, 2; P.G., 7, 848.*

[25] St. Theodore of Studium; "Epist. ad Paschalem"; P.G., 99, 1151, 1154.

[26] St. Maximus Confessor, "Epist. ad Petrum"; P.G., 91, 144.

[27] John of Jerusalem, "Epist. ad Abbatem Albanorum," quoted by Staub, n. 996.

d) SOZOMEN (died about 447). Sozomen in his Church History describes the controversy concerning the divinity of the Holy Spirit and then says: "When this question was being agitated and the heat of controversy was daily increasing, the matter was brought to the attention of the bishop of Rome, who wrote to the Churches of the East that the three Persons of the Trinity are of the same substance and of equal dignity. This doctrine, he said, must be confessed by the bishops of the East as by those of the West. The question having been thus decided by the Roman Church, peace was restored, and the question seemed finally at an end."[28]

e) ST. GREGORY OF NAZIANZUS (died 390). Timothy, a disciple of Apollinarius, was condemned for heresy by Pope Damasus, but his followers in Cappadocia spread the report that his doctrines were later approved by Rome. St. Gregory says: "If those who hold the views of Apollinarius have either now or formerly been received, let them prove it, and we shall be content. For it is evident that they can only have been so received as assenting to the orthodox faith, for this were impossible on any other terms."[29] These words prove that St. Gregory accepted approval by Rome as an infallible test of the true faith; if those accused of heresy can show that they have been approved at Rome, he is content to admit them to communion, because such approval "were impossible without assent to the orthodox faith."

f) GREEK LITURGY. In the Greek Liturgy, Pope Sylvester is addressed as the divinely constituted head of the Church, a teacher rendered infallible through the power of the Holy Spirit: "O father Sylvester, thou didst stand forth a pillar of fire, . . . an overshadowing cloud, and didst deliver the faithful from the Egyptian error (Arianism), and didst lead them to the divine light by thy ever *infallible teachings.* As divine head of the sacred Fathers thou didst establish the most sacred dogma and didst close the mouth of heretics. . . . Tongues which consented to error were put to shame *by the power of the Holy Ghost, who wrought in thee.*"[30]

The testimony of the councils and these few quotations from the many Fathers of the East and the West who could be cited in this matter, prove conclusively that the Vatican Council did "faithfully adhere to the tradition received from the beginning of the Christian faith." In defining the doctrine of papal infallibility, it introduced nothing new, but simply defined a doctrine held by the universal Church in all ages.

---

[28] Sozomen, "Church History," vi, 22; P.G., 67, 1347.
[29] St. Gregory Nazianaen, "Epist. ad Cledonium"; P.G., 37, 178.*
[30] Nilles, "Kalendarium Manuale," I, 51, 106 sq.

ART. II. OBJECTIONS AGAINST PAPAL INFALLIBILITY

The doctrine of papal infallibility is completely overthrown if even one pope is found to have erred in his teachings. But history testifies that not only one, but many have actually erred in their teachings concerning faith or morals. For example, the following may be mentioned:

a) LIBERIUS (352-356) signed an heretical formula of faith drawn up at Sirmium by the Arians.

b) ZOSIMUS (414-418) approved the heretical teachings of Pelagius and Celestius and declared that they contained nothing contrary to the Catholic faith.

c) HORMISDAS (514-523) and John II (532-535) taught contradictory doctrines, since Hormisdas declared it heretical to say that "one of the most Holy Trinity was crucified," whereas John II approved the formula as an expression of Catholic doctrine.

d) VIGILIUS (538-555) at first approved what are known as the Three Chapters, and afterwards condemned them as heretical.

e) HONORIUS I (625-638) approved the doctrine of the Monothelites, who taught that there is but one will in Christ. On this account he was condemned as a heretic by the Council of Constantinople in 680, and the condemnation was approved by Pope Leo II.

f) ZACHARIAS (741-752) ordered a certain Virgilius to be excommunicated, because he taught that there are people living on the opposite side of the world.

g) JOHN XXII (1316-1334) fell into heresy concerning the Beatific Vision.

h) GALILEO was condemned as a heretic for teaching that the earth moves around the sun.

. ANSWER. It is true that the doctrine of papal infallibility could not be maintained if one single Pope had ever erred in teaching *ex cathedra,* as explained above; but the promise of Christ precludes such a possibility and history offers no evidence to the contrary. The alleged examples of erroneous teaching present no difficulty, because the requisites for an *ex cathedra* definition of faith are lacking in every instance, and in very few cases was any error really taught. This becomes evident upon examination.

a) POPE LIBERIUS was sent into exile by the Arian Emperor Constantius, but was afterward allowed to return to his see. It is claimed that he obtained his release by signing an heretical creed, drawn up at Sirmium by the Arian party, who denied the divinity of the Son by teaching that He is like the Father, but not of the same nature. The nature of the creed signed by Liberius is a matter of conjecture. In fact, it is by no means certain that he signed any creed at all. Sozomen, the Church historian, is our principal source of information in this matter. If his testimony be accepted, the creed was not heretical except through a false interpretation made possible by the omission of the disputed terms *homoousios* and *homoiousios*. And Sozomen further states that the Pope first demanded a confession from all present, that "those who say the Son is not like the Father *in substance and in all things,* are cut off from communion in the Church."[31] If this be true, Liberius can be accused of nothing more than imprudence in signing a document open to false interpretation.

Even granting that Liberius actually signed an heretical creed on that occasion, this would prove nothing against the doctrine of papal infallibility. All admit that the signing, if done at all, was done under fear and compulsion, after the Pope had been broken by the hardships of exile. An act performed under such circumstances was not free and, therefore, not valid.[32]

b) ZOSIMUS. Pelagius and Celestius appealed to Pope Zosimus to examine their teachings and to correct them, if found erroneous. The Pope, deceived by this false pretense of good faith, ordered them to be treated with charity, as they were innocent of intentional wrong-doing in the matter; but he never approved their errors. Hence St. Augustine says: "They were approved on account of their willingness to amend; not on account of their false doctrines."[33]

c) HORMISDAS. John Maxentius and a number of Scythian monks of Constantinople sponsored the saying that "One of the Trinity was crucified," and wished to have it inserted into the Creed. Hormisdas refused to sanction this, partly because the formula was open to heretical interpretation, but more particularly because its sponsors, who were even then suspected of heresy, displayed an unbecoming spirit in the matter. John II afterwards approved the formula in its Catholic sense that Our Lord, who was one of the three divine Persons, suffered in His human nature.[34] In the days of Hormisdas, many interpreted it to mean that Our Lord has but one nature, the divine, in which He suffered.

d) VIGILIUS. The *Three Chapters,* strictly speaking were propositions condemning the works of Theodore of Mopsuestia, the works of Theodoret of Cyrus against St. Cyril, and a letter written by Ibas of Edessa to Maris of Persia; but the works themselves were also known

---

[31] Sozomen, "Church History," iv, 15; P.G., 67, 1131.
[32] Cf. Catholic Encyclopedia, art. "Liberius."
[33] St. Augustine, "Contra Pelagianos"; P.L., 44, 547.
[34] Hormisdas, "Epist. ad Possessorem"; P.L., 63, 490; John II, "Epist. ad Senatores"; P.L., 66, 20-21.

as the *Three Chapters*. There is no doubt that these works contained heretical teachings. Vigilius refused to condemn them because, being ignorant of Greek, he did not recognize their real nature. Upon learning that they were heretical, he condemned them, but soon after withdrew the decree as inopportune. Finally, under changed circumstances, he reissued the decree of condemnation. The Pope's prudence in the matter may be questioned, but not his faith. At no time did he *approve* the works, and always condemned their errors even while refusing to condemn the works as a whole.[35]

e) HONORIUS I. The charge of heresy against Honorius is based upon certain statements in his letters to Sergius of Constantinople. These statements are claimed to be a denial of the two wills in Christ and because of this denial he was condemned as a heretic by the Council of Constantinople.

Before considering the statements themselves, it should be noted that Honorius disclaimed any intention of issuing a dogmatic decree in the matter. He says that "in order to remove any scandal, we should neither *define* nor *preach* one or two operations." Moreover, the documents were private letters to Sergius, advising him to act prudently in the use of newly devised terms, lest they be misinterpreted. Consequently there was no *ex cathedra* definition of faith; first, because it was not intended as such, and secondly, because it was not issued for the universal Church. The letters in question were merely a matter of personal advice requested by Sergius, but even as such, they contain no error of Doctrine.

At that time the terms *will* and *operation* were coming into use in the East in reference to Our Lord. The Eutychians taught that Christ has but one nature and, therefore, but *one will*. The Nestorians held that there are two persons in Christ and therefore, *two wills*. Catholics were also using these terms, but in a different sense; they said that Christ has *two wills*, or *operations*, one corresponding to His human, the other to His divine nature, but these two *wills* are one in the sense that the human cannot be at variance with the divine. This confusion in the use of terms lent itself to misunderstandings and controversy and greatly disturbed the minds of the people. For this reason Sergius, archbishop of Constantinople, wrote to Pope Honorius for advice in the matter. In his reply, Honorius plainly teaches that there are *two wills in Christ*, —the one human, the other divine,—but that they are one in the sense of being in harmony one with the other. He then advises Sergius that

---

[35] Cf. Catholic Encyclopedia, art. "Vigilius" and "Three Chapters."

it were better to avoid entirely the use of such newly invented terms that may easily lead the people into error.[36]

This advice was simply approving the sentiments expressed by Sergius himself in his letter to the Pope, and, under the circumstances described by Sergius, would have been given by any prudent man; but it seems that the heretics continued to spread their false doctrines under the pleas that they had not been condemned. For this reason, the Council of Constantinople condemned Honorius as an abettor of heresy. He had not actually taught any heretical doctrine, but his failure to condemn it promptly and decisively made its propagation easier. This, at least, is the sense in which Pope Leo says that he approved the condemnation by the council: "Theodore, Cyrus, and Sergius were punished by eternal condemnation, . . . along with Honorius, who *did not repress* the flame of heretical doctrine, as becomes the Apostolic authority, but favored it by negligence." He gives the same explanation in a letter to the Emperor Constantius: "Honorius did not illumine this Apostolic Church by the doctrine of Apostolic tradition, but permitted it to be defiled by profane treason."[37]

f) ZACHARIAS. Virgilius, a priest or bishop of Germany, had been accused of heresy in regard to the existence of *people beneath the earth*, and Zacharias directed St. Boniface to depose him if he were found guilty of the charge. There is no question of an *ex cathedra* definition of faith; it was simply an order for St. Boniface to proceed with canonical punishment if the case demanded it. We cannot even say that Zacharias committed an error in the matter, since we know nothing of the doctrine except what can be gathered from the slight reference to it by Zacharias himself. He says: "If it shall be proved that he teaches there is another world and other people beneath the earth, . . . let him be deposed."[38] The mention of *another* world and *other* people makes it probable that Virgilius had fallen into the error of those who taught the existence of people on the opposite side of the world who were not descended from Adam and therefore not subject to original sin.

g) JOHN XXII. Before ascending the papal throne, John had written works in which he maintained that the souls of the just do not enjoy the Beatific Vision until after the resurrection of the body. After becoming Pope, he still maintained the opinion as probable, but distinctly stated that he did so in his capacity as a private theologian. He justified

[36] Honorius, "Epist. ad Sergium"; P.L., 80, 474-476.
[37] Leo II, "Epist. ad Hispaniae Episcopos," P.L., 96, 414. Cf. also Mann, "Lives of the Popes," Vol. I, pp. 330 sq.
[38] Zacharias, "Epist. ad Bonifacium," P.L., 89, 946.

this action on the ground that the question had never been defined by the Church and was, therefore, open for discussion by theologians. The question of infallibility is in no way involved in the matter, which was not definitely decided until the time of Pope Benedict XII.[39]

h) THE GALILEO CASE. The condemnation of Galileo is brought forth as undeniable proof for almost every charge against the Church, but it has no bearing whatever on the question of papal infallibility. The condemnation was made by the Congregation of the Index in 1616 and approved by Paul V in the ordinary routine manner; but no theologian ever dreamed that such decrees are infallible; they are not intended to be such. The congregation made a mistake, but that has nothing to do with papal infallibility.[40]

---

[39] Cf. Straub, "De Ecclesia Christi," n. 1045; Jungmann, "Dissertationes Historicae," 32, n. 10.

[40] Cf. Vacandard, "Etudes de Critque," Series I, pp. 339 sqq.; D'Ales, "Dictionnaire Apologetique," art. "Galilee"; Catholic Encyclopedia, art. "Galilei."

CHAPTER XVI

The Extent of Infallibility

The extent of infallibility refers to the truths that may be defined by the Church with infallible authority. Some truths are directly subject to the infallible authority of the Church by their very nature; others only indirectly because of their connection with the former. The one set of truths constitute the primary, the other secondary extent of infallibility.

ART. I. PRIMARY EXTENT OF INFALLIBILITY

REVEALED TRUTHS. Since infallibility is nothing more nor less than protection from error in teaching and explaining truth, it extends primarily and directly to all the truths committed to the teaching authority of the Church. This includes the whole body of Christian Revelation,—the deposit of faith,[1]—for Christ said to His Apostles: "Teaching them to observe all that I have commanded you."[2] He also promised them the Spirit of truth to preserve them from error in teaching these truths; "He will teach you all things, and bring to your mind whatever I have said to you."[3] It is evident then that infallibility extends directly and primarily to all revealed truths, whether of faith or morals.

FAITH AND MORALS. Theologians frequently refer to *matters of faith* and *matters of morals*. The former includes all those revealed truths proposed for belief rather than practice, since they are not immediately concerned with the direction of our lives. The latter embraces truths directly and immediately concerned with our actions, and necessary for leading a Christian life, but as they also are revealed, they must be believed no less firmly than the others.

COROLLARIES. Since the infallibility of the Church extends to all revealed truths, she must be infallible in determining the sources of revelation and in explaining their meaning. Therefore,

a) The Church is infallible in determining the canon of Sacred Scripture, i.e., in deciding what books are divinely inspired and, therefore, to be received as the word of God. Inspiration is a fact that can be known

---

[1] St. Paul was the first to use this term in reference to the body of revealed truths. He said to Timothy: "Custodi depositum." (1 Tim. vi, 20; cf. 2 Tim. i, 14.)
[2] Matt. xxviii, 20.
[3] John xiv, 26.

by revelation only; consequently the Church, being infallible in defining revealed truth, is necessarily infallible in defining what works belong to Holy Scripture.

b) The Church is infallible in expounding the true sense of revealed truth, whether written or unwritten, because the Church being infallible in teaching revealed truth, must likewise be infallible in interpreting the words through which it is revealed. Furthermore, there could be no certain knowledge of revealed truth, unless there were also certain knowledge of the true meaning of the words in which it is embodied.

c) The Church is infallible in selecting terms suitable to convey the truths which she defines. Truths can be set forth in words only, i.e., by means of creeds and dogmatic decrees. Therefore, to be infallible in teaching, the Church must also be infallible in choosing words that accurately express her meaning without ambiguity.

d) The Church is infallible in condemning doctrines opposed to revealed truth, because in knowing the truth with infallible certainty, she knows with like certainty that its contradictory is false. It is metaphysically impossible for the contradictory of a true proposition to be anything but false.

e) The Church is infallible in explaining the laws and precepts of God and the Evangelical Counsels of Our Lord, since these are all matters of divine revelation.

ART. II. SECONDARY EXTENT OF INFALLIBILITY

Since the Church is endowed with infallible authority for the express purpose of preserving intact the deposit of revealed truth and for expounding it without error, she must also be infallible in judging of doctrines and facts so intimately bound up with revealed truths that they cannot be denied or questioned without endangering revealed truth itself. Such doctrines and facts constitute the secondary object or extent of infallibility. They fall within the province of infallibility only in so far as they are connected with revealed truth. This secondary or indirect extent of infallibility includes especially (a) theological conclusions, (b) truths of the natural order, (c) dogmatic facts, and (d) general disciplinary matters.

a) THEOLOGICAL CONCLUSIONS. A theological conclusion is a proposition logically deduced from premises, one of which is a revealed truth, the other a truth known by reason, e.g., Christ is true man (revealed truth); but man is composed of body and soul (truth known by reason); therefore, Christ has a human body and a human soul (theological conclusion). The infallible authority of the Church necessarily extends to such conclusions, for otherwise the deposit of faith could not be preserved intact. "If the Church were infallible in revealed truths, but not in matters inseparably connected with them, she would be like a commander ordered to defend a city without authority to make fortifications or to destroy the machinery of war prepared by the enemy."[4]

b) NATURAL TRUTHS. Faith necessarily presupposes many truths of the purely natural order; such, for example, as the spirituality of the soul, the possibility of revelation and miracles, and also the possibility of attaining certain knowledge through human testimony. "There are also truths and conceptions, and even terms of such nature that revealed truths cannot be set forth and properly explained without them. Such, for instance, are the notions of substance, person, transubstantiation."[5] The Church must have infallible authority in regard to all such natural truths, in so far as they are connected with revealed truth, because without such authority she could not preserve and expound revelation with infallible security.

c) DOGMATIC FACTS. A dogmatic fact is one that has not been revealed, yet is so intimately connected with a doctrine of faith that without certain knowledge of the fact there can be no certain knowledge of the doctrine. For example, was the Vatican Council truly ecumenical? Was Pius IX a legitimate pope? Was the election of Pius XI valid? Such questions must be decided with certainty before decrees issued by any council or pope can be accepted as infallibly true or binding on the Church. It is evident, then, that the Church must be infallible in judging of such facts, and since the Church is infallible in believing as well as in teaching, it follows that the practically unanimous consent of the bishops and faithful in accepting a council as ecumenical, or a Roman Pontiff as legitimately elected, gives absolute and infallible certainty of the fact.

Whether a particular book or document contains heresy or true doctrine is also a dogmatic fact. Hence, the pope is infallible in condemning books as heretical if the condemnation is issued as an *ex cathedra* decision. "We do not maintain," says Tanquerey, "that the pope is infallible in judging a book to be the work of this or that author, or that the author meant to convey the ideas expressed in his work. But we do maintain that the pope can determine with infallible accuracy the sense which the words of the author actually do convey,

[4] Van Noort, "De Ecclesia Christi," n. 88.
[5] Dorsch, "De Ecclesia Christi," p. 333.

when considered in the context, and that he can judge with infallible certainty whether that sense is heretical or not."[6]

The Church, and therefore the Pope also, can declare with infallible authority that a particular version of Holy Scripture is authentic, i.e., he can declare that it contains no mistakes or corruptions of the original affecting doctrines of faith or morals. The Latin Vulgate has been declared free from all such mistakes and corruptions and made the official version of the Church. This does not mean that it contains no mistakes or corruptions whatsoever, as is evident from the fact that a commission was appointed some years ago to bring out a revised edition; but it does mean that it contains no substantial mistakes and corruptions that could in any way affect doctrine.

d) DISCIPLINARY MATTERS. Under this head are included the laws and precepts established by ecclesiastical authority for the regulation of worship or for the guidance of the faithful throughout the world. Such laws and precepts are necessarily subject to the infallible authority of the Church, because of their intimate connection with doctrines of faith and morals. For example, the law prescribing Communion under one species presupposes the doctrine that Our Lord is present whole and entire under either form, and the laws concerning the exposition of relics likewise presuppose that veneration of them is licit. Hence in making laws, the Church implicitly passes a twofold judgment:—one of doctrine, the other of prudence; she judges that the law is not opposed to any revealed truth and that, under the circumstances, it will assist and guide the faithful in the performance of their Christian duties. The Church is necessarily infallible in this doctrinal judgment, for if she were not, the faithful might be led into errors of doctrine at any time. But there is no promise that the rulers of the Church shall always enjoy the greatest degree of prudence; consequently, there is no guarantee that their laws and precepts will always be the best possible under the circumstances. Neither is the Church infallible in applying her laws to particular cases. The pope, for instance, may be mistaken in declaring a particular marriage valid or invalid.

COROLLARIES. a) The prayers prescribed or approved for universal use in public worship cannot be opposed to any revealed truth. Hence, the axiom, *Lex orandi est lex credendi*,—the rule of prayer is the rule of faith.

b) In the solemn approbation of religious orders the Church is in-

---

fallible in declaring that their practices and regulations are adapted to the promotion of Christian perfection.

c) The Church is also infallible in canonizing saints, for, as Benedict XIV says: "The universal Church cannot be led into error concerning matters of morals by the Supreme Pontiff; but this would be the case if he were not infallible in the canonization of saints."[7] In the act of canonization, the Church proclaims the saint a model of virtue; she commands all the faithful to honor him, and exhorts all to imitate his life. If the Church could be mistaken in this matter, the faithful would be led into grievous error by imitating the life of a sinner and by honoring one who is forever estranged from the friendship of God.

d) Before canonizing a person the Church usually demands evidence that a certain number of miracles have been performed through his or her intercession. Since the Church uses her authority to judge of the authenticity of these miracles, she may do so with an infallible judgment if she wishes. This, however, is not the custom of the Church either before canonization or in the act of canonization. The decree concerns the sanctity of the person canonized, not the authenticity of the miracles performed; they are merely an incentive for the Church to exercise her infallible authority in canonizing the person in question.[8]

e) The Church could also use her infallible authority to determine the genuineness of relics exposed for the veneration of the faithful, but this is rarely if ever done. The veneration paid to relics is, in reality, an honor paid to the person whom they represent or call to mind and cannot be affected by any defect in the relics. For this reason the authenticity of relics can scarcely ever be a matter of such importance as to demand the exercise of infallible authority on the part of the Church.

CONCLUSION. The infallible authority of the Church is primarily and directly concerned with revealed truths only; secondarily, with every doctrine or fact necessary for the proper understanding or faithful preservation of revealed truth. All are equally certain when defined by the Church, but they beget different kinds of faith. Revealed truths, when defined, become the object of divine and Catholic faith; they must be accepted on the authority of God who revealed them. Natural truths defined by the Church become the object of ecclesiastical faith; they are not accepted on the authority of God directly, but on the infallible authority of the Church defining them.

---

[7] Benedict XIV, "De Canoniz. et Beatific. Servorum Dei."
[8] Straub, "De Ecclesia Christi," n. 917.

CHAPTER XVII

CHURCH AND STATE

The Church, being an external society, must come into daily contact with the various civil powers that direct the temporal destinies of man. Her members are their members; her mission is closely allied to theirs, and like them, she also must employ certain material means to attain the purpose of her existence. These intimate relations beget certain mutual rights and duties between Church and State and also determine the powers of the pope in regard to civil rulers. Order and clearness in investigating these matters will be obtained most easily by considering (1) the various theories advanced at different times on the subject, (2) the Catholic doctrine from which are deduced, (3) the mutual rights and duties of Church and State, with (4) some practical application of the principles established, and (5) the powers of the Roman Pontiff in regard to secular rulers.

ART. I. VARIOUS THEORIES ADVANCED ON CHURCH AND STATE

I. MARSILIUS OF PADUA. According to the Teaching of the *Defensor Pacis,* the joint work of Marsilius and Jean de Jandum, all power, whether civil or ecclesiastical, resides in the people, who delegate it to the civil authorities to be exercised in their name. Consequently, the Church can exercise no authority except by permission of the civil power, which has complete jurisdiction over it. In refuting this doctrine of absolute subjection to the State, Augustus Triumphus went to the opposite extreme by giving the Church supreme power in both temporal and spiritual matters. He taught that temporal rulers are mere agents of the Roman Pontiff, who holds supreme temporal and spiritual power over the whole world.

II. THE REFORMERS. The so-called Reformers of the sixteenth century were forced to confer all spiritual authority upon secular princes in order to obtain their assistance and protection. A non-Catholic writer says that "the maxim, *cuius regio, eius,* religio,[1] the pithy definition of territorialism which makes the religion of the people dependent on the religion of the ruler of the country, became the leading principle in all Protestant States on the Continent. . . . Furthermore, as the bishops

---

[1] A phrase meaning that the religion of a country must be that of its ruler.

everywhere protested against the Reformation, the episcopal authority and jurisdiction had, in the Protestant countries, to be conferred on the civil ruler. . . . The Church became a mere department of his government."[2] The Church of England declares that "the King's Majesty hath the chief power in this realm of England and his other dominions . . . over all estates in this realm whether they be ecclesiastical or civil."[3] According to this doctrine of the Reformers, the "State is supreme, the Church its servant."[4]

III. GALLICANISM. The doctrines of Gallicanism, if put into practice, would logically lead to the institution of national Churches, subject to the civil power. Its advocates held that civil rulers are completely independent of Church authority in the administration of their office; that the civil power has the right of *vigilance* and *influence* in ecclesiastical affairs, and that the decrees and constitutions of the Roman Pontiff have no force unless approved by the king and published with his authority. This approval was known as the *royal placet* or *exequatur.*

The doctrine itself is known as Gallicanism, because its advocates proclaimed it for the French Church only. They did this on the idea that the authority of the pope was limited in France by ancient custom and by Church canons. The principles of Gallicanism were first systemized by Guy Coquille and Pierre Pithou in a work edited in 1594 under the title, *Liberties of the Gallican Church.* Under the influence of Louis XIV, these principles were reduced to four articles and published in 1682 as the *Declaration of the French Clergy,* although they were signed by only thirty-four out of the hundred and thirty-five prelates of France.[5]

IV. FEBRONIANISM. Nicholas von Hontheim, writing under the name of Justinus Febronius, set forth serious errors regarding the constitution of the Church and its relation to the State. According to his doctrine, all powers must be subordinated to the State, which is absolute. From this principle he deduced the right of the State to regulate the external affairs of the Church,—to convoke councils, reform Church discipline, grant and revoke immunities, administer the goods of the Church and receive appeals from the judgment of ecclesiastical authorities.

V. JOSEPHISM. Emperor Joseph II of Austria, influenced by Gallicanism, Febronianism, and the teachings of Voltaire, introduced the system known to history as *Josephism.* It was simply an attempt to

---

[2] Schaff-Herzog, art. "Church and State."
[3] The Thirty-nine Articles, Art. xxxvii.
[4] Schaff-Herzog, art. "Church and State."
[5] Cf. Catholic Encyclopedia, art. "Gallicanism"; Devivier-Sasia, "Christian Apologetics," Vol. II, p. 163 sqq.

create a national Church subject to the State, or, as one of his supporters expressed it, to make "the Church a department of the police, which must serve the aims of the State until such time as the enlightenment of the people permit its release by the secular police."[6] According to this policy the State is the administrator of all church property and has authority to regulate, change, or suppress anything in divine worship or in the government of the Church that is not essential to religion. As the State was sole judge in the matter, it turned out that religion had very few "essentials." Joseph interfered with Church services to such an extent that Frederick the Great dubbed him "our brother sacristan."

VI. LIBERALISM. Rationalists and materialists, assuming the title of *Liberals,* teach that the State is supreme and absolute in its powers; from it all rights are derived, and to its power everything must be subjected. The individual exists for the State, not the State for the individual. This doctrine makes the Church a mere private corporation, existing at the pleasure of the State, and subject to the State in every respect. It is a return to the pagan idea of the State as a divinity to be worshipped.[7]

The teaching of Modernism is closely allied to Liberalism on the subject of Church and State and logically leads to it. The Church, according to the Modernists, is not a divine institution, but a society of the faithful, which arose through evolutionary processes. Consequently it must be a private society, having neither rights nor authority other than those granted by the State. Pius X says "that since the phenomena of faith must be subject to science, so they say, so must the Church be subject to the State in its temporal concerns. Perhaps they have not openly asserted this as yet, but they are logically forced to admit it."[8]

VII. MODIFIED LIBERALISM. The advocates of this theory maintain that Church and State are completely independent of each other both in their existence and in their activities. Their motto is "A free Church in a free State,"—a phrase that tickles the ear and serves to cover up much false doctrine. Taken at its face value, the phrase expresses a fundamental truth concerning the relations of Church and State, but it is interpreted to mean that religion is an affair of the individual alone, and that the State should give no thought to religion in any of its acts or counsels, since anything is right and just that the popular will demands or consents to. All powers of the State and every right of the individual flow from the consent of the people.

---

[6] Sonnenfels, quoted by Catholic Encyclopedia, art. "Joseph II."
[7] Cf. Ryan and Millar, "The State and the Church," p. 195 sqq.
[8] Pius X, "Pascendi Domici Gregis," Sept. 7, 1907; Denzinger, n. 2093.

Theoretically, this form of Liberalism grants complete freedom of worship and equal rights to all forms of religion; practically, however, it results in an attempt to overthrow all religion. Those who advocate separation of Church and State on account of peculiar circumstances which obtain in various countries, cannot be classed as Liberals in the sense just explained. Separation is often necessary to avoid greater evils.

RESUME. The ancient world subordinated religion and the priesthood to the State, and at Rome the emperor assumed the title and office of *"Pontifex Maximus."* This idea of State supremacy clung for a time to the Christian emperors, especially in the East, where they meddled to a considerable extent in ecclesiastical affairs. During the Middle Ages there was a decided tendency to subject the State to the Church by placing temporal power in the hands of the Pope. A non-Catholic historian says: "It was characteristic of the whole period known as the Middle Ages that the State was too weak to stand alone, and consequently sought support in the spiritual authority of the Church."[9] This resulted in a dependence of the State upon the Church and gave to her considerable temporal power, which saved the peoples of the West from absolutism such as that exercised by the ancient state.

The Reformation of the sixteenth century brought about a reversal of this relation between Church and State by subjecting religion to political power. Comte describes this absorption of religion by the State as a "relapse into barbarism."[10] This change, brought about by the Reformation, gradually developed into the doctrine of State absolutism, which culminated in the teachings of Hegel, who declared the State the highest manifestation of Universal Reason, which all persons and institutions must serve and magnify.[11] The system commonly advocated today proclaims Church and State completely independent of each other in their existence, aims, and activities. While some of these systems may be the best obtainable under given circumstances, they are all false in principle and opposed to the teaching of the Church.

ART. II. CATHOLIC DOCTRINE ON CHURCH AND STATE

Catholic doctrine concerning the relations of Church and State may be summarized in three propositions: (a) Church and State are distinct and perfect societies, each supreme in its own province; (b) the State is *indirectly* subordinate to the Church, and (c) Church and State should be joined in mutual and friendly cooperation.

---

[9] Hans Delbruck, quoted by Mausbach, "Catholic Moral Teaching," p. 345.
[10] A. Comte, quoted by Mausbach, "Catholic Moral Teaching," p. 347.
[11] F. W. Hegel, "Philosophic des Rechts," quoted by Ryan and Millar, "The State and the Church," p. 198.

1. Church and State Distinct and Perfect Societies

I. DISTINCT SOCIETIES. Under the Christian dispensation, Church and State are separate and distinct societies, as all admit, and this distinction is a matter of divine institution, as is evident from the origin and purposes of the two societies and from the nature of the means employed to attain those purposes.

a) ORIGIN. Both State and Church have God for their author, for, as St. Paul says, "For there exists no authority except from God, and those who exist have been appointed by God."[12] Yet the two societies owe their existence to God in quite different senses. Civil power considered in the abstract is from God; the Church in its concrete form is of divine institution.

Man was created to live in the society of his fellowmen and cannot live happily without it; in fact, he can scarcely eke out an existence without the cooperation of others. Therefore, civil authority which is absolutely necessary for men to live together in peace and security, is from God, who gave man his social nature and social instincts. But the particular form which civil government assumes, depends upon the will of man. God wills that there be civil government with authority to rule, but He does not determine whether this government shall be a monarchy, a republic, or a pure democracy. The condition of the Church is quite different, since Christ directly established it in the concrete form under which it exists; He not only gave the authority, but also determined the particular form of government, and left no authority to change it in the least. It is evident, then, that the distinction between State and Church is of divine institution and cannot be abolished by any human authority.

b) PURPOSE. The civil power, being a natural society, is ordained for the attainment of a natural end; *viz.,* the happiness of its citizens in this life. It would also have been the duty of the State to provide for man's eternal happiness if God had not ordained otherwise; but since man is destined for a supernatural happiness, the State, being a purely natural society, is not sufficient to attain this end. For this reason the Church was instituted to provide for man's eternal happiness, leaving to the State, as its immediate end, the temporal well-being and happiness of its citizens. The purposes of the two societies are thus separate and distinct: the one temporal, the other eternal; the one natural, the other supernatural.

c) MEANS EMPLOYED. The means employed by the State to attain its end are all of the natural order; those employed by the Church

---

[12] Rom. xiii, 1.

are both natural and supernatural, the principal ones being supernatural, such as Revelation, the Sacraments, divine authority, infallibility, and the like.

II. PERFECT SOCIETIES. Church and State are not only distinct, they are also independent societies,—independent in their origin, in their existence, and in the means employed to attain their respective ends. Christ indicated this when He said: "Render therefore to Caesar the things that are Caesar's, and to God the things that are God's."[13] It is evident, then, that both Church and State fulfill all the requirements for a perfect society;[14] neither depends upon the other or upon any other society for its existence or for the means to attain its end. Furthermore the ends to be attained are different and not subordinated to any other end in the same order. Therefore, both Church and State are perfect societies, each supreme in its own sphere, as Leo XIII explicitly teaches: "God has divided the care of the human race between two powers, the ecclesiastical and the civil; one placed over divine things, the other over human. Each is supreme in its own sphere, and each is confined within certain limits defined by its very nature; . . . therefore each has a world of its own, as it were, in which to exercise its proper function."[15]

2. The State Indirectly Subordinate to the Church

SUBORDINATE. Church and State being distinct societies, must be of equal or unequal rank. In other words, the relation between them must be that of *coordination* or *subordination,* but societies cannot be truly *coordinate* unless they belong to the same order and are concerned about the same end, e.g., sovereign States are coordinate societies; so also are similar political subdivisions of a State, or independent corporations engaged in the same line of business. It is immediately evident, therefore, that Church and State cannot be coordinate, since they belong to different orders and are concerned about different ends. The one is supernatural, the other natural; the one is concerned with man's eternal happiness, the other with his temporal well-being. Consequently, one must be *subordinated* to the other, and in precisely the same manner that the ends to be attained by the two societies are subordinated one to the other.

Since man was created for eternal happiness, all temporal things must

---

[13] Matt. xxii, 21.
[14] See above, Ch. i, Art. iv.
[15] Leo XIII, "Immortale Dei," Nov. 1, 1885; Denzinger, n. 1866.

subserve that end. Temporal happiness and material well-being are not things to be sought after for themselves alone; right reason demands that they be used as a means to man's last end, or at least, that they be not opposed to that end, for, as Christ has said, "what does it profit a man, if he gain the whole world, but suffer the loss of his own soul."[16] Therefore, as man's temporal happiness and prosperity must be subordinate and subservient to his eternal happiness, so also must the State, which provides for the former, be subordinate and subservient to the Church, which provides for the latter. Hence Boniface VIII declared that "sword should be subject to sword; the temporal authority to the spiritual power, for, as the Apostle says, *there is no power but from God, and those that are from God are ordered.* But they would not be ordered if sword were not subject to sword and the lower directed by the higher to a supreme end."[17]

INDIRECT SUBORDINATE. Subordination may be *direct* or *indirect*. A society is *directly* subordinated to another when it has the same end in view and its sphere of action falls within that of the superior society. For example, the political divisions of a nation are directly subordinate to the nation itself, and the dioceses of the Church to the Church as a whole. In direct subordination the superior society has jurisdiction over the inferior with authority to prescribe its course of action and to approve or nullify any of its acts. There can be no question of such subordination of State to Church. The State, being a perfect society, supreme in its own order, is not and cannot be directly subject to the Church.

Indirect subordination can occur only when the societies concerned have different aims in view and distinct spheres of action, i.e., when the one is not included within the other. Under these conditions subjection of one society to another may arise from three different sources,—its members, the end it has in view and the means to attain that end.

a) If the members of a society happen to be subject to another and higher authority, the society itself is thereby indirectly subjected to that higher authority: it has no right to take any action that would cause its members to violate their duties to the higher authority. The State is thus indirectly subject to the Church, in so far as its citizens happen to be subject to the higher spiritual authority of the Church. This sort of subordination is only indirect and negative; it demands that the State refrain from any action that would cause her citizens or rulers to violate their duties to the Church or interfere in any way with the

---

[16] Matt. xvi, 26.
[17] Boniface VIII, "Unam Sanctam," Nov. 18, 1302; Denzinger, n. 469.

Church's exercise of spiritual authority over every single member, be he the humblest citizen in the land or the king on his throne.

b) A society is also indirectly subject to another if the end it has in view is subordinated to that of the other society. But the temporal happiness of man, the end directly sought by the State, is necessarily subordinate and subservient to his eternal happiness, to be obtained through the Church. Therefore, the State has neither the right nor the authority to seek any temporal happiness or material prosperity for its citizens detrimental to their eternal welfare, and since there can be no true temporal prosperity except that which leads to eternal happiness indirectly by providing for true temporal happiness. Consequently, the State is indirectly subject to the Church in this matter both *negatively* and *positively*, i.e., the State must not only refrain from anything that would impede the Church in her mission of salvation, it must also assist the Church indirectly by providing a temporal prosperity that will be conducive to the eternal welfare of her citizens.

c) Finally, a society is indirectly subject to another if the means it employs to attain its end are in any way connected with the attainment of a higher good for its members in that other society. The State is therefore indirectly subject to the Church in this respect, since right reason demands that the State cede to the Church whatever is necessary for her preservation and the proper attainment of her higher purpose,—the eternal salvation of man. Moreover, the actions of civil officials in carrying out the duties of their office often have a moral aspect that affects the spiritual welfare committed to the care of the Church. Consequently, the Church has direct jurisdiction over the official acts of civil authorities in regard to the moral aspect of those acts if the persons in question happen to be subjects of the Church. In this matter, therefore, the Church also exercises an indirect authority over the State.

COROLLARY. The Church has jurisdiction over all things pertaining to the salvation of man and to those only. Consequently the Church has sole jurisdiction in purely spiritual matters, but in temporal matters that neither impede her work in saving souls nor are necessary for that work, she has absolutely no jurisdiction. Temporal things consecrated to God or to the worship of God, and all things necessary for the proper fulfillment of her mission, are subject to the authority of the Church, and therefore removed from that of the State. Consequently, the Church has an inherent right to acquire and possess churches, schools, hospitals, orphanages, cemeteries, and the like, together with sufficient funds for their proper maintenance, and the State has no right to tax such properties, since they are not subject to State Authority. The Church also has the right to exempt from the jurisdiction of the State all persons consecrated to God by the reception of Orders or by religious profession. Such exemption is known as *privilegium fori,* because persons so exempt have the privilege of being tried for any crime in the courts (*forum*) of the Church and punished by her authority, if found guilty.

Leo XIII briefly stated these principles in the following words: "The nature and scope of that connection (between Church and State) can be determined only by having regard to the nature of each power, and by taking account of the relative excellence and nobility of their purpose. One has for its proximate and chief object the well-being of this mortal life; the other the everlasting joys of Heaven. Therefore, whatever in things human is sacred in character, whatever belong by nature or by reason of the end to which it is referred, to the salvation of souls, or to the worship of God, is subject to the power and judgment of the Church. Whatever is to be ranged under civil and political order, is rightly subject to civil authority. Jesus Christ Himself has given command that what belongs to Caesar must be rendered to Caesar, and that what belongs to God is to be rendered to God."[18]

In case a conflict of rights should occur, or a controversy arise between Church and State concerning the limits of their respective jurisdictions in particular cases, the State as the inferior society would be obliged, theoretically, to yield to the judgment of the Church. In practice, however, the Church desires that such matters be settled by mutual agreement. "There are occasions," says Leo XIII, "when another method of concord is available for the sake of peace and liberty. We mean, when rulers of the State and the Roman Pontiff come to an understanding touching some special matter. At such times the Church gives signal proof of her motherly love by showing the greatest possible kindness and indulgence." Agreements of this sort between Church and State concerning matters of more or less permanent nature are known as *concordats,* and correspond to treaties between nations.

3. Church and State in Mutual Support

The prevailing doctrine today advocates complete separation of Church and State allowing each to go its way without regard to the other. The opposite extreme is union of Church and State, in which one absorbs the other and exercises all authority, both civil and ecclesi-

---

[18] Leo XIII, "Immortale Dei," Nov. 1, 1885; Denzinger, n. 1866.

astical. Both extremes are wrong in principle and opposed to Catholic teaching. The fact that Christ instituted the Church as a society distinct from the State and independent of it, proves that they should not be united in such wise that either dominates or absorbs the other. On the other hand, complete separation is detrimental to both, and, therefore, contrary to the will of Christ.

With societies as with individuals, complete separation is lawful only when just rights and duties are not thereby violated. Persons bound by mutual rights and duties may not disregard them by complete separation, especially if the rights of others are involved. Husband and wife, for example, owe to each other certain duties which neither may lawfully evade by separation without consent of the other. Even mutual consent of the parties will not make separation lawful when the rights of children are concerned. The relation between Church and State is similar to that between husband and wife. Both were instituted to promote the common welfare of mankind,—the Church to care for his spiritual needs, the State for his temporal welfare. But neither of these can be properly provided for unless the other be taken into consideration. This fact gives rise to mutual rights and duties between Church and State, and if these are not fulfilled by friendly cooperation, the subjects of both societies must suffer injury. Leo XIII compares the ideal union between Church and State to that between body and soul in man: "Even in physical things, although of a lower order, the Almighty has so combined the forces and springs of nature with tempered action and wondrous harmony, that no one of them clashes with another, and all of them most fitly and aptly work together for the great purpose of the universe. There must, accordingly, exist between these two powers (Church and State) a certain orderly connection, which may be compared to the union of body and soul in man."[19]

The nature and extent of this ideal union between Church and State is easily deduced from their mutual rights and duties, as described in the following article; but what it shall be in any particular case will depend upon various circumstances. The principles remain the same, but their application will differ, because it often happens that insistence upon a theoretical right may cause harm rather than good. In such cases it is the part of prudence to avert the greater evil by forgoing the use of a right whose exercise is not absolutely essential.

---

[19] Leo XIII, "Immortale Dei," Nov. 1, 1885.

ART. III. MUTUAL RIGHTS AND DUTIES

I. THE STATE. a) RIGHTS. Since the State is a perfect society, supreme in its own sphere, it has the right to free and untrammeled action in those things pertaining to its jurisdiction, such as selecting the form of government, making necessary laws, providing for the common defense, making public improvements and the like. In a word, the State has an inherent right to free action in everything tending to promote the common good of its citizens, providing nothing is done contrary to the laws of God or the good of the Church. In certain matters of a mixed nature both State and Church have rights and duties that must be carefully distinguished. Education and marriage belong to this class and demand special attention, because they are matters of constant concern to Church and State alike.

Education tends to promote the welfare of society and the security of the State, especially in a representative government, where the people participate in it through the right of ballot. Consequently, the State has a just right to demand suitable instruction, to establish and maintain schools to impart such instruction, and to require all children to attend them, unless their education is otherwise provided for. The State also has the right to demand reasonable proficiency in all private schools and to see to it that nothing detrimental to the common good is taught or inculcated in them, and, since morality is necessary for the common good, the State has the right and also the duty to see to it that nothing contrary to morality is taught in any school or inculcated by books, newspapers, theaters, or other agencies. But since it belongs to the Church to teach faith and morals, the State must seek guidance from her in these matters and accept her judgment.

Since the peace and security of the nation depends to a large extent upon the peace and security of the family, the State has a just right to regulate marriage in its civil effects. For this purpose it may demand publicity for all marriages by means of an official license or the publication of banns and by a public registration of all marriages performed. The State also has authority to regulate the rights of husband and wife in regard to the ownership and inheritance of property, and to protect the rights of children by demanding that parents give them proper care and education. The State has no right to interfere with marriage as a Sacrament by prescribing how it shall be solemnized or by establishing diriment impediments. These matters were committed to the authority of the Church, when Christ raised marriage to the dignity of a Sacrament. It should be noted, however, that the marriage of unbaptized persons is not a Sacrament and that the contracting parties are not subject to Church authority; consequently, it belongs to the State to regulate such marriages, but in no case can it grant an absolute divorce, since this is contrary to the law of Christ.

b) DUTIES TO CHURCH. Since civil society, no less than the individual, owes its existence to God, the State as such is obliged to acknowledge and honor Him by public worship of a social character. "The State," says Leo XIII, "is clearly bound to act up to the manifold and weighty duties linking it to God, by the public profession of religion. Nature and reason, which command every one to worship God devoutly in holiness because we belong to Him and must return to Him from whom we came, also bind the civil community by a similar law. For men living together in society are under the power of God no less than individuals, and society no less than individuals, owes gratitude to God, who gave it being and maintains it, and whose ever bounteous goodness enriches it with countless blessings. As no one is allowed to be amiss in the service due to God, and as the chief duty of all men is to cling to religion in its teachings and its practice, . . . it is a public crime to act as though there were no God. So, too, is it a sin in the State to act as though religion were something beyond its scope or of no practical benefit."[20] These same principles were proclaimed by Pius IX when he condemned the teaching that "The best interests of society and civil progress demand that governments be organized and ruled with no more regard to religion than if it did not exist, or at least with no distinction between true and false religion."[21]

The State, as well as the individual, must recognize and worship God in the manner prescribed by Him; it may not "out of many forms of religion adopt that one which chimes in with its fancy, for we are bound absolutely to worship God in that way which He has shown to be His will."[22] In fine, the State as such is obliged to profess and protect the true religion of Christ, which is found in the Catholic Church alone. Moreover, as the State is bound to acknowledge and worship God, it is also obliged to prohibit and repress, as far as possible, whatever is opposed to His honor and glory, i.e., whatever is opposed to the natural or positive law of God and the good of His Church. The State must frame its laws and regulate its practices according to right reason and the truths of Revelation, as interpreted by the Church, the divinely appointed teacher and interpreter of all revealed truth.

The duties of the State in matters of religion, which we have deduced

[20] Leo XIII, "Immortale Dei," Nov. 1, 1885.
[21] Pius IX, "Quanta Cura," Dec. 8, 1864; Denzinger, n. 1689.
[22] Leo XIII, "Immortale Dei," Nov. 1, 1885.

from its dependence upon God, *"the King of kings and Lord of lords,"* may also be inferred from its one chief duty, that of providing for the temporal happiness and prosperity of its citizens. This happiness must be in accord with man's nature as a rational creature of God destined for eternal happiness. Therefore, as St. Thomas says, "it is the duty of the king (or civil authorities) to provide for the good of the people in a manner that will lead to eternal happiness in Heaven; he must command those things which will lead to eternal happiness, and forbid, as far as possible, whatever is opposed to its attainment."[23] But as man can attain eternal happiness only through the practice of true religion in the Catholic Church, it is the duty of the State to protect and promote the interests of the Church in order to promote the true temporal interests of its subjects.

Again, it is the duty of the State to protect every natural and civic right of its subjects; for this especially are governments organized and maintained. But the right of every man to acquire truth, whether natural or revealed, and the right to attain his supreme destiny through the practice of true religion, are fundamental and innate, and the State is obliged to protect them in the only way possible,—by protecting and promoting the interests of the Church divinely appointed to teach and save mankind. Finally, the State is obliged in justice to the people to provide for its own security and preservation, but true religion is the very foundation of all society, for the rights of man are not secure when the rights of God are contemned. Society without morality cannot continue long in peace and happiness, and without religion there can be no morality; wherefore the State secures its own position and strengthens its own authority by encouraging and promoting true religion, and every attack upon true religion is an attack upon the very foundations of civil government. On this account heresy was formerly punished as a crime against the State, just as blasphemy or violation of the Sunday are punished by the State in many places at the present time.

II. THE CHURCH. a) RIGHTS. The Church being a perfect society, supreme in its own sphere, has the right to free and unimpeded action in everything that is necessary for the salvation of souls,—in teaching, in the administration of the Sacraments, in matters of discipline and worship, and in the education of the clergy. She also has the right to acquire and administer church property, to open schools, and to see to it that nothing contrary to faith or morals is taught in the State schools. She likewise has a right to protection and assistance on the part of the State.

---

[23] St. Thomas Aquinas, "De Rege et Regno," I, xv.

b) DUTIES TOWARD THE STATE. The Church is bound in justice to recognize the supremacy of the State in purely temporal things and to leave to secular authority complete control of such affairs. The Fourth Lateran Council is explicit on this matter: "Since we do not wish the laity to invade the rights of the clergy, so neither do we wish the clergy to usurp the rights of the laity. Therefore, we forbid all clerics to make the liberty of the Church a pretext for extending their jurisdiction at the expense of secular justice. Let them remain content with approved constitution and customs, by which the things of Caesar are rendered to Caesar, and the things of God to God."[24]

The Church is also obliged to assist the State by inculcating public honesty and respect for lawful authority, and by promoting peace and tranquillity, all of which tend both to the spiritual and to the temporal welfare of the people. When necessary, the Church must also assist the State in warding off impending dangers that threaten Church and State alike, as often happens in time of war or hostile invasion. The history of our own country is an eloquent witness to the manner in which the Church has always fulfilled this duty to the government. Finally, the Church owes the duty of prayer for the State and its authorities. She must pray, as St. Paul commands, "for kings, and for all in high positions, that we may lead a quiet and peaceful life in all piety and worthy behavior."[25] The Church conscientiously fulfilled this duty even to the pagan emperors of Rome during the worst days of persecution, and continues to pray for all civil rulers in her public and private devotions.

CONCLUSION. The most superficial examination of the mutual rights and duties flowing from the very nature of the two societies must convince any thinking man that the ideal relation of Church and State is that of friendly cooperation, for, as Ivo of Chartres says, "when the civil and ecclesiastical powers agree, the world is well ruled and the Church flourishes and bears fruit. But when there is discord, everything fails miserably."[26] This ideal may be difficult to realize in practice, and history bears witness that it has seldom if ever been realized in the past, partly because the agents through which both powers must work are human beings with all the innate frailties of human nature, but ideals are not to be abandoned because they are seldom realized in their fullness. If such were the case, the progress of nations and the betterment of the human race would have to be abandoned as mere idle dreams.

Union of cooperation and mutual support is undoubtedly the ideal

---

[24] Mansi, T. xxii, col. 1027.
[25] 1 Tim. ii, 2-3.
[26] Ivo of Chartres, "Epist. ad Paschalem"; P.L., 162, 246.

relation of Church and State, yet separation must be preferred to a so-called union that amounts to subjection of the Church to the State, for separation with freedom is better far than union with slavery. Attempted unions in the past generally have led to subjection, and present experiences are far from satisfactory. The ideal is, perhaps, more nearly realized in the United States than in any other part of the world today, and this in spite of our protestations of complete separation. The State recognizes its duty to God and religion by proclaiming a day of national thanksgiving, by opening sessions of Congress and State legislatures with prayer, by appointing chaplains for army and navy, by protecting freedom of worship and the rights of the Church to own and administer her property without taxation, to educate her clergy, and to conduct schools for her children. Both national and State governments, it is true, recognize all religions alike, and secure equal rights to all, contrary to the principles of right reason, since truth alone has rights and falsehood can only be tolerated to avoid greater evils. But under the conditions prevailing in this country, the government could not prudently act otherwise, even if it so wished. In fact, any other course would be unjust to vast numbers living in good faith, because at the very inception of the government a solemn contract was made to recognize all religions alike in order to avoid greater evils.

ART. IV. PRACTICAL APPLICATION OF PRINCIPLES

Present conditions in the religious and political world seem to preclude all hope of attaining ideal relations between Church and State, yet there are certain rights for which the Church may reasonably demand recognition and respect. What these rights are, and what action the Church may take to enforce them against an unwilling government, must be determined from the circumstances of the case, and will depend largely upon whether the State in question is Catholic or non-Catholic, Christian, or non-Christian.

a) CATHOLIC STATE. In a Catholic State the Church must demand recognition of all her rights, and may reasonably insist that all of them be respected, unless special circumstances prevent the State from fulfilling certain duties toward her. But should the State unjustly refuse to respect the rights of the Church, her course of action is evident, for in this case the authorities of the State and, at least, a large majority of the people are Catholics, directly subject to the spiritual jurisdiction of the Church. This makes it possible for the Church to enforce respect for her rights by means of ecclesiastical punishments, which have generally proved effective in the past. But if such means were not sufficient, the Church could justly call upon other Catholic nations to defend her rights by force of arms. The prudence of such action would have to be judged from the circumstances of the case.

b) NON-CATHOLIC STATE. In a Christian State that is professedly non-Catholic, the Church cannot expect recognition of all her rights from the simple fact that she is not recognized as the true Church of Christ; but she can reasonably demand freedom of worship for Catholic subjects of the State and freedom for herself in teaching and making converts. The reasonableness of these demands follow from the fundamental Protestant doctrine of private interpretation and freedom to worship God according to the dictates of one's conscience, which a Protestant State could not consistently deny to any of its subjects. According to the same principle, the Church can reasonably demand recognition as a private society in the State, with all the rights and privileges accorded such societies.

But should the State refuse to respect even these demands of the Church, there is practically no means to enforce them. Theoretically, of course, the authorities and people of the State are subject to the jurisdiction of the Church, for, according to the supposition, they are baptized Christians. But they do not recognize this subjection, and cannot be expected to recognize it so long as they do not recognize the Church herself. This fact would render ecclesiastical punishments of no use whatever, unless enforced by the arms of Catholic nations, but the laws of prudence and charity would limit such action to cases of the most extreme necessity. It would always produce great harm and seldom, if ever, any good.

c) NON-CHRISTIAN STATE. In a non-Christian State force of arms wielded by other nations is the only means of defense against unjust invasion of the rights of the Church, for neither rulers nor people in such a State are subject in any way to the authority of the Church. Such force may be justly used to protect the right of the Church to preach the Gospel and bring souls to Christ, because all men, whether Christians or pagans, Jews or Gentiles, are subject to Christ, who commanded the Gospel to be preached to every creature and commissioned the Church to carry out this mission. Therefore, if a non-Christian State forbids the Gospel to be preached to its subjects, or to be accepted by them, the Church may call upon other nations to interfere by force of arms, if necessary. Both Catholic and Protestant nations have often intervened in this manner to protect missionaries and converts and thus secure freedom for the Gospel in pagan lands.

d) INDIFFERENT STATE. There is a growing tendency today for

governments to assume an attitude of complete indifference toward all religions. Such an attitude cannot be defended as an abstract principle by Catholics, but it may often be necessary through force of circumstances. A State may be compelled to tolerate false religions and hold all religions equal before the law, in order to preserve social peace and tranquillity. Where such conditions exist, Catholics may and do advocate a policy of religious indifference on the part of the State,—not as an abstract right, but as the least objectionable condition possible under the circumstances.

ART. V. THE ROMAN PONTIFF AND SECULAR RULERS

The supreme authorities in Church and State must stand in the same relation to each other as the societies over which they rule. From this we deduce the following principles: (1) secular rulers are indirectly subject to the Roman Pontiff; (2) the Roman Pontiff is exempt from all civil jurisdiction; and (3) temporal power is necessary to secure this exemption.

1. Secular Rulers Indirectly Subject to Roman Pontiff

Boniface VIII decreed that all men are subject to the Roman Pontiff, and the context shows that he had temporal rulers especially in mind, for the whole document is designed to prove that the civil power must be subject to the spiritual. He says: "If the worldly power deviates from the right path, it shall be judged by the spiritual; but if the supreme spiritual power deviates, it can be judged by God alone, as the Apostles testifies: *The spiritual man judges all things, but he himself is judged by no one.* . . . Therefore, we declare, say, define, and pronounce that it is necessary for salvation that every human creature be subject to the Roman Pontiff."[27]

Taken by themselves, these words of Pope Boniface might suggest a direct and complete subjection of temporal to spiritual rulers, but they have always been interpreted by theologians and by the Church herself as referring to an indirect subjection only. Membership in the Church, which is necessary for salvation, can be neither acquired nor retained without submission to the spiritual authority of her supreme head. For this reason Pope Boniface rightly says that subjection to the Roman Pontiff is necessary for every human creature, be he the meanest subject in the land or the mightiest monarch on his throne. All Catholic rulers, *as members of the Church,* are directly subject to the spiritual

---

[27] Boniface VIII, "Unam Sanctam," Nov. 18, 1302; Denzinger, n. 469.

authority of the Pope; *as civil rulers,* they are indirectly subject to the same authority, in so far as their official acts have a moral bearing. Since the Roman Pontiff has the right and duty of teaching faith and morals to the whole Church and to every member of the Church, it is his duty to instruct Catholic kings and rulers concerning the morality of all their acts, both private and official. It is his duty to decide what is contrary to the laws of God or the Church, and what is necessary for the protection of public and private morality. If a Catholic ruler violates the laws of God or of the Church, either in private or by official acts, the pope must admonish and punish him, if necessary, by excommunication, interdict, or other ecclesiastical censure, just as he would punish any other member of the Church. It is evident, then, that temporal rulers in their official capacity are subject to the authority of the pope only indirectly; he has no jurisdiction over their official acts except in so far as these acts have a moral bearing. The pope cannot forbid any act on the part of a civil ruler, unless that act be sinful; neither can he command any act, unless its omission would be a sin against the laws of God or the Church.

COROLLARY I. The jurisdiction of the Roman Pontiff extends to all subjects of the Church, and, therefore, to all validly baptized rulers of the State, whether Catholic or non-Catholic; but any attempt to exercise this authority over non-Catholic rulers would seldom, if ever, be expedient, for the simple reason that it is not recognized by them and would produce no good effect. Unbaptized rulers, not being subjects of the Church, are not subject to the authority of the Roman Pontiff, except as noted below, but it must not be concluded that on this account they are in a better position than Catholic rulers. On the contrary, their position is far inferior; they are bound by the laws of God in all their official acts, but are deprived of the infallible authority of the Church to guide them.

COROLLARY II. All civil rulers, whether Christian or non-Christian, may become indirectly subject to the authority of the Roman Pontiff through his spiritual jurisdiction over their subjects. The duty of the Roman Pontiff obliges him to instruct all the faithful in their duties, both private and civic. Therefore, if a law of the State is contrary to the law of God, the pope is bound in conscience to instruct the faithful that it cannot be obeyed, and if the conditions of government are such that the citizens are no longer bound by their oath of allegiance, it is the Pope's right to declare that fact to his own subjects for their spiritual guidance, and if all, or a large majority of the citizens be Catholics, this declaration would be equivalent to deposition of the ruler. In this sense only does the Pope, as such, have power to depose civil rulers. The same power is claimed by Protestants, but it operates in a different manner. With them each individual would have recourse to his own private judgment whether he is bound to allegiance or not, and might easily be misled in the matter by passion or interest. In such a case Catholics would have recourse to the judgment of the Roman Pontiff, to give them an authoritative decision, but in either case the results would be the same so far as the government authorities are concerned.

In the Middle Ages the popes seem to have exercised a direct power of deposing kings and emperors, but this was done by virtue of international law or custom, recognized at that time by all as conferring such authority upon the Pope as head and father of Christian nations.

2. The Roman Pontiff Exempt From Civil Authority

The Roman Pontiff is not subject to any power on earth, whether civil or ecclesiastical. This follows of necessity from his position as supreme head of the Church, which is subject to no authority save that of Christ alone. "Being supreme head of the Church, he cannot be judged by any other ecclesiastical power, and as the Church is a spiritual society superior to any temporal power whatever, he cannot be judged by any temporal ruler. Therefore, the supreme head of the Church can direct and judge the rulers of temporal powers, but he can neither be directed nor judged by them without a perversion of due order founded in the very nature of things."[28] This doctrine is taught by the Fathers and incorporated in the canons of the Church: "The first See is judged by no one."[29] A synod of bishops held in Rome in 503, to investigate charges against Pope Symmachus, declared that "God wished the causes of other men to be decided by men, but He reserved to His own tribunal, without question, the ruler of this See."[30]

This complete exemption of the Roman Pontiff from all civil jurisdiction is of divine institution, for Christ himself conferred it upon St. Peter and his successors, at least implicitly, when He entrusted to them the supreme authority, which necessarily implies such exemption. Some also see an explicit exemption from civil authority in the words of Christ concerning the payment of tribute: "What dost thou think, Simon? From whom do the kings of the earth receive

---

[28] Cardinal Bellarmine, "De Romano Pontifice," ii, 26.
[29] "Codex Juris Canonici," can. 1556.
[30] Ennodius of Ticino, "Apologia"; P.L., 63, 200.

tribute or customs; from their own sons, or from others?" And he
said, "From others." Jesus said to him, "The sons then are exempt.
But that we may not give offense to them, . . . give it to them for me
and for thee."[31] Christ here clearly proclaims His exemption from
earthly powers and seems to include St. Peter in the same.

3. Temporal Power Necessary

The claim to temporal power on the part of the Roman Pontiff is
not a pretension to exercise temporal dominion over the nations of
the world, as many non-Catholics falsely believe. It is simply claiming
the right to a territory, large or small, free from the dominion of any
other power, in which the Pope may be free to rule the Church without
let or hindrance. Such power is necessary because of the unique position of the pope as a person exempt from all human authority. In
civil society, as well as in the Church, all persons must be classed as
subjects or rulers, but if the pope were not the ruler of his own territory, he would find himself in the strange position of being neither
subject nor ruler; of being in society without forming any part of it.
Such a position could not be maintained without grave danger to his
freedom in governing the Church. If he were a subject, or even an
honored guest of any temporal ruler, his freedom of communication
with all parts of the Church and with other nations might be seriously
hampered at any time, or even lost entirely in times of war. He would
also be open to the suspicion of being unduly influenced by his host.
Such suspicion would greatly discredit his power and bring harm to
the Church, as happened during the residence of the Popes at Avignon
in France. For this reason the bishops gathered in Rome for the allo-
cution of Pius IX, on June 9, 1862, unanimously declared that "it is
indeed necessary for the Roman Pontiff, as head of the whole Church,
to be subject to no prince, nor even the guest of a prince. He should
have his own dominion and his own kingdom, so that he may protect
and spread the Catholic faith, rule and govern the Christian common-
wealth in noble and peaceful freedom."[32]

Our Lord conferred no temporal kingdom upon St. Peter; consequently, we cannot say that temporal power is a matter of divine
institution; but it is conditionally of divine right, for, since the pope is
exempt from all temporal power by divine right, whatever is necessary
to protect and preserve this immunity is also of divine right, but only on

---

[31] Matt. xvii, 24-26.
[32] Quoted from Dorsch, "De Ecclesia Christi," p. 467; cf. Leo XIII, "Inscrutabili,"
April 21, 1878.

condition that other suitable means cannot be found to serve the same purpose. Temporal power seems to be the only possible means to secure the necessary freedom and independence of the pope in the government of the Church; but whether this power should be restricted to a small territory, as at present, or extended to a larger dominion, as formerly, must be judged from circumstances. Either condition presents many advantages over the other, and both also have disadvantages.

Exemption from civil authority is a matter of divine right for the Roman Pontiff, but its actual enjoyment is not absolutely necessary for the existence or mission of the Church, and, as a matter of fact, was not always enjoyed by the popes. St. Peter and his successors for the first three centuries were exempt from civil authority, but could not enjoy the privilege while paganism ruled the world and persecution raged on every side. At the beginning of the fourth century, when paganism was practically overthrown, divine Providence so ordered affairs that the chief pastors of the Church began to reap the benefits of their privilege by means of civil exemption and power conferred upon them. This was really the beginning of temporal power, which steadily increased, until it was explicitly and solemnly recognized by Charlemagne in the ninth century.[33] From that time it continued with varying fortunes, until the capture of Rome by Garibaldi, in 1870, when nothing but the Vatican and the territory immediately surrounding it was left to the Popes.

On June 8, 1929, a Concordat (treaty) was ratified between the Holy See and the Italian Government. This assured the Holy Father of complete liberty and independence in the spiritual government of the diocese of Rome and of the Catholic Church throughout the world. It also recognized *de jure* and *de facto* international sovereignty of the Holy See with absolute jurisdiction over the State called the City of the Vatican. It also recognized complete ownership by the Holy Father of several properties, mostly churches in and around the city of Rome.

So long as this arrangement is not disturbed by some hostile force the situation of the Pope in regard to temporal power will be secure. He now has complete freedom to rule the Church without the cares and responsibilities of governing a nation as in the times prior to 1870. It was to attain this situation that when the Concordat was being drawn up Pope Pius XI requested that the Vatican City be limited to its present size,—an area of about 108 acres.[34]

---

[33] Cf. De Maistre, "Du Pape," Vol. I, Ch. 7; T. W. Allies, "The See of Peter and the Wandering of the Nations."

[34] Cf. Acta Apostolicae Sedis, Vol. xxi, p. 209 sq. Catholic Encyclopedia Dictionary edited by Donald Attwater: Art. Vatican, City of.

INDEX

Aaron, priesthood of, 35
Abercius, inscription of, 211
Abiron, punishment for schism, 155
Abram, name changed to Abraham, 174
Adam, head of the human race, 114
  mystical body of, 114
  Christ, the second, 114
Adults, conditions for membership in the Church, 126
Africa, growth of Church in, 92
  number of Protestants in, 92
African, bishops write to Pope Celestine, 219
Agatho, synodal letter of, 276
Alexander, excommunicated by St. Paul, 142
Alexandrians, synagogue of, 5
Allies, T. W., Mystical Body of Christ, 115
Ambrose, papal Infallibility, 280
  Peter's primacy, 176
  unicity of Church, 20
Ambrosiaster, Peter's primacy, 193
Anabaptists, holiness of Church, 59
Anacletus, Pope succeeded Linus, 210
Ananias, punishment of, 142
Andronicus, mentioned as apostle, 164
Androutsos, Chrestos; on infallibility of Church, 249
Angel, meaning of word, 163
Anglican Church, established by Parliament, 102
  lack of authority, 100
  lack of unity of doctrine, 99
  lack of succession, 102
  parties in, 99
Anglicans, and apostolicity, 79
  the Branch Theory, 180
  Church and State, 294
  the Continuity Theory, 101
  Infallibility, 262
  reject Catholic doctrines, 102
  reject five Sacraments, 102
  reject works of supererogation, 59
Anicetus, Pope, and Easter question, 211
Anselm, St., see of, 100
Antichrist and end of world, 75 sq., 231
  false Miracles of, 65
Antioch, patriarch of, 217, 234
  schism in, 204
Apiarius appeals to Rome, 219
Apostle, meaning of term, 163
  term in Old Testament, 163
  term in New Testament, 163
  term in St. Paul, 163

Apostles, authority to teach, 10
  commissioned by Christ, 10 sq.
  confirmed in Grace, 166
  constitute Bishops, 154
  gift of miracles, 167
  infallible, 165
  jurisdiction of, 166
  light of world, 177
  ministers of Christ, 155
  obedience to, 10
  personally chosen by Christ, 163
  powers to govern, 10
  power to sanctify, 10
  prerogatives of, 165
  receive sole authority, 153
  subject to St. Peter, 193 sq.
  succeeded by bishops, 157
  witnesses for Christ, 164
Apostles' Creed, 44, 68
Apostolic See, 79, 232, 281
Apostolicity, of Church, 29, 77 sq.
  of doctrine, 78, 80
  errors regarding, 79 sq.
  as Mark of Church, 88
  of ministry, 77 sq., 80
  nature of, 77
  of origin, 77, 80
  lacking in Orthodox Eastern Church, 103
  lacking in Protestantism, 99
  of succession, 77, 80
  of succession in Catholic Church, 94
Appointment of bishops, 233
Appolinaris condemned, 204
Approbation for preaching, 246
Arcadius, papal legate, 203
Archbishop, 234
Arian heresy, 76, 95, 268
Arimini, Council of, 267
Arnold, Thomas, on power of binding and loosing, 184
Articles of Anglican Church revised, 102.
Ascanius of Tarragona on infallibility, 279
Athanasius, St., appeals to Rome, 207
  on Arian heresy, 95
  on Catholicity of Church, 72
  on infallibility, 254, 263
  on visibility of Church, 41
Attributes of Church, 29 sq.
Augsburg Confession on visibility, 38
Augustine, St., on Catholicity, 68, 70, 71, 72, 75
  St. Cyprian, 224

extent of Church, 4
indefectibility, 34
infallibility, 254, 255, 264, 267, 280
membership in Church, 119, 124, 129, 135
ministerial powers, 148
Pelagius and Celestius, 284
synagogue and church, 5, 17, 35
soul of church, 117
temporal punishment, 144
visibility, 41
Augustine, Charles, Confirmation of Councils, 239
Aurelian, Emperor and Roman Primacy, 208
Aurelius of Carthage to Pope Zosimus, 240
Authority of Church, 140 sq.
Apostles alone receive, 153
formal cause of Church, 107
governing, 10, 153 sq.
lack of in Anglican Church, 100
subjection to necessary, 126
Avignon, Popes at, 312

Baptism, concorporation with Christ, 58
door to Church, 28, 137
by heretics, 222
necessity of means, 135
priesthood of laity, 155
rite of initiation, 11, 125, 135
Sacrament of, 56
Baptized, the invalidly, 132
Barlow, Consecrates Parker, 102
Barnabas, an Apostle, 164 sq.
Barry, Charles, on lack of authority in Anglican Church, 100
Basil, the Great, appeals to Rome, 205
Battifol, P., the Twelve, 170
Becket, Thomas a, see of, 100
Beckwith, C. A., on nature of Church, 7
Bellarmine, Card., Catholicity of Church, 73
doubtful Pope, 229
infallibility, 273
membership in Church, 132, 133
properties of the Church, 45
salvation out of Church, 137
Benedict XII, Beatific Vision, 287
Benedict XIV, Canonizing of Saints, 292
membership in Church, 127
Billot, Card., occult heretics and schismatics, 133
Billuart, C. R., occult heretics and schismatics, 133
"Binding and loosing," meaning of terms, 182 sq.
power of, 182
symbol of primacy, 184
Bishop, meaning and use of term, 161 sq.
Bishop of bishops, 207, 224

Bishops, appointment of, 233
appointed by Elizabeth, 102
Constituted by Apostles, 154
Custodians of Faith, 268
infallibility of, 266 sq.
jurisdiction of, 233
lists of, 163
removed by Elizabeth, 102
schismatic, 234
successors of Apostles, 157 sq., 231 sq.
teachers, 260 sq.
not mere vicars of Pope, 234
Body, Mystical, of Adam, 114
of Christ, 19, 20
Boniface, St. Consults Pope Zacharias, 283, 286
Boniface VIII, Church and State, 299, 309
membership in Church, 135
temporal punishments, 144
Books, censorship of, 245
imprimatur for, 246
prohibition of, 245
Bozius, Oratorian, Properties of Church, 45
Branch Theory, 39, 47, 100
Bride of Christ, 61
Broad Church, 100
Buddeus, J. F., Visibility of Church, 38
Bullinger, H., Marks of Church, 84
Burger, Rulers of Church, 152

Called, the, 4
Callistus, Pope, 207
Calvin, John, Marks of Church, 83
membership in Church, 121
Michael Servetus (note), 144
rulers of Church, 151
visibility, 38
Canon Law on temporal punishment, 143
Canonizing of Saints, 292
Canons, Cathedral, 162
Cardinals, 228, 234
Carthage, synods of, 222 sq.
Catechumens, not members of Church, 127
Catherine of Siena, 98
Catholic, distinctives term, 67
meaning of, 68
Roman, meaning of, 94
Catholic Church, apostolicity of, 94
Catholicity of, 93
Causative sanctity, 92
Civilizing influence of, 92
eminent sanctity in, 91
fecundity of, 91
manifestative sanctity of, 90
unity of faith in, 89
unity of government in, 90
unity of worship in, 90

Catholic doctrine on Church and State, 296
Catholicity, absolute, 73
  de facto, 69
  de jure, 69
  diffusion, 69
  formal, 70
  lacking in Orthodox Churches, 103
  lacking in Protestantism, 99
  mark of true Church, 86 sq.
  mark of Messianic Kingdom, 70
  moral, 72
  perfect, 74 sq.
  perpetual, 73
  physical, 72
  simultaneous, 72
  successive, 72
  in Catholic Church, 93
Catholics, Number of in Africa, 92
  number of in China, 92
  in world, 94
Cause of Church, efficient, 107
  final, 21, 107
  formal, 107
  material, 107, 120
Cause of Mystical Body, formal, 107
  material, 107, 120
Celestine I, Condemns Nestorius, 202
  hailed as voice of Peter, 278
  orders Apiarius reinstated, 219
Celestine V resigns, 228
Celestius appeals to Rome, 283 sq.
Censorship of Books, 245
Ceremonies of Old Law, 16
Ceylon, growth of Church in, 92
Chalcedon, Council of, Primacy of Rome, 201 sq., 217
  infallibility, 264, 277
Channels of Grace, 113
Chapman, Dom, Primacy of Rome, 214
Chapter, Cathedral, 162
Chapters, the Three, 284
Character, baptismal, 129
Charismata, 160
Charlemagne, Confirms temporal power of pope, 313
Chiliasm, 31
China, growth of Church in, 92
Christ, the second Adam, 114
  mystical Body of, 109 sq.
  second coming of, 14
  Confers power on Apostles, 10, 146 sq.
  Contrasted with Moses, 12
  founds Church, 9 sq.
  founds but one Church, 18
  the Foundation, 177
  frequents Temple, 16
  fullness of, 113
  Head of Church, 44
  Light of world, 177
  Personal reign of, 31

  powers of, 146
  the Rock, 177
  the Vine, 58
  visible, 44
Christianity and Church, 23
Chrysostom, St. John, indefectibility, 34
  Primacy of Rome, 192
  visibility, 41
Church, derivation and uses of term, 3
  apostolicity of, 29, 77 sq.
  attributes of, 29
  authority of, 140 sq., 243
  Body of Christ, 19, 108 sq.
  Catholicity of, 13, 29, 67 sq., 74
  and Christianity, 23
  door to, 28, 137
Church, errors regarding nature of, 7
  eschatological kingdom, 8, 14
  a fortress, 176
  Head of, 44, 110 sq.
  of Holy Spirit, 35
  indefectibility of, 29, 31
  institution of, 9 sq.
  Joannine, 31
  and the Jews, 75
  and the Kingdom, 25, 27 sq.
  magisterium of, 243
  marks of, 82 sq.
  members of, 121 sq., 127 sq.
  membership in, 119, 121 sq., 125, 136
  militant, 3
  miracles in, 62
  object of faith, 44
  of Old Law, 4
  parables of, 42
  Pauline, 31
  period of preparation, 76
  perpetuity of, 29
  persecuted, 13
  Petrine, 31
  pillar and ground of truth, 255
  powers of, 130, 146 sq.
  purpose of, 21, 107
Church and prosperity, 96
  rights of, 305
  rulers of, 151 sq.
  salvation out of, 119, 136 sq.
  sanctity of, 29, 56 sq.
  a society, 9 sq., 22 sq.
  soul of, 115 sq.
  spouse of Christ, 19
  Subjects of, 129
  suffering, 3
  symbols of, 11, 41
  and State, 293 sq.
  and Synagogue, 4, 12, 13, 17, 34
  triumphant, 3
  unicity of, 18 sq.
  unity of, 29, 45
  unity of doctrine in, 52
  unity of government in, 47

unity of worship in, 54
visibility of, 29, 36, 39 sq.
Church of England. See Anglican Church
Churches, Protestant, See Protestantism
Citra, Council of, Membership in Church, 136
Clement of Rome, succeeds Anacletus, 210
   bishops and deacons, 161
   Roman Primacy, 213
Clement of Alexandria, holiness of Church, 58
   unicity of Church, 20
Clement VI, Rome and Papacy, 230
Clement VII (Robert of Geneva), 95
Clement XII, membership in Church, 122
Commission to Apostles, 9 sq.
Comprehensiveness, glorious, 100
Comte, A., Church and State, 296
Conciliar Theory, 239
Conclusions, theological, 289
Concordats, 301
Confirmation of Councils, 238
Conscience, freedom of, 54
Constance, Council of, elects Pope, 229
   temporal punishment, 143
Constantinople, First Council, Roman Primacy, 217
   Second Council of, and Honorius I, 283, 285
   Third Council, infallibility, 276
   Fourth Council of, infallibility, 276
Constantius exiles Liberius, 283
Continuity theory, 101
Convocation of Councils, 236
Coquille Guy, Gallicanism, 294
Core, punished for schism, 155
Corea, growth of Church in, 92
Cornelius Pope, election of, 228
Cornelius a Lapide, occult heretics, 133
Councils, Celebration of, 237
   Confirmation of, 237 sq.
   Convocation of, 236 sq.
Councils, ecumenical, 236
   infallibility of, 260
   kinds of, 236
   nature of, 235
   presidency of, 238
   utility of, 241 sq.
Counsels, evangelical, 59, 98, 289
Coverdale, at consecration of Parker, 102
Creed, Augsburg, 38
   Apostles', 44
   Dositheus, 103
   Mogbila, 103
   Nicene, 45
Crete, Titus in, 154, 156

Custodians of faith, 268
Cyprian, St., Apostolicity, 81
   Controversy with St. Stephen, 222
   election of Cornelius, 228
   institution of Church, 11
   membership in Church, 136
   Primacy of Rome, 193, 195, 208, 221
   unicity of Church, 20
   unity of Church, 49, 53
Cyrenians, synagogue of, 5
Cyril of Alexandria, St., Papal delegate. 202
   Creed of Ephesus, 265
   soul of Church, 116
Cyril of Jerusalem, St., Catholic Church, 68
   Catholicity, 71
   infallibility, 254

D'Ailly, Peter, Supremacy of Councils, 240.
Damasus, Pope, annulled decrees of Arimini, 239
   condemned Eustateus and Appolinaris, 204
   confirmed election of Nectarius, 204
   deposed Maxinius, the Cynic, 204
   Roman Primacy, 198
Daniel, prophet, abrogation of Old Law, 35
   universality of kingdom, 69, 71
Dathan, punished for schism, 155
Deacons, Order of, 160
Declaration of French Clergy, 294
Defensor Pacis, 151, 293
DeMaistre, Protestant lack of unity, 97
Deposing power of Pope, 310 sq.
DeSan, Catholicity of Church, 87
Devotions of B. V. Mary, effects of, 92
Didache, bishops and deacons, 161
   unicity of church, 20
Diffusion of Catholic Church, 69, 93
Dignities, ecclesiastical, 234
Diocese, ruler of, 235
Dionysius of Alexandria, Roman Primacy, 207
Dioscorus of Alexandria,
   presided at Robber Council, 201
   deposed at Chalcedon, 201
Divorce, effects of, 98
Doctors, order in early church, 159
Doctrine, apostolicity of, 77, 80
   unity of, 46
Doctrines, fundamental, 47, 50
Dominicum, 5
Donatists, and holiness of Church, 59
Dorsch, Aemil, membership in Church, 132, 133
Dotes, of Church, 29
Duchesne, L., Roman Primacy, 213

Easter Question, 211
Eastern Church and Primacy of Peter, 192
Ecclesia, origin and meaning of word, 3 sq.
Education, rights of Church and State, 303.
Edwardine ritual reformed, 102
Election of Pope, 228
Eligibility to Papacy, 227
Elizabeth declared head of Church, 101
    makes and unmakes bishops, 102
Elymas healed by St. Paul, 63
Emperors convene and preside over Councils, 241
Eneas healed by St. Peter, 63
England, Church of,
    See Anglican Church
Epaphroditus called apostle, 163
Ephesus, Council of, condemned Nestorius, 203
    and infallibility, 265, 278
    and Roman Primacy, 203
Ephrem Syrus, St., Primacy of Peter, 174, 176, 192
Episcopate of divine origin, 231
    and Roman Primacy, 225
Episcopus, origin, and meaning of term, 161
    dispute regarding use of, 161 sq.
Eucharist, source of unity, 58
Eugene IV on baptism, 125
Eusebius gives lists of bishops, 163
Eustatius appeals to Rome, 204, 205
Eutyches appeals to Rome, 201
Evangelists, order in early church, 159
Excommunicates, 130
    subjects of church, 132
Excommunication, nature and kinds of, 130 sq.
    power of in church, 130
Eybel on power of pope, 226
Ezechiel, prophet, holiness of church, 60

Facts, dogmatic, 290
Faith, necessity of internal, 50
    objective, 50
    profession, 53, 125
    subjective, 50
    unity of, 50, 89
Febronius, Church and State, 294
    Councils, 240
    powers of Pope, 226
    rulers of Church, 152
Fecundity of Catholic Church, 91
Felicissimus of Carthage, 208
Fichte, threefold Church, 31
Finlay, Peter, Branch Theory, 100
    lack of authority in, Anglican Church, 100

Firmilian, Controversy with St. Stephen, 222
Florence, Council of, infallibility, 276
    ministerial powers, 149
    Roman Primacy, 230
Fortunatus of Carthage, 208
Franzelin, Card., membership in Church, 133
Freedom of Conscience, 54
    of worship, 54
Freeman, E. A., Continuity theory, 101
Fulgentius, infallibility, 279
Fullness of Christ, 113
Fundamental Doctrines, 47, 50
Fundamentalists, 31

Galileo condemned as heretic, 287
Gallican Liberties, 294
Gallicanism, 294
Gallicans, ecumenical Councils, 240
    infallibility, 272
Garizim, Mount, 43
Garibaldi seizes papal states, 313
"Gates of hell," meaning of, 33
Gelasius I, Confirmation of Councils, 239
    Roman Primacy, 240
Genuineness of relics, determined, 292
Gerson, supremacy of Councils, 240
Glossolalia, 167
Gog and Magog persecute Church, 76
Gore, Anglican Bishop, apostolicity, 79
    primacy of Peter, 173
Government, authority of, 10
    monarchical in Church, 162
    threefold powers of, 140
    unity of, 47 sq.
    unity of in Catholic Church, 90
    unity of lacking in Orthodox Churches, 103
    unity of lacking in Protestantism, 97
Grace, Channels of, 113
    Condition for membership in Church, 122
Greek liturgy. See "Liturgy"
Gregory Great, St., extent of Church, 3
    infallibility, 263
    necessity of miracles, 67
    reproves John the Faster, 220 sq.
Gregory Nanzianzen, St., infallibility, 264, 282
    soul of Church, 116
    unity of government, 50
Gregory XI, Pope, 95

Harnack, A., kingdom of God, 27
    nature of Church, 8
Hart, R. L., fundamentalism, 31
Head, preëminence of, 111
    vivifying influence of, 111
    union with body, 112

of Church, 110 sq.
of human race, 114
Hegel, nature of State, 296
Hegesippus, gives list of bishops, 163
Henderson, E., meaning of "keys," 180
Heresy, Iconoclast, 281
  Monothelite, 283
  Nestorian, 285
  repression of, 245
Heretic, definition of, 128
  formal, 128
  manifest, 128
  material, 128
  occult, 128
Heretics, baptism by, 222
  membership in Church, 121 sq.
  subjects of Church, 129
High Church party, 99
Hilary, Pope appealed to by Ascanius, 279
Hillel, 183
Hodgkins assists at consecration of Parker, 102
Holiness, see "sanctity"
Holy Spirit, soul of Church, 115 sq.
  united with Church, 118
Homer, "shepherds of the people," 190
Hontheim, Nicholas von, see "Febronius"
Honor, primacy of, 172
Honorius I condemned as heretic, 283, 285
Hormisdas, Pope, infallibility, 263, 283, 284
Huss, John, membership in Church, 121
Hypostasis, 280

Ibas of Odessa, 284
Iconoclast heresy, 281
Ignatius Martyr, St., bishops succeed apostles, 158
  Catholic Church, 67
  deacons, 160
  membership in Church, 136
  monarchical government, 162
  unity of government, 49
Impeccability of Apostles, 166
Imprimatur for books, 246
Indefectibility, 29
India, growth of Church in, 92
Indifferentism, 76
Inerrancy, 247
Infallibility of Apostles, 165
  of bishops, 266 sq.
  of Church, 247 sq.
  of Councils, 260 sq.
  degrees of, 248
Infallibility, extent of, 288 sq.
  opponents of, 249
  and private judgment, 257
  of Synagogue, 256

Infallibility of Pope, 270 sq
  Conditions for, 270 sq.
  objections to, 283 sq.
  personal privilege, 272
  proofs for, 273 sq.
  source of, 272
Infants, Condition for membership in Church, 127
Iniquity, Mystery of, 76
Initiation, Condition for Membership in Church, 125
  rite of, 11, 125, 135
Innocent II, salvation of unbaptized, 132
Innocent III, Christ the Foundation, 179
Inspiration, 247
Institution of Church, 9 sq.
Irenaeus, St., Apostolicity of succession, 81
  bishops successors of Apostles, 159
  infallibility, 253
  power of miracles in Church, 64
  Primacy of Rome, 209
  unity of faith, 52
  unity of government, 49
  letter to Pope Victor, 211
Isaias, prophet, Catholicity of kingdom, 71
Islamism, foe of Church, 76
Israel, figure of Church, 4

James of Sarug, St., Primacy of Peter, 175
Jandun, Jean de, Church and State, 293
  rulers of Church, 151
Jansenists, infallibility, 262
Januarius, St., miracle of blood, 91
Jeremias, prophet, foretells New Covenant, 35
Jerome, St., abuse at Rome, 220
  Arian heresy, 95
  and Pope Damasus, 204
  indefectibility, 34
  infallibility, 280
  priesthood of laity, 155
  primacy of Rome, 204
Jerusalem, Council of, 141
  destruction foretold, 14 sq.
  and Papacy, 231
  patriarchate of, 234
  prophecies concerning, 231
Jews, enter Church, 75
  expect kingdom of God, 26
  persecute Church, 13
  religion of tolerated at Rome, 14
John, St., bishops successors of Apostles, 158
  membership in Church, 124
  monarchical government, 162
John the Faster, universal bishop, 220
John of Jerusalem, infallibility, 281
John II, infallibility, 283, 285

John XXII, Beatific Vision, 286
  and Louis of Bavaria, 151
Joseph II of Austria, 294
Josephism, 294
Judaizers, 191
Judicial powers of Church, 142 sq.
Julius I, Roman Primacy, 206
Jurieu, unity of doctrine, 47
Jurisdiction, of Apostles, 166
  of bishops, 233
  over heretics and schismatics, 129
  primacy of, 78, 172
  principal power, 149
  succession of, 78

Kepha, Aramaic for Peter, 176 sq.
Key-bearer, 179 sq.
Key of knowledge, 182
Keys, significance of, 180
Kingdom, eschatological, 14, 28
  of God, and the Church, 25 sq.
Kitchen of Landaff, 101
Knabenbauer, "binding and loosing," 184
  symbolism of keys, 181
Kyriakon, 5
Kyriakos, infallibility, 249

Lacordaire, Miracles, 67
  unity of Church, 90
Lambeth, Conference of, 100
Lamentabile, decree, Condemns errors
  of Modernism, 9
Lanciani, Rudolpho, St. Peter in Rome,
  199
Lateran, Council of, Corporal punish-
  ment, 143
  membership in Church, 134
Lecky, W. E. H., Devotion to B. V.
  Mary, 92
Leibnitz, confession, 93
Leo the Great, Council of Chalcedon,
  201 sq.
  infallibility, 279
  primacy of Peter, 193
  Robber Council, 201, 239
Leo II Condemns Honorius I, 283, 285,
  286
Leo XIII, Church and State, 298, 301,
  302, 304
  Confirmation of Councils, 239
  episcopate, 232
  nature of Church, 23
  perpetuity, 32
  soul of Church, 115
Lexorandi, 291
Liberalism, 295
Liberius, Pope, Roman Primacy, 205
  infallibility, 283
Liberties, Gallican, 294
Libertines, synagogue of, 5
Lightfoot, J. B. Ignatius, letter to Romans, 212 sq.

papal domination, 195
Linus, Pope, succeeds St. Peter, 210
Liturgy, Greek, primacy of Peter, 175,
  176, 192
  infallibility, 282
Liturgy, Syriac, primacy of Peter, 176,
  192
  Syro-chaldaic, primacy of Peter, 176,
  192
Louis of Bavaria and John XXII, 151
Louis XIV, and Gallicanism, 294
Loisy, a, nature of Church, 8
Loosing and binding, power of, 182 sq.
Lourdes, miracles at, 91
Low Church party, 100
Lowrie, Walter, inscription of Abercuis,
  211 sq.
Lucentius, papal legate, 202
Luther, membership in Church, 121
  rulers of church, 151
  visibility, 37
Lydda, miracles at, 63
Lyons, Council of, infallibility, 275
  temporal punishment, 143

Macaulay, lack of unity in Anglican
  Church, 100
Magisterium of Church, 244
Malachias, prophet, Catholicity of king-
  dom, 71
Manning, Cardinal, Soul of Church, 116
  union of Church and Holy Spirit, 119
Marcellus, exiled, 206
Macian of Arles deposed, 208
Maris of Persia, 284
Marks of Church, 82 sq.
  apostolicity as Mark, 88
  Catholicity as Mark, 86
  Claimed by Orthodox, 83
  Claimed by Protestants, 83
  lacking in Anglican Church, 99
  lacking in Orthodox Churches, 103
  lacking in Protestant Churches, 97 sq.
  persecution as a Mark, 88
  requisites for, 82 sq.
  sanctity as a Mark, 85
  unity as a Mark, 85
Marriage, rights of Church and state re-
  garding, 303
  sanctity of, 92
Marsiluis of Padua, Church and State,
  293
  Councils, 240
  Rulers of Church, 151
Martin V elected, 95, 240
Mary, reestablishes Catholic religion in
  England, 101
Mason, A. J., "binding and loosing," 184
  symbolism of keys, 181
Matthias elected, 156
Mauretania, Cyprian to Bishops of, 222

Maximus, Confessor, infallibility, 281
Maximus, the Cynic deposed, 204
Melanchthon, visibility, 38
Melitene, synod of deposes Eustatius, 205
Melitus of Antioch, 204
Members of Church, 121 sq., 129, 132
Membership in the Church, Conditions of, 125 sq.
   errors regarding, 121
   necessity for, 134
Methodists, divisions of, 98
Metropolitans, 235
Middleton, C., power of miracles in Church, 62, 64
Middleton, Edmund, primacy of Peter, 195
Mileve, Council of, Roman Primacy, 219
Ministry, Apostolic, 9, 22
   apostolicity, 78, 80
Miracles, false, 65
   gift of, 167
   of St. Januarius Blood, 91
   at Lourdes, 91
   power of in Church, 61
Modernist, Church and State, 295
   indefectibility, 30
   infallibility, 262
   nature of church, 8
Moffat, James, "shepherd My sheep," 190
Moghila, Creed of, 103
Monothelite heresy, 283
Moses contrasted with Christ, 12
Muratorian Fragment, Catholic Church, 68
Mystical Body of Christ, 19, 20, 57, 61, 109 sq., 113, 137 sq.
Mystery of iniquity, 76

Necessity of means, 134
   of precept, 134
Nectarius, election of Confirmed, 204
Need of the divine, 8
Nero, decree against Christians, 14
Nestorian heresy, 285
Nestorius, condemned, 203
Nicene Council, 6th canon of, 218
   monarchical government, 163
   Roman Primacy, 218 sq.
   unicity of Church, 18
Nicholas I, privileges of Roman See, 230
Novatians, and holiness of Church, 59
Numidia, Cyprian to bishops of, 222

Oath of royal supremacy, 101
Old Law, abrogation foretold, 35
   ceremonies of, 16
   relation to Church, 17
   stages of, 17
Operations in Christ, 285

Optatus of Mileve, St., Catholicity, 71
   succession, 103
Order, primacy of, 172
Orders, powers of, 149
   succession of, 78, 155 sq.
   in Orthodox Churches, 103 sq.
Orders, approval of religious, 291 sq.
Origen, Membership in Church, 136
   primacy of Peter, 192
Origin, Apostolicity of, 79 sq.
Orthodox, number of, 94
   succession of Orders, 104

Palmer, Wm., unity of government, 47
   visibility, 39
Palmieri, Dominico, Membership in Church, 132, 133
Papacy and Jerusalem, 231
   and Rome, 229 sq.
Papal legates at Ephesus, 203
   at Chalcedon, 201
Parables of the Church, 41 sq.
Parker, Consecrated, 102
   source of succession in Anglican Church, 102
Parliament establishes Church of England, 102
   rejects authority of Rome, 101
Parousia, 77 (note)
Parochialism, 235
Paschal, Pope, appealed to from East, 281
Paschasinus, papal legate, 201
Pastors, vicars of bishop, 235
Patriarchs, 235
Paul, St., an Apostle, 165
   Censures books, 246
   Compares Church with Synagogue, 14
   indefectibility, 33
   infallibility, 165, 253, 255
   inflicts temporal punishment, 145
   intimates Monarchical government, 163
   membership in Church, 123
   Mystical Body of Christ, 109 sq.
   power of miracles, 62
   profession of faith, 54
   rebukes St. Peter, 191
   sanctity of Church, 58
   successors of Apostles, 158
   unity of doctrine, 52
Paul of Samosata deposed, 208
Paulinus of Antioch, 204
Pedagogus, the Synagogue a, 35
Pelagius appeals to Rome, 283, 284
Pelagians and holiness of Church, 59
Percival, H. R., 6th Canon of Nicaea, 218
   28 Canon of Chalcedon, 217
   failure of Protestantism, 99
Perfect society, Conditions for, 23 sq.

Perpetuity of Church, Nature of, 29
Persecution as Mark of Church, 88
Peter, significance of name, 175 sq.
Peter, St., Chief pastor, 188
  confirmer of brethren, 185 sq.
  foundation of Church, 173
  head of "The Twelve," 170 sq.
  key-bearer, 179 sq.
  more than Apostle, 195
  powers, how limited, 185
  primacy of, 169 sq.
  rebuked by St. Paul, 191
  in Rome, 198 sq.
  successors, 198 sq.
Peter, St., holiness of Church, 60
  priesthood of laity, 155
  presbyters, 161
  visibility of Church, 44
Philip the deacon, 160
Philip, papal legate, 203, 278
Pithou, Pierre, Gallicanism, 294
Pius VI, rulers of the Church, 153
  temporal punishment, 143
Pius IX, membership in Church, 135
  salvation out of Church, 136
  temporal punishment, 143
  unity of government, 48
Pius X, Modernism, 295
Polycarp, and Easter question, 211
Polycrates, and Easter question, 211
Pontian, Pope, resigns, 228
Pontifex, Maximus, 207
Pontiff, Roman, See Pope
Pope, and Councils, 237
  deposing power, 310 sq.
  doubtful, 229
  election of, 228
  exempt from Civil power, 311
  infallibility, 270 sq.
  Primacy of, 198 sq.
  powers of, 225 sq.
  and secular rulers, 309 sq.
Pope, successor of St. Peter, 198 sq.
  supreme teacher, 244
  temporal power of, 312
Popes at Avignon, 312
Power, Coërcive, 142
  of government, 141
  judicial, 142
  legislative, 141
  ministerial, 148
  of Orders, 148 sq.
  principal, 149
  of sanctification, 10
Powers, of Christ, 146
  of Church, 146 sq.
  conferred on Apostles, 9 sq., 146
  of jurisdiction, 155 sq.
  of Orders, 155 sq.
  of Peter, 185
  of pope, 185, 225

Preaching, approbation for, 246
Predestination, 121 note
  as condition for Membership, 121
Preëminence of St. Peter, 169
Prerogatives of Apostles, 165
Presbyter, meaning of word, 161
  dispute regarding use of, 162
Presbyterium, 162
Presidency of Councils, 238
Priests, See Presbyter
Priesthood of laity, 155
Primacy, meaning of term and kinds of, 172
Primacy of Peter, 169 sq.
  Conferred, 188 sq.
  permanent institution, 195
  promised, 173
  proof from tradition, 191
Primacy of Pope, divine origin, 210
  eligibility to, 227
  and episcopate, 225 sq.
  loss of, 228 sq.
  objections to, 215 sq.
  powers of, how limited, 185
  proofs for, 200 sq.
Primates, 234
Profession of faith, Necessity of, 125
  unity of, 53
Projectus, papal legate, 203
Prokopovitch, deuterocanonical books, 103
Properties of the Church, 29, 45
Prophets, order in early Church, 159
Prosperity and the Church, 96
Protestant Episcopal Church, 99
Protestantism, lacks marks of true Church, 97
  moral failure, 99
Protestants, apostolicity, 99
  catholicity, 99
  indefectibility, 30
  infallibility, 249, 262
  kingdom of God, 27
  nature of Church, 7
  number of, 92, 94
  power of Miracles, 62
  rulers of Church, 151
  unicity, 18
  unity, 46
  visibility, 37
Pseudo-Ambrose, indefectibility, 34
Punishment, kinds of, 143
  right of Church to inflict, 143 sq.
Purpose of Church, 21, 107
Pusey, E. B., unity of government, 47

Rationalists, indefectibility, 30
Redemption, 21
Reformers, Church and State, 293
  temporal punishment, 144 note
Reinhard, visibility, 38

Relics, genuineness determined, 292
Resignation of Roman Pontiff, 228
Revelation, 247
Rights of Church and State, 303 sq.
of State against Church, 303, 306
Rimini, Council of, 95
Ritual, Edwardine, 101, 102
Rivington, Luke, Cyprians Controversy, 224
Rulers of Church, 151 sq.
secular, how subject to Church, 309 sq.
Ruling body in Church, 152
Robber Council annulled, 201
Robert of Geneva (Clement VII), 95
Rock, faith of Peter, 179
Peter the Rock, 173 sq.
symbol of jurisdiction, 175
Rome, destruction of foretold, 231
and Papacy, how Connected, 229 sq.
patriarchate of, 217, 218, 234
persecuted Christians, 14
tolerated Jewish religion, 14
Roman Catholic, meaning of, 94
Roman Pontiff, See Pope

Sabatier, formation of Church, 8
Sacraments, Channels of grace, 113
Saints, Canonizing of, 292
Salmon, G., infallibility, 257
Salvation out of Church, 119, 137
Sanctification, power of, 10
Sanctity, nature and kinds of, 56
Sanctity of Church, Causative, 58
eminent, 61
manifestative, 61
Sanctity of Church, Mark of, 85
moral, or personal, 59
ontological, 57
physical, 56
Sanctity in Catholic Church, 90
lack of in Protestant Churches, 98
Saphira, punishment of, 142
Sarai, name changed to Sara, 174
Sardica, Council of, Roman Primacy, 205
Satyr, brother of St. Ambrose, 280
Schelling, threefold Church, 31
Schism, sin of, 49
Western, 94, 239
Schismatic, definition and kinds of, 128
Schismatics, membership in Church, 128, 133
subjects of Church, 129
Schismatic Churches of East, not Catholic, 103
no legitimate succession, 103 sq.
no unity, 103
valid orders, 103 sq.
Scorey, assisted consecration of Parker, 102

See, Apostolic, 79, 232, 281
Seleucia, Council of, 95, 268
Semeria, Church and Synagogue, 18
Sergius of Constantinople, 285
Shepherd, symbol of ruler, 189
Siefert, F., Peter the Rock, 174
Sin, original, 114
Smith, E. W., lack of unity in Protestantism, 97
Social nature of kingdom, 27 sq.
Society, nature of, 6
formal element of, 6
material element of, 6
perfect, 23
Sonnenfels, Church and State, 295
Soul of Church, 115 sq.
membership in, 137
Sozomen, infallibility, 282
Liberius, 283 sq.
Spouse of Christ, 19, 58
Stahl, powers of the Church, 150
State and Church, 293 sq.
duties toward Church, 304
and education, 303
and marriage, 303
rights of, 303
subordinate to Church, 298
Stead, T. W., lack of Saints in Protestantism, 98
Stephen, St., Controversy with St. Cyprian, 222
Stowe, Chas. E., lack of unity in Protestantism, 98
Straub, Convocation of Councils, 238
Catholicity as mark, 87
infallibility, 273
membership in Church, 132, 133
Strauss, D. F., nature of Church, 8
Suarez, infallibility, 273
membership in Church, 133
Subjects of Church, 129, 145
Successors of Apostles, 154, 231
Successors of St. Peter, 198 sq.
Succession, apostolic, 77, 78, 79, 80, 231
formal, 77
of jurisdiction, 78, 155
material, 77
of Orders, 78, 155
none in Anglican Church, 102
in Catholic Church, 94
none in Orthodox Churches, 104
none in Protestant Churches, 99
Supererogation, works of, 59, 98
Supremacy, oath of, 101
Sylvester, Pope, 282
Symbols of Church, 11, 41
Synagogue, abrogation of, 35
compared with Church, 12 sq., 43
infallibility of, 256
meaning of term, 5
a preparation for Gospel, 13

Syriac Liturgy, see Liturgy
Syro-Chaldaic Liturgy, see Liturgy

Talmud, "binding and loosing," 183
Tanquerey, abrogation of Old Law, 17
  infallibility, 291
Teaching authority, 10, 243
  extent of, 244
  infallible, 243
  primacy of, 186
Temple frequented by Christ and
  disciples, 16
Temporal power of Pope, 312
Tertullian, apostolicity, 81
  infallibility, 255
  Primacy of Peter, 175
  Roman Primacy, 207
  successors of apostles, 159
  unity, 53
Theodoret of Cyrus, 284
Theodore of Mopsuestia, 284
Theodore of Studium, infallibility, 281
Theodosius Calls Robber Council, 201
Thomas Aquinas, nature of Church, 3
  fullness of Christ, 113
  impeccability of Apostles, 167
Three Chapters, 284
Thucydides, use of word "ecclesia," 3
Timothy condemned by Pope Damasus,
  282
Titus, bishop of Crete, 154, 156
Tolerati, 131
Tradition, value of, 268
Trent, Council of, "Door" of Church,
  125
  jurisdiction of bishops, 234
  priests part of hierarchy, 161
  rulers of Church, 153
  succession of powers, 157
Triumphus, Augustus, Church and State,
  293
Twelve, the, 154, 169
Tyana, synod of restores Eustatius, 205

Unbaptized not members of Church, 127
Unicity of Church, 18 sq.
Union with Holy Spirit, 118
Unity of Church, bonds of, 45
  errors regarding, 46
  of doctrine, 46, 89, 97, 103
  of government, 47, 89, 98, 103
  as mark of Church, 85
  of profession, 53

and Western Schism, 94
  of worship, 54
Urban VI, 95

Vatican Council, apostolicity, 79
  councils, 240
  infallibility, 248, 266, 272
  institution of Church, 9
  perpetuity, 31
  power of Pope, 225, 226
  Primacy of Peter, 172
  Primacy of Roman Pontiff, 196, 198
  unity of doctrine, 51
  unity of government, 48
  visibility, 39
Victor, Pope, Easter question, 211
Victorinus, primacy of Peter, 193
Vigilius, and the Three Chapters, 284
Vienna, Council of, Temporal Punishment, 143
Vincent Lerins, apostolic See, 232
  infallibility, 267
Visibility of Church, 36 sq.
  errors regarding, 37
  formal, 36
  material, 36
  objections to, 41 sq.
Vitalis of Antioch, 204
Vitandi, 131
Vulgate, authentic version of Scripture,
  291

Waterland, fundamental doctrines, 51
Weiss, B., Peter the Rock, 174, 176
Weizsäcker, nature of Church, 8
Westminster Confession, visibility, 38 sq.
Wilmers, Catholicity, 87
  membership in Church, 132
Worship, freedom of, 54
  in spirit and truth, 43
  unity of, 46, 54
  unity of in Catholic Church, 89
Wyclif, holiness of Church, 59
  membership in Church, 121

Zacharias, prophet, foretells Catholic
  kingdom, 71
Zacharias, Pope, infallibility, 283, 286
Zenobia of Palmyra, 209
Zosimus, Pope, Councils, 240
  infallibility, 283, 284
  restores Apiarius, 219
Zwingli, visibility, 38

15320345R00190

Printed in Great Britain
by Amazon